Fodor's 2002

The U.S. & British Virgin Islands

Handwritten notes:

HERTZE AIRPORT
1·340·774·1879

AMERICAN AIRLINES
1·800·433·7300

HOTEL # 84068601 $894.00
CAR # B897171155 $217.00

ETICKET # T66N FN DB 7E $898.00
AMERICAN AIRLINES # BETZNZ

The complete guide, thoroughly up-to-date

Packed with details that will make your trip

The must-see sights, off and on the beaten path

What to see, what to skip

City strolls, countryside adventures

Smart lodging and dining options

Essential local do's and taboos

Transportation tips

Key contacts, savvy travel tips

When to go, what to pack

Clear, accurate, easy-to-use maps

Books to read, background essays

Excerpted from *Fodor's Ca*

D0068013

Fodor's Travel Publications • New York, Toronto, London, Sydney, Auckland
www.fodors.com

Fodor's The U.S. & British Virgin Islands

EDITOR: Douglas Stallings

Editorial Contributors: Pamela Acheson, Carol M. Bareuther, Lynda Lohr

Editorial Production: Kristin Milavec

Maps: David Lindroth, *cartographer;* Robert Blake and Rebecca Baer, *map editors*

Design: Fabrizio La Rocca, *creative director;* Guido Caroti, *art director;* Jolie Novak, *senior picture editor;* Melanie Marin, *photo editor*

Cover Design: Pentagram

Production/Manufacturing: Robert Shields

Cover Photograph: Neil Rabinowitz/Corbis

Copyright

ISBN 0–679–00872–1

ISSN 1070–6380

"Beach Picnic" by Calvin Trillin. Excerpted from his book *Travels With Alice*, published by Ticknor & Fields. Copyright © 1989 by Calvin Trillin. Originally appeared in different form in *Travel & Leisure*. "Me? The Dad? On a Spring-Break Cruise" by Bob Payne (*Sail* Magazine, 1992) is reproduced by permission of the author.

Important Tip

Although all prices, opening times, and other details in this book are based on information supplied to us at press time, changes occur all the time in the travel world, and Fodor's cannot accept responsibility for facts that become outdated or for inadvertent errors or omissions. So **always confirm information when it matters,** especially if you're making a detour to visit a specific place.

Special Sales

Fodor's Travel Publications are available at special discounts for bulk purchases for sales promotions or premiums. Special editions, including personalized covers, excerpts of existing guides, and corporate imprints, can be created in large quantities for special needs. For more information, contact your local bookseller or write to Special Markets, Fodor's Travel Publications, 280 Park Ave., New York, NY 10017. Inquiries from Canada should be directed to your local Canadian bookseller or sent to Random House of Canada, Ltd., Marketing Department, 2775 Matheson Boulevard East, Mississauga, Ontario L4W 4P7. Inquiries from the United Kingdom should be sent to Fodor's Travel Publications, 20 Vauxhall Bridge Road, London SW1V 2SA, England.

CONTENTS

On the Road with Fodor's   *v*

About Our Writers *v*

Don't Forget to Write *v*

Smart Travel Tips A to Z   *x*

1   **Destination: The Virgin Islands**   *1*

Something for Everyone *2*

What's Where *3*

Pleasures and Pastimes *4*

New and Noteworthy *5*

Fodor's Choice *5*

2   **United States Virgin Islands**   *7*

St. Thomas *12*

St. Croix *42*

St. John *62*

U.S. Virgin Islands A to Z *78*

3   **British Virgin Islands**   *91*

Tortola *93*

Virgin Gorda *111*

Jost Van Dyke *121*

Peter Island *122*

Anegada *123*

Other British Virgin Islands *125*

British Virgin Islands A to Z *127*

4   **Portraits of the Virgin Islands**   *133*

"Beach Picnic," by Calvin Trillin *134*

"Me? The Dad? On a Spring-Break Cruise?" by Bob Payne *138*

"Exploring the Waters of the USBVI" by Gary Goodlander *141*

Further Reading *152*

Index   *153*

Contents

Maps

The Virgin Islands *vi–vii*
The Caribbean *viii–ix*
United States Virgin Islands
  10–11
St. Thomas *14–15*
Charlotte Amalie *36*
St. Croix *44–45*
St. John *64–65*
British Virgin Islands *94–95*
Tortola *96–97*

Virgin Gorda *112–113*
United States Virgin Islands
  Anchorages *143*
British Virgin Islands Anchor-
  ages *144–145*
United States Virgin Islands
  Dive and Snorkel Sites
  148–149
British Virgin Islands Dive and
  Snorkel Sites *150–151*

ON THE ROAD WITH FODOR'S

THE MORE YOU KNOW before you go, the better your trip will be. The island's most fascinating small museum (or its most original local jewelry designer or trendiest beach bistro) could be just around the corner from your hotel, but if you don't know it's there, it might as well be on the other side of the globe. That's where this book comes in. It's a great step toward making sure your next trip lives up to your expectations. As you plan, check out the Web as well. Guidebooks have been helping smart travelers find the special places for years; the Web is one more tool. Whatever reference you consult, be savvy about what you read, and always consider the source. Images and language can be massaged to make places appear better than they are. And one traveler's quaint is another's grimy. Here at Fodor's, and at our on-line arm, Fodors.com, our focus is on providing you with information that's not only useful but also accurate and on target. Every day Fodor's editors put enormous effort into getting things right, beginning with the search for the right contributors—people who have objective judgment, broad travel experience, and the writing ability to put their insights into words. There's no substitute for advice from a like-minded friend who has just come back from where you're going, but our writers, having seen all corners of the U.S. and British Virgin Islands, are the next best thing. They're the kind of people you'd poll for tips yourself if you knew them.

About Our Writers

Our success in achieving our goals—and in helping to make your trip the best of all possible vacations—is a credit to the hard work of our extraordinary writers and editors.

Pamela Acheson spent 18 years in New York City as a publishing executive before heading south to divide her time between Florida and the Caribbean. She writes extensively about both areas and is a regular contributor to *Travel & Leisure*, *Caribbean Travel & Life*, *Fodor's Florida*, *Fodor's Walt Disney World*, and *Fodor's U.S. and British Virgin Islands*. She's the author of *The Best of the British Virgin Islands*, *The Best of St. Thomas and St. John*, *The Best of the Bahamas*, *The Best Romantic Escapes in Florida* (with her husband, Richard Myers), and *More of the Best Romantic Escapes in Florida*.

St. Thomas–based writer and dietitian **Carol M. Bareuther** publishes two weekly columns on food, cooking, and nutrition in the *Virgin Islands Daily News* and serves as the USVI stringer for the Reuters News Service International. She also writes about sports and travel for *Islands' Nautical Scene*, *All At Sea*, *Southern Boating*, *Caribbean Travel & Life*, and other publications. She's the author of two books, *Sports Fishing in the Virgin Islands* and *Virgin Islands Cooking*.

Lynda Lohr is a veteran mainland and USVI photojournalist who has spent the last 15 years living in St. John and who contributes regularly to national, regional, and local magazines, newspapers, and Web sites. She, her significant other, and their two cats recently moved into their new home-with-a-view at Ajax Peak. Although they're still building the house, it's finished enough to provide protection from any hurricanes that blow their way.

We would like to thank the British Virgin Islands Tourist Board and the U.S.V.I. Government Tourist Offices for helping keep us up-to-date.

Don't Forget to Write

Your experiences—positive and negative—matter to us. If we have missed or misstated something, we want to hear about it. We follow up on all suggestions. Contact the U.S. & British Virgin Islands editor at editors@fodors.com or c/o Fodor's, 280 Park Avenue, New York, New York 10017. And have a fabulous trip!

Karen Cure
Editorial Director

The Virgin Islands

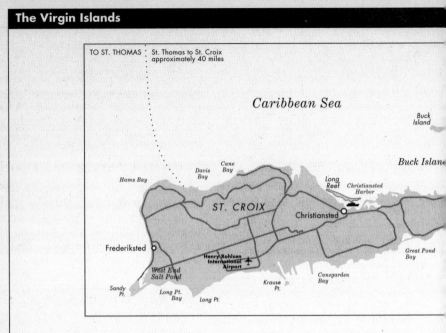

TO ST. THOMAS · St. Thomas to St. Croix approximately 40 miles

Caribbean Sea

Buck Island

Buck Islan

Davis Bay

Cane Bay

Hams Bay

Long Reef

Christiansted Harbor

ST. CROIX

Christiansted

Frederiksted

Great Pond Bay

West End Salt Pond

Henry Rohlsen International Airport

Sandy Pt.

Long Pt. Bay

Long Pt.

Krause Pt.

Canegarden Bay

A T L A N T I C   O C E A N

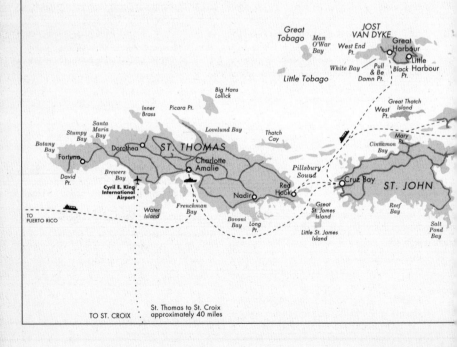

Great Tobago

Man O'War Bay

JOST VAN DYKE

West End Pt.

Great Harbour

White Bay

Pull & Be Damn Pt.

Little Black Harbour Pt.

Little Tobago

Big Hans Lollick

Picara Pt.

Inner Brass

Great Thatch Island

West Pt.

Santa Maria Bay

Lovelund Bay

Thatch Cay

Mary Pt.

Stumpy Bay

Dorothea

ST. THOMAS

Cinnamon Bay

Botany Bay

Fortuna

Charlotte Amalie

Pillsbury Sound

Cruz Bay

ST. JOHN

David Pt.

Brewers Bay

Cyril E. King International Airport

Nadir

Red Hook

Great St. James Island

Reef Bay

TO PUERTO RICO

Water Island

Frenchman Bay

Bovoni Bay

Long Pt.

Little St. James Island

Salt Pond Bay

TO ST. CROIX   St. Thomas to St. Croix approximately 40 miles

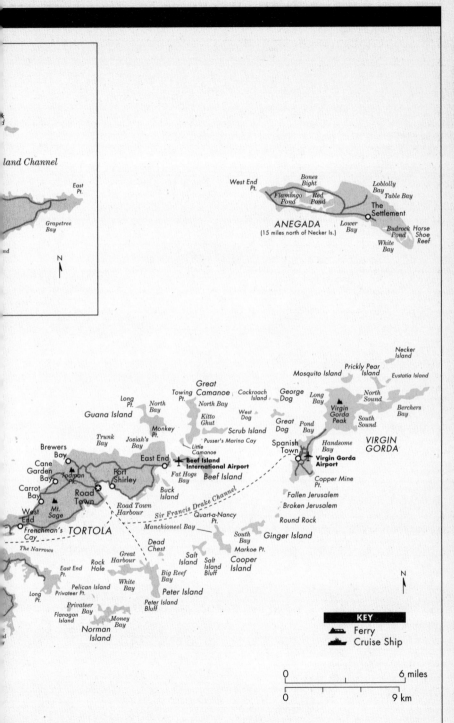

land Channel

East
Pt.

Grapetree
Bay

N

ANEGADA
(15 miles north of Necker Is.)

West End
Pt.

Bones
Bight

Flamingo
Pond

Red
Pond

Loblolly
Bay

Table Bay

The
Settlement

Lower
Bay

Budrock
Pond

Horse
Shoe
Reef

White
Bay

Necker
Island

Prickly Pear
Island

Mosquito Island

Eustatia Island

Long
Bay

North
Sound

Berchers
Bay

**Great
Camanoe**

Towing
Pt.

North
Pt.

Cockroach
Island

George
Dog

Virgin
Gorda
Peak

South
Sound

Guana Island

Long
Pt.

North
Bay

North Bay

West
Dog

Great
Dog

Pond
Bay

**VIRGIN
GORDA**

Kitto
Ghut

Scrub Island

Handsome
Bay

Trunk
Bay

Josiah's
Bay

Monkey
Pt.

Pusser's Marina Cay

Spanish
Town

Brewers
Bay

Little
Camanoe

**Beef Island
International Airport**

**Virgin Gorda
Airport**

East End

Cane
Garden
Bay

Todman
Pt.

Fort
Shirley

Fat Hogs
Bay

Beef Island

Copper Mine
Pt.

Carrot
Bay

**Road
Town**

Buck
Island

Fallen Jerusalem

Mt.
Sage

Road Town
Harbour

Quart-a-Nancy
Pt.

Broken Jerusalem

West
End

Sir Francis Drake Channel

Round Rock

Frenchman's
Cay

Manchioneel Bay

TORTOLA

South
Bay

Ginger Island

The Narrows

Dead
Chest

Markoe Pt.

East End
Pt.

Rock
Hole

Great
Harbour

Salt
Island

Salt
Island
Bluff

**Cooper
Island**

Long
Pt.

Pelican Island

Privateer Pt.

White
Bay

Big Reef
Bay

Peter Island

Privateer
Bay

Peter Island
Bluff

Flanagan
Island

Money
Bay

**Norman
Island**

N

KEY	
	Ferry
	Cruise Ship

0   6 miles

0   9 km

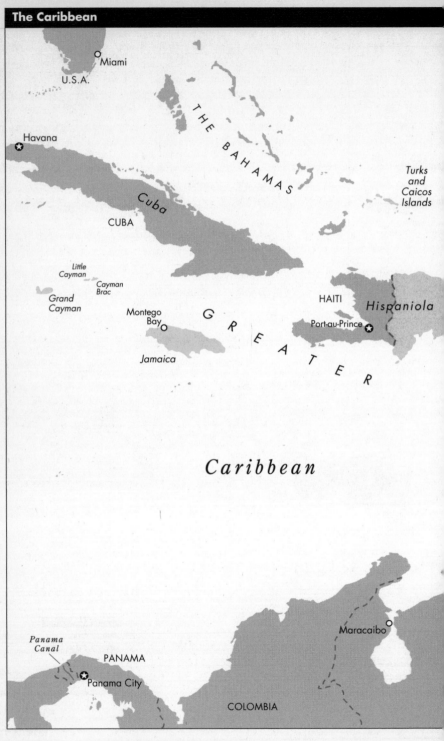

Miami

U.S.A.

THE BAHAMAS

Havana

Turks
and
Caicos
Islands

Cuba

CUBA

*Little
Cayman*

*Cayman
Brac*

*Grand
Cayman*

Montego
Bay

G R E A T E R

HAITI

Hispaniola

Port-au-Prince

Jamaica

Caribbean

*Panama
Canal*

PANAMA

Maracaibo

Panama City

COLOMBIA

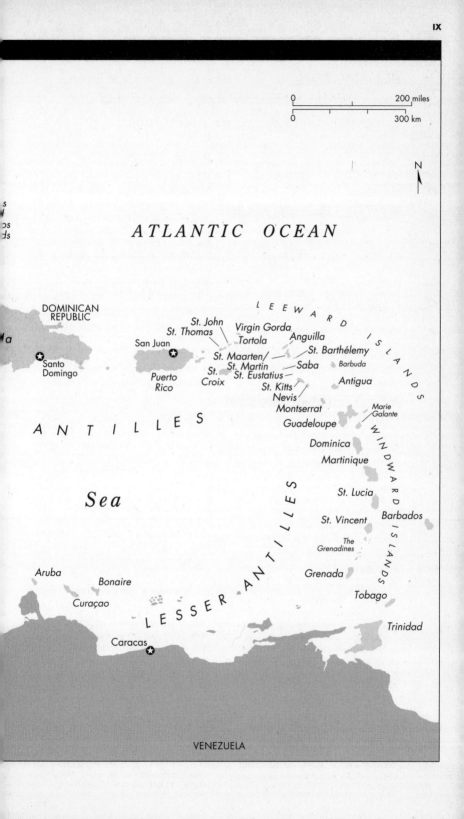

ATLANTIC OCEAN

0   200 miles
0   300 km

N

DOMINICAN REPUBLIC

LEEWARD ISLANDS

St. John
St. Thomas
Virgin Gorda
Tortola
San Juan
Anguilla
St. Barthélemy
Santo Domingo
St. Maarten/
St. Martin
Saba
Barbuda
St. Eustatius
St. Croix
Puerto Rico
St. Kitts
Antigua
Nevis
Montserrat
Marie Galante
Guadeloupe

ANTILLES

Dominica
Martinique

Sea

WINDWARD ISLANDS

St. Lucia
St. Vincent
Barbados
The Grenadines

Aruba
Bonaire
Grenada
Tobago

Curaçao
LESSER ANTILLES
Trinidad

Caracas

VENEZUELA

SMART TRAVEL TIPS A TO Z

Basic Information on Traveling in the Caribbean, Savvy Tips to Make Your Trip a Breeze, and Companies and Organizations to Contact

For island-specific information (including local phone numbers) see the A to Z sections in individual island chapters.

ADDRESSES

"Whimsical" might best describe Caribbean addresses. Street names change for no apparent reason, and most buildings have no numbers. Addresses throughout this guide may include cross streets, landmarks, and other directionals. But to find your destination, you might have to ask a local—and be prepared for such directions as, "Go down so, and take a right at the fish market. Stay on that road past the church and take a left after the river."

AIR TRAVEL

BOOKING

When you book, **look for nonstop flights** and **remember that "direct" flights stop at least once.** Try to avoid connecting flights, which require a change of plane. The more connections you make, the more likely your luggage won't keep up with you. For more booking tips and to check prices and make on-line flight reservations, log on to www.fodors.com.

CARRIERS

There are direct flights from the U.S. to both St. Thomas and St. Croix, with connecting ferry service to St. John. There are no direct flights to the BVI from the United States; rather, you connect in San Juan for a small hop over to Tortola or Virgin Gorda. American Airlines flies several times daily to the USVI, with most direct flights connecting in Miami or via American Eagle connecting flights through San Juan, Puerto Rico, to Tortola or Virgin Gorda. US Airways flies direct from Philadelphia to St. Thomas and St. Croix. Delta, Continental, and United also have flights to the USVI or to San Juan, where you

can pick up a connecting or code-share flight to the USVI or BVI. Air Sunshine flies back and forth from St. Thomas and San Juan to Beef Island/Tortola and Virgin Gorda. Air St. Thomas flies between St. Thomas and San Juan and Virgin Gorda. Cape Air flies from San Juan to both St. Thomas and St. Croix, and from St. Thomas to Tortola. Clair Aero Services flies back and forth to St. Thomas from Beef Island/Tortola.

LIAT flies to St. Thomas and Tortola from many other Caribbean islands with connections to flights from Europe and the U.K.

➤ MAJOR AIRLINES: **Air Sunshine** (☎ 800/327–8900; 800/435–8900 in Florida, WEB www.airsunshine.com). **Air St. Thomas** (☎ 800/522–3084). **American Airlines** (☎ 800/433–7300, WEB www.aa.com). **Cape Air** (☎ 800/352–0714, WEB www.flycapeair.com). **Clair Aero Services** (☎ 340/776–7790 in the U.S. and the USVI). **Continental** (☎ 800/231–0856, WEB www.continental.com). **Delta** (☎ 800/241–4141, WEB www.delta-airlines.com). **LIAT** (☎ 800/468–0482, WEB www.liatairline.com). **United Airlines** (☎ 800/538–2929, WEB www.united.com). **US Airways** (☎ 800/428–4322, WEB www.usairways.com).

CHECK-IN & BOARDING

Checking in, paying departure taxes (which is *not* included in your airfare in the BVI), clearing security, and boarding can take much longer than you expect at island airports. From some smaller islands there's often only one flight per day going in the direction you're headed; if you miss it, you'll miss your connecting flight. If you are leaving on a major carrier from the U.S. Virgin Islands, you must clear customs before you depart, so allow time for this. Have your sales slips handy to facilitate filling out the U.S. Customs forms. Especially when heading home, **get to the airport at least 1½ hours ahead of time** (2 hours if you plan to squeeze in some duty-free shopping).

Assuming that not everyone with a ticket will show up, airlines routinely overbook planes. When everyone does, airlines ask for volunteers to give up their seats. In return, these volunteers usually get a certificate for a free flight and are rebooked on the next flight out. If there are not enough volunteers, the airline must choose who will be denied boarding. The first to get bumped are passengers who checked in late and those flying on discounted tickets, so **get to the gate and check in as early as possible,** especially during peak periods.

Always **bring a government-issued photo I.D. to the airport;** a passport is best. You will be asked to show it before you are allowed to check in.

CUTTING COSTS

The least expensive airfares to the Caribbean must usually be purchased in advance and are nonrefundable. It's smart to **call a number of airlines, and when you are quoted a good price, book it on the spot**—the same fare may not be available the next day. Always **check different routings** and look into using different airports. Travel agents, especially low-fare specialists, are helpful.

Use the Internet to compare fares and schedules and buy tickets. Most airlines offer discounts or bonus frequent flyer miles if you purchase tickets online. General travel sites, such as www.expedia.com or www.travelocity.com, let you compare current fares for all airlines serving a particular destination and will also book your flights. In fact, many airline sites now show you competitive routings and fares. You can also **bid for cheaper fares over the Internet** through companies such as www.priceline.com, which are legitimate sources for seats on major airlines. The more flexible you are with your timing and destination, the better the deal you can make.

Consolidators are another good source. They buy tickets for scheduled international flights at reduced rates from the airlines, then sell them at prices that beat the best fare available directly from the airlines, usually without restrictions. Sometimes you can even get your money back if you need to return the ticket. Carefully read the fine print detailing penalties for changes and cancellations, and **confirm your consolidator reservation with the airline.**

➤ CONSOLIDATORS: **Cheap Tickets** (☎ 800/377–1000, WEB www.cheaptickets. com). **Discount Airline Ticket Service** (☎ 800/576–1600). **Unitravel** (☎ 800/325–2222). **Up & Away Travel** (☎ 212/889–2345). **World Travel Network** (☎ 800/409–6753).

ENJOYING THE FLIGHT

For more legroom, **request an emergency-aisle seat.** Don't sit in the row in front of the emergency aisle or in front of a bulkhead, where seats may not recline. If you have dietary concerns, **ask for special meals when booking.** These can be vegetarian, low-cholesterol, lactose-free, or kosher, for example. On long flights, try to maintain a normal routine to help fight jet lag. At night, **get some sleep;** by day **eat light meals, drink water** (not alcohol), **do isometric exercises,** and **move around the cabin** to stretch your legs. For additional jet-lag tips consult *Fodor's FYI: Travel Fit & Healthy* (available at bookstores everywhere).

FLYING TIMES

The flight from New York to San Juan, Puerto Rico, takes 3½ hours; from Miami to San Juan it's 1½ hours. Nonstop flights from London to Antigua are about 7 hours, with another hour from Antigua to the USBVI. Once you've arrived in the USBVI, hops between the islands take 10 to 20 minutes.

HOW TO COMPLAIN

If your baggage goes astray or your flight goes awry, complain right away. Most carriers require that you **file a claim immediately** before leaving the baggage claim area. Be sure to get a receipt for your baggage check, which the airline may retain, and a phone number (not reservations) where you may inquire about the status of your bag. Although it's a special nuisance when you're en route to your vacation destination, it's good to know that lost bags are merely delayed and rarely lost forever.

➤ AIRLINE COMPLAINTS: U.S. Department of Transportation **Aviation Consumer Protection Division** (✉ C-75, Room 4107, Washington, DC 20590, ☎ 202/366–2220, WEB www. dot.gov/airconsumer). **Federal Aviation Administration Consumer Hotline** (☎ 800/322–7873).

RECONFIRMING

Be sure to **reconfirm your flights on interisland carriers.** You may be subject to a small carrier's whims: If no other passengers are booked on your flight, you may be requested (actually, told) to take another flight or departure time that's more convenient for the airline, or your plane may make unscheduled stops to pick up more clients or cargo. It's all part of the excitement—and unpredictability—of Caribbean travel. In addition, regional carriers use small aircraft with limited baggage space, and they often impose weight restrictions; **travel light,** or you could be subject to outrageous surcharges or delays in getting very large or heavy luggage, which may have to follow on another flight.

AIRPORTS

The major airports are Beef Island International Airport on Tortola, Cyril E. King International Airport on St. Thomas, and Henry Rohlsen International Airport on St. Croix. There are smaller airports (so small that they don't have phone numbers; call the individual airlines if you need information) on Anegada and Virgin Gorda.

➤ AIRPORT INFORMATION: **Beef Island International Airport** (☎ 284/495–2525); **Cyril E. King International Airport** (☎ 340/774–5100); **Henry Rohlsen International Airport** (☎ 340/778–0589).

DUTY-FREE SHOPPING

Both St. Thomas and St. Croix airports have gift shops where you can pick up last-minute gifts or liquor, but since all items purchased in the USVI are duty-free, you won't find any bargains at the airports. Prices may be lower and the selection greater at off-airport stores. In the BVI, do your shopping in town because airport merchandise consists primarily of T-shirts.

BIKE TRAVEL

The USBVI offer a variety of biking terrains. You can wheel through some truly gorgeous scenery on St. Croix. On St. Thomas, St. John, and the BVI, steep hills and roads that lack shoulders make the going more difficult, but you can always cool off with a swim. Note, however, that traffic moves at a good clip on most islands, and drivers aren't always at their most polite when they encounter cyclists. You can rent mountain bikes in St. Croix and Tortola for about $7.50 an hour.

BIKES IN FLIGHT

Most airlines accommodate bikes as luggage, provided they are dismantled and boxed. Airlines sell bike boxes, which are often free at bike shops, for about $5 (it's at least $100 for bike bags). International travelers can sometimes substitute a bike for a piece of checked luggage at no charge; otherwise, the cost is about $100. Domestic and Canadian airlines charge $25–$50.

BOAT & FERRY TRAVEL

For more information, *see* Arriving and Departing by Boat *in* the A to Z section at the end of each chapter.

BUS TRAVEL

St. Thomas's mainland-size Vitran buses are comfortable (and no-smoking) but slow; service is limited to east–west runs to and from Charlotte Amalie. St. John's buses meet departing ferries. St. Croix has Vitran buses with limited service to key destinations. The fees range from 75¢ to $1 (one way), depending on your destination. On St. Croix and Tortola, taxi vans with reasonable fares and regular schedules and routes are also an option.

CAMERAS & PHOTOGRAPHY

Frothy waves in a turquoise sea and palm-lined crescents of beach are relatively easy to capture on film if you **don't let the brightness of the sun on sand and water fool your light meter.** You must compensate or else work early or late in the day when the light isn't as brilliant and contrast isn't such a problem. Try to **capture expansive views** of waterfront, beach, or village scenes; consider shooting down onto the shore from a clearing on a hillside or from a rock on the beach. Or **zoom in on something colorful,** such as a delicate tropical flower or a craftsman at work—but always **ask permission to take pictures of locals or their property. Use a disposable underwater camera** to make your snorkeling and diving adventures more memorable. The *Kodak Guide to Shooting Great Travel Pictures* (available at bookstores everywhere) is loaded with tips.

➤ PHOTO HELP: **Kodak Information Center** (☎ 800/242–2424).

EQUIPMENT PRECAUTIONS

Keep your film and tape out of the sun, and be advised that sand and sea water are no friends to most camera workings. Carry an extra supply of batteries, and **be prepared to turn on your camera or camcorder** to prove to airport security personnel that the device is real. **Keep all film, exposed or unexposed, in your hand luggage.** High-tech security scanners used on checked luggage in some airports can adversely affect film. Always **ask for hand inspection of film,** which becomes clouded after successive exposures to airport X-ray machines, and **keep videotapes away from metal detectors.** Although thievery isn't a major concern in the Caribbean, don't invite problems: **never leave your gear unattended on the beach or in a rental car,** and **lock up your camera or video equipment when you leave your hotel room.**

FILM & DEVELOPING

Film, batteries, and one-time-use cameras are available in camera stores, souvenir shops, hotel boutiques, and pharmacies—although such items can cost twice as much as at home. In all but the most remote areas, you can find 24-hour film-developing services, as well.

CAR RENTAL

Rates range from $50 a day/$300 a week for an economy car with air-conditioning, automatic transmission, and unlimited mileage to $80 a day/$400 a week for a four-wheel drive vehicle. Both the USVI and the BVI have major companies (with airport locations) as well as numerous local companies (near the airports, in hotels, and in the main towns). Most provide pick-up service; some ask that you take a taxi to their headquarters.

➤ MAJOR AGENCIES: **Alamo** (☎ 800/522–9696; 020/8759–6200 in the U.K., WEB www.alamo.com). **Avis** (☎ 800/331–1084; 800/879–2847 in Canada; 02/9353–9000 in Australia; 09/525–1982 in New Zealand; 0870/606–0100 in the U.K., WEB www.avis.com). **Budget** (☎ 800/527–0700; 0870/607–5000 in the U.K., through affiliate Europcar, WEB www.budget.com). **Dollar** (☎ 800/800–6000; 0124/622–0111 in the U.K., through affiliate Sixt Kenning; 02/9223–1444 in Australia, WEB www.dollar.com). **Hertz** (☎ 800/654–3001; 800/263–0600 in Canada; 020/8897–2072 in the U.K.; 02/9669–2444 in Australia; 09/256–8690 in New Zealand, WEB www.hertz.com) **National Car Rental** (☎ 800/227–7368; 020/8680–4800 in the U.K., where it is known as National Europe, WEB www.nationalcar.com).

CUTTING COSTS

Ask about required deposits and cancellation penalties. Plan to **pay by credit card to avoid a hefty cash deposit.** If you're traveling during a holiday period, **make sure that a confirmed reservation guarantees you a car.** To get the best deal, **book through a travel agent who will shop around.**

INSURANCE

When driving a rented car you are generally responsible for any damage to or loss of the vehicle as well as for any property damage or personal injury that you may cause. Before you rent, see what coverage your personal auto-insurance policy and credit cards provide.

THE GOLD GUIDE / SMART TRAVEL TIPS

REQUIREMENTS & RESTRICTIONS

An international driver's license or a temporary permit, which you can get at rental agencies or local police offices upon presentation of a valid license and a small fee, is often required.

SURCHARGES

Before you pick up a car in one city and leave it in another, **ask about drop-off charges or one-way service fees,** which can be substantial. This may be relevant in the larger islands with several large cities, such as Puerto Rico or the Dominican Republic. Note, too, that some rental agencies charge extra if you return the car before the time specified in your contract. To avoid a hefty refueling fee, **fill the tank just before you turn in the car.**

CAR TRAVEL

A car gives you mobility. You'll be able to spend an hour browsing at that cozy out-of-the-way shop instead of the 10 minutes allotted by your taxi driver. You can beach-hop without searching for a ride, and you can sample that restaurant you've heard so much about that's a half-hour (and an expensive taxi ride) away. On parts of some of the islands, you may need to rent a four-wheel-drive vehicle to really get out and about.

EMERGENCY SERVICES

To reach police, fire, or ambulance, dial 911 in the USVI and 999 in the BVI. There are no emergency-service companies such as AAA in the BVI. Before driving off into the countryside, **check your rental car for tire-changing equipment,** including an inflated spare.

GASOLINE

Gas is expensive, though at $1.25 a gallon in St. Croix, considerably less expensive than in many parts of the United States. However, prices rise to about $2 a gallon on other islands. The USVI stations sell gas by the gallon; in the BVI, you'll buy it by the liter. Most stations take major credit cards. Gas stations are found at key points on St. Croix and St. Thomas; on Tortola, Virgin Gorda, and St. John, and other islands, be sure to fill up before you leave the main towns. Most stations are open from early morning until early evening. On smaller islands, they may be closed on Sunday.

ROAD CONDITIONS

Island roads, particularly in mountainous regions that experience heavy tropical rains, are often potholed and bumpy—as well as narrow, winding, and hilly. **Drive with extreme caution,** especially if you venture out at night. You won't see guardrails on every hill and curve, although the drops can be frighteningly steep. And pedestrians (including children and the elderly) and livestock often share the roadway with vehicles.

ROAD MAPS

Main roads and those that go to major attractions are paved, but those to your rental villa may not be. Your best defense is a map, which you can get at rental agencies or tourist offices. Before setting out to a remote location, write down complete directions.

RULES OF THE ROAD

Driving in the USBVI can be tricky. Traffic moves on the left in *both* the USVI and BVI. (The BVI obviously followed the British tradition; no one knows why the USVI followed suit.) Except for the odd right-hand drive car in the BVI, cars on both the BVI and USVI have left-hand drive, the same as cars on the U.S. mainland. This means the driver sits on the side of the car next to the road's edge, a position that makes some people nervous. Note that you may turn left from the left-hand lane when the light is red.

Buckle up before you turn the key. Police in the USVI are notorious for giving $25 tickets to unbelted drivers and front-seat passengers. The police are a bit lax about drunk driver enforcement, but why risk it? Take a taxi or appoint a designated driver when you're out on the town.

Drivers throughout the island often stop in the middle of the road to chat with people or pick up passengers. Watch out for such situations. Traffic moves at about 10 mph in town; on major highways—in St. Croix, for example—you can fly along at 50 mph. On other roads, the speed limit may be less. Traffic jams in major towns such as Christiansted on St. Croix and Charlotte Amalie on St. Thomas aren't unheard of. Try to avoid the 7:30 AM–9 AM and 4 PM–6 PM rush hours.

Main roads in the USVI carry route numbers, but locals may not know them, nor are they always marked. (Be prepared for such directions as "turn left, at the big tree.") Few USVI secondary roads have signs; throughout the BVI, roads aren't very well marked either. Parking laws are enforced in all major towns. Your best bet is to park in public lots found on all the islands. There are no meters, but there are still fees on some islands, with some lots charging a mere 50¢ an hour. And never, ever park in a space for disabled drivers or block its access in the USVI unless you have a handicap sticker for your windshield. Police give out $1,000 tickets for this offense.

CHILDREN IN THE CARIBBEAN

The USBVI are family-friendly destinations. With endless beaches and outdoor activities, children can run off lots of their excess energy. The beach is also a great place for kids to meet other kids. For general advice about traveling with children, consult *Fodor's FYI: Travel with Your Baby* (available in bookstores everywhere).

If you are renting a car, don't forget to **arrange for a car seat** when you reserve.

FLYING

If your children are two or older, **ask about children's airfares.** As a general rule, infants under two not occupying a seat fly at greatly reduced fares or even for free. When booking, **confirm carry-on allowances** if you're traveling with infants. In general, for babies charged 10% of the adult fare you are allowed one carry-on bag and a collapsible stroller; if the flight is full, the stroller may have to be checked or you may be limited to less.

Experts agree that it's a good idea to use safety seats aloft for children weighing less than 40 pounds. Airlines set their own policies: U.S. carriers usually require that the child be ticketed, even if he or she is young enough to ride free, since the seats must be strapped into regular seats. Do **check your airline's policy about using safety seats during takeoff and landing.** And since safety seats are not allowed everywhere in the plane, get your seat assignments early.

When reserving, **request children's meals or a freestanding bassinet** if you need them. But note that bulkhead seats, where you must sit to use the bassinet, may lack an overhead bin or storage space on the floor.

FOOD

Even if your youngsters are picky eaters, meals in the Caribbean shouldn't be a problem. Baby food is easy to find (although often pricier than you might find at home, and brands may be limited), and hamburgers and hot dogs are available at many resorts. When kids want a taste of home, you'll find McDonald's, KFC, and Pizza Hut on St. Thomas and St. Croix. On all islands menus offer pasta and vegetarian dishes, pizza, sandwiches, and ice cream—all of which appeal to kids. Supermarkets have cereal, snacks, and other packaged goods you'll recognize from home. At outdoor markets, a few dollars will buy you enough bananas, mangoes, and other fresh fruit to last your entire vacation. Just watch out for overly spicy food that may upset children's sensitive stomachs.

LODGING

Most USBVI hotels allow children under a certain age to stay in their parents' room for free, but some charge for them as extra adults; be sure to **find out the cutoff age for children's discounts** when booking. Cribs are usually available, but ask before you book. Many of the larger hotels—try Little Dix Bay and Bitter End Yacht Club in the BVI, Chenay Bay Beach Resort, Sapphire Beach Resort and Marina, the Westin Resort, and Caneel Bay Resort in the USVI—offer children's programs that include supervised care and such activities as beach time, snorkeling, games, and movies. Some include meals. Your hotel may also offer evening baby-sitting service or have a list of approved local sitters for you to call.

For the most kid-friendly vacation, **consider booking a condo or a villa.** Your children will have room to stretch out, they can help themselves to snacks and drinks in the fridge, and their antics won't disturb anyone but you. The campgrounds at Cinnamon Bay and Maho Bay in St. John, Brewers Bay on Tortola, and White Bay on Jost Van Dyke also provide good opportunities for kids to meet other kids.

➤ BEST CHOICES: **Bitter End Yacht Club and Marina** (☎ 284/494–2746 or 800/872–2392) on Virgin Gorda; **Brewers Bay Campground** (☎ 284/494–3463) on Tortola; **Caneel Bay Resort** (☎ 340/776–6111 or 888/767–3966) on St. John; **Chenay Bay Resort** (☎ 340/773–2918 or 800/548–4457) on St. Croix; **Cinnamon Bay Campground** (☎ 340/776–6330 or 800/539–9998) on St. John; **Little Dix Bay** (☎ 284/495–5555) on Virgin Gorda; **Maho Bay Camps** (☎ 340/776–6240, 212/472–9453, or 800/392–9004) on St. John; **Renaissance Grand Beach Resort** (☎ 340/775–1510 or 800/468–3571) on St. Thomas; **Sapphire Beach Resort and Marina** (☎ 340/775–6100 or 800/524–2090) on St. Thomas; **Westin Resort, St. John** (☎ 340/693–8000 or 800/808–5020); **White Bay Campground** (☎ 284/495–9312) on Jost Van Dyke.

PRECAUTIONS

Don't underestimate the tropical sun. Throughout the day, even away from the beach, lather plenty of sunscreen—with a sun protection factor (SPF) of 15 or higher—on all exposed areas. Small children should also wear a hat. Mosquito bites can become infected when scratched, so **use bug spray** and avoid the problem. To prevent dehydration, **carry plenty of bottled water** at the beach and on sightseeing excursions.

To avoid immigration problems if your child carries a different last name, **bring identification that clarifies the family relationship** (e.g., a birth

certificate identifying the parent or a joint passport). If a child is traveling without both birth parents, a notarized letter should accompany the child from the nonpresent parent(s) authorizing permission for the child to travel.

SIGHTS & ATTRACTIONS

There are numerous attractions that children love; Coral World Marine Park on St. Thomas, which teaches kids about the undersea world around the island; the guided hikes and early evening slide shows and talks offered by the Virgin Islands National Park on St. John; the St. Croix Aquarium's touch tank, where kids can touch sea creatures; and Ft. Christianvaern's old guns and military exhibits on St. Croix.

Places that are especially appealing to children are indicated by a rubber-duckie icon (☺) in the margin.

SUPPLIES & EQUIPMENT

Disposable diapers are available throughout the USVI, but you may not find your favorite brand. To make sure you have the supplies you need, bring them from home. The farther you get from St. Thomas and St. Croix, the smaller the selection and the higher the prices; but grocery stores in the USBVI are your best bet for all baby supplies. Stores on all USBVI islands have nice selections of beach and educational toys and children's books about the marine and Caribbean environment. It's also easy to find children's bathing suits, but the prices will probably be higher than they are at home.

COMPUTERS ON THE ROAD

Bring an adapter for your laptop plug. Adapters are inexpensive, and some models have several plugs suitable for different systems throughout the world. Some hotels lend adapters to guests to use during their stay.

At the airport, **be prepared to turn on your laptop** to prove to security personnel that the device is real. The security X-ray machines aren't damaging to a laptop, but **keep computer disks away from metal detectors.** In your hotel, **stow away and lock up your laptop when you're out of the**

room. Although thievery isn't a major concern in the Caribbean, don't invite a problem.

CONSUMER PROTECTION

Whenever shopping or buying travel services in the Caribbean, **pay with a major credit card,** if possible, so you can cancel payment or get reimbursed if there's a problem. If you're doing business with a particular company for the first time, **contact your local Better Business Bureau and the attorney general's offices** in your state and (for U.S. businesses) the company's home state as well. Have any complaints been filed? Finally, if you're buying a package or tour, always **consider travel insurance** that includes default coverage (☞ Insurance).

➤ BBBs: **Council of Better Business Bureaus** (✉ 4200 Wilson Blvd., Suite 800, Arlington, VA 22203, ☎ 703/276–0100, FAX 703/525–8277, WEB www.bbb.org).

CRUISE TRAVEL

St. Thomas is the USBVI's most popular cruise destination, but ships also call at St. Croix, St. John, and Tortola. You'll find numerous activities available through your ship, including trips to beaches, sailing and kayaking adventures, and shopping excursions. The tours allow you to see a lot in a little time. Don't be afraid, however, to strike out on your own. Taxis can whisk you to downtown shopping areas, or you can walk—a great opportunity to see the sights at a slower pace. To learn how to plan, choose, and book a cruise-ship voyage, check out Cruise How-to's on www.fodors.com and consult *Fodor's FYI: Plan & Enjoy Your Cruise* (available in bookstores everywhere).

➤ CRUISE LINES: **American Canadian Caribbean Line** (✉ Box 368, Warren, RI 02885, ☎ 401/247–0955 or 800/556–7450, WEB www.accl-smallships. com). **Carnival Cruise Lines** (✉ 3655 N.W. 87th Ave., Miami, FL 33178, ☎ 305/599–2600 or 800/227–6482, WEB www.carnival.com). **Celebrity Cruises** (✉ 1050 Caribbean Way, Miami, FL 33122, ☎ 305/539–6000 or 800/437–3111, WEB www.celebritycruises.com). **Clipper Cruise Line** (✉ 7711 Bonhomme Ave., St. Louis, MO 63105, ☎ 314/727–2929 or 800/325–0010, WEB www.clippercruise. com). **Club Med** (✉ 75 Valencia Ave., Coral Gables, FL 33134, ☎ 800/258–2633 or 888/CLUBMED, WEB www. clubmed.com). **Costa Cruise Lines** (✉ World Trade Center Bldg., 80 S.W. 8th St., Miami, FL 33130, ☎ 305/358–7325 or 800/462–6782, WEB www.costacruises.com). **Crystal Cruises** (✉ 2049 Century Park E, Suite 1400, Los Angeles, CA 90067, ☎ 310/783–9300 or 800/446–6620, WEB www.crystalcruises.com). **Cunard Line** (✉ 6100 Blue Lagoon Dr., Suite 400, Miami, FL 33126, ☎ 305/463–3000 or 800/7–CUNARD, WEB www. cunardline.com). **Disney Cruise Line** (✉ 210 Celebration Pl., Suite 400, Celebration, FL 34747, ☎ 407/566–3500, WEB www.disneycruise.com). **Holland America Line** (✉ 300 Elliott Ave. W, Seattle, WA 98119, ☎ 206/281–3535 or 800/426–6593, WEB www.hollandamerica.com). **Lindblad Expedition** (✉ 720 5th Ave., New York, NY 10019, ☎ 800/762–0003, WEB www.lindblad.com). **Norwegian Cruise Line** (✉ 7665 Corporate Center Dr., Miami, FL 33126, ☎ 305/436–4000 or 800/327–7030, WEB www.ncl.com). **Princess Cruises** (✉ 10100 Santa Monica Blvd., Suite 1800, Los Angeles, CA 90067, ☎ 310/553–1770 or 800/421–0522, WEB www.princesscruises.com). **Radisson Seven Seas Cruises** (✉ 600 Corporate Dr., Suite 410, Fort Lauderdale, FL 33334, ☎ 954/776–6123 or 800/477–7500, WEB www.rssc.com). **Regal Cruises** (✉ 300 Regal Cruises Way, Box 1329, Palmetto, FL 34221, ☎ 941/721–7300 or 800/270–7245, WEB www.regalcruises.com). **Renaissance Cruises** (✉ 350 Las Olas Blvd., Fort Lauderdale, FL 33302, ☎ 877/549–1124, WEB www.renaissancecruises. com). **Royal Caribbean Cruise Line** (✉ 1050 Caribbean Way, Miami, FL 33132, ☎ 305/539–6000 or 800/327–6700, WEB www.royalcaribbean. com). **Seabourn Cruise Line** (✉ 6100 Blue Lagoon Dr., Suite 400, Miami, FL 33126, ☎ 305/463–3000 or 800/929–9391, WEB www.seabourn.com). **Silversea Cruises** (✉ 110 E. Broward Blvd., Fort Lauderdale, FL 33301, ☎ 954/522–4477 or 800/722–9055, WEB www.silverseacruises.com). **Star Clippers** (✉ 4101 Salzedo St.,

Coral Gables, FL 33146, ☎ 305/442–0550 or 800/442–0551, WEB www.star-clippers.com). **Windjammer Barefoot Cruises** (✉ 1759 Bay Rd., Miami Beach, FL 33139, ☎ 800/327–2602, WEB www.windjammer.com). **Windstar Cruises** (✉ 300 Elliott Ave. W, Seattle, WA 98119, ☎ 206/281–3535 or 800/258–7245, WEB www.windstarcruises.com).

➤ ORGANIZATIONS: **Cruise Lines International Association** (CLIA; ✉ 500 5th Ave., Suite 1407, New York, NY 10110, ☎ 212/921–0066, WEB www.cruising.org).

CUSTOMS & DUTIES

When shopping, **keep receipts** for all purchases. Upon reentering the country, **be ready to show customs officials what you've bought.** If you feel a duty is incorrect or object to the way your clearance was handled, note the inspector's badge number and ask to see a supervisor. If the problem isn't resolved, write to the appropriate authorities, beginning with the port director at your point of entry.

IN THE USBVI

Visitors to the USVI arriving from the continental United States or Puerto Rico don't need to pass through customs. Those arriving from any other point of origin do, but it's a quick process. Items of a personal nature may be brought into the USVI duty-free; any items of significant commercial value may be subject to a 6% duty.

All visitors to the BVI must pass through customs, but the lines are short and the inspectors speedy. Personal items may be brought into the BVI duty-free; any items of significant commercial value may be subject to a duty, which varies by the item.

IN AUSTRALIA

Australian residents who are 18 or older may bring home $A400 worth of souvenirs and gifts (including jewelry), 250 cigarettes or 250 grams of tobacco, and 1,125 ml of alcohol (including wine, beer, and spirits). Residents under 18 may bring back $A200 worth of goods. Prohibited items include meat products. Seeds, plants, and fruits need to be declared upon arrival.

➤ INFORMATION: **Australian Customs Service** (Regional Director, ✉ Box 8, Sydney, NSW 2001, Australia, ☎ 02/9213–2000, FAX 02/9213–4000, WEB www.customs.gov.au).

IN CANADA

Canadian residents who have been out of Canada for at least seven days may bring home C$500 worth of goods duty-free. If you've been away fewer than seven days but more than 48 hours, the duty-free allowance drops to C$200; if your trip lasts 24–48 hours, the allowance is C$50. You may not pool allowances with family members. Goods claimed under the C$500 exemption may follow you by mail; those claimed under the lesser exemptions must accompany you. Alcohol and tobacco products may be included in the seven-day and 48-hour exemptions but not in the 24-hour exemption. If you meet the age requirements of the province or territory through which you reenter Canada, you may bring in, duty-free, 1.14 liters (40 imperial ounces) of wine or liquor *or* 24 12-ounce cans or bottles of beer or ale. If you are 16 or older you may bring in, duty-free, 200 cigarettes and 50 cigars. Check ahead of time with Revenue Canada or the Department of Agriculture for policies regarding meat products, seeds, plants, and fruits.

You may send an unlimited number of gifts worth up to C$60 each duty-free to Canada. Label the package UNSOLICITED GIFT—VALUE UNDER $60. Alcohol and tobacco are excluded.

➤ INFORMATION: **Revenue Canada** (✉ 2265 St. Laurent Blvd. S, Ottawa, Ontario K1G 4K3, Canada, ☎ 613/993–0534 or 800/461–9999 in Canada, FAX 613/991–4126, WEB www.ccra-adrc.gc.ca).

IN NEW ZEALAND

Homeward-bound residents 17 or older may bring back NZ$700 worth of souvenirs and gifts. Your duty-free allowance also includes 4.5 liters of wine or beer; one 1,125-ml bottle of spirits; and either 200 cigarettes, 250 grams of tobacco, 50 cigars, or a combination of the three up to 250 grams. Prohibited items include meat products, seeds, plants, and fruits.

➤ INFORMATION: **New Zealand Customs** (Custom House, ✉ 50 Anzac Ave., Box 29, Auckland, New Zealand, ☎ 09/300–5399, FAX 09/359–6730, WEB www.customs.govt.nz).

IN THE U.K.

Although some Caribbean nations are part of the British Commonwealth, they are not part of the European Union (EU) with regard to customs. If you're a U.K. resident, you may bring home from countries outside the European Union, duty-free, 200 cigarettes or 50 cigars; 1 liter of spirits or 2 liters of fortified or sparkling wine or liqueurs; 2 liters of still table wine; 60 ml of perfume; 250 ml of toilet water; plus £136 worth of other goods, including gifts and souvenirs. Prohibited items include meat products, seeds, plants, and fruits.

➤ INFORMATION: **HM Customs and Excise** (✉ Dorset House, Stamford St., Bromley, Kent BR1 1XX, U.K., ☎ 020/7202–4227, WEB www.hmce. gov.uk).

IN THE U.S.

U.S. residents who have been out of the country for at least 48 hours and who have not used the $600 allowance or any part of it in the past 30 days may bring home $600 worth of foreign goods duty-free. This allowance, higher than the standard $400 exemption, applies to the two dozen countries in the Caribbean Basin Initiative (CBI). If you visit a CBI country and a non-CBI country, such as Martinique, you may still bring in $600 worth of goods duty-free, but no more than $400 may be from the non-CBI country. If you're returning from the U.S. Virgin Islands (USVI), the duty-free allowance is $1,200. If your travel included the USVI and another country—say, the Dominican Republic—the $1,200 allowance still applies, but at least $600 worth of goods must be from the USVI.

U.S. residents 21 and older may bring back 1 liter of alcohol duty-free (if you have visited the USVI, the exemption is 6 liters as long as 1 has been manufactured in the USVI). In addi-

tion, regardless of your age, you are allowed 200 cigarettes and 100 non-Cuban cigars. Antiques, which the U.S. Customs Service defines as objects more than 100 years old, enter duty-free, as do original works of art done entirely by hand, including paintings, drawings, and sculptures.

You may also mail or ship packages home duty-free: up to $200 worth of goods for personal use, with a limit of one parcel per addressee per day (except alcohol or tobacco products or perfume worth more than $5); label the package PERSONAL USE and attach a list of its contents and their retail value. Do not label the package UNSOLICITED GIFT or your duty-free exemption will drop to $100. Mailed items do not affect your duty-free allowance on your return.

➤ INFORMATION: **U.S. Customs Service** (✉ 1300 Pennsylvania Ave. NW, Washington, DC 20229, WEB www. customs.gov; inquiries ☎ 202/354–1000; complaints c/o ✉ 1300 Pennsylvania Ave. NW, Room 5.4D, Washington, DC 20229; registration of equipment c/o ✉ Resource Management, ☎ 202/927–0540).

DINING

Everything from fast food to fine cuisine in elegant settings are available in the USBVI, and prices run about the same as what you'd pay in New York or any other major city. Most chefs at top-of-the-line restaurants and even some small spots went to a major culinary school, which means innovative and interesting cuisine similar to what you might find in the United States. Don't be afraid to sample local dishes at the roadside restaurants located on all the islands. Throughout the book, the restaurants we list are the cream of the crop in each price category. *For price charts and details on island specialties and dress codes, see the Dining sections in individual island chapters.*

MEALS & SPECIALTIES

Your hotel is your best bet for breakfast in the USBVI, where you'll easily find American-style food. Local restaurants serve fish and other heavy dishes for breakfast. Other meals are similar to those in the U.S.

For fast food, island style, try a paté from a roadside stand. It's a fried pastry filled with conch, salted fish, or hamburger, which islanders call meat. Maubi, made from tree bark, is a unique drink popular in the USBVI.

MEALTIMES

Most restaurants open for lunch from around 11:30 AM to about 3 PM; they serve dinner from around 6:30 PM to about 10 PM. Unless otherwise noted, the restaurants listed in this guide are open daily for lunch and dinner.

PAYING

Major restaurants take at least two major credit cards, most often Mastercard and Visa, but that off-the-beaten path spot you've heard so much about may accept only cash.

RESERVATIONS & DRESS

Reservations are always a good idea: we mention them only when they're essential or not accepted. Book as far ahead as you can, and reconfirm as soon as you arrive. We mention dress only when men are required to wear a jacket or a jacket and tie. Beach attire is universally frowned upon in restaurants throughout the Caribbean.

WINE, BEER & SPIRITS

Top-notch restaurants offer good selections of fine wines. Beer and spirits are available on all islands at all kinds of restaurants and roadside stands, but you may not find the brand you prefer.

DISABILITIES & ACCESSIBILITY

The USBVI are sometimes difficult destinations for travelers with disabilities. The islands are hilly, and the pavement uneven in some places. It may be difficult to visit all areas of most of the USBVI's attractions; call first to make sure it has ramps and that you'll be able to access the entire attraction.

LODGING

Many hotels and resorts have accessible ground-floor guest rooms; others, particularly newer ones, offer some guest rooms with extra-wide doors and bathrooms with grab-bars and easily accessible shower stalls. Some hotels may also help arrange rentals of special equipment. Be sure to **make your special needs known when reserving your room.** It's also wise to ask whether access to the beach, pool, lobby, and dining areas requires the use of stairs and whether alternative ramps or elevators are available.

➤ BEST CHOICE IN THE BVI: Little Dix Bay (☎ 284/495–5555, WEB www. littledixbay.com) on Tortola.

➤ BEST CHOICES IN THE USVI: **Caneel Bay Resort** (☎ 340/776–6111 or 888/767–3966) on St. John; **Hibiscus Beach Hotel** (☎ 340/773–4042 or 800/442–0121) on St. Croix; **Marriott's Frenchman's Reef Resort and Morning Star Beach Resorts** (☎ 340/ 776–8500 or 800/524–2000) on St. Thomas; **Renaissance Grand Beach Resort** (☎ 340/775–1510 or 800/ 468–3571) on St. Thomas.

RESERVATIONS

When discussing accessibility with an operator or reservations agent, **ask hard questions.** Are there any stairs, inside *or* out? Are there grab bars next to the toilet *and* in the shower/tub? How wide is the doorway to the room? To the bathroom? Are there many stairs between the guest room and the restaurant, beach, or other public areas? For the most extensive facilities meeting the latest legal specifications, **opt for newer accommodations.**

TRANSPORTATION

At all USBVI airports passengers board and disembark aircraft directly from and onto the tarmac, which requires negotiating a steep staircase. It can be a rather long walk to immigration, customs, and the airport exit. Be sure to **request wheelchairs or escort assistance when booking your flight.** Taxis and specially adapted rental cars are the most practical option for sightseeing. The Virgin Islands Coalition of Citizens with Disabilities offers information on USVI Dial-A-Ride services and special parking permits.

➤ LOCAL RESOURCES: **The Virgin Islands Coalition of Citizens with Disabilities** (☎ 340/776–1277).

➤ COMPLAINTS: **Aviation Consumer Protection Division** (✉ C-75, Room

4107, Washington, DC 20590, ☎ 202/366–2220, WEB www.dot.gov/airconsumer) for airline-related problems. **Civil Rights Office** (✉ U.S. Department of Transportation, Departmental Office of Civil Rights, S-30, 400 7th St. SW, Room 10215, Washington, DC 20590, ☎ 202/366–4648, FAX 202/366–9371, WEB www.dot.gov/ost/docr/index.htm) for problems with surface transportation. **Disability Rights Section** (✉ U.S. Department of Justice, Civil Rights Division, Box 66738, Washington, DC 20035-6738, ☎ 202/514–0301 or 800/514–0301; 202/514–0383 TTY; 800/514–0383 TTY; FAX 202/307–1198, WEB www.usdoj.gov/crt/ada/adahom1.htm) for general complaints.

TRAVEL AGENCIES

In the United States, the Americans with Disabilities Act requires that travel firms serve the needs of all travelers. Some agencies specialize in working with people with disabilities.

➤ TRAVELERS WITH MOBILITY PROBLEMS: **Access Adventures** (✉ 206 Chestnut Ridge Rd., Scottsville, NY 14624, ☎ 716/889–9096, dltravel@prodigy.net), run by a former physical-rehabilitation counselor. **CareVacations** (✉ 5-5110 50th Ave., Leduc, Alberta T9E 6V4, Canada, ☎ 780/986–6404 or 877/478–7827, FAX 780/986–8332, WEB www.carevacations.com), for group tours and cruise vacations. **Flying Wheels Travel** (✉ 143 W. Bridge St., Box 382, Owatonna, MN 55060, ☎ 507/451–5005 or 800/535–6790, FAX 507/451–1685, WEB www.flyingwheelstravel.com). **Tomorrow's Level of Care** (✉ Box 470299, Brooklyn, NY 11247, ☎ 718/756–0794 or 800/932–2012), for nursing services and medical equipment.

➤ TRAVELERS WITH DEVELOPMENTAL DISABILITIES: **New Directions** (✉ 5276 Hollister Ave., Suite 207, Santa Barbara, CA 93111, ☎ 805/967–2841 or 888/967–2841, FAX 805/964–7344, WEB www.newdirectionstravel.com). **Sprout** (✉ 893 Amsterdam Ave., New York, NY 10025, ☎ 212/222–9575 or 888/222–9575, FAX 212/222–9768, WEB www.gosprout.org).

DISCOUNTS & DEALS

Visit during the off-season, when prices usually plummet at even the glitziest resorts; you'll realize savings of up to 50% between April 15 and December 15. Moreover, you'll usually find fewer tourists, it's easier to rent a car, the water tends to be calmer and clearer, and you might stumble onto local festivals.

Remember that your budget will go further on some islands (Dominica or Saba, for example) than on others (St. Barths or Anguilla). And more developed islands (St. Thomas, St. Maarten/St. Martin, Aruba, Puerto Rico, Jamaica, Grand Cayman) tend to be more competitive and creative in their package pricing. You'll also find small hotels or those that are a short walk from the beach offer very pleasant accommodations that are priced considerably lower than their larger, beachfront neighbors.

Be a smart shopper and **compare all your options** before making decisions. A plane ticket bought with a promotional coupon from travel clubs, coupon books, and direct-mail offers or on the Internet may not be cheaper than the least expensive fare from a discount ticket agency. And always keep in mind that what you get is just as important as what you save.

DISCOUNT RESERVATIONS

To save money, **look into discount reservations services** with toll-free numbers, which use their buying power to get a better price on hotels, airline tickets, even car rentals. When booking a room, always **call the hotel's local toll-free number** (if one is available) rather than the central reservations number—you'll often get a better price. Always ask about special packages or corporate rates.

When shopping for the best deal on hotels and car rentals, **look for guaranteed exchange rates,** which protect you against a falling dollar. With your rate locked in, you won't pay more, even if the price goes up in the local currency. (Note, however, that the currency of most Caribbean islands is fixed in value relative to the U.S. dollar, so this is not generally a critical issue for U.S. visitors.

➤ AIRLINE TICKETS: ☎ **800/FLY–ASAP.**

➤ HOTEL ROOMS: **Hotel Reservations Network** (☎ 800/964–6835, WEB www.hoteldiscount.com). **Players Express Vacations** (☎ 800/458–6161, WEB www.playersexpress.com). **Turbotrip.com** (☎ 800/473–7829, WEB www.turbotrip.com).

PACKAGE DEALS

Don't confuse packages and guided tours. When you buy a package, you travel on your own, just as though you had planned the trip yourself. Fly-drive packages, which combine airfare and car rental, are often a good deal. When you join a guided tour, you travel with a group, and everyone follows the same itinerary.

ECOTOURISM

St. John has the Virgin Islands National Park, which helps to keep a lid on development, and a coterie of environmental activists, who help to keep the island green. The park offers guided hikes in St. John, and the St. Croix Environmental Association and the Nature Conservancy run hikes through pristine areas of St. Croix. None of the BVI is very developed, and Tortola and other islands have national parks.

ETIQUETTE & BEHAVIOR

Cover up when you're not at the beach; Virgin Islanders are modest folks. Say good morning, good afternoon, or good night to start your conversation off right. Casual clothes are generally fine, but men should wear a tie and jacket and women a lightweight suit when dealing with government offices, insurance companies, and the like. Only wear shorts to the most casual of marine-related businesses.

GAY & LESBIAN TRAVEL

Gay and lesbian travelers are welcome in the USBVI, but some unfriendly attitudes still exist. It's wise to avoid public displays of affection in local bars, where the men aren't shy about making their views known. Ask at your hotel for advice on places to go. St. Thomas has a thriving gay community, and you'll be made very welcome. St. Croix has several gay-friendly resorts perfect for couples as well as singles.

➤ GAY- & LESBIAN-FRIENDLY TRAVEL AGENCIES: **Different Roads Travel** (✉ 8383 Wilshire Blvd., Suite 902, Beverly Hills, CA 90211, ☎ 323/651–5557 or 800/429–8747, FAX 323/651–3678, lgernert@tzell.com). **Kennedy Travel** (✉ 314 Jericho Tpke., Floral Park, NY 11001, ☎ 516/352–4888 or 800/237–7433, FAX 516/354–8849, WEB www.kennedytravel.com). **Now Voyager** (✉ 4406 18th St., San Francisco, CA 94114, ☎ 415/626–1169 or 800/255–6951, FAX 415/626–8626, WEB www.nowvoyager.com). **Skylink Travel and Tour** (✉ 1006 Mendocino Ave., Santa Rosa, CA 95401, ☎ 707/546–9888 or 800/225–5759, FAX 707/546–9891, WEB www.skylinktravel.com), serving lesbian travelers.

GUIDEBOOKS

Plan well and you won't be sorry. Guidebooks are excellent tools—and you can take them with you. You may want to check out *Fodor's Exploring Caribbean* (full color) and *Fodor's Caribbean Ports of Call.*

HEALTH

FOOD & DRINK

While you might find some unpleasant tasting tap water, food and water in the USBVI is safe. If you do get a mild case of diarrhea it should respond to Imodium (known generically as loperamide) or Pepto-Bismal (not as strong), both of which can be purchased over the counter. However, be aware that these medications can complicate more serious infections. Drink plenty of purified water or tea—chamomile is a good folk remedy. In severe cases, rehydrate yourself with a salt-sugar solution (½ teaspoon salt and 4 tablespoons sugar per quart of water). Also note that ciguatera, a toxin found in some reef fish (particularly kingfish), can be a problem at local restaurants.

PESTS & OTHER HAZARDS

Mosquitoes can be a problem here, particularly after a spate of showers. Off! insect repellant is readily available, but you may want to bring something stronger. Also a nuisance are the little pests from the sand-flea family known as no-see-ums. You don't realize you're being had for dinner until it's too late, and these bites stay, and itch, and itch, and itch. No-see-ums start getting hungry around 3 PM and are out in force by sunset. They're always more numerous in shady and wooded areas (such as the campgrounds on St. John). **Take a towel along for sitting on the beach, and keep reapplying insect repellant.** If you can't find any repellant and are desperate, blot a cloth with vodka or gin and dab the itch.

Beware of the manchineel tree, which grows near the beach and has green applelike fruit that is poisonous and bark and leaves that burn the skin.

SUN PROTECTION

Even if you've never been sunburned in your life, believe the warnings and **use sunscreen** in the USBVI. If you're dark-skinned, start with at least an SPF of 15 and keep it on. If you're fair-skinned, use a sunscreen with a higher SPF and stay out of the sun during the midday. Rays are most intense between 11 and 2, so move under a sea-grape tree (although you can still burn here) or, better yet, take a shady lunch break. You can also burn in this part of the world when it's cloudy, so putting sunscreen on every day no matter what the weather is the best strategy.

SWIMMING & DIVING

For the safest swim, pick a beach where there's a lifeguard. Most of the time, the water is lagoonlike calm, but during storms, big surf can kick up. Use caution—the undertow can make it difficult to get back to shore.

You can rent tanks and dive equipment from local dive shops, but a trip on their dive boat will take you to the best locations in the safest way. In the water, **watch out for black, spiny sea urchins**; stepping on one is guaranteed to be painful for quite some time. The good news is they are usually found in reef areas where you'll be snorkeling, so you aren't likely to step on one by accident. **Familiarize yourself with the various types of coral** before you go out. The fire coral, which can give you a bad burn if you scrape

against it, is particularly nasty. If you do get burned, **apply ammonia to the spot as soon as possible.**

Do not fly within 24 hours of scuba diving.

INSURANCE

The most useful travel-insurance plan is a comprehensive policy that includes coverage for trip cancellation and interruption, default, trip delay, and medical expenses (with a waiver for pre-existing conditions).

Without insurance you will lose all or most of your money if you cancel your trip, regardless of the reason. Default insurance covers you if your tour operator, airline, or cruise line goes out of business. Trip-delay covers expenses that arise because of bad weather or mechanical delays. Study the fine print when comparing policies.

If you're traveling internationally, a key component of travel insurance is coverage for medical bills incurred if you get sick on the road. Such expenses are not generally covered by Medicare or private policies. U.K. residents can buy a travel-insurance policy valid for most vacations taken during the year in which it's purchased (but check pre-existing-condition coverage). British and Australian citizens need extra medical coverage when traveling overseas.

Always **buy travel policies directly from the insurance company**; if you buy them from a cruise line, airline, or tour operator that goes out of business you probably will not be covered for the agency or operator's default, a major risk. Before making any purchase, **review your existing health and homeowner's policies** to find what they cover away from home.

➤ TRAVEL INSURERS: In the U.S.: **Access America** (✉ 6600 W. Broad St., Richmond, VA 23230, ☎ 804/285–3300 or 800/284–8300, FAX 804/673–1586, WEB www.previewtravel.com), **Travel Guard International** (✉ 1145 Clark St., Stevens Point, WI 54481, ☎ 715/345–0505 or 800/826–1300, FAX 800/955–8785, WEB www.noelgroup.com).

SMART TRAVEL TIPS

THE GOLD GUIDE / SMART TRAVEL TIPS

➤ INSURANCE INFORMATION: In the U.K.: **Association of British Insurers** (✉ 51–55 Gresham St., London EC2V 7HQ, U.K., ☎ 020/7600–3333, FAX 020/7696–8999, WEB www.abi.org.uk). In Canada: **Voyager Insurance** (✉ 44 Peel Center Dr., Brampton, Ontario L6T 4M8, Canada, ☎ 905/791–8700 or 800/668–4342 in Canada). In Australia: **Insurance Council of Australia** (✉ Level 3, 56 Pitt St., Sydney NSW 2000, ☎ 03/9614–1077, FAX 03/9614–7924). In New Zealand: **Insurance Council of New Zealand** (✉ Box 474, Wellington, New Zealand, ☎ 04/472–5230, FAX 04/473–3011, WEB www.icnz.org.nz).

LODGING

Decide whether you want to pay the extra price for a room overlooking the ocean or pool. At less expensive properties, location may mean a difference in price of only $10–$20 per room; at luxury resorts, however, it could amount to as much as $100 per room. Also **find out how close the property is to a beach.** At some hotels you can walk barefoot from your room onto the sand; others are across a road or a 10-minute drive away.

Nighttime entertainment is often alfresco in the USBVI, so if you go to sleep early or are a light sleeper, **ask for a room away from the dance floor.** Air-conditioning isn't a necessity on all islands, many of which are cooled by trade winds, but it can be a plus if you enjoy an afternoon snooze or are bothered by humidity. Breezes are best in second-floor rooms, particularly corner rooms. If you like to sleep without air-conditioning, make sure that windows can be opened and have screens. If you're staying away from the water, make sure the room has a ceiling fan and that it works. In even the most luxurious resorts, there are times when things simply *don't* work; it's a fact of Caribbean life. No matter how diligent the upkeep, humidity and salt air take their toll, and cracked tiles and chipped paint are common everywhere.

The lodgings we list are the cream of the crop in each price category. We always list the available facilities—but we don't specify whether they cost

extra. When pricing accommodations, always ask what's included and what costs extra. All hotels listed have rooms with private baths unless otherwise noted.

Assume that hotels operate on the **European Plan** (EP, with no meals), unless we specify that they offer the **Breakfast Plan** (BP, with full breakfast daily), **Continental Plan** (CP, with a Continental breakfast), the **Full American Plan** (FAP, with all meals), or the **Modified American Plan** (MAP, with breakfast and dinner), or are **all-inclusive** (including all meals and most activities).

APARTMENT & VILLA RENTALS

If you want a home base that's roomy enough for a family and comes with cooking facilities, **consider a furnished rental.** These can save you money, especially if you're traveling with a group. Home-exchange directories sometimes list rentals as well as exchanges.

➤ INTERNATIONAL AGENTS: **At Home Abroad** (✉ 405 E. 56th St., Suite 6H, New York, NY 10022, ☎ 212/421–9165, FAX 212/752–1591, WEB member.aol.com/athomabrod/index.html). **Hideaways International** (✉ 767 Islington St., Portsmouth, NH 03801, ☎ 603/430–4433 or 800/843–4433, FAX 603/430–4444, WEB www.hideaways.com; membership $129). **Hometours International** (✉ Box 11503, Knoxville, TN 37939, ☎ 865/690–8484 or 800/367–4668, WEB thor.he.net/˜hometour). **Vacation Home Rentals Worldwide** (✉ 235 Kensington Ave., Norwood, NJ 07648, ☎ 201/767–9393 or 800/633–3284, FAX 201/767–5510, WEB www.vhrww.com). **Villas and Apartments Abroad** (✉ 1270 Ave. of the Americas, 15th floor, New York, NY 10020, ☎ 212/897–5045 or 800/433–3020, FAX 212/897–5039, WEB www.vaanyc.com). **Villas International** (✉ 950 Northgate Dr., Suite 206, San Rafael, CA 94903, ☎ 415/499–9490 or 800/221–2260, FAX 415/499–9491, WEB www.villasintl.com).

CAMPING

Camping in the USBVI is limited to established campgrounds. Except for the National Park Service's Cinnamon

Bay Campground on St. John, all are privately operated. Camping is a big draw on St. John, so be sure to make reservations as early as possible. most campgrounds do not have hot showers, game rooms, or swimming pools; instead, your entertainment comes on the beach and along hiking trails.

➤ CAMPGROUNDS: In the USVI, Cinnamon Bay Campground (☎ 340/776–6330 or 800/539–9998) on St. John; Maho Bay Camps (☎ 340/776–6240, 212/472–9453, or 800/392–9004) on St. John. In the BVI, Brewers Bay Campground (☎ 284/494–3463) on Tortola; White Bay Campground (☎ 284/495–9312) on Jost Van Dyke.

HOME EXCHANGES

If you would like to exchange your home for someone else's, **join a home-exchange organization,** which will send you its updated listings of available exchanges for a year and will include your own listing in at least one of them. It's up to you to make specific arrangements.

➤ EXCHANGE CLUBS: HomeLink International (✉ Box 47747, Tampa, FL 33647, ☎ 813/975–9825 or 800/638–3841, FAX 813/910–8144, WEB www.homelink.org; $98 per year). Intervac U.S. (✉ Box 590504, San Francisco, CA 94159, ☎ 800/756–4663, FAX 415/435–7440, WEB www.intervacus.com; $93 yearly fee includes one catalogue and on-line access).

HOTELS

Several major hotel chains have properties in the USVI, but all those in the BVI.

➤ TOLL-FREE NUMBERS: Best Western (☎ 800/528–1234, WEB www.bestwestern.com). Choice (☎ 800/221–2222, WEB www.hotelchoice.com). Colony (☎ 800/777–1700, WEB www.colony.com). Divi Resorts (☎ 888/367–3484, WEB www.diviresorts.com). Hilton (☎ 800/445–8667, WEB www.hilton.com). Holiday Inn (☎ 800/465–4329, WEB www.basshotels.com). Le Meridien (☎ 800/543–4300, WEB www.lemeridien-hotels.com). Marriott (☎ 800/228–9290, WEB www.marriott.com). Renaissance Hotels & Resorts (☎ 800/468–3571, WEB www.renaissancehotels.com).

Ritz-Carlton (☎ 800/241–3333, WEB www.ritzcarlton.com). Westin Hotels & Resorts (☎ 888/625–5144, WEB www.starwood.com). Wyndham Hotels & Resorts (☎ 800/822–4200, WEB www.wyndham.com).

MAIL & SHIPPING

Airmail between the USBVI and cities in the United States or Canada takes 7–14 days; surface mail can take 4–6 weeks. Airmail to the United Kingdom takes 2–3 weeks; to Australia and New Zealand, 3–4 weeks. For island-specific information on post office locations, postal rates, and opening hours, *see* Telephones and Mail *in* A to Z sections of individual island chapters.

OVERNIGHT SERVICES

Courier services (such as Airborne, Federal Express, UPS, and others) operate in the USBVI, although not every company serves each island. "Overnight" service is more likely to take two or more days, because of the limited number of flights on which packages can be shipped.

MEDIA

NEWSPAPERS & MAGAZINES

The New York Times and *USA Today* are available mid-morning at most major hotels. Local daily newspapers in the USVI include the *Daily News,* the *Independent,* and the *Avis.* On St. John, the *Tradewinds* comes out weekly, and the *St. John Times* is published monthly. The *Beacon* comes out twice a week and the *Island Sun* weekly in the BVI.

RADIO & TELEVISION

Many islanders depend on the radio to stay up to date. WSTA at 1340 AM and WVWI at 1000 AM on St. Thomas and WSTX at 970 AM or 100.3 FM on St. Croix are popular. In the BVI, tune into ZBVI (pronounced Zed BVI) at 780 AM. Cable television is available nearly everywhere.

MONEY MATTERS

The U.S. dollar is the currency on both the USVI and BVI. Prices throughout this guide are given for adults. Substantially reduced room rates, meal charges, and admission fees are almost always available for children, students, and senior citizens.

ATMS

Chase Bank has ATMs at all its locations on both the USVI and the BVI, as do branches of Scotia Bank. You'll also find ATMs at Banco Popular branches throughout the USVI. Beware that Chase Bank's ATM in St. John, the only one on the island, often runs out of money on long holiday weekends.

CREDIT CARDS

Major credit cards are widely accepted at hotels, restaurants, shops, car-rental agencies, other service providers, and ATM machines throughout the Caribbean. The only places that might not accept them are open-air markets or tiny shops in out-of-the-way villages. Villa renters should be forewarned that villa managers may not accept credit cards.

It's smart to **write down (and keep separate) the number of the credit card(s) you're carrying** and the toll-free number to call in case the card is lost or stolen.

Throughout this guide, the following abbreviations are used: **AE,** American Express; **D,** Discover; **DC,** Diner's Club; **MC,** MasterCard; and **V,** Visa.

TRAVELER'S CHECKS

Traveler's checks are a good idea, but get them in small denominations—$20 or $50. Restaurants and most shops will accept them, and your hotel will cash them for you. In rural areas and small villages you'll need cash. Lost or stolen checks can usually be replaced within 24 hours. To ensure a speedy refund, buy your own traveler's checks—don't let someone else pay for them: irregularities such as this can cause delays. The person who bought the checks should make the call to request a refund.

PACKING

Make sure you can handle your luggage. There are no carts at USBVI airports, and porters can be scarce. Small interisland planes have very limited carry-on space. Suitcases that fit under seats on major carriers just won't fit in these tiny places, so check your luggage and pack some toiletries, a change of clothes, and perhaps a bathing suit in your carry-on bag—just in case your checked luggage doesn't make the connection until a later flight (which may be the next day). Regional carriers let you tote your luggage to the plane, where the pilot or first mate will stow it away. If you're worried about losing your bags, this is a good practice to follow.

Travel light. Dress on the islands is generally casual. Bring loose-fitting clothing made of natural fabrics to see you through days of heat and humidity. Pack a beach cover-up, both to protect yourself from the sun and as something to wear to and from your hotel room. On all islands, bathing suits and immodest attire are frowned upon off the beach. A sun hat is advisable, but you don't have to pack one—inexpensive straw hats are available everywhere. For shopping and sightseeing, bring walking shorts, jeans, T-shirts, long-sleeve cotton shirts, slacks, and sundresses. Night time dress can range from really informal to casually elegant, depending on the establishment. A tie is practically never required, but a jacket may be appropriate in the fanciest restaurants and casinos. You may need a light sweater or long-sleeve T-shirt for breezy nights (or overly air-conditioned restaurants) or for the ferry ride home after a day in the sun.

In your carry-on luggage, **pack an extra pair of eyeglasses or contact lenses** and **enough of any medication you take** to last the entire trip. You may also ask your doctor to write a spare prescription using the drug's generic name, since brand names may vary from country to country. In luggage to be checked, **never pack prescription drugs or valuables.** To avoid customs delays, carry medications in their original packaging. And don't forget to carry with you the addresses of offices that handle refunds of lost traveler's checks. Check *Fodor's How to Pack* (available in bookstores everywhere) for more tips.

CHECKING LUGGAGE

How many carry-on bags you can bring with you is up to the airline.

Most allow two, but not always, so make sure that everything you carry aboard will fit under your seat or in the overhead bin, and get to the gate early. Note that if you have a seat at the back of the plane, you'll probably board first, while the overhead bins are still empty.

If you are flying internationally, note that baggage allowances may be determined not by piece but by weight—generally 88 pounds (40 kilograms) in first class, 66 pounds (30 kilograms) in business class, and 44 pounds (20 kilograms) in economy.

Airline liability for baggage is limited to $1,250 per person on flights within the United States. On international flights it amounts to $9.07 per pound or $20 per kilogram for checked baggage (roughly $640 per 70-pound bag) and $400 per passenger for unchecked baggage. You can buy additional coverage at check-in for about $10 per $1,000 of coverage, but it excludes a rather extensive list of items, shown on your airline ticket.

Before departure, **itemize your bags' contents** and their worth, and label the bags with your name, address, and phone number. (If you use your home address, cover it so potential thieves can't see it readily.) Inside each bag, **pack a copy of your itinerary.** At check-in, **make sure that each bag is correctly tagged** with the destination airport's three-letter code. If your bags arrive damaged or fail to arrive at all, file a written report with the airline before leaving the airport.

PASSPORTS & VISAS

When traveling internationally, **carry your passport** even if you don't need one (it's always the best form of I.D.) and **make two photocopies of the data page** (one for someone at home and another for you, carried separately from your passport). If you lose your passport, promptly call the nearest embassy or consulate and the local police.

ENTERING THE USBVI

Upon entering the USBVI, U.S. and Canadian citizens are required to present some proof of citizenship, if not a passport then a birth certificate or citizenship certificate as well as a valid, government-issued photo ID. A voter registration card or simply a driver's license is not enough. Australian, New Zealand, and U.K. citizens—or citizens of other countries—must have a valid passport. All visitors must have a return or ongoing ticket.

PASSPORT OFFICES

The best time to apply for a passport or to renew is in fall and winter. Before any trip, check your passport's expiration date, and, if necessary, renew it as soon as possible. Current U.S. passport holders may renew by mail; forms are available at local post offices or can be printed from the Internet.

➤ AUSTRALIAN CITIZENS: **Australian Passport Office** (☎ 131–232, WEB www.dfat.gov.au/passports).

➤ CANADIAN CITIZENS: **Passport Office** (☎ 819/994–3500 or 800/567–6868 in Canada, WEB www.dfait-maeci.gc.ca/passport).

➤ NEW ZEALAND CITIZENS: **New Zealand Passport Office** (☎ 04/494–0700, WEB www.passports.govt.nz).

➤ U.K. CITIZENS: **London Passport Office** (☎ 0870/521–0410, WEB www.ukpa.gov.uk) for fees and documentation requirements and to request an emergency passport.

➤ U.S. CITIZENS: **National Passport Information Center** (☎ 900/225–5674; calls are 35¢ per minute for automated service, $1.05 per minute for operator service; WEB www.travel.state.gov/npicinfo.html).

REST ROOMS

Rest rooms in hotels, restaurants, and public buildings are, as a rule, clean and well-equipped. Pay toilets aren't customary nor are staffed rest rooms. Some beaches, particularly those that get a lot of traffic, have modern amenities.

SAFETY

In the USVI, ask hotel staff members about the wisdom of venturing off the beaten path. Although it may seem like a nice night for a stroll back to your hotel from that downtown restaurant, it's better to take a taxi than face in incident. Although local police go to great lengths to avoid it, crime does happen. The BVI has seen less crime than its neighbors to the west, but gain, better safe than sorry.

Follow the same precautions that you would anywhere. Look around before using the ATM. Keep tabs on your pocketbook; put it on your lap—not the back of your chair—in restaurants. Stow valuable jewelry or other items in the hotel safe when you leave your room; hotel and villa burglaries do occur infrequently. Deserted beaches on St. John and the BVI are usually safe, but think twice about stopping at that luscious strand of lonely sand on St. Croix and St. Thomas. Hotel or public beaches are your best bets. Never leave your belongings unattended at the beach or on the seats of your rental car.

SENIOR-CITIZEN TRAVEL

In the off-season, many hotels in the USBVI may offer substantial rate reductions. While they're usually not for seniors alone, it never hurts to ask. To qualify for age-related discounts, **mention your senior-citizen status up front** when booking hotel reservations (not when checking out) and before you're seated in restaurants (not when paying the bill). When renting a car, ask about promotional car-rental discounts, which can be cheaper than senior-citizen rates.

➤ EDUCATIONAL PROGRAMS: **Elderhostel** (✉ 11 Ave. de Lafayette, Boston, MA 02111-1746, ☎ 877/426–8056, FAX 877/426–2166, WEB www.elderhostel.org). **Interhostel** (✉ University of New Hampshire, 6 Garrison Ave., Durham, NH 03824, ☎ 603/862–1147 or 800/733–9753, FAX 603/862–1113, WEB www.learn.unh.edu).

SHOPPING

St. Thomas, and to a lesser extent St. Croix and St. John, is a duty-free shopper's paradise. Liquor, jewelry, and electronic items all shout for your attention when you browse through the shopping areas. Check prices before you leave home. You may do better on electronics at stateside outlet stores. For interesting and eclectic merchandise you won't find at a stateside mall, poke around in cluttered shops without the big names. Don't expect to bargain with the merchants.

KEY DESTINATIONS

The prime St. Thomas shopping districts are historic downtown Charlotte Amalie and the Havensight Mall next to the cruise-ship pier. On St. Croix, Christiansted and Frederiksted both have many shops. St. John's Cruz Bay has two charming malls with a string of shops in between. For shopping on Tortola, head to Road Town. You'll find shops adjacent to marinas and in hotels on both the USVI and BVI.

SMART SOUVENIRS

Although duty-free goods may tempt you, the real finds are tucked away in small shops where the owner has scoured the ends of the earth to stock his or her store. Look for jams and jellies made in the USBVI, local artwork in various styles, and handcrafted jewelry in all price ranges.

WATCH OUT

USBVI shopkeepers are honest as a whole, but there's always a bad banana or two in the bunch. If you're buying a big-ticket item, ask for a guarantee. Be particularly careful when shopping the vendor's plaza on St. Thomas: once in a while, someone tries to pass off fake designer goods as the real thing. U.S. citizens returning home must **consume tropical fruits and other produce, smoke those Cuban cigars, and (with rare exceptions) leave the bouquets of flowers behind** before heading home.

STUDENTS IN THE USBVI

Students are especially fond of the BVI in general and of St. John in the USVI. Camping on these islands cuts costs considerably. At Maho Bay Camps, in St. John, anyone can work four hours a day at whatever needs doing in exchange for a tent and reduced-price food. In addition, interisland ferry trips are affordable, so students can often island-hop their way from St. Thomas, which has a major airport, to St. John and on to the BVI.

➤ I.D.s & SERVICES: **Council Travel**
(CIEE; ✉ 205 E. 42nd St., 15th floor,
New York, NY 10017, ☎ 212/822–
2700 or 888/268–6245, FAX 212/822–
2699, WEB www.councilexchanges.org)
for mail orders only, in the United
States. **Maho Bay Camps** (☎ 340/
776–6240, 212/472–9453, or 800/
392–9004) on St. John. **Travel Cuts**
(✉ 187 College St., Toronto, Ontario
M5T 1P7, Canada, ☎ 416/979–2406;
800/667–2887 in Canada, FAX 416/
979–8167, WEB www.travelcuts.com).

➤ ORGANIZATIONS: **International
Education Resource Center** (IERC; ✉
860 E. 216th St., Bronx, NY 10467;
☎ 718/231–8333 or 718/515–0093,
FAX 718/547–9210). **School for Field
Studies** (✉ 16 Broadway, Beverly,
MA 01915, ☎ 978/927–7777, FAX
978/927–5127).

TELEPHONES

Phone and fax service to and from
the USBVI is up-to-date and efficient.
Phone cards are used throughout the
islands; you can buy them (in several
denominations) at many retail shops
and convenience stores. They must be
used in special card phones, which
are also widely available.

AREA & COUNTRY CODES

The area code for the USVI is 340; for
the BVI, 284. The country code is 1
for the United States and Canada, 61
for Australia, 64 for New Zealand,
and 44 for the United Kingdom.

DIRECTORY ASSISTANCE &
OPERATOR ASSISTANCE

In the USVI, dial 913 to reach the
operator. In the BVI, dial 119. In both
locations, dial 0 for advice on how to
place your call.

INTERNATIONAL CALLS

Calling the United States and Canada
from the USBVI is just like making a
long distance call within those countries: dial 1, plus the area code. To
reach Europe, Australia, and New
Zealand, dial 011 followed by the
country code.

LOCAL CALLS

Local calls from USBVI pay phones
run 25¢, although some privately
owned phones are now charging 35¢.
Calls from the USVI to the BVI and

vice versa are charged as international
toll calls.

LONG-DISTANCE SERVICES

AT&T, MCI, and Sprint access codes
make calling long distance relatively
convenient, but you may find the
local access number blocked in many
hotel rooms. First ask the hotel operator to connect you. If the hotel operator balks, ask for an international
operator, or dial the international
operator yourself. One way to im-
prove your odds of getting connected
to your long-distance carrier is to
travel with more than one company's
calling card (a hotel may block Sprint,
for example, but not MCI). If all else
fails, call from a pay phone.

TIME

The USBVI are in the Atlantic Standard Time zone, which is one hour
later than Eastern Standard or four
hours earlier than GMT. During
Daylight Savings Time, between April
and October, Atlantic Standard is the
same time as Eastern Daylight Time.

TOURS & PACKAGES

Because everything is prearranged on
a prepackaged tour or independent
vacation, you'll spend less time planning—and often get it all at a good
price.

BOOKING WITH AN AGENT

Travel agents are excellent resources.
But it's a good idea to collect brochures from several agencies as
some agents' suggestions may be
influenced by relationships with tour
and package firms that reward them
for volume sales. If you have a special
interest, **find an agent with expertise
in that area**; ASTA has a database of
specialists worldwide.

Make sure your travel agent knows
the accommodations and other services of the place they're recommend-
ing. Ask about the hotel's location,
room size, beds, and whether it has a
pool, room service, or programs for
children, if you care about these. Has
your agent been there in person or
sent others whom you can contact?

Do some homework on your own,
too: local tourism boards can provide
information about lesser-known and

small-niche operators, some of which may sell only direct.

BUYER BEWARE

Each year consumers are stranded or lose their money when tour operators—even large ones with excellent reputations—go out of business. So **check out the operator.** Ask several travel agents about its reputation, and try to **book with a company that has a consumer-protection program.** (Look for information in the company's brochure.) In the United States, members of the National Tour Association and the United States Tour Operators Association are required to set aside funds to cover your payments and travel arrangements in the event that the company defaults. It's also a good idea to choose a company that participates in the American Society of Travel Agents' Tour Operator Program (TOP); ASTA will act as mediator in any disputes between you and your tour operator.

Remember that the more your package or tour includes the better you can predict the ultimate cost of your vacation. Make sure you know exactly what is covered, and **beware of hidden costs.** Are taxes, tips, and transfers included? Entertainment and excursions? These can add up.

➤ TOUR-OPERATOR RECOMMENDATIONS: **American Society of Travel Agents** (ASTA; ☎ 800/965–2782 24-hr hot line, FAX 703/739–7642, WEB www.astanet.com). **National Tour Association** (NTA; ✉ 546 E. Main St., Lexington, KY 40508, ☎ 859/226–4444 or 800/682–8886, WEB www.ntaonline.com). **United States Tour Operators Association** (USTOA; ✉ 342 Madison Ave., Suite 1522, New York, NY 10173, ☎ 212/599–6599 or 800/468–7862, FAX 212/599–6744, WEB www.ustoa.com).

VOLUNTEER VACATIONS

A volunteer vacation can add an incalculable dimension to your regular "time off." You become a part of other people's lives forever by digging with archaeologists, helping to build an island's infrastructure, improving its health-care facilities, teaching its children, consulting with its local businesses, or saving its environment.

Volunteer vacations aren't free but may be tax-deductible. Fees range from a few hundred to several thousand dollars, depending on the program and its duration, and cover most expenses while you're there. Round-trip transportation is often your own responsibility.

Organizations include Earthwatch, which arranges for you to participate in scientific research; Global Volunteers, which offers opportunities in education, construction, and business; and Habitat for Humanity, which puts you to work building homes.

➤ VOLUNTEER ORGANIZATIONS: **Earthwatch** (✉ 3 Clocktower Pl., Suite 100, Box 75, Maynard, MA 01754, ☎ 800/776–0188). **Global Volunteers** (✉ 375 E. Little Canada Rd., St. Paul, MN 55117, ☎ 800/487–1074). **Habitat for Humanity** (✉ 121 Habitat St., Americus, GA 31709, ☎ 800/422–4828).

TRANSPORTATION
AROUND THE USBVI

You have several options for getting around the USBVI. Taxis in both places are on the expensive side, but considering that it's often difficult to find places because the roads aren't well marked, it may be your best option. Vehicle rentals are also expensive, but a good bet for adventurous travelers who like to explore. Except on St. John, where reliable bus service follows the main road from Cruz Bay to Salt Pond, buses in St. Thomas and St. Croix don't keep to their schedule. There is no bus service in the BVI. Hotels often provide transportation from the airport to the hotel, and some offer low-priced or free shopping and beach shuttles.

TRAVEL AGENCIES

A good travel agent puts your needs first. Look for an agency that has been in business at least five years, emphasizes customer service, and has someone on staff who specializes in your destination. In addition, **make sure the agency belongs to a professional trade organization.** The American Society of Travel Agents (ASTA), with more than 26,000 members in some 170 countries, is the largest and most influential in the field. Operating under the motto "Without a travel agent, you're on your own," it maintains and enforces a strict code of ethics and will step in to help mediate any agent-client disputes if necessary. ASTA also maintains a Web site that includes a directory of agents.

➤ LOCAL AGENT REFERRALS: **American Society of Travel Agents** (ASTA; ☎ 800/965–2782 24-hr hot line, FAX 703/739–7642, WEB www.astanet. com). **Association of British Travel Agents** (✉ 68–71 Newman St., London W1T 3AH, U.K., ☎ 020/7637–2444, FAX 020/7637–0713, WEB www. abtanet.com). **Association of Canadian Travel Agents** (✉ 130 Albert St., Suite 1705, Ottawa, Ontario K1P 5G4, Canada, ☎ 613/237–3657, FAX 613/237–7502, WEB www.acta.net). **Australian Federation of Travel Agents** (✉ Level 3, 309 Pitt St., Sydney NSW 2000, Australia, ☎ 02/9264–3299, FAX 02/9264–1085, WEB www.afta.com.au). **Travel Agents' Association of New Zealand** (✉ Box 1888, Wellington 10033, New Zealand, ☎ 04/499–0104, FAX 04/499–0827, WEB www.taanz.org.nz).

VISITOR INFORMATION

For general information on the islands, contact these tourist offices before you go.

➤ USVI: UNITED STATES VIRGIN ISLANDS DEPARTMENT OF TOURISM: **USVI Government Tourist Office** (✉ 245 Peachtree St., Center Ave. Marquis One Tower MB-05, Atlanta, GA 30303, ☎ 404/688–0906; ✉ 500 N. Michigan Ave., Suite 2030, Chicago, IL 60611, ☎ 312/670–8784; ✉ 3460 Wilshire Blvd., Suite 412, Los Angeles, CA 90010, ☎ 213/739–0138; ✉ 2655 Le Jeune Rd., Suite 907, Coral Gables, FL 33134, ☎ 305/442–7200; ✉ 1270 Ave. of the Americas, Room 2108, New York, NY 10020, ☎ 212/332–2222; ✉ Hall of Streets, #298, 444 N. Capital St. NW, Washington, DC 20006, ☎ 202/624–3590; ✉ 60 Washington St., San Juan, Puerto Rico 00907, ☎ 787/722–8023; ✉ 703 Evans Ave. Suite 106, Toronto, Ontario, Canada M9C 5E9, ☎ 416/233–1414; ✉ Molasses House, Clove Hitch Quay, Plantation Wharf, York Place, London SW11 3TW, U.K., ☎ 020/7978–5262; WEB www.usvi.net).

➤ BVI: BRITISH VIRGIN ISLANDS TOURIST BOARD: **BVI Tourist Board (U.S.)** (✉ 370 Lexington Ave., Suite 1605, New York, NY 10017, ☎ 212/696–0400 or 800/835–8530; ✉ 3450 Wilshire Blvd., Suite 1202 Los Angeles, CA 90010, ☎ 213/736–8931; ✉ 3390 Peachtree Rd. NE, Suite 1000, Atlanta, GA 30326, ☎ 404/240–8018); **BVI Tourist Board (U.K.)** (✉ 55 Newman St., London W1P 3PG, U.K., ☎ 011–44–207–947–8200).

➤ U.S. GOVERNMENT ADVISORIES: **U.S. Department of State** (✉ Overseas Citizens Services Office, Room 4811 N.S., 2201 C St. NW, Washington, DC 20520, ☎ 202/647–5225 for interactive hot line, WEB travel.state. gov/travel/html); enclose a self-addressed, stamped, business-size envelope.

WEB SITES

Do check out the World Wide Web when you're planning your trip. You'll find everything from weather forecasts to virtual tours of various islands. Be sure to **visit Fodors.com** (www.fodors.com), a complete travel-planning site. You can research prices and book plane tickets, hotel rooms, rental cars, vacation packages, and more. In addition, you can post your pressing questions in the Travel Talk section and, in the site's Rants & Raves section, read comments about some of the restaurants and hotels in this book—and chime in yourself. Other planning tools include a currency converter and weather reports, and there are loads of links to other travel resources.

On the USVI Department of Tourism's Web site (www.usvi.net) you need only pick a palm tree to access information on St. Croix, St. Thomas, or St. John. In addition to the usual lodging, dining, and shopping categories, the BVI Tourism Bureau's site (www.bviwelcome.com) has a separate "At Sea" category, a nod to the popularity of water sports on these islands. And of course every Caribbean traveler should bookmark

THE GOLD GUIDE / SMART TRAVEL TIPS

the Caribbean Tourism Organization's comprehensive site (www.caribtourism.com).

WHEN TO GO

The high season in the USBVI is traditionally winter—from December 15 to the week after the St. Thomas Carnival, usually the last week in April—when northern weather is at its worst. During this season, you're guaranteed the most entertainment at resorts and the most people with whom to enjoy it. It's also the most fashionable, the most expensive, and the most popular time to visit—and most hotels are heavily booked. You must make reservations at least two or three months in advance for the very best places (sometimes a year in advance for the most exclusive spots). Hotel prices drop 20%–50% after April 15; airfares and cruise prices also fall. Saving money isn't the only reason to visit the USBVI during the off-season. Summer is usually one of the prettiest times of the year; the sea is even calmer, and things move at a slower pace (except for the first two weeks of August on Tortola when the BVI celebrates Carnival). The water is clearer for snorkeling and smoother for sailing in the Virgin Islands in May, June, and July.

CLIMATE

Weather in the USBVI is a year-round wonder. The average daily temperature is about 80F, and there isn't much variation from the coolest to the warmest months. Rainfall averages 40 to 44 inches per year. But in the tropics, rainstorms tend to be sudden and brief, often erupting early in the morning and at dusk.

In May and June what's known as the Sahara Dust sometimes moves through, making for hazy spring days and spectacular sunsets.

Toward the end of summer, of course, hurricane season begins in earnest, with the first tropical wave passing by in June. Islanders pay close attention to the tropical waves as they form and travel across the Atlantic from Africa. In an odd paradox, tropical storms passing by leave behind the sunniest and clearest days you'll ever see. (And that's saying something in the land of zero air pollution.)

➤ FORECASTS: **Weather Channel Connection** (☎ 900/932–8437), 95¢ per minute from a Touch-Tone phone.

The following are average daily maximum and minimum temperatures for the Virgin Islands.

CLIMATE IN THE VIRGIN ISLANDS

Jan.	86F	25C	May	88F	31C	Sept.	92F	33C
	74	23		75	24		76	24
Feb.	86F	25C	June	88F	31C	Oct.	92F	33C
	74	23		75	24		76	24
Mar.	87F	30C	July	95F	35C	Nov.	86F	25C
	71	22		77	25		72	22
Apr.	87F	30C	Aug.	95F	35C	Dec.	86F	25C
	71	22		77	25		72	22

HOW TO
USE THIS GUIDE

Great trips begin with great planning, and this guide makes planning easy. It's packed with everything you need—insider advice on hotels and restaurants, cool tools, practical tips, essential maps, and much more.

COOL TOOLS

Fodor's Choice Top picks are marked throughout with a star.

Great Itineraries These tours, planned by Fodor's experts, give you the skinny on what you can see and do in the time you have.

Smart Travel Tips A to Z This special section is packed with important contacts and advice on everything from how to get around to what to pack.

Good Walks You won't miss a thing if you follow the numbered bullets on our maps.

Need a Break? Looking for a quick bite to eat or a spot to rest? These sure bets are along the way.

Off the Beaten Path Some lesser-known sights are worth a detour. We've marked those you should make time for.

POST-IT® FLAGS
Dog-ear no more!

"Post-it" is a registered trademark of 3M.

Favorite restaurants • Essential maps •
Frequently used numbers • Walking tours
• Can't-miss sights • Smart Travel
Tips • Web sites • Top shops • Hot
ses • Smart contacts
beaten-path spots •
s • Essential maps •
Walking
• Smart
ops • Hot
nightclubs • Addresses • Smart contacts •
Events • Off-the-beaten-path spots • Favorite
restaurants • Essential maps • Frequently
used numbers • Walking tours •

ICONS AND SYMBOLS

Watch for these symbols throughout:

★	Our special recommendations
✕	Restaurant
🏠	Lodging establishment
✕🏠	Lodging establishment whose restaurant warrants a special trip
☺	Good for kids
☞	Sends you to another section of the guide for more information
✉	Address
☎	Telephone number
FAX	Fax number
WEB	Web site
🎫	Admission price
☉	Opening hours
$-$$$$	Lodging and dining price categories, keyed to strategically sited price charts. Check the index for locations.
①❶	Numbers in white and black circles on the maps, in the margins, and within tours correspond to one another.

ON THE WEB

Continue your planning with these useful tools found at **www.fodors.com**, the Web's best source for travel information.

"Rich with resources." —*New York Times*

"Navigation is a cinch." —*Forbes* "Best of the Web" list

"Put together by people bursting with know-how."
—*Sunday Times* (London)

Create a Miniguide Pinpoint hotels, restaurants, and attractions that have what you want at the price you want to pay.

Rants and Raves Find out what readers say about Fodor's picks—or write your own reviews of hotels and restaurants you've just visited.

Travel Talk Post your questions and get answers from fellow travelers, or share your own experiences.

On-Line Booking Find the best prices on airline tickets, rental cars, cruises, or vacations, and book them on the spot.

About our Books Learn about other Fodor's guides to your destination and many others.

Expert Advice and Trip Ideas From what to tip to how to take great photos, from the national parks to Nepal, Fodors.com has suggestions that'll make your trip a breeze. Log on and get informed and inspired.

Smart Resources Check the weather in your destination or convert your currency. Learn the local language or link to the latest event listings. Or consult hundreds of detailed maps—all in one place.

1 DESTINATION: THE VIRGIN ISLANDS

SOMETHING FOR EVERYONE

SEPARATED BY ONLY a narrow channel of shimmering water patrolled by flotillas of pelicans and pleasure craft, the United States and British Virgin Island groups are nevertheless a world apart. It isn't just the obvious: a tale of two traditions and governments. Indeed, clearing customs is usually a formality (although it's taken very seriously), and the U.S. dollar is the official currency on both sides of the "border." Rather, it's the individual look and feel that set them apart, the atmosphere they determinedly cultivate—and the differing breeds of visitors this attracts—an atmosphere perhaps too glibly defined as American verve versus British reserve.

Though the islands are closely grouped, the vegetation and terrain vary widely. The USVI are largely lush and tropical. On St. John, where two-thirds of the land is under U.S. National Park Service protection, there are more than 250 species of trees, vines, shrubs, flowers, and other plant life. Each of the three major USVI— St. John, St. Thomas, and St. Croix—is really a collection of ecosystems, ranging from tropical seacoast to mountain, rain forest to desert. The flowering trees are particularly superb: frangipani, flamboyant, hibiscus, and lignum vitae blanket the hills and rolling fields with a dainty blue, pink, yellow, and white quilt.

In contrast, the BVI's largest island, Tortola, lost lots of its vegetation to the farmer's field. This gives it a very different look than that of the heavily forested St. John, just a 2-mi boat ride away. Its high peaks culminate with see-forever views at Sage Mountain National Park. Virgin Gorda is fringed with monumental boulders whose exact origins are still shrouded in mystery. These are the "cactus tropics," dotted with agave and other spiny plants and enlivened by the vibrant colors of an occasional wild hibiscus or bougainvillea tree.

Both island groups are steeped in history. The USVI are graced with the rich architectural legacy of the original Danish settlers, including the picturesque ruins of their sugar plantations. Christiansted and Frederiksted, the two main towns on St. Croix, feature delightful red-roof gingerbreads in coral and canary yellow, fronted by shaded galleries and stately colonnades. The old sugar estates on St. Croix are the islands' best preserved and most elegant. Caribbean ghost towns unto themselves, they're crawling and cracked with undergrowth, the haunting grandeur of their double stairways eloquently attesting to St. Croix's former prosperity.

If their architectural remains aren't as spectacular, the BVI have an incomparable *air* of history. In the 17th and 18th centuries the islands' numerous cays, rocks, secret coves, and treacherous reefs formed the perfect headquarters for raiding corsairs and privateers, among them the infamous Edward "Blackbeard" Teach, Captain Kidd, and Sir Francis Drake. The nautical spirit lives on, and today these pirate hideaways attract legions of "yachties." The calm, iridescent waters of the BVI are among the world's most popular sailing destinations. In fact, the islands, forested by masts and flecked with sails, are perhaps best experienced by boat—what better way to explore every rainbow-colored coral reef or gleaming scimitar of white sand (replete with beach bar)? The favorite sport may well be motoring to a private cove, waving if it's occupied, and cruising to the next.

But ultimately the greatest differences between the USVI and the BVI are the ways in which they've been developed. Step off the plane in St. Thomas and you know you're in a consumer society where bigger is better. Posters hawking products and fast-food franchises dominate the lush surroundings. Charlotte Amalie, the bustling capital, pulsates with legendary duty-free shopping and by far the most active nightlife in the area. You'll discover more pristine pockets on pastoral St. Croix, which by comparison resembles a friendly small town. The odd isle out in the USVI equation is tranquil, sleepy St. John, the closest American island to the BVI in distance and temperament. But even here the development and pace often exceed that of its British cousins.

With so many options for the tourist dollar, competition among USVI properties is fierce. The constant upgrading of facilities, added amenities, and attractive package rates translate into tremendous values. If you want all the comforts and conveniences (and convenience stores) of home—with tropical sun and exotic accent—head for the USVI.

Although tourism is as much the number-one industry on the BVI as it is on the USVI, you'd never know it. On these quiet, unhurried islands, there are few major developments and no high-rises or traffic lights. Cruise ships do visit regularly, but far fewer stop here than at the USVI. Though there are repeated promises (viewed more as threats by locals) from the tourist office to deepen the harbor and lengthen the airport runways (now scheduled to happen by 2003), there's a tacit understanding that it's precisely their comparatively undeveloped state that makes the BVI such desirable vacation spots.

By many tourism standards, the BVI are *not* a bargain. The hotels tend to be small and exclusive; many were built by industrial barons and shipping magnates as hideaways for themselves and friends. But true luxury is often understated. It isn't necessarily blow-dryers and satellite TVs in every room. Rather, it's the privacy, the relaxed, easygoing pace, the personalized service, and the ambience.

Expatriates on both sets of islands often delight in taking potshots at their neighbors. You'll find many passionate devotees and repeat visitors who wouldn't dream of crossing the border. USVI detractors point to the swarming crowds and comparatively high crime rate on St. Thomas and St. Croix. BVI critics cite the boring lifestyle and the difficulty of getting top-notch goods even on Tortola. The USVI have been disparaged as "entry-level Caribbean" and "Detroit with palm trees." Their aficionados will counter, "There's a reason the British Home Office once called the BVI 'the least important part of the Empire.'"

The rivalry only demonstrates how popular the islands are with their respective fans. Luckily, whichever you prefer, there's always the advantage of proximity. In the Virgin Islands you can truly have the best of both worlds.

–Jordan Simon

A freelance writer who has traveled throughout the Caribbean, Jordan Simon has written for Elle, Travel & Leisure, Modern Bride, *and* Fodor's Caribbean.

WHAT'S WHERE

The U.S. Virgin Islands

ST. THOMAS➤ Because it's the transportation hub of the Virgin Islands, many visitors at least land on hilly St. Thomas. Those who stay longer may have come for its legendary shopping or the wide variety of water sports, activities, and accommodations. The bustling port of Charlotte Amalie is the main town; about ¼ mi off its shores is Water Island, which was made the fourth Virgin Island in 1996 when the U.S. Department of the Interior transferred it to the territorial government. Up-and-coming Red Hook sits on St. Thomas's eastern tip. The island's western end is relatively wild, and hotels and resorts rim its southern and eastern shores.

ST. CROIX➤ The largest of the USVI, St. Croix is 40 mi south of St. Thomas. Plantation ruins, reminiscent of the days when it was a great producer of sugar, dot the island. Its northwest is covered by a lush rain forest, its drier East End spotted with cacti. The restored Danish port of Christiansted and the more Victorian-looking Frederiksted are its main towns; Buck Island, off the northeast shore, attracts many day visitors.

ST. JOHN➤ Only 3 mi from St. Thomas but still a world apart, St. John is the least developed of the USVI. Although two-thirds of its tropical hills remain protected as national parkland, a bit of hustle and bustle has come to Cruz Bay, the main town. Accommodations range from world-class luxury resorts to top-notch vacation villas to back-to-basics campgrounds.

The British Virgin Islands

TORTOLA➤ A day might not be enough to tour this island—all 10 sq mi of it—not because there's so much to see and do but because you're meant to relax while you're here. Time stands still even in Road Town, the biggest community, where the hands of the central square's clock occasionally move, but never tell the right time. The harbor, however, is busy with sailboats—this is the charter-boat capital of the world. Tortola's roads dip and curve and lead to lovely, secluded accommodations.

VIRGIN GORDA➤ Progressing from laid-back to more laid-back, mountainous and arid Virgin Gorda fits right in. Its main road sticks to the center of the island, connecting the odd-shaped north and south appendages; sailing is the preferred mode of transportation. Spanish Town, the most noteworthy settlement, is on the southern wing, as are The Baths. Here smooth, giant boulders are scattered about the beach and form delightful sea grottoes just offshore.

OTHER ISLANDS➤ **Jost Van Dyke,** a sparsely populated island northwest of Tortola, has a disproportionate number of surprisingly lively bars and is a favorite haunt of yachties. Hilly **Peter Island** also attracts sailors with its wonderful anchorages. Flat **Anegada** lurks 20 mi northeast of Virgin Gorda. It rises just 28 ft above sea level, but its reef stretches out underwater, practically inviting wrecks. The scores of shipwrecks that encircle the island attract divers and a bounty of fish.

PLEASURES AND PASTIMES

Beaches

With their warm, clear days, unspoiled sandy strands, and beautiful turquoise water, the Virgin Islands are a beach bum's paradise. Even if you're not a connoisseur, a day or two on the sand is central to a complete vacation here.

Your accommodation may border a beach or provide transportation to one nearby, but you have other options. You could spend one day at a lively, touristy beach that has plenty of water-sports facilities and is backed by a bar and another at an isolated cove that offers nothing but seclusion. Of course, these beaches are just jumping-off points to the underwater world.

In the USVI, public access to beach waters is guaranteed but land access to them isn't, effectively restricting some areas to resort guests. On St. Thomas, Magens Bay is among the prettiest (but also the liveliest) public beaches, and Hull Bay is the only place to surf. St. Croix's west-end beaches are popular, and the calm waters of Isaac Bay, on the more isolated East End, can give you a stretch all to yourself. Beautiful Trunk Bay, St. John, gets a lot of day-trip cruise-ship passengers; Salt Pond Bay is remote and mostly undeveloped.

Nowhere in the BVI will you find crowds to match those at the most popular USVI beaches, but Cane Garden Bay on Tortola probably comes the closest. Apple Bay and Josiah's Bay, also on Tortola, are good for surfing, and Long Bay (West) is quieter. Virgin Gorda's beaches are easiest to get to from the water but are also approachable from land. Swimming among the rock formations at The Baths is a priority for many visitors, but this area can be crowded. On the smaller BVI, the lovely beaches are most likely sparsely populated by those who have dropped anchor and made their way in.

Historic Sites

Columbus, pirates, European colonizers, and plantation farmers and their slaves are among the people who have left their marks on these islands, all of which are benefiting the tourism industry, a relatively recent development.

In Charlotte Amalie, St. Thomas, Fort Christian (1672), Blackbeard's Castle (1679), the Synagogue of Beracha Veshalom Vegmiluth Hasidim (1833), and the Danish Consulate (1830) are some noteworthy sights that give glimpses into the town's past. St. Croix's countryside is dotted with ruins of plantation great houses and sugar mills. St. John, too, has several plantations in varying degrees of decay.

Die-hard sightseers will find less to keep them busy in the British Virgin Islands. Numbering among the historic sights, however, are Tortola's Mt. Healthy National Park, an old plantation site, and Copper Mine Point, the ruins of a 400-year-old mine on Virgin Gorda.

Nightlife

Although you'll never be too far from a Jimmy Buffett tune, the nightlife establishments in the Virgin Islands do their share to provide something for everyone. Yachties congregate, not surprisingly, at the waterfront bars, where live guitar music may accompany the rum drinks. BVI watering holes, especially those on Jost Van Dyke, are most likely to be true beach bars. Steel-drum, calypso, and reggae music—as well as broken-bottle dancing—are common in shows at larger hotels. Musicians also often play impromptu in the street, and if you look around you may come across a piano bar or a jazz band.

Shopping

Charlotte Amalie, St. Thomas, is *the* place to shop. As the Virgin Islands' main commercial center, it has the best selection of just about everything. Bargain hunters drool over the duty-free allowances and the lack of sales tax; liquor, china, crystal, and jewelry are especially popular buys. But you should also seek out artwork, crafts, and spices that are sold locally throughout the islands.

Water Sports

Whether you chart a boat or head out on a day-sail, traveling by boat is a relaxing and efficient way to see the islands. Wrecks and reefs make the islands as interesting underwater as above. For pointers on how to plan a trip that involves sailing, scuba diving, or snorkeling, *see* "Exploring the Waters of the USBVI" *in* Chapter 4.

NEW AND NOTEWORTHY

➤ St. Thomas: If you're itching to keep in touch with family and friends back home, the Little Switzerland store in Charlotte Amalie now has an Internet café with free access.

In 2001 the U.S. Senate lifted the ban on tobacco products bought in the USVI. Now you can bring your duty-free tobacco back home with you—legally.

➤ St. Croix: A boardwalk now wraps around Christiansted Harbor from the Holger Danske Hotel to Fort Christianvaern. Part of an improvement expected to extend all the way to Gallows Bay, the boardwalk is a pleasant place for a stroll and to people watch.

Henry E. Rohlsen International Airport was expanded and remodeled in 2001. The main terminal is now comfortably air-conditioned.

➤ St. John: Stop by the island's newest shopping center, the Market Place. On Route 104, this attractive concrete and stone building includes the island's largest supermarket, Starfish, a drug store, video rental store, and something you won't find in Cruz Bay—easy parking.

➤ Tortola/Beef Island: Construction continues on the expanded runway and improved passenger facilities at the Beef Island Airport, which should be finished by 2003.

FODOR'S CHOICE

Beaches

⭐ **Magens Bay, St. Thomas,** a long, lovely loop of white sand.

⭐ **Palm-fringed Dead Man's Bay, Peter Island,** conducive to romance.

⭐ **Smuggler's Cove, Tortola,** for its good snorkeling and view of Jost Van Dyke.

⭐ **Spring Bay or The Baths, Virgin Gorda,** where you can swim among unique rock formations—essential to a Virgin Gorda vacation.

⭐ **Trunk Bay, St. John,** beautiful, if at times crowded. Its snorkeling trail is a big draw.

Hotels

⭐ **Biras Creek Hotel, Virgin Gorda.** The setting and service here are exceptional. $$$$

⭐ **Caneel Bay Resort, St. John.** Civilized and luxurious, Caneel Bay draws the same visitors year after year. $$$$

⭐ **Long Bay Beach Resort, Tortola.** Accommodations range from hillside rooms to beachside cabanas on stilts—all positioned to take advantage of the spectacular setting. $$$$

⭐ **Ritz-Carlton, St. Thomas.** Built like an Italian villa, there's elegance everywhere, from the marbled-floor reception area to a pool that seems to flow right into the sea. $$$$

★ **Sunterra Carambola Beach Resort, St. Croix.** Room decor is tasteful but not overdone, and all rooms look out on a garden or an exquisite ecru beach. *$$$$*

★ **The Villas of Fort Recovery Estates.** With a remote, beachside setting and a friendly, helpful staff, this resort has the ingredients for a great vacation. *$$$$*

★ **Hotel 1829, St. Thomas.** Romance and classic elegance abound at this historic, Spanish-style inn. *$$$*

★ **Admiral's Inn, St. Thomas.** This charming inn sprawls down a hillside in Frenchtown. *$$*

Restaurants

★ **Brandywine Bay, Tortola.** The Tuscan food and the romantic setting here are both big draws. *$$$–$$$$*

★ **Sugarmill Restaurant, Tortola.** Candlelight and stone walls decorated with island art combined with superb cuisine create a romantic evening in this 360-year-old mill. *$$$–$$$$*

★ **Raffles, St. Thomas.** Sandra Englesburger's one-woman culinary show is well worth the price of admission. *$$$*

★ **Top Hat, St. Croix.** The delicious Danish dishes here include a delicious fried Camembert with lingonberries. *$$$*

★ **Virgilio's, St. Thomas.** This intimate, elegant hideaway serves the best northern Italian food on the island, right down to its cappuccino. *$$$*

★ **Skinny Legs Bar and Restaurant, St. John.** Sitting in the midst of Coral Bay's nautical scene, this is the best place to go for burgers, beers, and the like. *$$*

Music, Nightlife, Bars

★ **Any bar on Jost Van Dyke.** You can't go wrong on this island, which does its best to entertain the charter-yacht crowd.

★ **Bath and Turtle, Virgin Gorda.** Good island bands play on Wednesday and Sunday evenings.

★ **Blue Moon, St. Croix.** You'll find great live jazz every Friday night.

★ **Bomba's Surfside Shack, Tortola.** This is one of the island's liveliest spots. On full moons, the music plays all night long.

★ **Old Mill Entertainment Complex, St. Thomas.** Whether you want rock-til-you-drop partying or a tamer piano bar or just jazz, this place offers it all.

★ **Quito's Gazebo, Tortola.** The surf is the perfect accompaniment to whatever's playing: ballads, reggae, or Quito Rhymer's love songs.

Scenic Views

★ **Annaberg Plantation, St. John,** provides a glimpse into the island's history and gorgeous views of the BVI and the sound that runs from St. Thomas eastward.

★ **The beautiful parade of cruise ships** out of St. Thomas's Charlotte Amalie harbor is a sight to behold.

★ **Sailing into Red Hook (St. Thomas) from St. John at sunset** makes for a mellow start to your evening in town.

★ **Sunsets from the Skyworld observation tower, Tortola,** are especially colorful. If the sky is clear, you may even see St. Croix.

2 UNITED STATES VIRGIN ISLANDS

Mornings at the Squirrel Cage coffee shop on St. Thomas aren't much different from those in coffee shops back home. A cop stops by to joke with the waitress and collect his first cup of coffee; a high-heeled secretary runs in for the paper and some toast; a store clerk lingers over a cup of tea to discuss politics with the cook. But is the coffee shop back home in a bright pink hole-in-the-wall of a 19th-century building, steps from a park abloom with frangipani— in January? Are bush tea and johnnycake served alongside oatmeal and omelets?

Updated by
Carol
Bareuther and
Lynda Lohr

T'S THE COMBINATION of the familiar and the exotic found in St. Thomas, St. Croix, and St. John—the United States Virgin Islands (USVI)—that defines this "American paradise" and explains much of its appeal. The effort to be all things to all people—while remaining true to the best of itself—has created a sometimes paradoxical blend of island serenity and American practicality in this U.S. territory 1,000 mi (1,600 km) from the southern tip of the U.S. mainland.

The images you'd expect from a tropical paradise are here: Stretches of beach arc into the distance, and white sails skim across water so blue and clear it stuns the senses. Red-roof houses color the green hillsides as do the orange of the flamboyant tree, the red of the hibiscus, the magenta of the bougainvillea, and the blue stone ruins of old sugar mills. Towns of pastel-tone villas, decorated with filigree wrought-iron terraces, line narrow streets that climb from the harbor. Amid all the images you can find moments—sometimes whole days—of exquisite tranquillity: an egret standing in a pond at dawn, palm trees backlighted by a full moon, sunrises and sunsets that send your spirits soaring with the frigate bird flying overhead.

Chances are that on one of the three islands you'll find your own idea of paradise. Check into a beachfront condo on the east end of St. Thomas, eat burgers, and watch football at a beachfront bar and grill. Or stay at an 18th-century plantation great house on St. Croix, dine on Danish delicacies, and go horseback riding at sunrise. Rent a tent or a cottage in the pristine national park on St. John, take a hike, kayak off the coast, read a book, or just listen to the sounds of the forest. Or dive deep into "island time" and learn the art of limin' (hanging out, Caribbean-style) on all three islands.

Idyllic though they may be, these bits of volcanic rock in the middle of the Caribbean Sea haven't entirely escaped such worries of overdevelopment as trash, crime, and traffic. Isolation and limited space have, in fact, accentuated these problems. What, for example, do you do with 76 million cans and bottles imported annually when the nearest recycling plant is across 1,000 mi (1,600 km) of ocean? Despite these dilemmas wildlife has found refuge here. The brown pelican is on the endangered list worldwide but is a common sight in the USVI. The endangered native boa tree is protected, as is the hawksbill turtle, whose females lumber onto the beaches to lay eggs.

Preserving its own culture while progressing as a tourist destination is another problem. The islands have been inhabited by Taíno Indians (on St. John and St. Thomas); Carib Indians (on St. Croix); Danish settlers and Spanish pirates; traders and invaders from all the European powers; Africans brought in as slaves; migrants from other Caribbean islands; and, finally, Americans, first as administrators, then as businesspeople and tourists. All these influences are creating a more homogeneous culture, and with each passing year the USVI lose more of their rich, spicy, Caribbean personality.

Sailing into the Caribbean on his second voyage in 1493, Christopher Columbus came upon St. Croix before the group of islands that would later be known as St. Thomas, St. John, and the British Virgin Islands (BVI). He named St. Croix "Santa Cruz" (called Ay Ay by the Carib Indians already living there) but moved on quickly after he encountered the fierce residents. As he approached St. Thomas and St. John, he was impressed enough with the shapely silhouettes of the numerous islands and cays (including the BVI) to name them after Ursula and her 11,000 virgins, but he found the islands barren and moved on to explore Puerto Rico.

Over the next century, as it became clear that Spain couldn't defend the entire Caribbean, other European powers began to settle the islands. In the 1600s the French were joined by the Dutch and the English on St. Croix, and St. Thomas had a mixture of European residents in the early 1700s. By 1695 St. Croix was under the control of the French, but the colonists had moved on to what is today Haiti. The island lay virtually dormant until 1733, when the Danish government bought it—along with St. Thomas and St. John—from the Danish West India Company. At that time settlers from St. Thomas and St. John moved to St. Croix to cultivate the island's gentler terrain. St. Croix developed a plantation economy, but St. Thomas's soil was ill suited to agriculture. There the harbor became internationally known because of its size and ease of entry; it's still hailed as one of the most beautiful seaports in the world.

Plantations depended on slave labor, of which there was a plentiful supply in the Danish West Indies. As early as 1665, agreements between the Brandenburger Company (which needed a base in the West Indies from which to ship the slaves it had imported from Africa) and the West India Company (which needed the kind of quick cash it could collect in duties, fees, and rents from the slave trade) established St. Thomas as a primary slave market.

It's from the slaves who worked the plantations that most Virgin Islanders are descended. More than likely the salesclerk who sells you a watch and the waitress who serves your rum punch can trace their lineage to ancestors captured in Africa some 300 years ago and brought to the West Indies, where they were sold on the block, priced according to their comeliness and strength. Most were captured along Africa's Gold Coast, from the tribes of Asante, Ibo, Mandika, Amina, and Wolof. They brought with them African rhythms in music and language, herbal medicine, and such crafts as basketry and wood carving. The West Indian–African culture comes to full bloom at Carnival time, when playing *mas* (with abandon) takes precedence over all else.

Yet you can still see the influence of the early Danish settlers here, too. It's reflected in the language and architecture; in common surnames such as Petersen, Jeppesen, and Lawaetz; and in street names such as Kongen's Gade (King Street) and Kronprindsen's Gade (Prince Street). The town of Charlotte Amalie was named after a Danish queen. The Lutheran Church is the state church of Denmark, and Frederick Lutheran Church on St. Thomas dates from 1666. Other peoples have left their marks on the USVI as well. Jewish settlers came to the territory as early as 1665; they were shipowners, chandlers, and brokers in the slave trade. Today their descendants coexist with nearly 1,500 Arabs—95% of whom are Palestinian. You'll also find many East Indians, who are active members of the business community. Immigrants from Puerto Rico and the Dominican Republic make up close to half of St. Croix's population. Transplants from Caribbean countries to the south continue to arrive, seeking better economic opportunities.

St. Thomas, St. Croix, and St. John were known collectively as the Danish West Indies until the United States bought the territory in 1917 during World War I, prompted by fears that Germany would establish a U-boat base in the western hemisphere. The name was changed to the United States Virgin Islands, and almost immediately thereafter British-held Tortola and Virgin Gorda—previously known simply as the Virgin Islands—hastily inserted "British" on the front of their name.

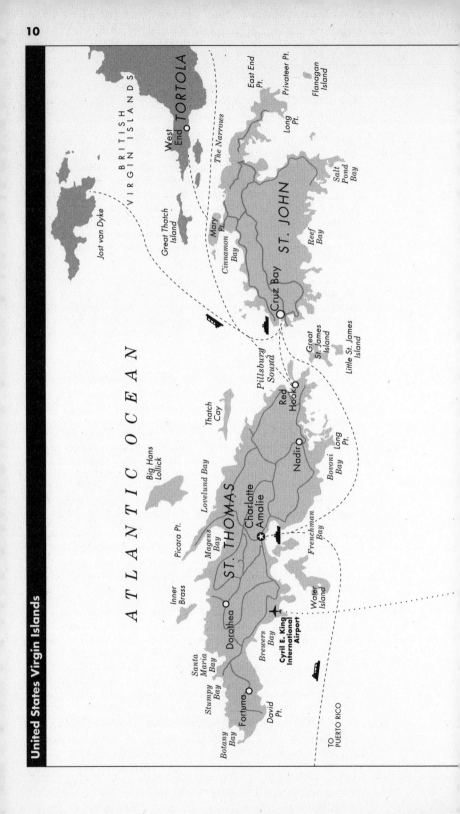

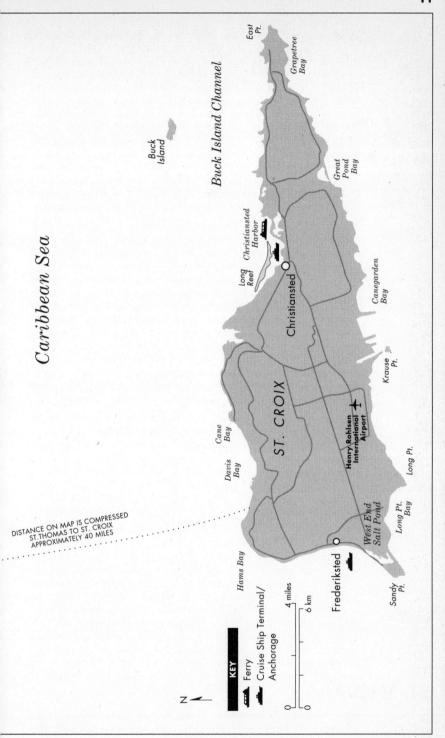

Caribbean Sea

Buck Island Channel

East Pt.

Grapetree Bay

Buck Island

Great Pond Bay

Christiansted Harbor

Long Reef

Canegarden Bay

Christiansted

Krause Pt.

ST. CROIX

Cane Bay

Henry Rohlsen International Airport

Long Pt.

Davis Bay

West End Salt Pond

Long Pt. Bay

DISTANCE ON MAP IS COMPRESSED
ST. THOMAS TO ST. CROIX
APPROXIMATELY 40 MILES

Hams Bay

Frederiksted

Sandy Pt.

KEY

Ferry

Cruise Ship Terminal/
Anchorage

4 miles

6 km

N

0

0

In the 1960s, Pineapple Beach Resort (today Renaissance Grand Beach Resort) was built on St. Thomas, and the Caneel Bay Resort on St. John, built in 1956, was expanded; and with direct flights from the U.S. mainland, the tourism industry was born. In 1960 the total population of all three islands was 32,000. By 1970 it had more than doubled to 75,000, as workers from throughout the Caribbean came to man the building boom. When the boom waned, the people stayed, bringing additional diversity to the territory but also putting a tremendous burden on its infrastructure. Today there are about 50,000 people living on 32-square-mi (83-square-km) St. Thomas (about the same size as Manhattan), 51,000 on the 84 square mi (216 square km) of pastoral St. Croix, and about 5,000 on 20-square-mi (52-square-km) St. John, two-thirds of which is a national park. The per capita income in the USVI is the highest in the West Indies. Just over 25% of the total labor force is employed by the government, and about 10% work in tourism.

Agriculture hasn't been a major economic factor since the last sugarcane plantation on St. Croix ceased operating in the 1960s, but a few farmers on St. Croix, St. Thomas, and St. John still produce some of the mangoes, pineapples, and herbs you'll find on your plate. The islands' cuisine reflects a dependency on a land that gives grudgingly of its bounty. Root vegetables such as sweet potato, hardy vegetables such as okra, and stick-to-your-ribs breads were staples 200 years ago, and their influence is still evident in the sweet potato stuffing (mashed potatoes, spices, and raisins), *fungi* (cornmeal and okra), and johnnycakes (deep-fried dough rounds made of cornmeal and white flour) that are ever-present on menus today. The fruits are sweet (slaves got energy to cut sugarcane from a sugar-water drink made from sugar apples). Beverages include not only rum but coconut water, fruit juices, and *maubi,* made from tree bark, and reputedly a virility enhancer.

The backbone of the economy is tourism, but at the heart of the islands is an independent, separate being: a rollicking hodgepodge of West Indian culture with a sense of humor that puts sex and politics in almost every conversation. Lacking a major-league sports team, Virgin Islanders follow the activities and antics of their 15 elected senators with the rabidity of Washingtonians following the Redskins. Loyalty to country and faith in God are the rules in the USVI not the exceptions. Prayer is a way of life, and ROTC is one of the most popular high-school extracurricular activities.

The struggle to preserve the predominantly black Caribbean-influenced culture is heating up in America's paradise. Native Virgin Islanders say they want access to more than just the beach when big money brings in big development. But the three islands are far from united in their goals, especially in light of a $1 billion deficit that threatens the autonomy of the local government and protection of the territory's number-one resource—scenic beauty. The ongoing conflict between progress and preservation here is no mere philosophical exercise, and attempts at resolutions display yet another aspect of the islands' unique blend of character.

ST. THOMAS

Updated by
Carol
Bareuther

If you fly to the 32-square-mi (83-square-km) island of St. Thomas, you land at its western end; if you arrive by cruise ship, you come into one of the world's most beautiful harbors. Either way, one of your first sights is the town of Charlotte Amalie. From the harbor you see an idyllic-looking village that spreads into the lower hills. If you were expecting a quiet hamlet with its inhabitants hanging out under palm trees, you've missed that era by about 300 years. Although other islands in the USVI developed plantation economies, St. Thomas cultivated its harbor, and it became a thriving seaport soon after it was settled by the Danish in the 1600s.

The success of the naturally perfect harbor was enhanced by the fact that the Danes—who ruled St. Thomas with only a couple of short interruptions from 1666 to 1917—avoided involvement in some 100 years' worth of European wars. Denmark was the only European country with colonies in the Caribbean to stay neutral during the war of the Spanish succession in the early 1700s. Thus, products of the Dutch, English, and French islands—sugar, cotton, and indigo—were traded through Charlotte Amalie, along with the regular shipments of slaves. When the Spanish wars ended, trade fell off, but by the end of the 1700s Europe was at war again, Denmark again remained neutral, and St. Thomas continued to prosper. Even into the 1800s, while the economies of St. Croix and St. John foundered with the market for sugarcane, St. Thomas's economy remained strong. This prosperity led to the development of shipyards, a well-organized banking system, and a large merchant class. In 1845 Charlotte Amalie had 101 large importing houses owned by the English, French, Germans, Haitians, Spaniards, Americans, Sephardim, and Danes.

Charlotte Amalie is still one of the most active cruise-ship ports in the world. On almost any day at least one and sometimes as many as eight cruise ships are tied to the dock or anchored outside the harbor. Gently rocking in the shadows of these giant floating hotels are just about every other kind of vessel imaginable: sleek sailing mono- and multihulls that will take you on a sunset cruise complete with rum punch and a Jimmy Buffett soundtrack, private megayachts that spirit busy executives away, and barnacle-bottom sloops—with laundry draped to dry over the lifelines—that are home to world-cruising gypsies. Huge container ships pull up in Sub Base, west of the harbor, bringing in everything from cornflakes to tires. Anchored right along the waterfront are the picturesque down-island sloops of the type that has plied the waters between the Greater Antilles and the Leeward Islands for hundreds of years. The sloops still deliver produce, but today they also return down-island with refrigerators, VCRs, and disposable diapers.

The waterfront road through Charlotte Amalie was once part of the harbor. Before it was filled to build the highway, the beach came right up to the back door of the warehouses that now line the thoroughfare. Two hundred years ago those warehouses contained indigo, tobacco, and cotton. Today the stone buildings house silk, crystal, linens, and leather. Exotic fragrances are still traded—but by island beauty queens in air-conditioned perfume palaces instead of through open market stalls. The pirates of old used St. Thomas as a base from which to raid merchant ships of every nation, though they were particularly fond of the gold- and silver-laden treasure ships heading to Spain. Pirates are still around, but today's versions use St. Thomas as a drop-off for their contraband: illegal immigrants and drugs.

With the exception of some private homes, the island's western end is still relatively wild. If you stay on the quiet north side, you'll go up the mountain along roads lined with giant ferns and philodendron, banana trees, and flamboyant trees that thrive in the cooler, wetter climate. The lush vegetation muffles the sound of all but the birds, and it's here you'll find many private villas for rent. In the drier areas to the south and east, the roads are lined with colossal cacti and succulents, punctuated by the bright colors of the hardy bougainvillea and hibiscus. The southeastern and far eastern ends of the island are flat, and this is where

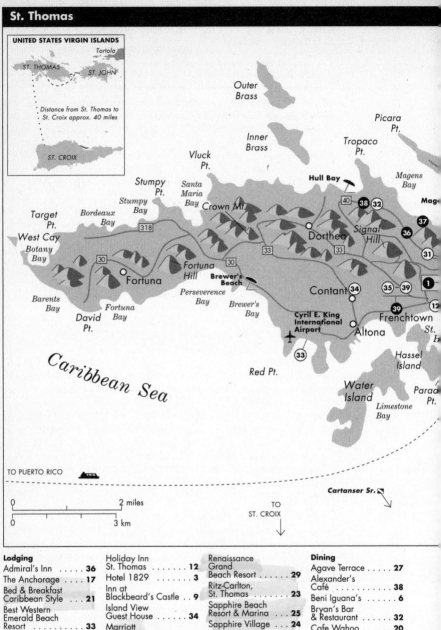

UNITED STATES VIRGIN ISLANDS

Tortola

ST. THOMAS   ST. JOHN

Distance from St. Thomas to
St. Croix approx. 40 miles

ST. CROIX

Outer
Brass

Picara
Pt.

Inner
Brass

Tropaco
Pt.

Magens
Bay

Vluck
Pt.

Hull Bay

Mag

Stumpy
Pt.

Santa
Maria
Bay

Crown Mt.

40 38 32

Stumpy
Bay

Dorthea

Signal
Hill

37

Target
Pt.

Bordeaux
Bay

318

36

West Cay

33

33

31

Botany
Bay

30

Fortuna
Hill

Brewer's
Beach

30

Contant 34

35 39

1

Fortuna

Perseverence
Bay

Brewer's
Bay

39

Frenchtown

12

Barents
Bay

Fortuna
Bay

Cyril E. King
International
Airport

Altona

St.

David
Pt.

Hassel
Island

Caribbean Sea

Red Pt.

33

Water
Island

Para
Pt.

Limestone
Bay

TO PUERTO RICO

Cartanser Sr.

0   2 miles

0   3 km

TO
ST. CROIX

Lodging

Admiral's Inn **36**
The Anchorage **17**
Bed & Breakfast
Caribbean Style . . . **21**
Best Western
Emerald Beach
Resort **33**
Blazing Villas **29**
Bluebeard's
Castle **1**
Bolongo Bay Beach
Club & Villas **14**
Elysian Beach
Resort **22**

Holiday Inn
St. Thomas **12**
Hotel 1829 . . . . . . **3**
Inn at
Blackbeard's Castle . **9**
Island View
Guest House **34**
Marriott
Frenchman's Reef
and Morning Star
Beach Resorts **13**
Point Pleasant
Resort **27**

Renaissance
Grand
Beach Resort **29**
Ritz-Carlton,
St. Thomas **23**
Sapphire Beach
Resort & Marina . . . **25**
Sapphire Village . . . **24**
Secret Harbour
Beach Resort
& Villas **16**
Villa Santana **2**
Wyndham Sugar
Bay Beach Club
& Resort **26**

Dining

Agave Terrace **27**
Alexander's
Café **38**
Beni Iguana's **6**
Bryan's Bar
& Restaurant **32**
Cafe Wahoo **20**
Craig & Sally's **39**
Duffy's Love
Shack **18**

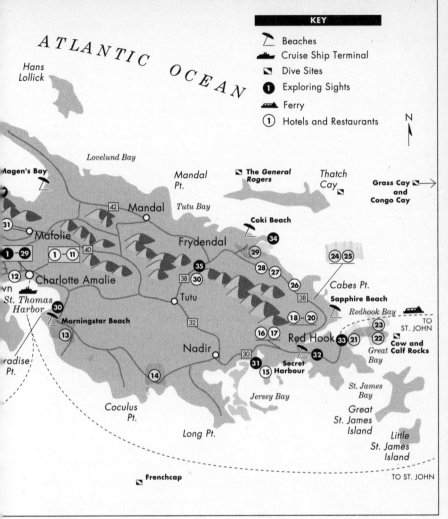

KEY

- ⚓ Beaches
- 🚢 Cruise Ship Terminal
- ◪ Dive Sites
- ❶ Exploring Sights
- 🚢 Ferry
- ① Hotels and Restaurants

N

ATLANTIC OCEAN

Hans Lollick

Magen's Bay

Lovelund Bay

Mandal Pt.

◪ **The** *General Rogers*

Thatch Cay

Grass Cay ◪ → and Congo Cay

Tutu Bay

42 Mandal

Coki Beach

Frydendal

34

31

Mafolie

①-29

①-⑪ 40

29

24 25

12

Charlotte Amalie

35

38 30

28 27

26

Cabes Pt.

Sapphire Beach

St. Thomas Harbor

Tutu

38

Redhook Bay

TO ST. JOHN

30

Morningstar Beach

32

18-20

23

adise Pt.

13

Nadir

16 17

Red Hook

33 21

22

Cow and Calf Rocks

30

Great Bay

14

31

15

Secret Harbour

32

St. James Bay

Jersey Bay

Great St. James Island

Coculus Pt.

Long Pt.

Little St. James Island

TO ST. JOHN

◪ **Frenchcap**

Gladys' Cafe **7**
Greenhouse Bar and Restaurant **4**
Hard Rock Cafe **5**
Hervé **8**
Hotel 1829 . . . . **3**
Molly Molone's **19**
The Pointe at Villa Olga **37**
Polli's **30**

Raffles **15**
Romanos **28**
Sib's Mountain Bar and Restaurant **31**
Tavern on the Waterfront **10**
Victor's New Hide-Out **35**
Virgilio's **11**

Exploring
Compass Point Marina **31**
Coral World Marine Park **34**
Drake's Seat **37**
Estate St. Peter Greathouse & Botanical Gardens **38**
Frenchtown **39**

Mountain Top **36**
Paradise Point Tramway **30**
Red Hook **33**
Tillett Gardens **35**
Virgin Islands National Park Headquarters **32**

you'll find the beachfront hotels and condominiums. At the eastern tip is Red Hook, a friendly village anchored by the marine community nestled at Red Hook harbor.

Lodging

Of the USVI, St. Thomas has the most rooms and the greatest variety of accommodations. You can let yourself be pampered at a luxurious south shore, east end, or west end resort—albeit at a price of $300 to more than $900 per night, not including meals. If your means are more modest, you will find fine hotels (often with rooms that have a kitchen and a living area) in lovely settings throughout the island. There are also guest houses and inns with great views (if not a beach at your door) and great service at about half the cost of the beachfront pleasure palaces. Many of these are east and north of Charlotte Amalie, in the Frenchtown area or overlooking hills—ideal if you plan to get out and mingle with the locals. There are also inexpensive lodgings (most right in town) that are perfect if you just want a clean room to return to after a day of exploring or beach-bumming.

Families often stay at an east end condominium complex. Although condos are pricey (winter rates average $240 per night for a two-bedroom unit, which usually sleeps six), they have full kitchens, and you can definitely save money by cooking for yourself—especially if you bring your own nonperishable foodstuffs. (Virtually everything on St. Thomas is imported, and restaurants and shops pass shipping costs on to you.) Though you may spend some time laboring in the kitchen, many condos ease your burden with daily maid service and on-site restaurants; a few also have resort amenities, including pools and tennis courts. The east end is convenient to St. John, and it's home to the boating crowd and some good restaurants. The prices below reflect rates in high season, which runs from December 15 to April 15. Rates are 25% to 50% lower the rest of the year.

CATEGORY	COST*
$$$$	over $200
$$$	$150–$200
$$	$100–$150
$	under $100

All prices are for a standard double room, excluding 8% tax.

Hotels

CHARLOTTE AMALIE

$$$$ 🏨 **Best Western Emerald Beach Resort.** On a white-sand beach across from the airport, this mini-resort has the feel of its much larger east-end cousins. Each room in the four pink three-story buildings has its own terrace or balcony, palms, and colorful flowers that frame an ocean view. Rooms are decorated in modern tropical prints and rattan. A plus: the resort is popular with businesspeople, so the pool and beach are rarely crowded. A minus: the noise from nearby jets taking off and landing can be heard intermittently over a three-hour period each afternoon. ⊠ *8070 Lindberg Bay, 00802,* ☎ *340/777–8800; 800/233–4936 direct to hotel,* FAX *340/776–3426,* WEB *www.emeraldbeach.com. 90 rooms. Restaurant, air-conditioning, pool, tennis court, beach. AE, D, MC, V. EP.*

$$$$ 🏨 **Bluebeard's Castle.** Though not exactly a castle, this large red-roof complex offers kingly comforts on a steep hill above town. All rooms are air-conditioned and have terraces. The hotel is a short ride from the shops of Charlotte Amalie and Havensight Mall, and there's free transportation to Magens Bay Beach and to town. ⊠ *Bluebeard's Hill (Box 7480), 00801,* ☎ *340/774–1600; 800/524–6599 direct to hotel,*

FAX *340/774–5134. 170 rooms. 3 restaurants, bar, air-conditioning, pool, 2 tennis courts, gym. AE, D, DC, MC, V. EP.*

$$$ 🏨 **Holiday Inn St. Thomas.** This harbor-front property is comfortable for business travelers as well as vacationers who want to be close to the duty-free shopping. Contemporarily furnished rooms have such amenities as coffeemakers, hair dryers, ironing boards and irons, cable TV, and phones. Complimentary features include a daily beach shuttle and an introductory dive lesson. ⊠ *Waterfront Hwy. (Box 640), 00804,* ☎ *340/774–5200; 800/524–7389 direct to hotel,* FAX *340/774–1231,* WEB *www.holidayinn.st-thomas.com. 140 rooms, 11 suites. Restaurant, bar, air-conditioning, in-room safes, refrigerators, pool, hair salon, gym, dive shop. AE, D, DC, MC, V. EP.*

$$$ 🏨 **Hotel 1829.** This historic Spanish-style inn is popular with visiting
★   government officials and people with business at Government House down the street. Rooms, on several levels (no elevator), range from elegant and roomy to quite small but are priced accordingly, so there's one for every budget. Author Graham Greene is said to have stayed here, and it's easy to imagine him musing over a drink in the small, dark bar. The second-floor botanical gardens and open-air champagne bar make a romantic spot for sunset viewing before dinner in the gourmet Hotel 1829 restaurant. Rooms count phones and TVs in their list of amenities. There's a tiny, tiny pool for cooling off, and the shops of Charlotte Amalie are close by. ⊠ *Government Hill (Box 1567), 00804,* ☎ *340/776–1829; 800/524–2002 direct to hotel,* FAX *340/776–4313,* WEB *www.hotel1829.com. 14 rooms. Restaurant, air-conditioning, refrigerators, pool. AE, D, MC, V, CP.*

$$$ 🏨 **Inn at Blackbeard's Castle.** This cozy hilltop inn is laid out around a tower from which, it's said, Blackbeard kept watch for invaders. It's an informally elegant place, where you can while away a Sunday morning reading the *New York Times.* Mahogany furnishings, including four-poster beds, lend a 17th-century feel to the place, yet each room has many modern conveniences. You can see stunning views of the harbor at Charlotte Amalie from the tower as well as from the open-air bar, the fresh-water pool, and the many outdoor terraces. ⊠ *Blackbeard's Hill (Box 6227), 00804,* ☎ *340/776–1234; 800/334–5771 direct to hotel,* FAX *340/776–4521,* WEB *www.blackbeardscastle.vi. 16 rooms. Restaurant, bar, air-conditioning, pool. AE, D, DC, MC, V. CP.*

$$ 🏨 **Villa Santana.** Built by General Santa Anna of Mexico, the villa (circa
★   1857) still provides a panoramic view of the harbor and plenty of West Indian charm. This landmark, close to town, has six villa-style rooms. Dark-wood furniture, plaster-and-stone walls, shuttered windows, cathedral ceilings, and interesting nooks contribute to the sense of romance and history. All units have full kitchens, TVs, and either four-poster or cradle beds; ceiling fans and natural trade winds keep things cool. Villas La Torre and La Mansion are split-level quarters with spiral staircases. ⊠ *2D Denmark Hill, 00802,* ☎ *340/776–1311,* FAX *340/776–1311,* WEB *www.st-thomas.com/villasantana. 6 rooms. Kitchenettes, fans, pool, croquet. AE, CP.*

EAST END

$$$$ 🏨 **Elysian Beach Resort.** The coral-color villas here are situated along a hill all the way to the edge of Cowpet Bay. Rooms are decorated in muted tropical floral prints and have terraces, TVs, and phones; some have full kitchens. Activity centers on a kidney-shape pool with a waterfall and thatch-roofed pool bar. The Palm Court restaurant has a strong local following for the Sunday buffet brunch. ⊠ *Estate Nazareth (Box 51), Red Hook 00802,* ☎ *340/775–1000; 800/753–2554 direct to hotel,* FAX *340/776–0910. 175 rooms. 2 restaurants, 2 bars, air-conditioning, fans* ████████ *(some), pool, tennis court, health club, beach. AE, MC, V.*

$$$$ 🏨 **Point Pleasant Resort.** Stretching up a steep, tree-covered hill and affording a great view of Drake's Channel, this resort offers a choice of accommodations from simple bedrooms to multi-room suites. Units are in buildings hidden among the trees. All have striking views, balconies, and fully equipped kitchens. Although the "beach" is almost nonexistent, three good-size pools surrounded by decks are placed at different levels on the hill. The property also has a labyrinth of well-marked nature trails to explore. Every guest gets four hours free use of a car daily (you do need to pay the $20, per use, fuel and maintenance fee). If you like seafood, don't miss dinner at the Agave Terrace restaurant. ✉ *6600 Estate Smith Bay, No. 4, 00802,* ☎ *340/775–7200; 800/524–2300 direct to hotel,* FAX *340/776–5694,* WEB *www.point-pleasantresort.com. 95 suites. 2 restaurants, bar, kitchenettes, 3 pools, tennis court, gym, beach. AE, D, DC, MC, V. EP.*

$$$$ ★ 🏨 **Renaissance Grand Beach Resort.** The zigzag architectural angles spell luxury, and that's what you'll find everywhere, from the marble atrium lobby to the one-bedroom suites with whirlpool baths. The beach is excellent, and there's a fitness center with Nautilus machines. The lobby is often populated by those lucky business types whose companies favor the resort as a convention-and-conference center. Daily activities for children include iguana hunts, T-shirt painting, and sand-castle building. This tends to be a very busy hotel, with lots of people in the restaurants and on the beach. ✉ *Smith Bay Rd. (Box 8267), 00801,* ☎ *340/775–1510 or 800/468–3571,* FAX *340/775–3757,* WEB *www.renaissancehotels.com/sttsr. 290 rooms, 36 suites. 2 restaurants, snack bar, air-conditioning, 2 pools, barbershop, hair salon, 6 tennis courts, health club, beach, children's programs, business services. AE, D, DC, MC, V. EP, MAP.*

$$$$ 🏨 **Ritz-Carlton, St. Thomas.** This premier luxury resort resembles a villa in Venice and offers stunning ocean views through the lobby's glass doors. Guest rooms, in six buildings that fan out from the main villa, are spacious and tropically furnished. Elegance is everywhere, from the beautiful pool that appears to become one with the sea to the gourmet restaurant and casual alfresco lunch area. A multilingual staff and 24-hour room service enhance the sophisticated atmosphere. A $75-million renovation and expansion project, which should be completed by the end of 2001, will add 48 additional rooms, a full-service spa and fitness center, and 80 two- and three-bedroom private club residences. ✉ *6900 Great Bay Estate, 00802,* ☎ *340/775–3333 or 800/241–3333,* FAX *340/775–4444,* WEB *www.ritzcarlton.com. 148 rooms. 3 restaurants, 3 bars, air-conditioning, room service, pool, 3 tennis courts, health club, beach, children's programs, business services. AE, D, DC, MC, V. EP.*

$$$$ 🏨 **Sapphire Beach Resort & Marina.** On a clear day the lush, green mountains of the neighboring British Virgin Islands seem close enough to touch from this picturesque, red-roof resort. Room interiors, from the tropical bold-pattern rugs and comforters to full kitchenettes, were renovated in early 2000. A new five-building area in the center of the property will open in fall of 2001 with retail shops, a meeting area, and deli dining. The good news is that this construction doesn't obscure the beautiful beachside view. The fun family-oriented atmosphere here is highlighted by a Sunday beach party that thumps with rock and reggae and MeriStar's Fun Factory™ Kids Klub program, where 4- to 12-year-olds can enjoy such activities as arts and crafts, sing-alongs, and sand-castle building. Children under 12 eat free, while teens up to 18 also can sleep in their parents' room at no additional charge. ✉ *Sapphire Bay (Box 8088), 00801,* ☎ *340/775–6100; 800/524–2090 direct to hotel,* FAX *340/775–2403,* WEB *www.sapphirebeachstthomas.com. 171 suites. 4 restaurants, 2 bars, deli, air-conditioning, kitchenettes, 4* *tennis courts, health club, beach, marina, shops, children's programs, meeting room. AE, MC, V. EP, MAP.*

$$$$ 🏨 **Secret Harbour Beach Resort & Villas.** These beige buildings, which contain low-rise studios and suites, are tucked into the hillsides and along an inviting sandy cove. Watch marvelous sunsets from the balconies or the casual restaurant. All units have air-conditioning and maid service. Children under age 13 stay free, making this a family-friendly resort. ✉ *6280 Estate Nazareth, 00802-1104,* ☎ *340/775–6550; 800/ 524–2250 direct to hotel,* FAX *340/775–1501,* WEB *www.st-thomas. com/shb.vi. 49 suites, 15 studios. Restaurant, bar, air-conditioning, fans, kitchenettes, pool, 4 tennis courts, health club, beach, dive shop, snorkeling, windsurfing. AE, MC, V. CP.*

$$$$ 🏨 **Wyndham Sugar Bay Beach Club & Resort.** This warm, terra-cotta hillside resort is one of the island's most attractive. Most rooms overlook water; some have views of the British Virgin Islands. All are spacious and comfortable and have balconies, hair dryers, and coffeemakers. The beach is small, but there's a giant pool with waterfalls. ✉ *6500 Estate Smith Bay, 00802,* ☎ *340/777–7100; 800/927–7100 direct to hotel,* FAX *340/777–7200,* WEB *www.wyndham.com. 300 rooms, 9 suites. Restaurant, bar, air-conditioning, 3 pools, 2 tennis courts, health club, beach, snorkeling, windsurfing. AE, D, DC, MC, V. All-inclusive.*

FRENCHTOWN

$$ 🏨 **Admiral's Inn.** This charming inn sprawls down a hillside on the point
★ of land known as Frenchtown, just west of Charlotte Amalie. All rooms have wonderful town, ocean, or harbor views; the four ocean-view rooms have balconies and refrigerators. All units have rattan furniture; cream- or teal-color bedspreads; vertical blinds; coral, teal, and cream carpeting; and large, tiled vanity areas. The rocky shoreline is perfect for snorkeling, and the freshwater pool (there's bar service here) is surrounded by a large deck that's ideal for sunning. ✉ *Villa Olga, 00802,* ☎ *340/774–1376; 800/544–0493 direct to hotel,* FAX *340/774– 8010,* WEB *www.admirals-inn.com. 12 rooms. Restaurant, bar, kitchenettes (some), pool. AE, D, MC, V. CP.*

SOUTH SHORE

$$$$ 🏨 **Bolongo Bay Beach Club & Villas.** This 75-room, beachfront resort also includes the 20-room Bolongo Villas next door and the six-room Bolongo Bayside Inn across the street. All rooms—which include mini-suites and one- and two-bedroom units—have kitchens and balconies and are just steps from a strand of white-sand beach. The resort offers a choice of all-inclusive or semi-inclusive plans, which means you can pay less if you opt for fewer activities. The all-inclusive rate covers all meals and drinks, the use of tennis courts, and many water-sports activities—including an all-day sail and half-day snorkel trip on a yacht. There's a three-night minimum for the all-inclusive plan. ✉ *50 Estate Bolongo, 00802,* ☎ *340/775–1800; 800/524–4746 direct to hotel,* FAX *340/775–3208,* WEB *www.bolongo.com. 101 units. 2 restaurants, 2 bars, air-conditioning, kitchenettes, 3 pools, 2 tennis courts, health club, volleyball, beach, dive shop, dock, snorkeling, windsurfing, boating, jet skiing. AE, D, DC, MC, V. All-inclusive.*

$$$$ 🏨 **Marriott Frenchman's Reef and Morning Star Beach Resorts.** On a
★ prime harbor promontory east of Charlotte Amalie, you'll find these two sprawling, luxurious, full-service superhotels. Frenchman's Reef has 128 suites—each with glorious ocean and harbor views. The more elegant Morning Star rooms are in buildings nestled surfside along the fine white sand of Morning Star Beach. Guests at both resorts can work out at the Reef Health Club & Spa, which offers state-of-the-art equipment, therapeutic massages, and skin-care therapies. Dining is alfresco on American or gourmet Caribbean fare or oceanfront at the Tavern

on the Beach; there's also a lavish buffet served, overlooking the sparkling lights of Charlotte Amalie. Live entertainment and dancing, scheduled activities for all ages, and a shuttle boat to town make having fun easy. ⊠ *Estate Bakkeroe (Box 7100), 00801,* ☎ *340/776–8500; 800/524–2000 direct to hotel,* FAX *340/776–3054,* WEB *www.marriott-fr.vi. 373 rooms, 128 suites. 6 restaurants, 6 bars, snack bar, air-conditioning, 2 pools, spa, 4 tennis courts, health club, beach, children's programs. AE, D, DC, MC, V. EP.*

Guest Houses

CHARLOTTE AMALIE

🏠 **Island View Guest House.** In tropical foliage 545 ft (166 m) up on the face of Crown Mountain, this simply furnished bed-and-breakfast offers sweeping views of Charlotte Amalie harbor from the pool and shaded terraces. Continental breakfast is served daily; however, six rooms have kitchenettes. All rooms have phones, ceiling fans, TVs, and baths. The friendly office staff can arrange tours. ⊠ *Estate Contant (Box 1903), 00801,* ☎ *340/774–4270; 800/524–2023 direct to hotel,* FAX *340/774–6167,* WEB *www.st-thomas.com/islandviewguesthouse. 15 rooms. Fans, kitchenettes (some), pool. AE, MC, V. CP.*

Villas and Condominiums

EAST END

🏠 **The Anchorage.** Next to the St. Thomas Yacht Club and facing Cowpet Bay, these two- and three-bedroom villas are right on the beach. They have washing machines and dryers, and the complex has two lighted tennis courts, a freshwater pool, and an informal restaurant. ⊠ *Estate Nazareth (Antilles Resorts, Box 8529, 00801),* ☎ *340/775–2600; 800/874–7897 direct to hotel,* FAX *340/775–5901,* WEB *www.antillesresorts.com. 30 rooms. Dining room, air-conditioning, kitchenettes, pool, 2 tennis courts. AE, D, MC, V. EP.*

🏠 **Blazing Villas.** On the Renaissance Grand Beach Resort property, these cool pastel yellow, pink, green, and blue villas have their own garden patios and can be combined with other villas to create a four-bedroom, four-bath unit. All quarters have refrigerators, microwaves, and phones. You can use all the resort's facilities. ⊠ *Smith Bay Rd. (Box 502697), 00805,* ☎ *340/776–0760; 800/382–2002 direct to hotel,* FAX *340/776–3603,* WEB *www.blazingvillas.com. 19 rooms. 2 restaurants, snack bar, air-conditioning, refrigerators, 2 pools, 6 tennis courts, health club, beach, business services. AE, MC, V. EP.*

🏠 **Sapphire Village.** A stay in these high-rise units may take you back to the swinging-singles days of apartment-house living since many of the units are rented out long-term to refugees from northern winters. The best units overlook the marina and St. John; the beach is in sight and just a short walk down the hill. ⊠ *Sapphire Bay (Antilles Resorts, Box 8529, 00801),* ☎ *340/775–2600; 800/874–7897 direct to hotel,* FAX *340/775–5901,* WEB *www.antillesresorts.com. 35 units. Restaurant, pub, air-conditioning, kitchenettes, 2 pools. AE, D, MC, V. EP.*

🏠 **Bed & Breakfast Caribbean Style.** Honeymooners will enjoy the romantic feel of these private, elegantly decorated condos. Each unit has a king-size bed, a reading and video library, a porch with hammock, cable TV, and a phone. The kitchen comes stocked with a tempting variety of breakfast foods. There's a small pool on the property, and the beach and water sports are a five-minute walk away. Those seeking to tie the knot will find that making wedding arrangements, including professional photography, is a specialty of the owner. ⊠ *Estate Vessup Bay (6501 Red Hook Plaza, Suite 96, 00802),* ☎ *340/775–6131,* WEB *www.cstyle.co.vi. 3 units. Air-conditioning, kitchenettes, pool. AE, MC, V. EP.*

Private Homes

You can arrange private-home rentals through various agents. **Ca-lypso Realty** (⊠ Box 12178, 00801, ☎ 340/774–1620 or 800/747–4858, ⩫ www.calypsorealty.com) specializes in rental properties in St. Thomas. **McLaughlin-Anderson Villas** (⊠ 100 Blackbeard's Hill, Suite 3, 00802, ☎ 340/776–0635 or 800/537–6246, ⩫ www.mclaughli-nanderson.com), handles rental villas throughout the U.S. Virgin Islands, British Virgin Islands, and Grenada. Both specialize in luxury residences, and have Web sites and brochures that show photos of the properties they represent. Some villas are suitable for travelers with disabilities.

Dining

The beauty of St. Thomas and its sister islands has attracted a cadre of professionally trained chefs who know their way around fresh fish and local fruits. You can dine on everything from terrific, cheap local dishes such as goat water (a spicy stew) and fungi, to imports such as hot pastrami sandwiches and raspberries in crème fraîche.

In large hotels you'll pay prices similar to those in New York City or Paris. Fancy restaurants may have a token chicken or pasta dish under $20, but otherwise, main courses are pricey. You can, however, find good inexpensive Caribbean restaurants. To snack on some local fare, order a johnnycake or a thick slice of dumb bread (a dense round loaf often cut into triangles and filled with cheddar cheese) from any of the mobile food vans parked all over the island. Familiar fast-food franchises also abound.

If your accommodations have a kitchen and you plan to cook, you'll find good variety in St. Thomas's mainland-style supermarkets. Note, however, that grocery prices are about 20% higher than those on the mainland United States. As for drinking, outside the hotels a beer in a bar will cost between $2 and $3 and a piña colada $4 or more.

What to Wear

Dining on St. Thomas is informal. Few restaurants require a jacket and tie. Still, at dinner in the snazzier places, shorts and T-shirts are inappropriate; men would do well to wear slacks and a shirt with buttons. Dress codes on St. Thomas rarely require women to wear skirts, but you'll never go wrong with something flowing.

CATEGORY	COST*
$$$$	over $30
$$$	$20–$30
$$	$10–$20
$	under $10

per person for a main course at dinner

Charlotte Amalie

AMERICAN

$$ ✕ **Greenhouse Bar and Restaurant.** Watch the waterfront wake up at this large, bustling open-air restaurant, whose waitstaff looks like a bunch of all-American college kids on spring break. An eight-page menu features burgers, omelets, salads, sandwiches, and pizza that are served all day long, along with more upscale entrées such as peel-'n'-eat shrimp, Maine lobster, and Certified black Angus prime rib that are reasonably priced. The atmosphere is family-friendly, though the Wednesday night live reggae band that starts thumping at 10 PM draws a lively young-adult crowd that enjoys partying into the early morning hours. ⊠ *Waterfront Hwy. at Storetvaer Gade,* ☎ *340/774–7998. AE, D, MC, V.*

$$ ✗ **Hard Rock Cafe.** A hot spot from the day it opened, this waterfront restaurant is pretty much like its namesakes around the world. Rock-and-roll memorabilia abound, and the menu offers hamburgers, sandwiches, salads, and great desserts. Jerk pork tenderloin is a delicious Caribbean addition. Doors are open from 11 AM until 2 AM; there's always a wait for a table during prime meal times. ✉ *International Plaza on Waterfront,* ☎ *340/777–5555. AE, MC, V.*

ASIAN

$ ✗ **Beni Iguana's.** Here sushi is served as "edible art" in a charming Danish courtyard. Among the offerings are cucumber and avocado or scallop with scallion rolls, specialty big rolls such as the Kung Fooee (shiitake, cucumber, daikon, and flying-fish roe), and tuna or salmon sashimi. A pictorial menu board makes ordering by the piece, plate, or combination platter easy. ✉ *Grand Hotel Court, Tolbod Gade at Norre Gade,* ☎ *340/777–8744. No credit cards. Closed Sun.*

CARIBBEAN

$ ✗ **Gladys' Cafe.** Even if the local specialties—conch in butter sauce,
★ salt fish and dumplings, hearty red bean soup—didn't make this a recommended café, it would be worth coming for Gladys's smile. While you're here, pick up some of her hot sauce for $6 a bottle. ✉ *Waterfront at Royal Dane Mall,* ☎ *340/774–6604. AE. Closed Sun. No dinner.*

CONTINENTAL

$$$ ✗ **Hotel 1829.** You'll dine by candlelight flickering over stone walls
★ and pink table linens at this restaurant on the terrace of the Hotel 1829. The menu and award-winning wine list (325 varieties, 15 available by the glass) are extensive, from Caribbean rock lobster to rack of lamb. Many items—including a warm spinach salad—are prepared table-side, and the restaurant is justly famous for its dessert soufflés: chocolate, Grand Marnier, raspberry, or coconut, to name a few. ✉ *Government Hill near Main St.,* ☎ *340/776–1829. Reservations essential. AE, D, MC, V. Closed Sun.*

ECLECTIC

$$$ ✗ **Hervé.** French-trained Hervé Chassin's long experience in the St. Thomas restaurant industry has led to a menu that offers a delightful mix of Caribbean and Continental cuisine. In the warm glow of candlelight—at tables impeccably dressed with linen cloths, silver settings, and fine crystal—you can start off with crispy conch fritters served with a spicy-sweet mango chutney, and then choose from such entrées as fresh tuna encrusted with sesame seeds or succulent roast duck with a ginger and tamarind sauce. The passionfruit cheesecake is to die for. ✉ *Government Hill,* ☎ *340/777–9703. AE, MC, V. Closed Sun.*

$$$ ✗ **Tavern on the Waterfront.** White linen tablecloths, silver and crystal table settings, and a rich mahogany decor set the scene for an elegant meal at this second-floor, air-conditioned restaurant that overlooks the harbor. Tiger Woods, Michael Jordan, and Walter Cronkite have all supped here. The menu offers flavors from every corner of the globe. Try the soft-shell crabs with mango salsa or the tuna sushi for lunch. Dinner offerings include a two-pound Caribbean lobster specialty. Sunday is Latin night. ✉ *Waterfront at Royal Dane Mall,* ☎ *340/776–4328. AE, MC, V. Closed Sun.*

ITALIAN

$$$ ✗ **Virgilio's.** For the island's best Northern Italian cuisine, don't miss
★ this intimate, elegant hideaway tucked on a quiet side street. Eclectic art covers the two-story-high brick walls, and the sound of Italian opera music sets the stage for a memorable meal. Come here for more than 40 homemade pastas complemented by superb sauces—*cappellini* (very thin spaghetti) with fresh tomatoes and garlic, say, or spaghetti peas-

ant style (in a rich tomato sauce with mushrooms and prosciutto). House specialties are osso buco and tiramisu for dessert, expertly prepared by chef Ernesto Garrigos. ✉ *18 Main St.,* ☎ *340/776–4920. Reservations essential. AE, MC, V. Closed Sun.*

East End

ECLECTIC

$$$ ✕ **Raffles.** In a homey dining room, set in a quaint marina, owner-chef
★ Sandra Englesburger puts on a one-woman culinary show. Her from-scratch creations include a signature coconut shrimp appetizer, and entrées such as beef Wellington, mahimahi in a rich lobster sauce, and a two-day Peking duck. There are fresh fish and vegetarian specials daily. For dessert, try the chocolate paté—Belgian chocolate melted and frozen into a decadent treat. ✉ *41–6–1 Compass Point Marina,* ☎ *340/775–6004. Reservations essential. AE, MC, V. No lunch Apr.–Oct. Closed Mon.*

$ ✕ **Duffy's Love Shack.** If the floating bubbles don't attract you to this zany eatery, the lime-green shutters, loud rock music, and fun-loving wait staff sure will. It's billed as the "ultimate tropical drink shack," and the bartenders shake up such exotic concoctions as the Love Shack Volcano—a 50-ounce flaming extravaganza. Dining selections are just as trendy. Try the grilled mahimahi taco salad or jerk Caesar wrap. Thursday night features theme parties complete with giveaways. ✉ *Red Hook Plaza parking lot,* ☎ *340/779–2080. No credit cards.*

IRISH

$$ ✕ **Molly Molone's.** This casual, alfresco restaurant has a devout fol-
★ lowing of locals who live and work on boats docked nearby. You'll find such traditional Irish dishes as stew, and bangers and mash (sausage and mashed potatoes), as well as fresh fish, oversized deli sandwiches, and rich soups. Beware: the iguanas like to beg for table scraps—bring your camera. Upstairs, the same owners run A Whale of a Tale, a pricier seafood eatery that also serves freshly made pasta and fine wines. ✉ *American Yacht Harbor, Bldg. D, Red Hook,* ☎ *340/775–1270. MC, V.*

ITALIAN

$$$$ ✕ **Romanos.** Inside this huge, old stucco house is a delightful surprise:
★ a spare yet elegant setting and superb Northern Italian cuisine. Owner Tony Romano hasn't advertised since the restaurant opened in 1988, yet it's always packed. Try the pastas, either with a classic sauce or one of Tony's unique creations, such as a cream sauce with mushrooms, prosciutto, pine nuts, and Parmesan. ✉ *97 Smith Bay,* ☎ *340/775–0045. Reservations essential. MC, V. No lunch. Closed Sun.*

SEAFOOD

$$$ ✕ **Agave Terrace.** At this dimly lit, open-air pavilion restaurant in the Point Pleasant Resort, fresh fish is the specialty, served as steaks or fillets, and the catch of the day is listed on the blackboard. There are more than a dozen fish sauces to choose from, including teriyaki-mango and lime ginger. Come early and have a drink at the Lookout Lounge, which has breathtaking views of the British Virgins. The food enjoys as good a reputation as the view. ✉ *6600 Estate Smith Bay,* ☎ *340/775–4142. AE, MC, V. No lunch.*

$$$ ✕ **Cafe Wahoo.** The fish is so fresh at this open-air eatery that you may see it coming in from one of the boats tied up at the dock just steps away. For starters, try the house-cured vodka salmon with mango crème fraîche. Entrées include a rib-sticking wahoo bouillabaisse with scallops, shrimp, and green tip mussels all in a lobster bisque. Steak, poultry, and pasta lovers will find something to please on the menu, too. ✉ *American Yacht Harbor Marina, Red Hook,* ☎ *340/775–6350. AE, MC, V. No lunch.*

TEX-MEX

$ ✕ Polli's. You'll feel as if you're sitting deep within a tropical jungle at this open-air restaurant, where a parrot squawks a greeting to incoming diners. The menu is complete with jalapeño poppers (deep-fried cheese-stuffed hot peppers), chicken- or seafood-stuffed fajitas, and apple chimichangas for dessert. All entrées come vegetarian-style upon request. ⊠ *Tillett Gardens, Estate Tutu,* ☎ *340/775–4550. AE, MC, V.*

Frenchtown

AUSTRIAN

$$ ✕ Alexander's Café. This place is a favorite with the people in the restau-
★ rant business on St. Thomas—always a sign of quality. Alexander is Austrian, and the schnitzels are delicious and reasonably priced; pasta specials are fresh and tasty. Save room for strudel. Next door is Alexander's Bar & Grill, serving food from the same kitchen but in a more casual setting and at lower prices. ⊠ *24-A Honduras,* ☎ *340/776–4211. Reservations essential. AE, D, MC, V. Closed Sun.*

CARIBBEAN

$$ ✕ Victor's New Hide-Out. Although it's a little hard to find—it's up the hill between the Nisky shopping center and the airport—this landmark restaurant is worth the search. Native food—steamed fish, marinated pork chops, and local lobster—and native music are offered in a casual, friendly West Indian atmosphere. ⊠ *Sub Base,* ☎ *340/776–9379. AE, MC, V.*

ECLECTIC

$$$ ✕ The Pointe at Villa Olga. Set in the old Russian consulate great house at the tip of the Frenchtown peninsula, this restaurant offers superb views along with fresh fish, teriyaki dishes, lobster, and steaks grilled to order. A large salad bar, brimming with traditional salad fare, along with Mediterranean-style roasted vegetables and fresh-baked rustic breads, offers a meal in itself. ⊠ *Villa Olga,* ☎ *340/774–4262. AE, D, DC, MC, V.*

$$ ✕ Craig & Sally's. In the heart of Frenchtown, culinary wizard Sally
★ Darash creates menus with a passionate international flavor using fresh ingredients and a novel approach that makes for a delightful dining experience at this friendly casual eatery. Husband Craig maintains a 300-bottle wine list that's received *Wine Spectator*'s Award of Excellence. ⊠ *22 Honduras,* ☎ *340/777–9949. Reservations suggested. AE, MC, V. No lunch weekends. Closed Mon.–Tues.*

Northside

AMERICAN

$$ ✕ Sib's Mountain Bar and Restaurant. Here you'll find live music, football, burgers, barbecued ribs and chicken, and beer. This friendly two-fisted drinking bar, with a restaurant on the back porch, is a good place for a casual dinner after a day at the beach. Don't be surprised when the basil, tomatoes, or hot peppers you see the chef pick from the backyard garden wind up on your plate minutes later. ⊠ *Mafolie Hill,* ☎ *340/774–8967. AE, MC, V.*

ECLECTIC

$$ ✕ Bryan's Bar & Restaurant. Dramatic views of Hull Bay and Inner Brass Cay set the mood for your meal. Tuna, wahoo, and dolphinfish—caught daily by the island's French fishermen—are served grilled, fried, or broiled with a sauce that's a savory mix of garlic, onions, tomatoes, and fresh herbs. Baby-back ribs, 9-ounce beef burgers, and a children's menu means there's something for everyone. Sunday brunch draws a big local crowd, who come for everything from the steak and eggs to salmon quesadillas. Live music and lively billiard games keep the place jumping on weekends. ⊠ *Hull Bay Rd.,* ☎ *340/777–1262. AE, MC, V. No lunch.*

Beaches

All 44 St. Thomas beaches are open to the public, although you can only reach some of them by walking through a resort. Hotel guests frequently have access to lounge chairs and floats that are off-limits to nonguests; for this reason you may feel more comfortable at one of the beaches not associated with a resort, such as Magens Bay (which charges an entrance fee to cover beach maintenance) or Coki. Whichever one you choose, remember to remove your valuables from the car and keep them out of sight when you go swimming.

On Route 30 near the airport, **Brewer's Beach** is a long stretch of powdery white sand. Trucks that sell lunch, snacks, and drinks often park along the road bordering the beach.

Coki Beach, next to Coral World (turn north off Route 38), is a popular snorkeling spot for cruise-ship passengers; it's common to find a group of them among the reefs on the east and west ends of the beach. It's also a good place to dash in for a swim or just to do some people-watching. Don't leave valuables unattended in your car or on the beach.

On the north shore (Route 37), **Hull Bay** beach faces Inner and Outer Brass cays and attracts fishermen and beachcombers. With its rough Atlantic surf and relative isolation, Hull Bay is one of the island's best surfing spots. Take a break from the rigors of sightseeing at the Hull Bay Hideaway, a laid-back beach bar where a local band plays rock on Sunday afternoon.

On Route 35, **Magens Bay** is usually lively because of its spectacular crescent of white sand, more than ½ mi (¾ km) long, and its calm waters, which are protected by two peninsulas. It's often listed among the world's most beautiful beaches. (If you arrive between 8 AM and 5 PM, you'll have to pay an entrance fee of $3 per person.) The bottom is flat and sandy, so this is a place for sunning and swimming rather than snorkeling. On weekends and holidays the sounds of groups partying under the sheds fill the air. You'll also find a bar, bathhouses, a nature trail (unmarked and often overgrown), and a snack bar. East of the beach is Udder Delight, a one-room shop of the St. Thomas Dairies that serves a Virgin Islands tradition—a milk shake with a splash of Cruzan rum. Kids can enjoy virgin shakes, which have a touch of soursop, mango, or banana flavoring.

Close to Charlotte Amalie and fronting the Marriott Frenchman's Reef Hotel, the pretty curve of **Morning Star Beach** is where many young locals bodysurf or play volleyball. Snorkeling is good near the rocks when the current doesn't affect visibility.

At **Sapphire Beach** you'll find a fine view of St. John and other islands. The snorkeling is excellent at the reef to the right or east, near Pettyklip Point, and the Sapphire Beach Resort rents water-sports gear.

The condo resort at **Secret Harbor** doesn't at all detract from the attractiveness of the covelike beach. Not only is this east end spot pretty, it also has superb snorkeling—head out to the left, near the rocks.

Outdoor Activities and Sports

Participant Sports

BOATING AND SAILING

Calm seas, crystal waters, and close-by islands (perfect for picnicking, snorkeling, and exploring) make St. Thomas a favorite jumping-off spot for day- or weeklong sails or powerboat adventures. With more than 100 vessels from which to choose, St. Thomas is the charter-boat mecca of the U.S. Virgin Islands. You can go through a broker to book a sailing vessel with a crew or contact a charter company directly. Crewed charters start at $1,200 per person per week, while bareboat charters are less expensive and can start at $600 to $800 per person on a weekly basis, not including provisioning.

Blue Water Cruises (⊠ Box 322, Islesboro, ME 04848, ☎ 800/524–2020) is a brokerage with an excellent worldwide reputation. **Fan Fare Charters** (⊠ 6501 Red Hook Plaza, Suite 201, ☎ 340/715–1326), at the Vessup Bay Marina, is the only yacht rental business in the Virgin Islands to offer sailboats by the day as well as week. Day charter rates range from $220 to $450 for 30-ft to 50-ft yachts. In Red Hook, **Island Yachts** (⊠ 6100 Red Hook Quarter, 18B, ☎ 340/775–6666 or 800/524–2019), offers sail or power boats on either a bareboat or crewed basis. **Regency Yacht Vacations** (⊠ 5200 Long Bay Rd., ☎ 340/776–5950 or 800/524–7676), at the Yacht Haven Marina, is an outfitter that is expert at matching clients with yachts for a week-long crewed charter holiday. Bareboat sail and power boats, including a selection of stable trawlers, are available at **VIP Yacht Charters** (⊠ 6118 Estate Frydenhoj 58, ☎ 340/776–1510 or 800/524–2015), near Red Hook.

Nauti Nymph (⊠ 6501 Red Hook Plaza, Suite 201, ☎ FAX 340/775–5066 or ☎ 800/734–7345) has a large selection of powerboats for rent. Rates range from $295 to $370 a day and include snorkel gear, water skis, and outriggers.

CYCLING

On St. Thomas, hills are steep and roads don't have shoulders, but you'll never ride too far from a beautiful beach and cool swim. **St. Thomas Mountain Bike Adventure** (⊠ Box 7037, 00801, ☎ 340/776–1727) takes you on a 1½-hour cycle out past Magens Bay to Peterborg Point using Trek 830 21-speed mountain bikes. There are lots of photo opportunities: flora, fauna, and a lesser-seen side of Magens Bay's picturesque beach. Helmets, water, and a guide are provided; the cost is $35. **Water Island Bike Tours** (⊠ Box 308262, 00803, ☎ 340/714–2186) is a cycling adventure to the USVI's "newest" Virgin. You'll take a 10-minute ferry ride from Crown Bay Marina to Water Island before jumping on a Cannondale M-200 18-speed mountain bike for a three-hour tour over rolling hills on mostly paved roads. Helmets, water, a guide, and ferry fare are included in the $49 cost.

FISHING

Fishing here is synonymous with blue marlin angling—especially from June through October. Four 1,000-pound-plus blues, including three world records, have been caught on the famous North Drop, about 20 mi (32 km) north of St. Thomas. If you're not into marlin fishing, try hooking up sailfish in the winter, dolphinfish come spring, and wahoo in the fall.

At the **American Yacht Harbor** (⊠ 6100 Red Hook Plaza, ☎ 340/775–6454), you'll find charter boats *Blue Fin II, Marlin Prince,* and *Prowler.* The **Charter Boat Center** (⊠ 6300 Red Hook Plaza, ☎ 340/775–7990 or 800/866–5714) in Red Hook represents a wide range of sport fishing charters. Capt. Red Bailey's *Abigail III* bases out of the **Sapphire Beach Marina** (⊠ Sapphire Bay, ☎ 340/775–6100), along with several other charter operations. To really find the trip that will best suit you, walk down the docks at either American Yacht Harbor or Sapphire Beach Marina in the late afternoon and chat with the captains and crews.

GOLF

The **Mahogany Run Golf Course** (✉ Rte. 42, ☎ 340/777–5000) is open daily and often hosts informal weekend tournaments. A spectacular view of the British Virgin Islands and the challenging 3-hole Devil's Triangle attracts golfers to this Tom Fazio–designed par-70, 18-hole course.

HORSEBACK RIDING

Half Moon Stables (☎ 340/777–6088) offers hour-long rides along a secluded trail that winds through lush, green hills to a pebble-covered east end beach. Horses and ponies are available, and so are Western or English saddles. The cost is $55. There is a weight limit of 245 pounds. Children must be eight years or older.

PARASAILING

The Caribbean waters are so clear here that the outlines of coral reefs are visible from high in the sky. Parasailers sit in a harness attached to a parachute that lifts them off a boat deck until they're sailing up in the air. Parasailing trips average a 10-minute ride in the sky that costs $55 per person. Friends who want to ride along and watch pay $10 for the boat trip. **Caribbean Parasail and Watersports** (✉ 6501 Red Hook Plaza, ☎ 340/775–9360) makes parasailing pickups from every beachfront resort. They also rent jet skis, kayaks, and floating battery-powered chairs.

SCUBA DIVING AND SNORKELING

Dive sites feature wrecks such as the *Cartanser Sr.,* a beautifully encrusted World War II cargo ship sitting 35 ft deep (11 m deep), and the *General Rogers,* a 65-ft-deep (213-m-deep) Coast Guard cutter with a gigantic resident barracuda. Reef dives offer hidden caves and archways at **Cow and Calf Rocks,** coral-covered pinnacles at **Frenchcap,** and tunnels where you can explore undersea from the Caribbean to the Atlantic at **Thatch Cay, Grass Cay,** and **Congo Cay.** Many resorts and charter yachts offer dive packages. A one-tank dive starts at $40; two-tank dives are $55 or more. There are plenty of snorkeling possibilities, too. Nick Aquilar's *At-A-Glance Snorkeller's Guide To St. Thomas,* available at local souvenir shops, describes 15 idyllic spots in detail.

Aqua Action (✉ 6501 Red Hook Plaza, ☎ 340/775–6285) is a full-service, PADI five-star shop that offers all levels of instruction at Secret Harbour Beach Resort. **Blue Island Divers** (✉ Crown Bay Marina, Suite 505, ☎ 340/774–2001) is a full-service dive shop that offers both day and night dives to wrecks and reefs. **Chris Sawyer Diving Center** (☎ 340/777–7804 or 800/882–2965), at the American Yacht Harbor marina and the Renaissance Grand Beach Resort is a PADI five-star outfit that specializes in dives to the 310-ft-long RMS *Rhone,* in the British Virgin Islands. It also has a NAUI certification center that offers instruction up to dive master. **Snuba of St. Thomas** (✉ Coki Point, ☎ 340/693–8063) offers a cross between snorkeling and scuba diving: a 20-ft (6-m) air hose connects you to the surface.

SEA EXCURSIONS

Landlubbers and seafarers alike will enjoy the wind in their hair and salt spray in the air while exploring the waters surrounding St. Thomas. Several businesses can effortlessly book you on a half-day inshore light-tackle fishing trip for $300 to $400 for two anglers; a snorkel-and-sail to a deserted cay for the day that costs on the average $75 to $90 per person; or an excursion over to the British Virgin Islands starting at $100 per person plus $12 custom's fees. Contact the **Adventure Center** (✉ Marriott Frenchman's Reef Hotel, Estate Bakkeroe, ☎ 340/774–2990), for a soup-to-nuts choice of sea tours. The **Char-**

ter **Boat Center** (✉ 6300 Red Hook Plaza, ☎ 340/775–7990 or 800/
866–5714) specializes in day trips to the British Virgin Islands and day
or weeklong sailing charters. **Limnos Charters** (✉ 6100 Red Hook Plaza,
☎ 340/775–3203) offers one of the most popular British Virgin Islands
day trips, complete with lunch, open bar, and snorkel gear. Jimmy Love-
land at **Treasure Isle Cruises** (✉ 6616 Estate Nadir 30–31, ☎ 340/775–
9500), can set you up with everything from a half-day sail to a 10-day
multi-island sailing adventure that departs from St. Thomas.

SEA KAYAKING

Fish dart, birds sing, and iguanas lounge on the limbs of dense mangroves deep within a marine sanctuary on St. Thomas's southeast
shore. Many resorts on St. Thomas's eastern end have kayaks. **Virgin
Islands Ecotours** (✉ 2 Estate Nadir, on Rte. 32, ☎ 340/779–2155) offers 2½-hour guided trips on two-man sit-atop ocean kayaks; there are
stops for swimming and snorkeling. The cost is $50 per person.

STARGAZING

Without the light pollution so prevalent in more densely populated areas,
the heavens appear supernaturally bright. On a **Star Charters Astron-
omy Adventure** (✉ Nisky Mail Center, No. 693, ☎ 340/774–9211),
you can peer into the Caribbean's largest telescope—an 18-inch New-
tonian reflector—and learn the science and lore of the stars from a well-
informed celestial guide.

SUBMARINING

Dive 90 ft (28 m) under the sea to one of St. Thomas's most beautiful
reefs without getting wet. **Atlantis Submarines** (✉ Havensight Shopping Mall, Bldg. VI, ☎ 340/776–5650) are 46-passenger, air-conditioned
conduits to a watery world teeming with brightly colored fish, vibrant
sea fans, and an occasional shark. A guide narrates the two-hour jour-
ney, while a diver makes a mid-tour appearance for a fish-feeding
show. The cost is $75. No children less than 36 inches tall are allowed.

TENNIS

The Caribbean sun is hot, so be sure to hit the courts before 10 AM or
after 5 PM (many courts are lighted). You can indulge in a set or two
even if you're staying in a guest house without courts, since most hotels rent time to nonguests. **Marriott Frenchman's Reef Resort** (✉ Estate Bakkeroe, ☎ 340/776–8500 Ext. 6818) has two courts, with
nonguests charged $10 per hour per court. There are six courts at **Re-
naissance Grand Beach Resort** (✉ Smith Bay Rd., ☎ 340/775–1510)
that are lighted until 8 PM and rent for $8 per hour. Three courts are
available at the **Ritz-Carlton, St. Thomas** (✉ 6900 Great Bay Estate, ☎
340/775–3333), where nonguests can reserve lessons for $60 per hour
and $35 per ½ hour. Courts will be closed for part of 2002 as part of
the property's building expansion and renovation. **Sapphire Beach Resort** (✉ Sapphire Bay, ☎ 340/775–6100 Ext. 2131) has four courts
that fill up fast in the cool early morning hours. Tennis pro Cecil
Phillips gives lessons to nonguests at **Wyndham Sugar Bay** (✉ 6500
Estate Smith Bay, ☎ 340/777–7100) by appointment. Rates start at
$40 for a half-hour lesson. **Lindberg Bay Park** has two courts that are
open to the public; it's located opposite the Cyril E. King Airport. There
are two public tennis courts at **Sub Base** (next to the Water and Power
Authority), open on a first-come, first-served basis for no cost.

WINDSURFING

Expect some spills, anticipate the thrills, and try your luck clipping
through the seas. Most beachfront resorts rent Windsurfers and offer
one-hour lessons for about $60. One of the island's best-known inde-
pendent windsurfing companies is **West Indies Windsurfing** (✉ Ves-

sup Beach, No. 9, Nazareth, ☎ 340/775–6530), which helped organize the U.S. Windsurfing Association National Championships on St. Thomas in 1997.

Spectator Sports

HORSE RACING

The **Clinton Phipps Racetrack** (✉ Rte. 30 at Nadir 42, ☎ 340/775–4555) schedules races—especially on local holidays—with sanctioned betting. Be prepared for large crowds.

Shopping

St. Thomas lives up to its billing as a shopper's paradise. Even if shopping isn't your idea of how to spend a vacation, you still may want to slip in on a quiet day (check the cruise-ship listings—Monday and Saturday are usually the least crowded) to browse. Among the best buys are liquor, linens, china, crystal (most stores will ship), and jewelry. The amount of jewelry available makes this one of the few items for which comparison shopping is worth the effort. Local crafts include shell jewelry, carved calabash bowls, straw brooms, woven baskets, and dolls. Creations by local doll maker Gwendolyn Harley—like her costumed West Indian market woman—have been goodwill ambassadors bought by visitors from as far away as Asia. Spice mixes, hot sauces, and tropical jams and jellies are other native products.

There's no sales tax in the USVI, and you can take advantage of the $1,200 duty-free allowance per family member (remember to save your receipts). Although you'll find the occasional salesclerk who will make a deal, bartering isn't the norm.

Areas and Malls

The prime shopping area in **Charlotte Amalie** is between Post Office and Market squares; it consists of three parallel streets that run east–west (Waterfront Highway, Main Street, and Back Street) and the alleyways that connect them. Particularly attractive are the historic **Royal Dane Mall, A. H. Riise Alley,** and pastel-painted **International Plaza**—quaint alleys between Main Street and the Waterfront.

Vendors Plaza, on the waterfront side of Emancipation Gardens in Charlotte Amalie, is a central location for vendors selling handmade earrings, necklaces, and bracelets; straw baskets and handbags; T-shirts; fabrics; African artifacts; local foods; and fruit smoothies.

West of Charlotte Amalie, the pink-stucco **Nisky Center,** on Harwood Highway about ½ mi (¾ km) east of the airport, is more of a hometown shopping center than a tourist area, but there are a bank, a pharmacy, a record shop, and a Radio Shack.

Havensight Mall, next to the cruise-ship dock, may not be as charming as downtown Charlotte Amalie, but it does have more than 60 shops. You'll find an excellent bookstore, a bank, a pharmacy, a gourmet grocery, and smaller branches of many downtown stores. The shops at **Port of Sale,** which adjoins the Havensight Mall (its buildings are pink instead of the brown of the Havensight shops), feature discount items.

East of Charlotte Amalie, **Tillett Gardens** (✉ Estate Tutu, ☎ 340/775–1405) is an oasis of artistic endeavor across from the Tutu Park Shopping Center. The late Jim Tillett and then-wife Rhoda converted this old Danish farm into an artists' retreat in 1959. Today you can watch artisans produce silk-screen fabrics, pottery, candles, watercolors, gold jewelry, stained glass, and other handicrafts. Something special is often happening in the gardens as well: the Classics in the Gardens program is a classical music series presented under the stars, and Arts Alive is a visual-arts and crafts festival held four times yearly.

Tutu Park Shopping Center, across from Tillett Gardens, is the island's one and only enclosed mall. The 47 stores and food court are anchored by a Kmart and the Plaza Extra grocery store. Archaeologists have discovered evidence that Arawak Indians once lived near the mall grounds.

Red Hook has **American Yacht Harbor,** a waterfront shopping area with a dive shop, a tackle store, clothing and jewelry boutique, and a few restaurants. Don't forget **St. John.** A ferry ride (an hour from Charlotte Amalie or 20 minutes from Red Hook) will take you to the charming shops of **Mongoose Junction** and **Wharfside Village,** which specialize in unique, often island-made items.

Specialty Items

ART

A. H. Riise Caribbean Print Gallery. Historic and contemporary prints, posters, and photo note cards depicting West Indian life are sold here. ⊠ *37 Main St., at Riise's Alley,* ☎ *340/776–2303.*

Camille Pissarro Art Gallery. This second-floor gallery, in the birthplace of St. Thomas's famous artist, offers a fine collection of original paintings and prints by local and regional artists. ⊠ *14 Main St.,* ☎ *340/ 774–4621.*

Jonna White Gallery. Vividly colored tropical images drawn on handmade paper have been White's trademark since 1978. You can buy etchings, which run from small to large, framed or unframed. Shipping to the U.S. mainland is free. ⊠ *30 Main St.,* ☎ *340/774–1201.*

Mango Tango. Works by popular local artists—originals, prints, and note cards—are displayed (there's a one-person show at least one weekend a month) and sold here. You'll also find the island's largest humidor and a brand-name cigar gallery. ⊠ *Al Cohen's Plaza, atop Raphune Hill, ½ mi (¾ km) east of Charlotte Amalie,* ☎ *340/777–3060.*

BOOKS AND MAGAZINES

Dockside Bookshop. This place is packed with books for children, travelers, cooks, and historians, as well as a good selection of paperback mysteries, best-sellers, art books, calendars, and prints. It also carries a selection of books written in and about the Caribbean and the Virgin Islands. ⊠ *Havensight Mall,* ☎ *340/774–4937.*

Island Newsstand. This place has the largest selection of magazines and newspapers on St. Thomas. Expect to pay about 20% above stateside prices. ⊠ *Grand Hotel Court, Tolbod Gade at Norre Gade, Charlotte Amalie,* ☎ *340/774–0043.*

CAMERAS AND ELECTRONICS

Boolchand's. A variety of brand-name cameras, audio and video equipment, and binoculars is sold here. ⊠ *31 Main St.,* ☎ *340/776–0794;* ⊠ *Havensight Mall,* ☎ *340/776–0302.*

Royal Caribbean. Shop here for cameras, camcorders, stereos, watches, and clocks. ⊠ *33 Main St.,* ☎ *340/776–8166;* ⊠ *Havensight Mall,* ☎ *340/776–8890.*

CHINA AND CRYSTAL

A. H. Riise Gift Shops. A. H. Riise carries Waterford, Royal Crown, and Royal Doulton at good prices. For example, a five-piece place setting of Royal Crown Derby's Old Imari goes for less than $600. The branch at Riise's Alley also sells jewelry, pearls, perfumes, and watches—including an outstanding Rolex selection (Riise's is the exclusive retailer for Rolex in the USVI). ⊠ *37 Main St., at Riise's Alley,* ☎ *340/776–2303;* ⊠ *Havensight Mall,* ☎ *340/776–7713.*

The English Shop. This store offers figurines, cutlery, and china and crystal from major European and Japanese manufacturers, including Spode, Limoges, Royal Doulton, Portmeirion, Noritaki, and Wedgwood. You can choose what you like from the catalogs here, and shopkeepers will order and factory-ship it for you. (Be sure to keep your receipts in case something goes awry.) ⊠ *Havensight Mall,* ☎ *340/776–3776.*

Little Switzerland. All of this establishment's shops carry crystal from Baccarat, Waterford, Orrefors, and Riedel; china from Villeroy & Boch and Wedgwood, among others; and fine Swiss watches. There's also an assortment of cut-crystal animals, china and porcelain figurines, and many other affordable collectibles. They also do a booming mail-order business; ask for a catalog. ⊠ *Tolbod Gade, across from Emancipation Garden,* ☎ *340/776–2010;* ⊠ *3B Main St.,* ☎ *340/ 776–2010;* ⊠ *5 Main St., inside A. H. Riise Gift Mart,* ☎ *340/776–2010;* ⊠ *Dockside at Havensight Mall,* ☎ *340/776–2010.*

CLOTHING

Cosmopolitan. At this sophisticated clothing emporium, look for such top lines as Paul and Shark, Bally, Timberland, Sperry Topsider, Givenchy, and Nautica. ⊠ *Drake's Passage at the Waterfront,* ☎ *340/ 776–2040.*

Local Color. Men, women, and children will find something to choose from among such brand name wear as Jams World, Urban Safari, and St. John artist Sloop Jones's colorful, hand-painted island designs on cool dresses, T-shirts, and sweaters. There are also tropically oriented accessories such as big-brim straw hats, bold-color bags, and casual jewelry. (The Local Color Kids store in Hibiscus Alley has Fresh Produce T-shirts, shorts, and dresses along with toys, games and books.) ⊠ *Royal Dane Mall at the Waterfront,* ☎ *340/774–2280.*

Lover's Lane. With the motto "Couples that play together, stay together," this romantic second-floor shop sells sensuous lingerie, sexy menswear, and provocative swimwear. ⊠ *Waterfront Hwy. at Raadets Gade,* ☎ *340/777–9616.*

Nicole Miller Boutique. This world-renowned New York designer has created an exclusive motif for the USVI: a map of the islands, a cruise ship, and a tropical sunset. Find this print, and Miller's full line of other designs, on ties, scarves, boxer shorts, sarong skirts, and dresses at this chic boutique. ⊠ *24 Main St., at Palm Passage,* ☎ *340/774–8286.*

Pusser's Tropical & Nautical Co. Store. Here, tropical sports and travel clothing for men, women, and children all have a nautical theme. Look for bottles of Pusser's rum at the sales counter. ⊠ *Waterfront Hwy. at Riise's Alley,* ☎ *340/777–9281;* ⊠ *Across from Havensight Mall,* ☎ *340/774–9680.*

Tommy Hilfiger. Stop by this shop for classic American jeans and sportswear as well as trendy bags, belts, ties, socks, caps, and wallets. ⊠ *Waterfront Hwy. at Trompeter Gade,* ☎ *340/777–1189.*

FOODSTUFFS

Caribbean Chocolate. Everything at this confectionery tastes as good as it smells. A wide assortment of Godiva chocolates shares space with Caribbean rum balls, tropical-flavor saltwater taffy, colorful jelly beans, homemade fudge, and Caribbean coffees. ⊠ *Trompeter Gade,* ☎ *340/774–6675.*

Cost-U-Less. This store sells everything from soup to nuts, but in giant sizes and case lots. The meat and seafood department, however, has smaller, family-size portions. ⊠ *1 mi (1½ km) east of Charlotte Amalie on Rte. 38 (¼ mi / ½ km west of Rte. 39 intersection)*, ☎ 340/777–3588.

Fruit Bowl. For fruits and vegetables, this is the place. ⊠ *Wheatley Center,* ☎ *340/774–8565.*

Gourmet Gallery. Visiting millionaires buy their caviar here. There's also an excellent and reasonably priced wine selection, as well as specialty ingredients for everything from tacos to curries to chow mein. A full-service deli offers imported meats, cheeses, and in-store prepared foods that are perfect for a gourmet picnic. ⊠ *Crown Bay Marina,* ☎ *340/776–8555;* ⊠ *Havensight Mall,* ☎ *340/774–4948.*

Marina Market. You won't find a better fresh-meat and seafood department anywhere on the island. ⊠ *Across from Red Hook ferry,* ☎ *340/779–2411.*

Plaza Extra. This supermarket has a large selection of Middle Eastern foods. ⊠ *Tutu Park Shopping Center,* ☎ *340/775–5646.*

Pueblo Supermarkets. You'll find stateside brands of most products at these large supermarkets—but at higher prices because of shipping costs. ⊠ *Four Winds Plaza, across from Tillett Gardens,* ☎ *340/775–4655;* ⊠ *Sub Base, 1 mi (1½ km) north of Havensight Mall,* ☎ *340/774–4200;* ⊠ *Estate Thomas, 1 mi (1½ km) north of Havensight Mall,* ☎ *340/774–2695.*

HANDICRAFTS

Arabella's. St. Croix artist Jan Mitchell displays her vibrantly colored fused-glass platters and ornaments in this cheery store. You'll also find pottery, batiks, baskets, and watercolors from Virgin Islands and Caribbean artists, not to mention hot sauces, jams, and jellies too. ⊠ *Trompeter Gade,* ☎ *340/774–8041.*

Caribbean Marketplace. This is a great place to buy handicrafts from the Caribbean and elsewhere. Also look for Sunny Caribee spices, soaps, coffee, and teas from Tortola, and coffee from Trinidad. ⊠ *Havensight Mall,* ☎ *340/776–5400.*

Down Island Traders. These traders deal in hand-painted calabash bowls; finely printed Caribbean note cards; jams, jellies, spices, hot sauces, and herbs; teas made of lemongrass, passion fruit, and mango; coffee from Jamaica; and a variety of handicrafts from throughout the Caribbean. ⊠ *Waterfront Hwy. at Post Office Alley,* ☎ *340/776–4641.*

Native Arts and Crafts Cooperative. More than 40 local artists—including schoolchildren, senior citizens, and people with disabilities—create an ever-changing array of handcrafted items: African-style jewelry, quilts, calabash bowls, dolls, carved-wood figures, woven baskets, straw brooms, note cards, and cookbooks. ⊠ *Tolbod Gade, across from Emancipation Garden and next to visitors center,* ☎ *340/777–1153.*

Tropical Memories. The emphasis here is on Virgin Islands artists. There are prints, pottery, gorgeous glass trays, carved mahogany bowls, and scented soaps. ⊠ *Royal Dane Mall,* ☎ *340/776–7536.*

JEWELRY

Amsterdam Sauer. Many fine one-of-a-kind designs are displayed at this jeweler's three locations. ⊠ *14 Main St.,* ☎ *340/774–2222;* ⊠ *Havensight Mall,* ☎ *340/776–3828;* ⊠ *Ritz-Carlton Resort, 6900 Great Bay Estate,* ☎ *340/779–2308.*

When you pack your MCI Calling Card, it's like packing your loved ones along too.

Your MCI Calling Card is the easy way to stay in touch when you travel. Use it to call to and from over 125 countries. Plus, every time you call, you can earn frequent flier miles. So wherever your travels take you, call home with your MCI Calling Card. It's even easy to get one. Just visit **www.mci.com/worldphone**.

EASY TO CALL WORLDWIDE

1. Just enter the WorldPhone® access number of the country you're calling from.
2. Enter or give the operator your MCI Calling Card number.
3. Enter or give the number you're calling.

Aruba ❖	800-888-8
Bahamas ❖	1-800-888-8000

Barbados ❖	1-800-888-8000
Bermuda ❖	1-800-888-8000
British Virgin Islands ❖	1-800-888-8000
Canada	1-800-888-8000
Mexico	01-800-021-8000
Puerto Rico	1-800-888-8000
United States	1-800-888-8000
U.S. Virgin Islands	1-800-888-8000

❖ Limited availability.

EARN FREQUENT FLIER MILES

    HAWAIIAN MILES

MIDWEST EXPRESS AIRLINES   **///UNITED** Mileage Plus® US AIRWAYS DIVIDEND MILES

SEE THE WORLD
IN FULL COLOR

Fodor's Exploring Guides bring all the great sights vividly to life with hundreds of photographs, fascinating historical background, and colorful anecdotes. Detailed maps and practical information keep you headed in the right direction.

Pair a **Fodor's** Exploring Guide with your trusted Gold Guide for a complete planning package.

Blue Carib Gems. At family-owned and -run Blue Carib Gems, watch Alan O'Hara, Sr., polish Caribbean amber and larimar, agate, and other gems and mount them into gold and silver settings. Visit Alan, Jr., at the Wharfside Village branch on St. John. ✉ *2–3 Back St.,* ☎ *340/774–8525.*

Cardow's. An enormous "chain bar"—with gold chains in several lengths, widths, sizes, and styles—awaits you here, along with diamonds, emeralds, and other precious gems. You're guaranteed 30%–50% savings off U.S. retail prices, or your money will be refunded within 30 days of purchase. ✉ *33 Main St.,* ☎ *340/776–1140;* ✉ *Havensight Mall,* ☎ *340/774–0530 or 340/774–5905;* ✉ *Marriott Frenchman's Reef Resort, Estate Bakkeroe,* ☎ *340/774–0434.*

Colombian Emeralds. Well known in the Caribbean, this store offers set and unset emeralds as well as gems of every description. The watch boutique carries upscale Ebel, Tissot, and Jaeger LeCoultre brands. ✉ *30 Main St.,* ☎ *340/774–3400;* ✉ *Havensight Mall,* ☎ *340/774–2442.*

Diamonds International. Choose a diamond, emerald, or tanzanite gem and a mounting, and you'll have your dream ring set in an hour. Famous for having the largest inventory of diamonds on the island, this shop welcomes trade-ins, has a U.S. service center, and offers free diamond earrings with every purchase. ✉ *31 Main St.,* ☎ *340/774–3707;* ✉ *3 Drakes Passage,* ☎ *340/775–2010;* ✉ *7AB Drakes Passage,* ☎ *340/774–1516;* ✉ *Havensight Mall,* ☎ *340/776–0040;* ✉ *Wyndham Sugar Bay Beach Club & Resort,* ☎ *340/777–7100.*

H. Stern. The World Collection of jewels set in modern, fashionable designs and an exclusive sapphire watch have earned this Brazilian jeweler a stellar name. ✉ *12 Main St.,* ☎ *340/776–1939;* ✉ *32AB Main St.,* ☎ *340/776–1146;* ✉ *Havensight Mall,* ☎ *340/776–1223;* ✉ *Marriott Frenchman's Reef Resort, Estate Bakkeroe,* ☎ *340/776–3550.*

LEATHER GOODS

Coach Boutique. A whole wall of high-fashion handbags leads deeper into the store, where lightweight Tumi luggage of nylon or leather is so strong you can sit on it. There are also sporty canvas Kipling bags, all under $100. ✉ *34 Main St.,* ☎ *340/777–1469.*

Purses and Things. This "house of handbags" has a wide selection of sizes and great prices (you can buy a five-in-one leather clutch for only $20). Bargains are equally good on eel-skin goods. ✉ *International Plaza,* ☎ *340/777–9713.*

Zora's. Fine leather sandals made to order are the specialty here. There's also selection of made-only-in-the-Virgin-Islands backpacks, purses, and briefcases in durable, brightly colored canvas. ✉ *Norre Gade across from Roosevelt Park,* ☎ *340/774–2559.*

LINENS

Fabric in Motion. Fine Italian linens share space with Liberty's of London silky cottons, colorful batiks, cotton prints, ribbons, and accessories at this small shop. ✉ *Storetvaer Gade,* ☎ *340/774–2006.*

Mr. Tablecloth. The friendly staff here will help you choose from the floor-to-ceiling array of linens, from Tuscany lace tablecloths to Irish linen pillowcases. The prices will please. ✉ *6–7 Main St.,* ☎ *340/774–4343.*

LIQUOR AND TOBACCO

A. H. Riise Liquors. This Riise venture offers a large selection of tobacco (including imported cigars), as well as cordials, wines, and rare vintage Armagnacs, cognacs, ports, and Madeiras. It also stocks fruits in brandy and barware from England. ⊠ *37 Main St., at Riise's Alley,* ☎ *340/776–2303;* ⊠ *Havensight Mall,* ☎ *340/776–7713.*

Al Cohen's Discount Liquor. The wine selection at this warehouse-style store is very large. ⊠ *Across from Havensight Mall, Long Bay Rd.,* ☎ *340/774–3690.*

Rio Cigars. Find a wide selection of premium cigars and accessories, including A. Fuente, Romeo Y Juleta, Havana, and more. ⊠ *Royal Dane Mall,* ☎ *340/774–5877.*

MUSIC

Modern Music. Shop for the latest stateside and Caribbean CD and cassette releases, plus oldies, classical, and New Age music. ⊠ *Across from Havensight Mall,* ☎ *340/774–3100;* ⊠ *Nisky Center,* ☎ *340/777–8787.*

Parrot Fish Records and Tapes. A stock of standard stateside tapes and CDs, plus a good selection of Caribbean artists, including local groups, can be found here. For a catalog of calypso, *soca* (up-tempo calypso), steel band, and reggae music, write to Parrot Fish, Box 9206, St. Thomas 00801. ⊠ *Back St.,* ☎ *340/776–4514.*

PERFUME

Tropicana Perfume Shoppes. Tropicana has the largest selection of fragrances for men and women in all of the Virgin Islands. ⊠ *2 Main St.,* ☎ *340/774–0010.*

SUNGLASSES

Davante. You'll find an enormous eyewear collection tucked into this glittering, glamorous store. Filling prescriptions is no problem. ⊠ *A. H. Riise Mall,* ☎ *340/714–1220.*

Tropical Optical. Take your pick from among name-brand eyewear. A real plus here is prescription sunglasses, copied from your present eyewear, ready in a 1/2-for $99. ⊠ *International Plaza,* ☎ *340/777–5585.*

TOYS

Grandpa's Korner Emporium. Birds sing, dogs bark, and fish swim in this animated toyland. Adults have as much fun trying out the wares as do kids. ⊠ *International Plaza,* ☎ *340/777–4944;* ⊠ *Tutu Park Shopping Center,* ☎ *340/777–7533.*

Nightlife and the Arts

On any given night, especially in season, you'll find steel-pan orchestras, rock-and-roll, piano music, jazz, broken-bottle dancing (dancing atop broken glass), disco, and karaoke. Pick up a copy of the free, bright yellow *St. Thomas This Week* magazine when you arrive (you'll see it at the airport, in stores, and in hotel lobbies); the back pages list who's playing where. The Thursday edition of the *Daily News* carries complete listings for the upcoming weekend.

Nightlife

BARS

Epernay Bistro. This intimate night spot has small tables for easy chatting, wine by the glass, and a spacious dance floor. Mix and mingle with island celebrities. The action runs from 4 PM until the wee hours. ⊠ *24-A Honduras, Frenchtown,* ☎ *340/774–5348.*

The Greenhouse. Once this favorite eatery puts away the salt and pepper shakers at 10 PM, it becomes a rock-and-roll club with a DJ or live reggae bands raising the weary to their feet six nights a week. ⊠ *Waterfront Hwy. at Storetvaer Gade,* ☎ *340/774–7998.*

Iggies. Sing along karaoke-style to the sounds of the surf or the latest hits at this beachside lounge. There's often a DJ on weekends, when a buffet barbecue precedes the 9 PM music fest. Dance inside or kick up your heels under the stars. ✉ *50 Estate Bolongo,* ☎ *340/775–1800.*

Old Mill Entertainment Complex. In—you guessed it—an old mill, this is a rock-'til-you-drop late-night spot Thursday through Sunday. There's also a tamer piano bar and jazz club in the complex, as well as billiards and foosball tables. ✉ *193 Contant,* ☎ *340/776–3004.*

Island-style steel-pan bands are a treat that should not be missed. Pan music resonates after dinner on Thursday, Friday, and Sunday at the **Agave Terrace** (✉ Point Pleasant Resort, 6600 Estate Smith Bay, ☎ 340/775–4142). A live band and dancing under the stars is a big draw for locals and visitors alike at **Duffy's Love Shack** (✉ Red Hook Plaza parking lot, ☎ 340/779–2080). **Lord Rumbottoms Club** (✉ Bolongo Bay Beach Club & Villas, ☎ 340/775–1800) hosts a Carnival night complete with steel pan music on Wednesday. **Raffles** (✉ 41–6–1 Compass Point Marina, ☎ 340/775–6004) features open-mike night Thursday, jazz and blues Friday, and live guitar Saturday. On Monday night, catch pan music at the **Ritz-Carlton** (✉ 6900 Great Bay Estate, ☎ 340/775–3333).

The Arts

THEATER

Reichhold Center for the Arts. This amphitheater has its more expensive seats covered by a roof. Schedules vary, so check the paper to see what's on when you're in town. Throughout the year there's an entertaining mix of local plays, dance exhibitions, and music of all types. ✉ *Rte. 30, across from Brewers Beach,* ☎ *340/693–1559.*

Exploring St. Thomas

St. Thomas is only 13 mi (21 km) long and less than 4 mi (6½ km) wide, but it's extremely hilly, and even an 8- or 10-mi (13- or 16-km) trip could take several hours. Don't let that discourage you, though; the mountain ridge that runs east to west through the middle and separates the island's Caribbean and Atlantic sides has spectacular vistas.

Charlotte Amalie

Look beyond the pricey shops, T-shirt vendors, and bustling crowds for a glimpse of the island's history. The city served as the capital of Denmark's outpost in the Caribbean until 1917, an aspect of the island often lost in the glitz of the shopping district.

Emancipation Gardens, right next to the fort, is a good place to start a walking tour. Tackle the hilly part of town first: head north up Government Hill to the historic buildings that house government offices and have incredible views. Several regal churches line the route that runs west back to the town proper and the old-time market. Virtually all the alleyways that intersect Main Street lead to eateries that serve frosty drinks, sandwiches and burgers, and West Indian fare. You'll find public rest rooms in this area, too. Allow an hour for a quick view of the sights, two hours if you plan to tour Government House.

A note about the street names: in deference to the island's heritage, the streets downtown are labeled by their Danish names. Locals will use both the Danish name and the English name (such as Dronningens Gade and Norre Gade for Main Street), but most people refer to things by their location ("a block toward the Waterfront off Main Street" or "next to the Little Switzerland Shop"). It's best to ask for directions by shop names or landmarks.

Charlotte Amalie

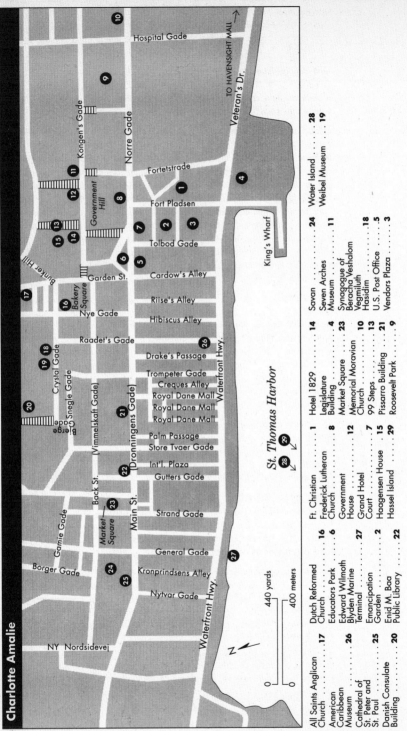

St. Thomas Harbor

All Saints Anglican Church 17
American Caribbean Museum 26
Cathedral of St. Peter and St. Paul 25
Danish Consulate Building 20
Dutch Reformed Church 16
Educators Park 6
Edward Wilmoth Blyden Marine Terminal 27
Emancipation Garden 2
Enid M. Baa Public Library 22
Ft. Christian 1
Frederick Lutheran Church 8
Government House 12
Grand Hotel Court 7
Haagensen House 15
Hassel Island 22
Hotel 1829 14
Legislature Building 4
Market Square 23
Memorial Moravian Church 10
99 Steps 13
Pissarro Building 21
Roosevelt Park 9
Savan 24
Seven Arches Museum 11
Synagogue of Beracha Veshalom Vegmiluth Hasidim 18
U.S. Post Office 5
Vendors Plaza 3
Water Island 28
Weibel Museum 19

0   440 yards
0   400 meters

Numbers in the margin correspond to points of interest on the Charlotte Amalie map.

SIGHTS TO SEE

⓱ All Saints Anglican Church. Built in 1848 from stone quarried on the island, the church has thick, arched window frames lined with the yellow brick that came to the islands as ballast aboard ships. Merchants left the brick on the waterfront when they filled their boats with molasses, sugar, mahogany, and rum for the return voyage. The church was built in celebration of the end of slavery in the USVI. ⊠ *Domini Gade,* ☎ *340/774–0217.* ⊙ *Mon.–Sat. 6–3.*

㉖ American Caribbean Museum. Learn about the Virgin Islands intriguing past via life-size replicas of historical figures and treasured artifacts. A 45-minute tour is led by knowledgable staff who encourage questions and delight in sharing true tales of the island's history from the days of the Amerindians to Danish transfer in 1917. Descriptive signs accompany each exhibit written in both English and Spanish. ⊠ *32 Raadets Gade,* ☎ *340/714–5150.* ⊙ *Daily 9–3.*

㉕ Cathedral of St. Peter and St. Paul. This building was consecrated as a parish church in 1848 and serves as the seat of the territory's Roman Catholic diocese. The ceiling and walls are covered with murals painted in 1899 by two Belgian artists, Father Leo Servais and Brother Ildephonsus. The San Juan–marble altar and side walls were added in the 1960s. ⊠ *Lower Main St.,* ☎ *340/774–0201.* ⊙ *Mon.–Sat. 8–5.*

⓴ Danish Consulate Building. Built in 1830, this structure housed the Danish Consulate until the Danish West India Company sold its properties to the local government in 1992. It now serves as home to the territory's governor. ⊠ *Take stairs north at corner of Bjerge Gade and Crystal Gade to Denmark Hill.*

⓰ Dutch Reformed Church. This church has an austere loveliness that's amazing considering all it has been through—founded in 1744, it burned down in 1804 and was rebuilt in 1844; it was then blown down by Hurricane Marilyn in 1995 and rebuilt in 1997. The unembellished cream-color hall gives you a sense of peace—albeit monochromatically. The only other color is the forest green of the shutters and the carpet. ⊠ *Nye Gade and Crystal Gade,* ☎ *340/776–8255.* ⊙ *Weekdays 9–5. Call ahead; doors are sometimes locked.*

❻ Educators Park. A peaceful place amid the town's hustle and bustle, the park has memorials to three famous Virgin Islanders: educator Edith Williams, J. Antonio Jarvis (a founder of the *Daily News*), and educator and author Rothschild Francis. The latter gave many speeches from here. ⊠ *Main St. across from U.S. Post Office.*

㉗ Edward Wilmoth Blyden Marine Terminal. Locally called "Tortola Wharf," you can catch the *Native Son* and other ferries to the BVI from here. The restaurant upstairs is a good place to watch the Charlotte Amalie harbor traffic and sip an iced tea. Next door is the ramp for the *Seaborne* seaplane, which offers commuter service and flightseeing tours to St. Croix and the BVI. ⊠ *Waterfront Hwy.*

❷ Emancipation Garden. Built to honor the freeing of slaves in 1848, the garden was refurbished to mark the 150th anniversary of emancipation in 1998. A bronze bust of a freed slave blowing a symbolic conch shell commemorates this anniversary. The gazebo here is used for official ceremonies. Two other monuments show the island's Danish-American tie—a bust of Denmark's King Christian and a scaled-down model of the U.S. Liberty Bell. ⊠ *Between Tolbod Gade and Ft. Christian.*

㉒ Enid M. Baa Public Library. Like so many structures on the north side of Main Street, this large pink building is a typical 18th-century town house. Merchants built their houses (stores downstairs, living quarters above) across from the brick warehouses on the south side of the street. The library was once the home of merchant and landowner Baron von Bretton. It's the island's first recorded fireproof building, meaning it was built of ballast brick instead of wood. Its interior of high ceilings and cool stone floors is the perfect refuge from the afternoon sun. You can browse through historic papers or just sit in the breeze by an open window reading the paper. ⊠ *Main St.,* ☏ *340/774–0630.* ⊙ *Weekdays 9–5, Sat. 9–3.*

 ❶ Ft. Christian. St. Thomas's oldest standing structure, this monument anchors the shopping district. It was built in 1672–1680 and now has U.S. National Landmark status. The clock tower was added in the 19th century. This remarkable building has, over time, been used as a jail, governor's residence, town hall, courthouse, and church.

Ft. Christian now houses **The Virgin Islands Museum,** where you can see exhibits on USVI history, natural history, and turn-of-the-20th-century furnishings. Local artists display their works monthly in the gallery. A gift shop sells local crafts, books, and other souvenir items. This is also the site of the Chamber of Commerce's Hospitality Lounge where you'll find public rest rooms, brochures, and a place you can stash your luggage for some last-minute shopping on the way to the airport. ⊠ *Waterfront Hwy. just east of shopping district,* ☏ *340/776–4566.* ▦ *Free.* ⊙ *Weekdays 8:30–4:30.*

❽ Frederick Lutheran Church. This historic church has a massive mahogany altar, and its pews—each with its own door—were once rented to families of the congregation. Lutheranism is the state religion of Denmark, and when the territory was without a minister, the governor—who had his own elevated pew—filled in. ⊠ *Norre Gade,* ☏ *340/776–1315.* ⊙ *Mon.–Sat. 9–4.*

⓬ Government House. Built as an elegant residence in 1867, today Government House serves as the governor's office, with the first floor open to the public. The staircases are of native mahogany, as are the plaques hand-lettered in gold with the names of the governors appointed and, since 1970, elected. Brochures detailing the history of the building are available, but you may have to ask for them.

The three murals at the back of the lobby were painted by Pepino Mangravatti in the 1930s as part of the U.S. government's Works Projects Administration. They depict Columbus's landing on St. Croix during his second voyage in 1493; the transfer of the islands from Denmark to the United States in 1917; and a sugar plantation on St. John.

A deputy administrator can take you on a tour of the second floor. You can call ahead for an appointment, or you can take a chance that an official will be in. It's worth the extra effort, if for no other reason than the terrace view. Imagine colonial affairs of state being conducted in the grandeur of the high-ceiling, chandeliered ballroom. In the reception room are four small paintings by Camille Pissarro, but unfortunately they're hard to appreciate because they're enclosed in frosted-glass cases. More interesting, and visible, is the large painting by an unknown artist that was found in Denmark and purchased by former governor Ralph M. Paiewonsky, who then gave it to Government House: it depicts a romanticized version of St. Croix. ⊠ *Government Hill,* ☏ *340/774–0001.* ▦ *Free.* ⊙ *Weekdays 8–5.*

❼ Grand Hotel Court. This imposing building stands at the head of Main Street. Once the island's premier hotel, it has been converted into offices and shops. ⊠ *Tolbod Gade at Norre Gade,* ☎ *340/776–0100.* ☉ *Weekdays 8–5, Sat. 9–noon.*

⑮ Haagensen House. Behind Hotel 1829, this lovingly restored home was built in the early 1800s by Danish entrepreneur Hans Haagensen and is surrounded by an equally impressive cookhouse, outbuildings, and terraced gardens. A lower level banquet hall now showcases an antique-print and photo gallery. ⊠ *Government Hill,* ☎ *340/774–9605.* 🖃 *$8.* ☉ *Daily 9–4.*

㉙ Hassel Island. East of Water Island in Charlotte Amalie harbor, Hassel Island is part of the Virgin Islands National Park, as it has the ruins of a British military garrison (built during a brief British occupation of the USVI during the 1800s) and the remains of a marine railway (where ships were hoisted into drydock for repairs). Also on Hassel Island is the shell of the hotel that writer Herman Wouk's fictitious character Norman Paperman tried to turn into his own paradise in the book *Don't Stop the Carnival.* There's a small ferry that runs from the Crown Bay Marina to the island; departure times are posted at Tickles Dockside Pub, and the fare is $3.

⑭ Hotel 1829. As its name implies, it was built in 1829, albeit as a residence of a prominent merchant named Lavalette rather than as a hotel. The building's bright coral-color exterior walls are accented with fancy black wrought iron, and the interior is paneled in a dark wood, which makes it feel delightfully cool. From the dining terrace there's an exquisite view of the harbor framed by tangerine-color bougainvillea. Be sure to visit Haagensen House, just behind the hotel, for a peek at another wonderfully restored 19th-century home. ⊠ *Government Hill,* ☎ *340/776–1829.*

❹ Legislature Building. Its pastoral-looking lime-green exterior conceals the vociferous political wrangling of the Virgin Islands Senate going on inside. Constructed originally by the Danish as a police barracks, the building was later used to billet U.S. Marines, and much later it housed a public school. You're welcome to sit in on sessions in the upstairs chambers. ⊠ *Waterfront Hwy. across from Ft. Christian,* ☎ *340/774–0880.* ☉ *Daily 8–5.*

㉓ Market Square. Formally called Rothschild Francis Square, this is a good place to find produce. A cadre of old-timers sells mangoes and papayas, strange-looking root vegetables, and herbs; sidewalk vendors offer a variety of African fabrics and artifacts and tie-dyed cotton clothes at good prices. ⊠ *North side of Main St. at Strand Gade.*

❿ Memorial Moravian Church. Built in 1884, it was named to commemorate the 150th anniversary of the Moravian Church in the VI. ⊠ *17 Norre Gade,* ☎ *340/776–0066.* ☉ *Weekdays 8–5.*

☾ ⑬ 99 Steps. This staircase "street," built by the Danes in the 1700s, leads to the residential area above Charlotte Amalie and Blackbeard's Castle. The castle's tower, built in 1679, was once used by the notorious pirate Edward Teach. Today this lookout serves at the backdrop for a trendy restaurant. If you count the stairs as you go up, you'll discover, as have thousands before you, that there are more than 99. ⊠ *Look for steps heading north from Government Hill.*

㉑ Pissarro Building. Home to several shops and an art gallery, this was the birthplace and childhood home of Camille Pissarro, who later moved to France and became an acclaimed impressionist painter. In the art gallery you'll find three original pages from Pissarro's sketchbook and two pastels by Pissarro's grandson, Claude.

⑨ Roosevelt Park. You'll see members of the local legal community head to the nearby court buildings while you rest on a bench in this park—a good spot to people-watch. The small monument on the park's south side is dedicated to USVI war veterans. Kids enjoy the playground made of wood and tires. ⊠ *Norre Gade.*

㉔ Savan. A neighborhood of small streets and houses, it was first laid out in the 1700s as the residential area for a growing community of middle-class black artisans, clerks, and shopkeepers. You'll find a row of Rastafarian shops along the first block and restaurants that sell *pate*—a delicious turnover-type pastry stuffed with meat or vegetables. ⊠ *Turn north off lower Main St. onto General Gade.*

⑪ Seven Arches Museum. This restored 18th-century home is a striking example of classic Danish–West Indian architecture. There seem to be arches everywhere—seven to be exact—all supporting a "welcoming arms" staircase that leads to the second floor and the flower-framed front doorway. The Danish kitchen is a highlight: it's housed in a separate building just off the main house, as were all cooking facilities in the early days (in case of fire). Inside the house you'll find mahogany furnishings and gas lamps. ⊠ *Government Hill, 3 bldgs. east of Government House,* ☎ *340/774–9295.* 🎟 *$5 (suggested donation).* 🕙 *10–4. By appointment only Aug.–Sept.*

⑱ Synagogue of Beracha Veshalom Vegmiluth Hasidim. The synagogue's Hebrew name translates to the Congregation of Blessing, Peace, and Loving Deeds. The small building's white pillars contrast with rough stone walls, as does the rich mahogany of the pews and altar. The sand on the floor symbolizes the exodus from Egypt. Since the synagogue first opened its doors in 1833, it has held a weekly Sabbath service, making it the oldest synagogue building in continuous use under the American flag and the second-oldest (after the one on Curaçao) in the western hemisphere. Next door, the Weibel Museum showcases Jewish history on St. Thomas. ⊠ *15 Crystal Gade,* ☎ *340/774–4312.* 🕙 *Weekdays 9–4.*

⑤ U.S. Post Office. While you buy your postcard stamps, contemplate the murals of waterfront scenes by *Saturday Evening Post* artist Stephen Dohanos. His art was commissioned as part of the Works Project Administration (WPA) in the 1930s. ⊠ *Tolbod Gade and Main St.*

③ Vendors Plaza. Here merchants sell everything from T-shirts to African attire to leather goods. Look for local art among the ever-changing selections at this busy market. ⊠ *West of Ft. Christian at the waterfront.* 🕙 *Weekdays 8–6, weekends 9–1.*

㉘ Water Island. This island, about ¼ mi (½ km) out in Charlotte Amalie Harbor, was once a peninsula of St. Thomas, but a channel was cut through so U.S. submarines could get to their base in a bay just to the west, known as Sub Base. On December 12, 1996, the U.S. Department of the Interior transferred 50 acres of the island, which included beaches and roads, to the territorial government, making it the fourth-largest of the USVI. A ferry goes between Crown Bay Marina and the island several times daily, at a cost of $3.

⑲ Weibel Museum. In this museum next to the synagogue, 300 years of Jewish history on St. Thomas are showcased. The small gift shop sells a commemorative silver coin celebrating the anniversary of the Hebrew congregation's establishment on the island in 1796. ⊠ *15 Crystal Gade,* ☎ *340/774–4312.* 🎟 *Free.* 🕙 *Weekdays 9–4.*

Around the Island

To explore outside Charlotte Amalie, you'll need to rent a car or hire a taxi. Your rental car should come with a good map; if not, pick up the "St. Thomas–St. John Road Map" at a tourist information center. Roads are marked with route numbers, but they're confusing and seem to switch numbers suddenly. If you stop to ask for directions, it's best to have your map in hand because locals probably know the road you're looking for by another name. Allow yourself a day to explore, especially if you want to stop for picture taking or to enjoy a light bite or refreshing swim. Most gas stations are on the island's more populated eastern end, so fill up before heading to the north side. And remember to drive on the left.

Although the eastern end has many major resorts and spectacular beaches, don't be surprised if a cow or a herd of goats crosses your path as you drive through the relatively flat, dry terrain. The north side of the island is more lush and hush—fewer houses and less traffic. Here you'll find roller-coaster routes (made all the more scary because the roads have no shoulders) and incredible vistas. Leave time in the afternoon for a swim at the beach. Pick up some sandwiches from delis in the Red Hook area for a picnic lunch, or enjoy a slice of pizza at Magens Bay. A day in the country will reveal the tropical pleasures that have enticed more than one visitor to become a resident.

Numbers in the margin correspond to points of interest on the St. Thomas map.

SIGHTS TO SEE

③¹ **Compass Point Marina.** It's fun to park your car and walk around this marina. The boaters—many of whom have sailed here from points around the globe—are easy to engage in conversation. ⊠ *Turn south off Red Hook Rd. at well-marked entrance road just east of Independent Boat Yard.*

③⁴ **Coral World Marine Park.** Coral World is home to an offshore underwater observatory that houses the Predator Tank, one of the world's largest coral-reef tanks, and an aquarium with more than 20 portholes providing close-ups of Caribbean sea life. *Sea Trekkin'* lets you tour the reef outside the park at a depth of 15 ft under the sea thanks to specialized high-tech headgear and a continuous air supply that's based on the surface. A guide leads the ½ hour tour and the narration is piped through a specialized microphone inside each trekker's helmet; the cost is $50 per person. The park also has several outdoor pools where you can touch starfish, pet a baby shark, feed stingrays, and view endangered sea turtles. In addition you'll find a mangrove lagoon and a nature trail full of lush tropical flora. Daily feedings and talks take place at most every exhibit. ⊠ *Coki Point, turn north off Rte. 38 at sign,* ☎ *340/775–1555,* WEB *www.coralworldvi.com.* ✆ *$18.* ☉ *Daily 9–5:30.*

③⁷ **Drake's Seat.** Sir Francis Drake was supposed to have kept watch over his fleet and looked for enemy ships from this vantage point. The panorama is especially breathtaking (and romantic) at dusk, and if you arrive late in the day you'll miss the hordes of day-trippers on taxi tours who stop here to take a picture and buy a T-shirt from one of the many vendors. ⊠ *Rte. 40.*

③⁸ **Estate St. Peter Greathouse & Botanical Gardens.** This unusual spot is perched on a mountainside 1,000 ft (306 m) above sea level, with views of more than 20 islands and islets. You can wander through a gallery displaying local art, sip a complimentary rum or Virgin Punch while looking out at the view, or follow a nature trail that leads through nearly 200 varieties of trees and plants, including an orchid jungle. ⊠ *Rte. 40, St. Peter Mountain Rd.,* ☎ *340/774–4999,* WEB *www.greathouse-mountaintop.com.* ✆ *$8.* ☉ *Mon.–Sat. 9–4:30.*

㊴ Frenchtown. Popular for its several bars and restaurants, Frenchtown also serves as home to the descendants of immigrants from St. Barthélemy (St. Barths). You can watch them pull up their brightly painted boats and display their equally colorful catch of the day along the waterfront. If you chat with them, you'll hear speech patterns slightly different from those of other St. Thomians. Get a feel for the residential district of Frenchtown by walking west to some of the town's winding streets, where tiny wooden houses have been passed down from generation to generation. ⊠ *Turn south off Waterfront Hwy. at the U.S. Post Office.*

㉟⃝ ㊱ Mountain Top. Stop here for a banana daiquiri and spectacular views from the observation deck more than 1,500 ft (459 m) above sea level. There are also shops that sell everything from Caribbean art to nautical antiques, ship models, and T-shirts. Kids will like talking to the parrots—and hearing them answer back. ⊠ *Head north off Rte. 33; look for signs,* WEB *www.greathouse-mountaintop.com.*

㉟⃝ ㉚ Paradise Point Tramway. Fly skyward in a gondola to Paradise Point, an overlook with breathtaking views of Charlotte Amalie and the harbor. There are several shops, a bar, and a restaurant. A ¼-mi (½-km) hiking trail leads to spectacular sights of St. Croix to the south. Wear sturdy shoes; the trail is steep and rocky. ⊠ *Rte. 30 at Havensight,* ☎ *340/774–9809.* ⊠ *$12.* ⊙ *Daily 7:30–4:30.*

㉝ Red Hook. In this nautical mecca you'll find fishing and sailing charter boats, dive shops, and powerboat rental agencies at the American Yacht Harbor marina. There are also several bars and restaurants, including Molly Molone's, Duffy's Love Shack, and Cafe Wahoo. Two grocery stores and two delis offer picnic fixings—from sliced meats and cheeses to rotisserie-cooked chickens, gourmet salads, and fresh baked breads.

㉟ Tillett Gardens. Clustered in a booming shopping area, you'll find a colony where local artisans craft stained glass, pottery, gold jewelry, and ceramics. Tillett's paintings and silk-screened fabrics are also on display and for sale. The gardens encircle a shaded courtyard with fountains and Polli's Mexican restaurant. ⊠ *Rte. 38 across from Tutu Park Shopping Center,* ☎ *340/775–1929,* WEB *www.tillettgardens.com.* ⊠ *Free.*

㉜ Virgin Islands National Park Headquarters. This facility consists of a dock, a small grassy area with picnic tables, and a visitor center where maps and brochures are available. Iguanas are common here. If you see one, hold out a hibiscus flower, which is this prehistoric-looking creature's favorite food. ⊠ *Turn east off Rte. 32 at sign,* ☎ *340/775–6238.* ⊙ *Weekdays 8–5.*

ST. CROIX

Updated by
Lynda Lohr

St. Croix, the largest of the three USVI at 84 square mi (218 square km), lies 40 mi (65 km) south of St. Thomas. But unlike the bustling island-city of St. Thomas, its harbor teeming with cruise ships and its shopping district crowded with bargain hunters, St. Croix has a slower pace and a more diverse economy, mixing tourism with light and heavy industry on rolling land that was once covered with waving carpets of sugarcane.

St. Croix's population has grown dramatically over the last 30 years, and its diversity reflects the island's varied history. The cultivation of sugarcane was more important here than on St. Thomas or St. John and continued as an economic force into the 1960s. After the end of slavery in 1848, the need for workers brought waves of immigrants from other Caribbean islands, particularly nearby Puerto Rico. St. Croix was divided into plantation estates, and the ruins of great houses and the more than 100 sugar mills that dot the land are evidence of an era when St. Croix was one of the greatest producers of sugar in the West Indies.

Tourism began and boomed in the 1960s, bringing visitors and migrants from the mainland United States (whom locals refer to as Continentals). In the late 1960s and early 1970s industrial development brought St. Croix yet another wave of immigrants. This time they came mostly from Trinidad and St. Lucia to seek work at the Hess oil refinery or at the south shore aluminum-processing plants.

St. Croix is a study in contrasting beauty. The island isn't as hilly as St. Thomas or St. John. A lush rain forest envelops the northwest, the eastern end is dry, and palm-lined beaches with startlingly clear aquamarine water ring the island. The capital, Christiansted, is a restored Danish port on a coral-bound northeastern bay. The tin-roof 18th-century buildings in both Christiansted and Frederiksted, on the island's western end, are either pale yellow, pink, or ocher—resplendent with bright blazes of bougainvillea and hibiscus. The prosperous Danes built well (and more than once, as both towns were devastated by fire in the 19th century), using imported bricks or blocks cut from coral, fashioning covered sidewalks (galleries) and stately colonnades, and leaving an enduring cosmopolitan air as their legacy.

Lodging

From plush resorts to simple beachfront digs, St. Croix's variety of accommodations is bound to suit every type of traveler. If you sleep in either the Christiansted or Frederiksted area, you'll be close to shopping, restaurants, and nightlife. Any of the island's other hotels will put you just steps from the beach. St. Croix has several small but special properties that offer personalized service. If you like all the comforts of home, you may prefer to stay in a condominium or villa. Room rates on St. Croix are competitive with those on other islands, and if you travel off-season, you'll find substantially reduced prices. Many properties offer honeymoon and dive packages that are also big money savers. Whether you stay in a hotel, a condominium, or a villa, you'll find up-to-date amenities, including cable TV.

Although a stay right in historic Christiansted may mean putting up with a little urban noise, you probably won't have trouble sleeping. Christiansted rolls up the sidewalks fairly early. The Frederiksted area is perfect for folks who want peace. A small, charming town—hardly more than a village—with a lovely waterfront, it has beaches within walking distance of its shops and restaurants. Solitude is guaranteed at hotels and inns outside the main towns. Old ruins dot the landscape where the green mountains meet the dark blue and turquoise sea.

For approximate costs, *see* the lodging price chart *in* St. Thomas.

Hotels

CHRISTIANSTED

$$$ ☒ **King's Alley Hotel.** In the center of Christiansted's hustle and bus-
★ tle, this small hotel (part of the King's Alley shopping and restaurant complex) mixes convenience with charm. The 12 premium rooms in the section across the courtyard have mahogany four-poster beds, Mexican tile floors, and Indonesian print fabrics. French doors open onto balconies with a view of the waterfront and the shopping arcade. The 23 standard rooms in the older section are a tad less interesting

St. Croix

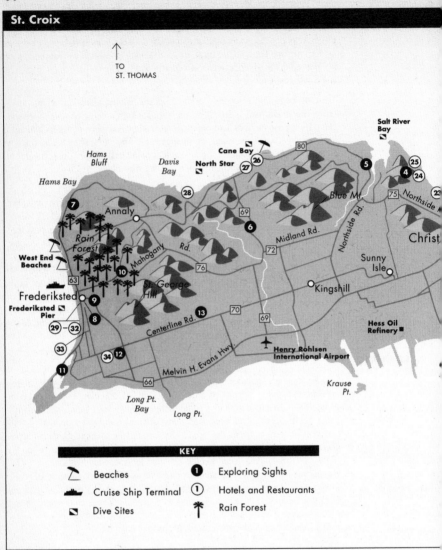

KEY

- ⌇ Beaches
- ⛴ Cruise Ship Terminal
- ◪ Dive Sites
- ❶ Exploring Sights
- ① Hotels and Restaurants
- 🌴 Rain Forest

Lodging

Breakfast Club **3**
Buccaneer **14**
Chenay Bay
Beach Resort **16**
Club St. Croix **21**
Colony Cove **23**
Cormorant
Beach Club **24**
Divi Carina Bay
Resort **19**

The Fredreiksted . . . **31**
Hibiscus Beach
Hotel **25**
Hilty House **11**
Hotel Caravelle **9**
King's Alley
Hotel **10**
Sandcastle on the
Beach **33**
Schooner Bay **13**

Sugar Beach **22**
Sunterra
Carambola
Beach Resort **28**
Tamarind
Reef Hotel **15**
Villa Madeleine **18**
Waves at Cane
Bay **26**

Dining

Blue Moon **29**
Breezez **21**
The Galleon **17**
Great House at
Villa Madeleine **18**
Harvey's **4**
Indies **5**
Kendricks **12**
Off the Wall **27**

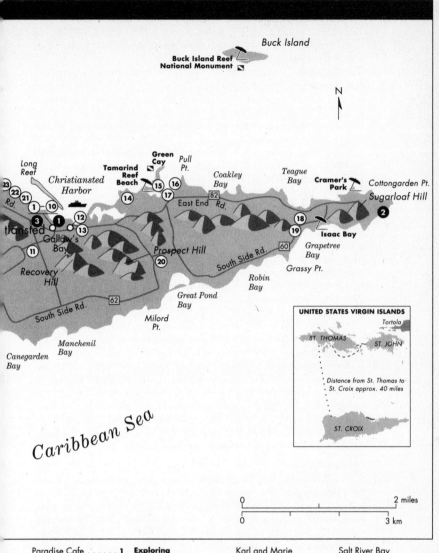

Buck Island

Buck Island Reef
National Monument

N

Green
Cay

Pull
Pt.

Long
Reef

Christiansted
Harbor

**Tamarind
Reef
Beach**

Coakley
Bay

Teague
Bay

**Cramer's
Park**

Cottongarden Pt.

Sugarloaf Hill

23
22
21
1
10

Rd.

14

15 16

17

East End Rd.

82

18

2

Christiansted

3
1
12
13

11

Gallow's
Bay

Prospect Hill

South Side Rd.

19

Isaac Bay

60

Grapetree
Bay

Grassy Pt.

20

Recovery
Hill

62

South Side Rd.

Milord
Pt.

Great Pond
Bay

Robin
Bay

Canegarden
Bay

Manchenil
Bay

Caribbean Sea

UNITED STATES VIRGIN ISLANDS

Tortola

ST. THOMAS

ST. JOHN

*Distance from St. Thomas to
St. Croix approx. 40 miles*

ST. CROIX

0   2 miles

0   3 km

Paradise Cafe **1**	
Pizza Mare **2**	
Le St. Tropez **30**	
South Shore
Cafe **20**	
Tivoli Gardens . . . **6**	
Top Hat **7**	
Turtle's Deli **32**	
Tutto Bene **8**	
Villa Morales **34**	

Exploring
Christiansted **1**
Estate Mount
Washington
Plantation **7**
Estate Whim
Plantation
Museum **12**
Frederiksted **8**
Judith's Fancy **4**

Karl and Marie
Lawaetz Museum **9**
Little Princess
Estate **3**
Mt. Eagle **6**
Point Udall **2**
St. Croix Leap **10**
St. George Village
Botanical
Gardens **13**

Salt River Bay
National
Historical Park
and Ecological
Preserve **5**
West End
Salt Pond **11**

but still attractive. The staff can arrange all sorts of activities: water sports, tours, golf, tennis. ⊠ *57 King St. (Box 4120), 00822,* ☎ *340/ 773–0103; 800/843–3574 direct to hotel,* FAX *340/773–4431,* WEB *www.kingsalley.com. 35 rooms. Air-conditioning, pool, dive shop, boating, fishing. AE, D, DC, MC, V. EP.*

$$ 🖫 **Hilty House.** For an alternative to beach and in-town lodgings, try this tranquil hilltop B&B. Built on the ruins of an 18th-century rum factory, it has the feel of a Florentine villa. You can escape to a patio and while-away an afternoon in sun or shade, or mingle with others in the immense great room, where a prix-fixe dinner is served on Friday (reservations essential). Unless you want to spend your entire vacation reading or sunning at the large tiled pool, however, you'll need a rental car to venture forth from here. ⊠ *Queste Verde Rd. (Box 26077), Gallows Bay, 00824,* ☎ FAX *340/773–2594. 4 rooms, 1 cottage. Dining room, pool. No credit cards. CP.*

$$ 🖫 **Hotel Caravelle.** The fetching, three-story Caravelle offers moderately priced in-town lodgings. Rooms are done in tasteful dusky blues and have floral-print bedspreads and curtains, vaulted ceilings, phones, and TV with free HBO. Baths are clean and fresh, though the unique tile in the showers is a holdover from when the hotel was built in 1968. Most rooms have some sort of ocean view; the best overlook the harbor. Owners Sid and Amy Kalmans are friendly and helpful. The Rum Runners, a casual terrace eatery, serves local and Continental cuisine. ⊠ *44A Queen Cross St., 00820,* ☎ *340/773–0687; 800/524–0410 direct to hotel,* FAX *340/778–7004,* WEB *www.hotelcaravelle.com. 43 rooms, 1 suite. Restaurant, bar, air-conditioning, refrigerators, pool, massage, gym, meeting room. AE, D, DC, MC, V. EP.*

$ 🖫 **Breakfast Club.** This rambling guest house is within walking distance of downtown. Rooms of various sizes and decors are clean, and each has a full kitchen and bath. Guests like to gather at the bar, and owner Toby Chapin includes gourmet breakfasts (featuring banana pancakes) in the room rates. ⊠ *18 Queen Cross St., 00820,* ☎ *340/773– 7383,* FAX *340/773–8642,* WEB *www.nav.to/thebreakfastclub. 7 rooms. Bar, air-conditioning (some), fans, kitchenettes, hot tub. MC, V. BP.*

EAST END

$$$$ 🖫 **The Buccaneer.** On the grounds of an old, 300-acre sugar plantation, this complex has it all: sandy beaches, swimming pools, golf, and many activities. A palm tree–lined main drive leads to the large, pink main building atop a hill; shops, restaurants, and guest quarters are scattered about rolling manicured lawns. The ambience and decor tend toward the Mediterranean, with tile floors, four-poster beds, massive wardrobes of pale wood, pastel fabrics, spacious marble baths, and local works of art. All rooms have such modern conveniences as hair dryers and cable TV. ⊠ *Rte. 82 (Box 25200), Gallows Bay, 00824,* ☎ *340/773–2100; 800/255–3881 direct to hotel,* FAX *340/778– 8215,* WEB *www.thebuccaneer.com. 138 rooms. 4 restaurants, air-conditioning, in-room safes, refrigerators, 2 pools, spa, 18-hole golf course, 8 tennis courts, jogging, 3 beaches, shops. AE, D, DC, MC, V. BP.*

$$$$ 🖫 **Chenay Bay Beach Resort.** The beachfront location and complimentary tennis and water-sports equipment (including kayaks) make this resort a real find—especially for families with active kids. Rooms are basic, with ceramic-tile floors, bright peach or yellow walls, rattan furnishings, and front porches. Gravel paths connect the terraced wood or stucco cottages with the shore, where you'll find a large L-shape pool, a protected beach, a picnic area, and a casual restaurant. The hotel offers an inexpensive day camp for children ages 4–12 and a shuttle to grocery stores and shopping areas. ⊠ *Rte. 82 (Box 24600), Christiansted 00824,* ☎ *340/773–2918; 800/548–4457 direct to hotel,*

FAX *340/773–6665,* WEB *www.chenaybay.com. 50 rooms. Restaurant, bar, picnic area, air-conditioning, kitchenettes, pool, hot tub, 2 tennis courts, volleyball, beach, snorkeling, baby-sitting, children's programs. AE, MC, V. EP.*

$$$$ 🏨 **Divi Carina Bay Resort.** Opt for a bottom-floor room at this ocean-front resort, and you're just steps from the water's edge. In all hotel rooms you'll fall asleep to the sound of the surf. A stay at the villas across the street puts you a two-minute walk from your morning swim. The rooms are fresh, with rattan and wicker furniture, white tile floors, sapphire and teal spreads, and sea-tone accessories that compliment the white walls. Small refrigerators and microwaves make this a comfy place to call home while you play the slot machines or blackjack at the island's only casino. The sea breeze keeps you cool, but when the humidity rises or on that rare day when the breeze dies, the ceiling fans or the air-conditioning will keep the air moving. For folks who just have to stay in touch, a desk and a data port on the phone make it easy to hook up your notebook computer. You're a long way from anywhere here, so if you're not content to just read a good book on your balcony or patio, hit the casino, or lounge at the pool or beach, you'll need a car to get around. ⊠ *25 Estate Turner Hole, Rte. 60, 00820,* ☎ *340/773–9700 or 800/823–9352,* FAX *340/773–6802,* WEB *www.divicarina.com. 126 rooms, 2 suites, 20 villas. 2 restaurants, 3 bars, deli, air-conditioning, fans, in-room data ports, in-room safes, refrigerators, pool, hot tub, 2 tennis courts, gym, beach, snorkeling, dock, billiards, casino, video games. AE, D, DC, MC, V. EP.*

$$$$ 🏨 **Villa Madeleine.** A West Indian plantation great house is the cen-
★ terpiece of this exquisite resort complex. Richly upholstered furniture, Asian rugs, teal walls, and whimsically painted driftwood set the mood in the billiards room, the library, and the sitting room. The great house sits on a hill, and there are villas on both sides of it. Each has a full kitchen and a pool. The decor is modern tropical: rattan furniture with plush cushions; rocking chairs; and, in some villas, bamboo four-poster beds. Special touches include pink-marble showers and hand-painted floral wall borders. Enjoy fine dining on the terrace at the Great House at Villa Madeleine or steak at the Turf Club. ⊠ *52 Kings St., off Rte. 82 at Teague Bay, Christiansted 00820,* ☎ *340/773–4850 or 800/237–1959,* FAX *340/773–8989,* WEB *www.teaguebayproperties.com. 43 villas. 1 restaurant, bar, air-conditioning, kitchenettes, tennis court, billiards, library. AE, MC, V. EP.*

$$$ 🏨 **Tamarind Reef Hotel.** At this casual, motel-like seaside spot, you can sunbathe at the large pool and sandy beach or snorkel in the reef, which comes right to the shore (serious swimming here is difficult). The spacious, modern rooms have rattan furniture, tropical-print drapes and spreads, and either a terrace or a deck with views of the water and St. Croix's sister islands to the north. Many rooms have basic kitchenettes—handy for preparing light meals—and three rooms have facilities for guests with disabilities. There's a snack bar just off the beach and a restaurant at the adjacent Green Cay Marina. ⊠ *Off Rte. 82, 5001 Tamarind Reef, 00820,* ☎ *340/773–4455; 800/619–0014 direct to hotel,* FAX *340/773–3989,* WEB *www.usvi.net/hotel/tamarind. 46 rooms. Snack bar, air-conditioning, kitchenettes, pool. AE, DC, MC, V. EP.*

FREDERIKSTED

$ 🏨 **The Frederiksted Hotel.** Don't be put off by the rather plain blue exterior. This modern, four-story hotel puts you right in the heart of Frederiksted and just steps from the town's restaurants and shops. The harbor is just across the street. In the inviting, tile courtyard, the glass tables and yellow chairs of the bar and restaurant crowd around a small freshwater swimming pool. Guest rooms have light-color rattan furniture, colorful print bedspreads, mini-fridges, and microwaves. Bathrooms are smallish, but bright and clean. ⊠ *442 Strand St., 00840,* ☎ *340/772–0500; 800/595–9519 (direct to hotel),* FAX *340/772–0500 Ext 151,* WEB *www.frederikstedhotel.com. 40 rooms. Restaurant, bar, air-conditioning, refrigerators, pool. AE, D, DC, MC, V. EP.*

OUTSIDE FREDERIKSTED

$$ 🏨 **Sandcastle on the Beach.** Right on a gorgeous strand of white beach, this laid-back resort caters mainly to gay and lesbian guests. Most are couples, but singles also enjoy the house-party atmosphere. There are several categories of rooms; most put you steps from the water, and most have sea views and kitchenettes. Room refurbishments are ongoing; finished rooms have a modern look with Mexican tile floors; the others are still a bit old-fashioned, but all are comfortable. Complimentary coffee, juice, and bagels or muffins are served on the patio each morning. ⊠ *127 Smithfield, Rte. 71, 00840,* ☎ *340/772–1205; 800/524–2018 direct to hotel,* FAX *340/772–1757,* WEB *www.gaytraveling.com/onthebeach. 6 rooms, 11 suites, 2 villas. Air-conditioning, fans, in-room VCRs, kitchenettes, 2 pools, beach, snorkeling. AE, D, MC, V. CP.*

NORTH SHORE

$$$ 🏨 **Cormorant Beach Club.** This small north-shore resort a few miles outside Christiansted offers a large, white beach for sunbathing and swimming and welcoming hospitality. All white-tiled rooms have large balconies, ceiling fans, cable TV, and queen- or king-size beds, with refrigerators for an extra charge; penthouse suites have a separate living room with 2 sofas and a wet bar. Two new beach bungalows have full kitchens and wooden decks. An open-air restaurant serves all meals with views of the water; the bar is a lively spot most nights. While gay-owned, the hotel's predominate mix of gay and lesbian couples and some singles happily coexists with a few straight couples too. ⊠ *4126 La Grande Princesse, 00820-4441,* ☎ *340/778–8920; 800/548–4460 direct to hotel,* FAX *340/778–9218,* WEB *www.cormorant-stcroix.com. 34 rooms, 4 penthouse suites, 2 beach bungalows. Restaurant, bar, air-conditioning, fans, in-room safes, kitchenettes (some), pool, massage, 2 tennis courts, gym, beach, snorkeling, meeting room. AE, D, DC, MC, V.*

$$$ 🏨 **Hibiscus Beach Hotel.** Rooms here are in five pink two-story buildings—each named for a tropical flower. Most rooms have ocean views, but those in the Hibiscus Building are closest to the water. All have such amenities as roomy balconies and cable TV, and all are tastefully decorated with white-tile floors, white walls, pink-stripe curtains, floral spreads, and fresh-cut hibiscus blossoms. Bathrooms are clean but nondescript—both the shower stalls and the vanity mirrors are on the small side. ⊠ *4131 Estate La Grande Princesse, off Rte. 752, 00820-4441,* ☎ *340/773–4042; 800/442–0121 direct to hotel,* FAX *340/773–7668,* WEB *www.1hibiscus.com. 37 rooms. Restaurant, air-conditioning, in-room safes, minibars, pool, beach, snorkeling. AE, D, MC, V. EP.*

$$$ 🏨 **Sunterra Carambola Beach Resort.** The 25 quaint, two-story, red-★ roof villas (including one that's wheelchair-accessible) are connected by lovely, lush arcades. Rooms are identical except for the view—ocean or garden. The decor is English country with a touch of Caribbean: terra-cotta floors, ceramic lamps, mahogany ceilings and furnishings, and rocking chairs and sofas upholstered in soothing floral fabrics. Each room has a patio and a huge bath (shower only). The two-bedroom suite, with its 3-ft-thick (1-m-thick) plantation walls and large patio, is the perfect Caribbean family dwelling. ⊠ *Rte. 80 (Box 3031), Kingshill 00851,* ☎ *340/778–3800 or 888/503–8760,* FAX *340/778–1682. 150 rooms, 1 cottage. 2 restaurants, deli, air-conditioning, pool, golf,*

4 tennis courts, gym, beach, dive shop, snorkeling, library. AE, D, DC, MC, V. CP.

$$$ ⊞ **Waves at Cane Bay.** Lapping waves lull you to sleep at this isolated inn. Although the beach here is rocky, Cane Bay Beach is next door, and the world-famous Cane Bay Reef is just 100 yards offshore (divers take note: this is a PADI resort). You can also sunbathe on a small patch of sand beside the very unusual pool: it's carved from the coral along the shore, and waves crash dramatically over its side, creating a foamy whirlpool on blustery days. Two peach and mint-green buildings house enormous, balconied guest rooms that are done in cream and soft pastel prints. ⊠ *Rte. 80 (Box 1749), Kingshill 00851,*☎ *340/778–1805; 800/545–0603 direct to hotel,* ☒ *340/778–4945,* WEB *www. canebaystcroix.com.12 rooms, 1 suite. Restaurant, bar, air-conditioning, in-room safes, kitchenettes, pool, snorkeling. AE, MC, V. EP.*

Cottages and Condominiums

$$$ ⊞ **Club St. Croix.** Popular with honeymooners, this complex's studio and one- and two-bedroom apartments are spacious and bright. Indian-print throw rugs and cushions complement the bamboo furniture and rough white-tile floors; glass-top tables and mirrored closet doors are lovely modern touches. Penthouses have loft bedrooms atop spiral staircases; studios have Murphy beds in their sitting rooms. All units have sundecks with waterfront views of Christiansted and Buck Island. On the beach you'll find the Breezez restaurant, a bar, and a dock. ⊠ *3230 Estate Golden Rock, Rte. 752, 00820,* ☎ *340/773–4800 or 800/524–2025,* ☒ *340/778–4009,* WEB *www.antillesresorts.com. 54 apartments. Restaurant, bar, air-conditioning, kitchenettes, pool, 3 tennis courts, beach, dock. AE, D, MC, V. EP.*

$$$ ⊞ **Colony Cove.** Next door to Sugar Beach, this condo-style resort has sunny apartments done up with pastel prints, white tile, and rattan furnishings. Each unit has two bedrooms, two baths, a balcony, a washer and dryer, and a kitchen so complete that it even has a lasagna pan. You'll find a large pool, a water-sports center, and tennis courts on the grounds, and you can walk along the beach to the restaurant next door. ⊠ *3221 Golden Rock, Rte. 752, 00820,* ☎ *340/773–1965 or 800/828– 0746 (direct to hotel),* ☒ *340/773–5397,* WEB *www.usvi.net/hotel/colony. 60 apartments. Snack bar, air-conditioning, kitchenettes, pool, 2 tennis courts, beach, snorkeling. AE, MC, V. EP.*

$$$ ⊞ **Schooner Bay.** This red-roof condo village climbs a hill above Gallows Bay and just outside Christiansted. Each modern two- or three-bedroom apartment has a balcony, a washer and dryer, and a full kitchen with a dishwasher and a microwave. Rattan furnishings are set on beige-tile floors; floral-print fabrics add splashes of color. Three-bedroom units have spiral staircases. Sun worshipers might be disappointed that the nearest beach is east, at the Buccaneer, but those with a yen to explore Christiansted will find the location ideal—within walking distance of downtown yet away from its bustle. ⊠ *5002 Gallows Bay, 00820,* ☎ *340/778–7670 or 888/868–7798,* ☒ *340/773– 4740,* WEB *www.stayinstcroix.com/schooner_bay.html. 40 apartments. Air-conditioning, fans, kitchenettes, 2 pools, tennis court. AE, MC, V. EP.*

$$$ ⊞ **Sugar Beach.** A stay here puts you on the beach at the north side of the island and just five minutes from Christiansted. The apartments, which range from studios to units with four bedrooms, are immaculate and breezy. Each has a full kitchen and a large patio or balcony with an ocean view; larger units have washers and dryers. Though the exteriors of these condos are ordinary beige stucco, the interiors are lovely (white with tropical furnishings). The pool is amid the ruins of a 250-year-old sugar mill. ⊠ *3245 Estate Golden Rock, Rte. 752, 00820,* ☎ *340/773–5345; 800/524–2049 direct to hotel,* ☒ *340/773–1359,* WEB *www.sugarbeachstcroix.com. 46 apartments. Air-conditioning,* *kitchenettes, pool, 2 tennis courts, beach, meeting rooms. AE, D, MC, V. EP.*

Private Homes and Villas

Renting a house gives you the convenience of home as well as top-notch amenities. Many houses have pools, hot tubs, and deluxe furnishings. Most companies meet you at the airport, arrange for a rental car, and provide helpful information. **The Collection** (☎ 856/751–2413) specializes in villas at Carambola. **Island Villas** (☎ 340/773–8821 or 800/626–4512, WEB www.stcroixislandvillas.com) rents villas across St. Croix. **Rent A Villa** (☎ 800/533–6863, WEB www.rentavillavacations.com) specializes in villas on the island's east end. **Richards & Ayer** (☎ 340/772–0420, WEB www.ayervirginislands.com) has villas on the island's west end. **Teague Bay Properties** (☎ 340/773–4850, WEB www.teague-bayproperties.com) specializes in villas on the eastern end of St. Croix.

Dining

Seven flags have flown over St. Croix, and each has left its legacy in the island's cuisine. You can feast on Italian, French, Danish, and American dishes; there are even Chinese and Mexican restaurants in Christiansted. Fresh local seafood is plentiful and always good; wahoo, mahimahi, and conch are popular. Island chefs often add Caribbean twists to familiar dishes. For a true island experience, stop at a local restaurant for goat stew, curry chicken, or fried pork chops. Regardless of where you eat, your meal will be an informal affair. But be forewarned, prices are a lot higher than you'd pay on the mainland.

For approximate costs, *see* the dining price chart *in* St. Thomas.

Christiansted

CARIBBEAN

$$ ✕ **Indies.** A historic courtyard full of tables covered with handmade
★ floral-print cloths is the setting for a wonderful dining experience. The menu of island-inspired dishes changes each day to take advantage of St. Croix's freshest bounties. Indulge in the crab cakes or the spicy Caribbean spring rolls to start, then the spice-rubbed chicken (every bite reveals a new, subtle flavor) or spiny lobster fresh from the sea. Enjoy live jazz Thursday, Friday, and Saturday evenings. ✉ 55–56 Company St., ☎ 340/692–9440. AE, D, MC, V. No lunch weekends.

$ ✕ **Harvey's.** The plain, even dowdy dining room has just 14 tables, and plastic floral tablecloths constitute the sole attempt at decor. But who cares? The food is delicious. Daily specials, such as mouthwatering goat stew and tender whelks in butter, served with heaping helpings of rice, fungi, and vegetables, are listed on the blackboard. Genial owner Sarah Harvey takes great pride in her kitchen, bustling out from behind the stove to chat and urge you to eat up. ✉ 11B Company St., ☎ 340/773–3433. No credit cards. Closed Sun. No dinner.

CONTEMPORARY

$$$ ✕ **Kendricks.** The chef at this open-air restaurant—a longtime favorite
★ with locals—conjures up creative, tasty cuisine. Try the Alaskan king crab cakes with lemon black pepper aïoli to start, or the warm *chipotle* pepper with garlic and onion soup. Move on to the house specialty: pecan-crusted roast pork loin with ginger mayonnaise. ✉ 21–32 Company St.,☎ 340/773–9199. AE, MC, V. Closed Sun. No lunch.

CONTINENTAL

$$$ ✕ **Top Hat.** Owned by a delightful Danish couple, this restaurant has
★ been serving international cuisine (with Danish specialties, of course) since 1970. Dishes include roast duck stuffed with apples and prunes, *frikadeller* (savory meatballs in a tangy cocktail sauce), conch beignets,

and smoked eel. The signature dessert is a rum-ice-cream-filled chocolate windmill whose blades turn. ⊠ *52 Company St.,* ☎ *340/773–2346. AE, D, DC, MC, V. No lunch.*

$$ ✕ **Tivoli Gardens.** Fresh breezes and bowers of hanging plants virtu-
★ ally transform this restaurant in the heart of Christiansted into a garden. The menu features steak, lobster, and more lobster. To make it easy to eat, the chef takes all the succulent meat from a whole lobster, puts it into half the lobster's shell, and drips butter over the top. For dessert try the bittersweet chocolate velvet—a chocoholic's dream that's closer to candy than cake. ⊠ *39 Strand St.,* ☎ *340/773–6782. MC, V. No lunch weekends.*

ECLECTIC

$$ ✕ **Paradise Cafe.** The exposed brick walls of this tiny, lively spot are splashed with colorful island prints. Stop in for breakfast, lunch, or supper: sandwiches and burgers are the big draw, though steak and the daily seafood special, often wahoo or mahimahi, are also popular. ⊠ *Company and Queen Cross Sts.,* ☎ *340/773–2985. No credit cards.*

ITALIAN

$$$ ✕ **Tutto Bene.** Its yellow walls, brightly striped cushions, and painted trompe l'oeil tables make Tutto Bene look more like a sophisticated Mexican cantina than an Italian cucina. One bite of the food, however, will clear up any confusion. Written on hanging mirrors is the daily menu, which includes such fare as veal Parmesan and seafood stew with a tasty fennel, cumin, tomato, and basil broth. Desserts are prepared by one of the island's finest pastry chefs. ⊠ *2 Company St.,* ☎ *340/773–5229. AE, MC, V.*

Outside Christiansted
ECLECTIC

$$ ✕ **Breezez.** This aptly named restaurant sits poolside at Club St. Croix condominiums. Visitors and locals are drawn by its reasonable prices, its very casual ambience, and its good food. This is *the* place to be for Sunday brunch, where the menu includes lobster rolls, burgers, and blackened prime rib with Cajun seasonings and horseradish sauce. For dessert, try the flourless chocolate torte—a wedge of rich chocolate served with a river of chocolate sauce. ⊠ *3220 Golden Rock, off Rte. 752,* ☎ *340/773–7077. AE, D, MC, V.*

ITALIAN

$ ✕ **Pizza Mare.** This trendy spot just may have the best pizza in all of
★ St. Croix. Residents gather for muffins in the morning as well as lasagna and meatball sandwiches for lunch or dinner. ⊠ *24 Estate Welcome, Rte. 82,* ☎ *340/773–3663. AE, D, MC, V. Closed Sun.*

East End
CONTEMPORARY

$$$ ✕ **Great House at Villa Madeleine.** The elegant restaurant at the Villa Madeleine resort serves such diverse cuisine as roasted ducking and macadamia-encrusted wahoo; there are also a number of fine beef dishes. The wine list is extensive. ⊠ *19A Teague Bay (Take Rte. 82 out of Christiansted, turn right at Reef Condominiums),* ☎ *340/778–7377. AE, D, MC, V. No lunch.*

ECLECTIC

$$$ ✕ **The Galleon.** Popular with locals and visitors, this dockside restaurant has something for everyone. Start with the Caesar salad or gravlax (fresh salmon with dill and pepper). Pasta lovers should sample the vegetable ravioli: the homemade pasta is filled not only with whatever grilled vegetable the chef gets in that day (the eggplant is especially good) but also with Parmesan, ricotta, and mozzarella cheeses. The osso buco and rack of lamb are legendary. ⊠ *Teague Bay (Take Rte. 82 out of Christiansted, turn left at sign for Green Cay Marina),* ☎ *340/773–9949. AE, MC, V. No lunch.*

$$ ✕ **South Shore Cafe.** This casual bistro sits near the Great Salt Pond on the island's south shore. Popular with locals for its good food and cozy ambience, the restaurant features dishes drawn from a variety of cuisines. Meat lovers and vegetarians can find common ground with a menu that runs from handmade pasta to prime rib. The selection isn't extensive, but the chef puts together a blackboard full of specials every day. ⊠ *Junction of Rtes. 62 and 624,* ☎ *340/773–9311. V. No lunch. Closed Mon.–Tues.*

Frederiksted

CARIBBEAN

$ ✕ **Villa Morales.** Locals come to this family-run spot for the food and the dancing (in the cavernous back room). The kitchen turns out such well-prepared Cruzan and Puerto Rican dishes as goat stew, conch, and baked chicken, but also steaks and fresh fish, all served with heaping helpings of fungi, rice, and beans. If you want lobster, be sure to reserve your order the day before. ⊠ *Plot 82C (off Rte. 70), Estate Whim,* ☎ *340/772–0556. D, MC, V. Reservations essential. Closed Sun.–Wed.*

DELICATESSENS

$ ✕ **Turtle's Deli.** Stop by this waterfront spot for a quick lunch or a take-out picnic. The sandwiches are creative, with names like the Beast—a warm roast beef sandwich topped with melted Swiss cheese, tomatoes, raw onions, horseradish, and mayonnaise served on roasted garlic bread. Add a fresh-baked cookie or two for dessert. ⊠ *625 Strand St.,* ☎ *340/772–3676. No credit cards. No dinner. Closed Sun.*

ECLECTIC

$$ ✕ **Blue Moon.** This terrific little bistro, popular for its live jazz on Friday night, has a changing menu that draws on Asian, Cajun, and local flavors. Try the seafood chowder or crab cakes with a spicy aïoli as an appetizer; the roasted vegetables and shrimp over linguine as an entrée; and the Almond Joy sundae for dessert. ⊠ *17 Strand St.,* ☎ *340/ 772–2222. AE, D, DC, MC, V. Closed Mon.*

$$ ✕ **Le St. Tropez.** A ceramic-tile bar and soft lighting add to the Mediterranean atmosphere at this pleasant bistro, tucked into a courtyard off Frederiksted's main thoroughfare. Seated either inside or on the adjoining patio, you can enjoy such items as grilled meats in delicate French sauces. The menu changes daily, often taking advantage of local seafood. The fresh basil, tomato, and mozzarella salad is heavenly. ⊠ *227 King St.,* ☎ *340/772–3000. AE, MC, V. No lunch Sat. Closed Sun.*

Cane Bay

ECLECTIC

$ ✕ **Off the Wall.** Divers fresh from a plunge at the north shore's popular wall gather at this breezy spot right on the beach. If you want to sit a spell before you order, a hammock beckons. Burgers, fish sandwiches, quesadillas, and Philly steak sandwiches join pizza and hot dogs on the menu. The potato salad that comes with your sandwich is as good as you'd get at home. You might find blues and jazz on Friday, Saturday, and Sunday nights. ⊠ *Rte. 80,* ☎ *340/778–4771. AE, MC, V.*

Beaches

Buck Island. A visit to this island, part of the U.S. National Park system, is a must. The beach is beautiful, but its finest treasures are those you can see when you plop off the boat and adjust your mask, snorkel, and flippers. To get here, you'll have to charter a boat or go on an organized trip.

Cane Bay. The waters aren't always gentle at this breezy north shore beach, but there are never many people around and the scuba diving and snorkeling are wondrous. You'll see elkhorn and brain corals, and less than 200 yards out is the drop-off called Cane Bay Wall.

Cramer's Park. This USVI territorial beach on the northeast coast (Route 82) is very popular with locals. It's a good spot for beach picnics and camping. Because of its isolation, though, it's not a good place to linger if you're traveling solo.

Isaac's Bay. This east-end beach is almost impossible to reach without a four-wheel-drive vehicle, but it's worth the effort. You'll find secluded sands for sunbathing, calm waters for swimming, and a barrier reef for snorkeling. You can also get here via footpaths from Jack's Bay.

Tamarind Reef Beach. Small but attractive Tamarind Reef Beach is east of Christiansted. Both Green Cay and Buck Island seem smack in front of you—an arresting view. The snorkeling is good.

West End Beaches. There are several unnamed beaches along the coast road north and south of Frederiksted. Just pull over at whatever piece of powdery sand catches your fancy. The beach at the Rainbow Beach Club, a five-minute drive outside Frederiksted on Route 63, has a bar, a casual restaurant, water sports, and volleyball.

Outdoor Activities and Sports

CYCLING

A bike tour to some of the island's top sights adds a new dimension to your vacation and helps you stay in shape. **St. Croix Bike and Tours** (✉ Strand Square Courtyard, Frederiksted, ☎ 340/772–1351) offers two tours; both cost $35. One heads through historic Frederiksted before cycling on a fairly flat road to Hamm's Bluff. The second, for heartier folks, takes you up and through the rain forest. Bikes rent for $7.50 for the first hour; $2.50 for each additional hour.

FISHING

In the past quarter century, some 20 world records—many for blue marlin—have been set in these waters. Sailfish, skipjack, bonito, tuna (allison, blackfin, and yellowfin), and wahoo are abundant. A charter runs about $100 an hour per person, with most boats going out for four-, six- or eight-hour trips. **Mile Mark Charters** (✉ 59 King's Wharf, Christiansted, ☎ 340/773–2628 or 800/523–3483) will take you out on a 38-ft powerboat, the *Fantasy*. **S.C.O.R.E./VI Divers** (✉ 11–12 Strand St., Christiansted, ☎ 340/773–6045 or 877/773–60453) will take you fishing on either their 29-ft *Tarpon* or 36-ft *Tarpon Shark II*.

GOLF

St. Croix's courses welcome you with spectacular vistas and well-kept greens. Check with your hotel or the tourist board to determine when major celebrity tournaments will be held. There's often an opportunity to play with the pros. The **Buccaneer**'s (✉ off Rte. 82 at Teague Bay, ☎ 340/773–2100) 18-hole course is conveniently close to (east of) Christiansted. The **Reef Golf Course** (☎ 340/773–8844), in the northeastern part of the island, has 9 holes. The spectacular 18-hole course at **Sunterra Carambola Beach Resort** (✉ Rte. 80, ☎ 340/778–5638), in the northwest valley, was designed by Robert Trent Jones Sr.

HIKING

Although you can set off by yourself on a hike through a rain forest or along a shore, a guide will point out what's important and tell you why. The **Nature Conservancy** (✉ 52 Estate Little Princess, Box 1066, Christiansted, 00821, ☎ 340/773–5575) has two-hour hikes to Jack's and Isaac's bays, on the east end. The cost is $10 per person. The non-profit **St. Croix Environmental Association** (✉ Arawak Bldg., Suite 3, Gallows Bay, 00820, ☎ 340/773–1989) offers treks through several ecological treasures, including Estate Mt. Washington, Estate Caledonia, in the rain forest, and Salt River. The cost is $20 per person for a two-hour hike.

HORSEBACK RIDING

Well-kept roads and expert guides make horseback riding on St. Croix pleasurable. At Sprat Hall, near Frederiksted, Jill Hurd runs **Paul and Jill's Equestrian Stables** (✉ Rte. 58, ☎ 340/772–2880 or 340/772–2627) and will take you clip-clopping through the rain forest, pastures, and hilltops (explaining the flora, fauna, and ruins on the way). A two-hour ride costs $50.

KAYAKING

Caribbean Adventure Tours takes you on trips through Salt River National Park and Ecological Preserve, one of the island's most pristine areas. A daytime ecotour runs $45, a moonlight trip is $40, and a combination kayaking and biking trip runs $50. (✉ Columbus Cove Marina, Rte. 80, ☎ 340/773–4599).

SAILING

Day sail to Buck Island aboard a charter boat. Most leave from the Christiansted waterfront or from Green Cay Marina. They stop for a snorkel at the island's eastern end before dropping anchor off a gorgeous sandy beach for a swim, a hike, and lunch. The best trips are on catamarans, which can drop anchor just off shore. A full-day trip runs about $65 with lunch included on most trips. A half-day sail costs about $35 to $50. **Big Beard's Adventure Tours** (☎ 340/773–4482) takes you on a catamaran, the *Renegade* or the *Flyer,* from the Christiansted Waterfront to Buck Island for snorkeling before dropping anchor at a private beach for a barbecue lunch. **Buck Island Charters** (☎ 340/773–3161) trimaran *Teroro II* leaves Green Cay Marina for full- or half-day sails. Bring your own lunch. **Mile Mark Charters** (☎ 340/773–2628 or 800/523–3483) departs from the Christiansted waterfront for half- and full-day trips on a variety of boats.

SCUBA DIVING AND SNORKELING

At **Buck Island,** a short boat ride from Christiansted or Green Cay Marina, the reef is so spectacular it's been named a national monument. You can dive right off the beach at **Cane Bay,** which has a spectacular drop-off. **Frederiksted Pier** is home to a colony of seahorses, creatures seldom seen in the waters off the Virgin Islands. At **Green Cay,** just outside Green Cay Marina in the east end, you'll see colorful fish swimming around the reefs and rocks. Two exceptional **north shore sites** are North Star and Salt River, which you can reach only by boat. You can float downward through a canyon filled with colorful fish and coral.

The island's dive shops take you out for one- or two-tank dives. Plan to pay about $50 for a one-tank dive and $70 for a two-tank dive, including equipment and an underwater tour. **Anchor Dive Center** (✉ Salt River Marina, Rte. 801, ☎ 340/778–1522 or 800/532–3483; ✉ Christiansted Wharf, ☎ 340/773–3307 or 800/532–3483) takes divers to 35 sites, including the wall at Salt River Canyon and Buck Island Reef National Monument. It also offers PADI certification. **Cane Bay Dive Shop** (✉ Rte. 80, Cane Bay, ☎ 340/773–9913 or 800/338–3843) takes you on boat and beach dives along the north shore. The famed wall is just 150 yards from their shop. **Dive Experience** (✉ Strand St., Christiansted, ☎ 340/773–3307 or 800/235–9047) is a five-star PADI training facility that offers everything from introductory dives to certification. It also runs trips to the north shore walls and reefs. **Scuba**

West (☎ 340/772–3701 or 800/352–0107) operates out of Frederiksted. Although it runs trips to reefs and wrecks, its specialty is the seahorses that live around the Frederiksted Pier. **V. I. Divers Ltd.** (☎ 340/773–6045 or 877/773–6045) is near the water at 11–12 Strand Street. It's a PADI international outfit that will take you to your choice of 28 sites.

TENNIS
The public courts in Frederiksted and out east at Cramer Park are in questionable shape. It's better to pay a fee and play at one of the hotel courts. Costs vary by resort, but count on paying at least $10 an hour. **Buccaneer Hotel** (⊠ Rte. 82, ☎ 340/773–2100) has eight courts (two lighted), plus a pro and a full tennis shop. **Chenay Bay Beach Resort** (⊠ Rte. 82, ☎ 340/773–2918) has two courts (no lights). **Club St. Croix** (⊠ Rte. 752, ☎ 340/773–4800) has three lighted courts. **Sunterra Carambola Beach Resort** (⊠ Rte. 80, ☎ 340/778–3800) has four lighted courts.

WINDSURFING
St. Croix's trade winds make windsurfing a breeze. Most hotels rent Windsurfers and other water-sports equipment to nonguests. **St. Croix Watersports** (⊠ Hotel on the Cay, ☎ 340/773–7060) offers Windsurfer rentals, sales, and rides; parasailing; and a wide range of water-sports equipment, such as Sea Doos and kayaks. Renting a windsurfer runs about $25 an hour.

Shopping

Areas and Malls
Although St. Croix doesn't offer as many shopping opportunities as St. Thomas, the island does have an array of small stores with unique merchandise. In Christiansted the best shopping areas are the **Pan Am Pavilion** and **Caravelle Arcade** off Strand Street, **Kings Alley Walk,** and along **King** and **Company streets.** These streets give way to arcades filled with boutiques. **Gallows Bay** has a blossoming shopping area in a quiet neighborhood. Stores are often closed on Sunday.

The best shopping in Frederiksted is along **Strand Street** and in the side streets and alleyways that connect it with **King Street.** Most stores close Sunday except when a cruise ship is in port.

Specialty Items
BOOKS
The Bookie. This shop carries paperback novels, stationery, newspapers, and cards. Stop in for the latest gossip and to find out about upcoming events. ⊠ *1111 Strand St., Christiansted,* ☎ *340/773–2592.*

Undercover Books. For Caribbean books or the latest good read, try this bookstore across from the post office in the Gallows Bay shopping area. ⊠ *5030 Anchor Way,* ☎ *340/719–1567.*

CLOTHING
From the Gecko. Come here for the hippest clothes on St. Croix, from superb batik sarongs to hand-painted silk scarves. ⊠ *1233 Queen Cross St., Christiansted,* ☎ *340/778–9433.*

Coconut Vine. Pop into this store at the start of your vacation, and you'll leave with enough comfy cotton or rayon batik men's and women's clothes to make you look like a local. Although the tropical designs and colors originated in Indonesia, they're perfect for the Caribbean. ⊠ *King's Alley, Christiansted,* ☎ *340/773–1991.*

Soul of Africa. The leopard- or zebra-trimmed clothing will catch your eye at this store. Elegant silk jackets and batik bedspreads in unique patterns also fill the shelves. ⊠ *Kings Alley, Christiansted,* ☎ *340/773–3099.*

The White House/Black Market. This contemporary store sells clothes in all-white, black, and natural colors. Look for exquisite lingerie, elegant evening wear, and unusual casual outfits. ⊠ *8B Kings Alley Walk, Christiansted,* ☎ *340/773–9222.*

FOODSTUFFS

If you've rented a condominium or a villa, you'll appreciate that St. Croix offers excellent shopping at its stateside-style supermarkets. Fresh vegetables, fruits, and meats arrive frequently. Try the open-air stands strung out along Route 70 for island produce.

Cost-U-Less is a warehouse-type store across from Sunshine Mall with a large, well-priced selection of liquor. It does not charge a membership fee. ⊠ *Rte. 70, outside Frederiksted,* ☎ *340/692–2220.*

Plaza Extra sells Middle Eastern foods in addition to the usual grocery store items. The newest supermarket on the island is the mid-island branch. ⊠ *United Shopping Plaza, Rte. 70, Frederiksted,* ☎ *340/778–6240;* ⊠ *Rte. 70, mid-island,* ☎ *340/719–1870.*

Pueblo is a stateside-style market with locations all over the island. ⊠ *Orange Grove Shopping Center, Rte. 75, Christiansted,* ☎ *340/773–0118;* ⊠ *Sunny Isle Shopping Center, Rte. 70, mid-island,* ☎ *340/778–5005;* ⊠ *Villa La Reine Shopping Center, Rte. 75, La Reine,* ☎ *340/778–1272.*

Schooner Bay Market is on the smallish side, but has good quality deli items. ⊠ *Rte. 82, outside Christiansted,* ☎ *340/773–3232.*

GIFTS

Gone Tropical. Whether you're looking for inexpensive souvenirs of your trip or a special, singular gift, you'll probably find it here. On her travels about the world, owner Margo Meacham keeps her eye out for items with which to stock her shop—from tablecloths and napkins in bright Caribbean colors to carefully crafted metal birds. ⊠ *5 Company St., Christiansted,* ☎ *340/773–4696.*

Island Webe. The coffees, jams, and spices—produced locally or elsewhere in the Caribbean—here will tempt your taste buds. Small *mocko jumbie* dolls depict an African tradition transported to the islands during slave days (they represent the souls of the ancestors of African slaves). The fabric dolls wearing Caribbean costumes will delight kids of all ages. Turn the double dolls upside down to see a white face on one side and a black one on the other. ⊠ *210 Strand St., Frederiksted,* ☎ *340/772–2555.*

Royal Poinciana. You'll find island seasonings and hot sauces, West Indian crafts, bath gels, and herbal teas at this attractive shop. Shop here for tablecloths and paper goods in tropical brights. ⊠ *1111 Strand St., Christiansted,* ☎ *340/773–9892.*

HANDICRAFTS

Folk Art Traders. Owners Patty and Charles Eitzen travel to Cuba as well as Haiti, Jamaica, and elsewhere in the Caribbean to find treasures for their shop. The baskets, ceramic masks, pottery, jewelry, and sculpture they find are unique examples of folk-art traditions. ⊠ *1B Queen Cross St., at Strand St., Christiansted,* ☎ *340/773–1900.*

HOUSEWARES

St. Croix Landmarks Museum Store. If a mahogany armoire or cane-backed rocker catches your fancy, the staff will arrange to have it shipped to your mainland store at no charge from its mainland warehouse. Furniture aside, this store has one of the largest selections of local art along with Caribbean-inspired bric-a-brac in all prices ranges. ⊠ *5A King St., Christiansted,* ☏ *340/713–8102.*

Textiles with a Story. Oriental rugs mingle with island-inspired batiks at this store that speaks of an Arabian souk. Comfy pillows in varied motifs and colors invite you to rest. ⊠ *52 King St., Christiansted,* ☏ *340/692–9867.*

JEWELRY

Colombian Emeralds. Specializing—of course—in emeralds, this store also carries diamonds, rubies, sapphires, and gold. A branch store, **Jewelers' Warehouse** (⊠ 1 Queen Cross St., Christiansted, ☏ 340/773–5590), is across the street. The chain, the Caribbean's largest jeweler, offers certified appraisal and international guarantees. ⊠ *43 Queen Cross St., Christiansted,* ☏ *340/773–1928 or 340/773–9189.*

Crucian Gold. This store, in a small courtyard of a West Indian–style cottage, carries the unique gold creations of St. Croix native Brian Bishop. His trademark piece is the Turk's Head ring (a knot of interwoven gold strands). ⊠ *59 King's Wharf, Christiansted,* ☏ *340/773–5241.*

Karavan West Indies. The owner here designs her own jewelry and also sells an assortment of tchotchkes, including handmade Christmas ornaments. ⊠ *5030 Anchor Way, Gallows Bay,* ☏ *340/773–9999.*

Sonya's. Sonya Hough opened this store in 1964 to showcase her jewelry creations; now she runs it with her daughter, Diana. Sonya invented the hook bracelet, popular among locals. With hurricanes hitting the island so frequently, she has added an interesting decoration to these bracelets: the swirling symbol used in weather forecasts to indicate these storms. ⊠ *1 Company St., Christiansted,* ☏ *340/778–8605.*

LEATHER GOODS

Kicks. This upscale shop carries a good, if small, selection of shoes and leather goods. ⊠ *57 Company St., Christiansted,* ☏ *340/773–7801.*

LIQUOR AND TOBACCO

Baci Duty Free Liquor and Tobacco. A walk-in humidor with a good selection of Arturo Fuente, Partagas, and Macanudo cigars is the centerpiece of this store. It also carries sleek Danish-made watches and Lladro Nao figurines. ⊠ *55 Company St., Christiansted,* ☏ *340/773–5040.*

Cruzan Rum Distillery. A tour of the company's factory culminates in a tasting of its products, all sold here at decent prices. ⊠ *West Airport Rd.,* ☏ *340/692–2280.*

Kmart. The two branches of this discount department store—a large one in the Sunshine Mall and a smaller one mid-island at Sunny Isle Shopping Center—carry a huge line of discounted, duty-free liquor. ⊠ *Sunshine Mall, Rte. 70, Frederiksted,* ☏ *340/692–5848;* ⊠ *Sunny Isle Shopping Center, Rte. 70,* ☏ *340/719–9190.*

PERFUMES

Violette Boutique. Perfumes, cosmetics, and skin-care products are the draws here. ⊠ *Caravelle Arcade, 38 Strand St., Christiansted,* ☏ *340/773–2148.*

Nightlife and the Arts

The island's nightlife is ever-changing, and its arts scene is eclectic—ranging from Christmastime performances of the *Nutcracker* to whatever local group got organized enough to put on a show. Folk-art traditions, such as quadrille dancers, are making a comeback. To find out what's happening, pick up the local newspapers—*V.I. Daily News* and *St. Croix Avis*—which are available at newsstands.

Nightlife

Christiansted has a lively and eminently casual club scene near the waterfront. **Hotel on the Cay** (⊠ Protestant Cay, ☎ 340/773–2035) has a West Indian buffet on Tuesday night in the winter season that features a broken-bottle dancer (a dancer who braves a carpet of broken bottles) and mocko jumbie characters. Easy jazz flows from the courtyard bar at **Indies** (⊠ 55–56 Company St., ☎ 340/692–9440) Thursday, Friday, and Saturday evenings. The **2 Plus 2 Disco** (⊠ 17 La Grande Princesse, ☎ 340/773–3710) spins a great mix of calypso, soul, disco, and reggae; there's live music on weekends in the winter.

Frederiksted has a couple of restaurants and clubs with a variety of weekend entertainment. **Blue Moon** (⊠ 17 Strand St., ☎ 340/772–2222), a waterfront restaurant, is the place to be for live jazz on Friday 9 PM– 1 AM.

Outside Frederiksted, **Off the Wall** (⊠ Rte. 80, Cane Bay, ☎ 340/778– 4471), has blues or jazz every Friday, Saturday, and Sunday from 6 PM to 9 PM.

The Arts

The **Whim Greathouse** (⊠ Rte. 70, ☎ 340/772–0598) hosts classical music concerts during the winter season.

Exploring St. Croix

Though there are things to see and do in St. Croix's two towns, Christiansted and Frederiksted (both named after Danish kings), there are lots of interesting spots in between them and to the east of Christiansted. Just be sure you have a map in hand (pick one up at rental-car agencies, or stop by the tourist office for an excellent one that's free). Many secondary roads remain unmarked; if you get confused, ask for help.

Numbers in the margin correspond to points of interest on the St. Croix map.

Christiansted and the East

Christiansted is a historic Danish-style town that always served as St. Croix's commercial center. Your best bet is to see the historic sights in the morning, when it's still cool. This two-hour endeavor won't tax your walking shoes and will leave you with energy to poke around the town's eclectic shops. Break for lunch at an open-air restaurant before spending as much time as you like shopping.

An easy drive (roads are flat and well marked) to St. Croix's eastern end takes you through some choice real estate. Ruins of old sugar estates dot the landscape. You can make the entire loop on the road that circles the island in about an hour, a good way to end the day. If you want to spend a full day exploring, you'll find some nice beaches and easy walks, with places to stop for lunch.

SIGHTS TO SEE

❶ **Christiansted.** In the 1700s and 1800s this town was a trading center for sugar, rum, and molasses. Today it's home to law offices, tourist shops, and restaurants, but many of the buildings, which start at the harbor and go up into the gentle hillsides, still date from the 18th century. You can't get lost. All streets lead gently downhill to the water, where a new boardwalk follows the harbor around. Still, if you want some friendly advice, stop by the **Visitors Center** (⊠ 53A Company

St., ☎ 340/773–0495) weekdays between 8 and 5 for maps and brochures.

Large, yellow **Ft. Christiansvaern** dominates the waterfront. Because it's so easy to spot, it makes a good place from which to begin a walking tour. In 1749 the Danish built the fort to protect the harbor, but the structure was repeatedly damaged by hurricane-force winds and was partially rebuilt in 1771. It's now a national historic site and the best preserved of the five remaining Danish-built forts in the Virgin Islands. It's also a convenient, free spot to park during the day. ⊠ *Hospital St.,* ☎ *340/773–1460.* ☞ *$2 (includes admission to Steeple Bldg.).* ◔ *8–5.*

When you're tired of sightseeing, stop at **D. Hamilton Jackson Park**—on the street side of Ft. Christiansvaern—for a rest. It's named for a famed labor leader, judge, and journalist who started the first newspaper not under the thumb of the Danish crown. ⊠ *Between Ft. Christiansvaern and the Danish Customs House.*

Built in 1830 on foundations that date from 1734, the **Danish Customs House**—near Ft. Christiansvaern—originally served as both a customs house and a post office (second floor). In 1926 it became the Christiansted Library, and it has been a National Park Service office since 1972. ⊠ *King St.,* ☎ *340/773–1460.* ◔ *Weekdays 8–5.*

Constructed in 1856, the **Scale House** was once the spot where goods passing through the port were weighed and inspected. It now serves as the Christiansted Historic Site's visitors center. ⊠ *King St.,* ☎ *340/773–1460.* ◔ *Weekdays 8–4:30, weekends and holidays 8:30–4:30.*

Built by the Danes in 1753, the **Steeple Building** was the first Danish Lutheran church on St. Croix. It's now a national park museum and contains exhibits that document the island's Indian habitation. It's worth the block-long walk from Ft. Christiansvaern to see the building's collection of archaeological artifacts, displays on plantation life, and exhibits on the architectural development of Christiansted, the early history of the church, and Alexander Hamilton, the first secretary of the U.S. Treasury, who grew up in St. Croix. ⊠ *Church St.,* ☎ *340/773–1460.* ☞ *$2 (includes admission to Ft. Christiansvaern).* ◔ *Daily 9–4:30.*

The **Post Office Building,** built in 1749, was once the Danish West India & Guinea Company warehouse. ⊠ *Church St.*

One of the town's most elegant structures, **Government House** was built as a home for a Danish merchant in 1747. Today it houses USVI government offices. If the building is open, slip into the peaceful inner courtyard to admire the still pools and gardens. A sweeping staircase leads you to a second-story ballroom, the site of official government functions. ⊠ *King St.,* ☎ *340/773–1404.* ◔ *Weekdays 8–5.*

Around the corner and down a block from Government House, the tanks at the **St. Croix Aquarium** contain an ever-changing variety of local sea creatures. Children are invited to explore the discovery room, with its microscopes, interactive displays, and educational videos. Children will enjoy the petting tank, where they can feel starfish relax to their touch. ⊠ *Caravelle Arcade,* ☎ *340/773–8995.* ☞ *$5.* ◔ *Tues.–Sat. 11–4.*

Built in 1735 as a slave market, today **the market,** housed in a wood and galvanized aluminum structure, is where farmers and others sell their goods every Wednesday and Saturday from 8 to 5. The market is a three-block walk from the aquarium and is a great place to end a walking tour. ⊠ *Company St.*

The **Buck Island Reef National Monument,** off the northeast coast, has pristine beaches that are just right for sunbathing, but there's some shade for those who don't want to fry. The spectacular snorkeling trail set in the reef allows close-up study of coral formations and tropical fish. After your arrival by charter boat, crew members give special attention to novice snorkelers and children. There's an easy hiking trail to the island's highest point, where you'll be rewarded for your efforts by spectacular views of the reef and St. John. Charter-boat trips leave daily from the Christiansted waterfront or from Green Cay Marina, about 2 mi (3 km) east of Christiansted. Check with your hotel for recommendations. ⊠ *North Shore,* ☎ *340/773–1460 (park headquarters),* WEB *www.nps.gov/buis.*

❷ Point Udall. This rocky promontory, the easternmost point in the United States, is about a half-hour's drive from Christiansted. A paved road takes you to an overlook with glorious views. More adventurous folks can hike down to the pristine beach below. On the way back, look for The Castle, an enormous mansion that can only be described as a cross between a Moorish mosque and the Taj Mahal. It was built by an extravagant recluse known only as the Contessa. ⊠ *Rte. 82.*

Between Christiansted and Frederiksted

A drive through the countryside between these two towns will take you past ruins of old plantations, many bearing whimsical names (Morningstar, Solitude, Upper Love) bestowed by early owners. The traffic moves quickly—by island standards—on the main roads, but you can pause and poke around if you head down some side lanes. It's easy to find your way west, but driving from north to south requires good navigation. Don't leave your hotel without a map. Allow an entire day for this trip so you'll have enough time for a swim at a north shore beach. Although you'll find lots of casual eateries on the main roads, pick up a picnic lunch if you plan to head off the beaten path.

SIGHTS TO SEE

❹ Judith's Fancy. In this upscale neighborhood you'll find the ruins of an old great house and tower of the same name, both remnants of a circa-1750 Danish sugar plantation. The "Judith" comes from the first name of a woman buried on the property. From the guard house at the neighborhood entrance, follow Hamilton Drive past some of St. Croix's loveliest homes. At the end of Hamilton Drive the road overlooks Salt River Bay, where Christopher Columbus anchored in 1493. A skirmish between members of Columbus's crew and a group of Carib Indians resulted in the first bloody encounter between Europeans and West Indians. The peninsula on the bay's east side is named for the event: Cabo de las Flechas (Cape of the Arrows). On the way back, make a detour left off Hamilton Drive onto Caribe Road for a close look at the ruins. ⊠ *Turn north onto Rte. 751, off Rte. 75.*

❸ Little Princess Estate. If the old plantation ruins decaying here and there around St. Croix intrigue you, a visit to this Nature Conservancy project will give you even more of a glimpse into the past. The staff has carved walking paths out of the bush that surrounds what's left of a 19th-century plantation. It's easy to stroll among well-labeled fruit trees and see the ruins of the windmill, the sugar and rum factory, and the laborers' village. This is the perfect place to reflect on St. Croix's agrarian past fueled with labor from African slaves. The property also has a community garden. ⊠ *Just off Rte. 75 (turn north at the Five Corners traffic light),* ☎ *340/773–5575.* ☜ *Free.* ☉ *9–2.*

❻ Mt. Eagle. This is St. Croix's highest peak (1,165 ft/356 m). Leaving Cane Bay and passing North Star Beach, follow the coastal road that dips briefly into a forest, then turn left on Rte. 69. Just after you make the turn, the pavement is marked with the words THE BEAST and a set of giant paw prints. The hill you're about to climb is the location of the famous Beast of the St. Croix Half Ironman Triathlon, an annual event during which participants must bike this intimidating slope. ☒ *Rte. 69.*

5 Salt River Bay National Historical Park and Ecological Preserve. This joint national and local park was dedicated in November 1993. In addition to sights with cultural significance, it encompasses a biodiverse coastal estuary with the largest remaining mangrove forest in the USVI, a submarine canyon, and several endangered species, including the hawksbill turtle and the roseate tern. Plans are afoot to create a museum, interpretive walking trails, and a replica of a Carib village. A ball court, used by the Caribs in worship ceremonies, was discovered at the spot where the taxis park. Take a short hike up the dirt road to the ruins of an old earthen fort for great views of Salt River Bay and the surrounding countryside. ☒ *Rte. 75 to Rte. 80.*

Frederiksted and Environs

St. Croix's second-largest town, Frederiksted, was founded in 1751. A stroll around its historic sights will take you no more than an hour. Allow a little more time if you want to browse in the few small shops. The area just outside town has old plantations, some of which have been preserved as homes or historic structures that are open to the public.

SIGHTS TO SEE

7 Estate Mount Washington Plantation. Several years ago, while surveying the property, the owners discovered the ruins of a sugar plantation beneath the rain-forest brush. The grounds have since been cleared and opened to the public. You can take a self-guided walking tour of the mill, the rum factory, and other ruins, and there's an antiques shop in what were once the stables. ☒ *Rte. 63 (watch for antiques shop sign),* ☎ *340/772–1026.* ☉ *Ruins open daily; antiques shop open by appointment only.*

☝ 12 Estate Whim Plantation Museum. The lovingly restored estate, with a windmill, cook house, and other buildings, will give you a sense of what life was like on St. Croix's sugar plantations in the 1800s. The oval-shape great house has high ceilings and antique furniture, decor, and utensils. Notice its fresh, airy atmosphere—the waterless stone moat around the great house was used not for defense but for gathering cooling air. The apothecary exhibit is the largest in all the West Indies. If you have kids, the grounds are the perfect place for them to stretch their legs, perhaps while you browse in the museum gift shop. ☒ *Rte. 70,* ☎ *340/772–0598,* WEB *www.stcroixlandmarks.com.* ☒ *$6.* ☉ *Mon.–Sat. 10–4.*

8 Frederiksted. The town is noted less for its Danish than for its Victorian architecture, which dates from after the slave uprising and the great fire of 1878. One long cruise-ship pier juts into the sparkling sea. It's the perfect place to start a tour of this quaint city. The **Visitors Center** (☒ Waterfront, ☎ 340/772–0357), right on the pier, was built in the late 1700s; the two-story gallery was added in the 1800s. The building once served as the customs house; today you can stop in weekdays from 8 to 5 and pick up brochures or view the exhibits on St. Croix.

On July 3, 1848, 8,000 slaves marched on the red-brick **Ft. Frederik** to demand their freedom. Danish governor Peter von Scholten, fearing they would burn the town to the ground, stood up in his carriage parked in front of the fort and granted them their freedom. The fort, completed in 1760, houses a number of interesting historical exhibits as well as an art gallery and a display of police memorabilia. It's within earshot of the Visitors Center. ⊠ *Waterfront,* ☎ *340/772–2021.* 🎫 *Free.* ⊙ *Weekdays 8:30–4:30.*

St. Patrick's Roman Catholic church, complete with three turrets, was built in 1843 of coral. Wander inside, and you'll find woodwork hand-crafted by Frederiksted artisans. The churchyard is filled with 18th-century gravestones. ⊠ *Prince St.*

St. Paul's Anglican Church (circa 1812) is a mix of Georgian and Gothic Revival architecture. The bell tower of exposed sandstone was added later. The simple interior has gleaming woodwork and a tray ceiling (it looks like an upside-down tray) popular in Caribbean architecture. ⊠ *Prince St.*

Built in 1839, **Apothecary Hall** is a good example of 19th-century architecture; its facade has both Gothic and Greek Revival elements. ⊠ *King Cross St.*

Stop at the **market** for fresh fruits and vegetables (be sure to wash or peel this produce before eating it) sold each morning, just as they have been for more than 200 years. ⊠ *Queen St.*

❾ Karl and Marie Lawaetz Museum. For a trip back in time, tour this circa-1750 farm. Owned by the prominent Lawaetz family since 1899, just after Karl arrived from Denmark, the lovely two-story house is in a valley at La Grange. A Lawaetz family member shows you the four-poster mahogany bed Karl and Marie shared, the china Marie painted, the family portraits, and the fruit trees that fed the family for several generations. Initially a sugar plantation, it was subsequently used to raise cattle and produce. ⊠ *Estate Little La Grange, Rte. 76, Mahogany Rd.,* ☎ *340/772–1539.* 🎫 *$6.* ⊙ *Wed.–Sun. 10–4.*

❿ St. Croix Leap. This workshop sits in the heart of the rain forest, about a 15-minute drive from Frederiksted. It sells a wide range of articles, including mirrors, tables, bread boards, and mahogany jewelry boxes crafted by local artisans. ⊠ *Rte. 76,* ☎ *340/772–0421.* ⊙ *Weekdays 8–5:30, Sat. 10–5.*

⓭ St. George Village Botanical Gardens. At this 17-acre estate you'll find lush, fragrant flora amid the ruins of a 19th-century sugarcane plantation village. There are miniature versions of each ecosystem on St. Croix, from a semiarid cactus grove to a verdant rain forest. ⊠ *Turn north off Rte. 70 at sign, Kingshill,* ☎ *340/692–2874,* 🕸 *www.sgvbg.com.* 🎫 *$6.* ⊙ *9–5.*

⓫ West End Salt Pond. A bird-watcher's delight, this salt pond attracts a vast variety of winged creatures, including flamingos. ⊠ *Veteran's Shore Dr.*

ST. JOHN

Updated by
Lynda Lohr

Beautiful and largely undisturbed St. John is 3 mi (5 km) east of St. Thomas across the Pillsbury Sound (a 20-minute ferry ride from Red Hook). In 1956 Laurance Rockefeller, who founded the Caneel Bay Resort, donated ⅔ of St. John's 20 square mi (53 square km) to the United States as a national park. Because of this, the island comes close to realizing that travel-brochure dream of "an unspoiled tropical paradise." It's covered with vegetation, including a bay-tree forest that once supplied St. Thomas with the raw material for its fragrant bay rum. Along St. John's north shore, clean, gleaming white-sand beaches fringe bay after bay, each full of iridescent water perfect for swimming, fishing, snorkeling, diving, and underwater photography.

In 1675 Jorgen Iverson claimed the unsettled island for Denmark. The British residents of nearby Tortola, however, considered St. John theirs, and when a small party of Danes from St. Thomas moved onto the uninhabited island, the British "invited" them to leave (which they did). Despite this, in 1717 a group of Danish planters founded the first permanent settlement at Coral Bay. The question of who owned St. John wasn't settled until 1762, when Britain decided that maintaining good relations with Denmark was more important than keeping St. John.

By 1728 St. John had 87 plantations and a population of 123 whites and 677 blacks. By 1733 there were more than 1,000 slaves working more than 100 plantations. In that year the island was hit by a drought, hurricanes, and a plague of insects that destroyed the summer crops. Everyone felt the threat of famine, particularly the slaves, whose living and working conditions were already harsh. Sensing the growing desperation, the landowners enacted even more severe measures in a misguided attempt to keep control. On November 23 the slaves revolted. With great military prowess, they captured the fort at Coral Bay, took control of the island, and held on to it for six months. During this time nearly a quarter of the island's population—black and white—was killed. The rebellion was eventually put down by 100 Danish militia and 220 Creole troops brought in from Martinique. Slavery continued until 1848, when slaves in St. Croix marched on Frederiksted to demand their freedom from the Danish government. After emancipation, St. John fell into decline, with its inhabitants eking out a living on small farms. Life continued in much the same way until the national park was established in 1956 and tourism became an industry.

Today St. John may well be the most racially integrated of the three USVI. Its 5,000 residents, black and white, have a strong sense of community that seems rooted in a desire to protect the island's natural beauty. Cruz Bay, the administrative capital, is home to the Virgin Islands National Park Visitors Center and a few small shopping centers. It's more a small West Indian village (calm except when cruise ships arrive) than a major urban hub, and its residents want to keep it that way. When the government tried to install the island's first traffic light here, the citizens successfully opposed it, claiming it would change the character of the island and do little to help traffic. The consensus that the island's natural resources are sacrosanct may be curbing excesses on private land as well. Except for Cruz Bay, most of St. John—even areas outside the national park—still has a natural, undeveloped feel to it. Here you can truly escape the pressures of modern life for a day, a week—perhaps, forever.

Lodging

St. John doesn't have many beachfront hotels, but that's a small price to pay for all the pristine sand. However, the island's two world-class resorts—Caneel Bay Resort and the Westin Resort, St. John—*are* on the beach. Sandy, white beaches string out along the north coast, which is popular with sunbathers and snorkelers and is the home to the Caneel Bay Resort and Cinnamon and Maho Bay campgrounds. Most villas are in the residential south shore area, a 15-minute drive from the north shore beaches. If you head east you'll come to the laid-back community of Coral Bay, where you'll find a few villas and cottages. A stay outside of Coral Bay will be peaceful and quiet.

If you're looking for West Indian–village charm, there are a few inns in Cruz Bay. Just know that when bands play at any of the town's bars (some of which stay open till the wee hours), the noise can be a problem. Your choice of accommodations also includes condominiums and

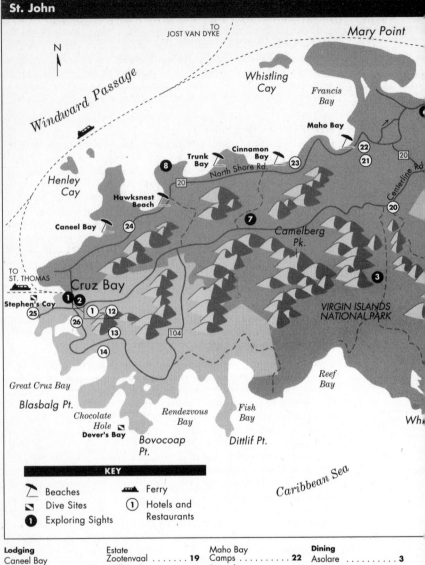

St. John

KEY

⚓ Beaches
◣ Dive Sites
❶ Exploring Sights
⚓ Ferry
① Hotels and Restaurants

Lodging

Caneel Bay
Resort **24**
Cinnamon Bay
Campground **23**
Coconut Coast
Villas **25**
Estate
Concordia **15**

Estate
Zootenvaal **19**
Gallows Point
Suite Resort **2**
Garden by
the Sea **26**
Harmony **21**

Maho Bay
Camps **22**
Serendip **13**
St. John Inn **12**
Westin Resort,
St. John **14**

Dining

Asolare **3**
Café Roma **1**
Chateau
Bordeaux **20**
Dinner with André . . . **9**
Ellington's **2**
Fish Trap **4**
La Tapa **10**
Lime Inn **5**

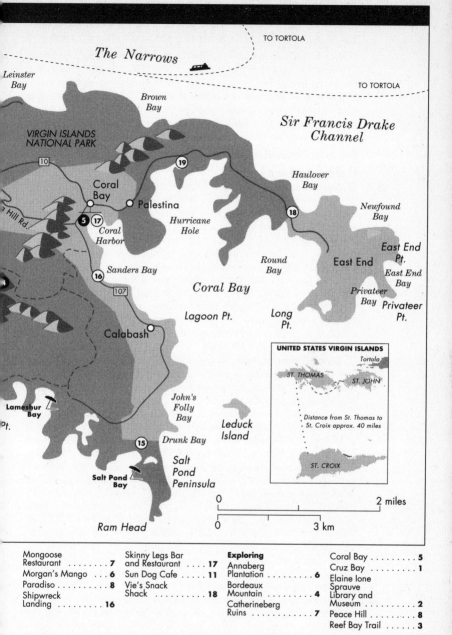

TO TORTOLA

The Narrows

Leinster Bay

Brown Bay

TO TORTOLA

Sir Francis Drake Channel

VIRGIN ISLANDS NATIONAL PARK

10

19

Coral Bay

Palestina

Hurricane Hole

Haulover Bay

18

Newfound Bay

Hill Rd.

5 **17**

Coral Harbor

Sanders Bay

16

107

Round Bay

East End

East End Pt.

East End Bay

Privateer Bay

Privateer Pt.

Coral Bay

Lagoon Pt.

Long Pt.

Calabash

John's Folly Bay

Leduck Island

UNITED STATES VIRGIN ISLANDS

Tortola

ST. THOMAS

ST. JOHN

Distance from St. Thomas to St. Croix approx. 40 miles

ST. CROIX

Lameshur Bay

Pt.

15

Drunk Bay

Salt Pond Peninsula

Salt Pond Bay

Ram Head

0   2 miles

0   3 km

Mongoose Restaurant **7**
Morgan's Mango **6**
Paradiso **8**
Shipwreck Landing **16**

Skinny Legs Bar and Restaurant **17**
Sun Dog Cafe **11**
Vie's Snack Shack **18**

Exploring
Annaberg Plantation **6**
Bordeaux Mountain **4**
Catherineberg Ruins **7**

Coral Bay **5**
Cruz Bay **1**
Elaine Ione Sprauve Library and Museum **2**
Peace Hill **8**
Reef Bay Trail **3**

cottages near town; two campgrounds, both at the edges of beautiful beaches (bring bug repellent); ecoresorts; and luxurious villas, often with a pool or a hot tub (sometimes both), and a stunning view.

If your lodging comes with a fully equipped kitchen, you'll be happy to know that St. John's handful of grocery stores sells everything from the basics to sun-dried tomatoes and green chilies—though the prices will take your breath away. If you're on a budget, consider bringing some staples (pasta, canned goods, paper products) from home. Hotel rates throughout the island, though considered expensive by some, do include endless privacy and access to most water sports.

For approximate costs, *see* the lodging price chart *in* St. Thomas.

Hotels and Inns

$$$$ 🏨 **Caneel Bay Resort.** Set on 170 lush peninsular acres—originally part
★ of the Danish West India Company's Durloo plantation—Caneel Bay Resort mixes a good bit of peace and quiet into its luxurious air. You won't find crowds or glitz; your room won't have a TV, or even a phone (though management will loan you a cellular). Instead, you'll discover spacious, restful rooms that are open to the breezes and are tastefully decorated with tropical furnishings; seven beaches, each more gorgeous than the last; and an attentive staff that will fill your every need. ⊠ *Rte. 20 (Box 720), Cruz Bay, 00830,* ☎ *340/776–6111 or 888/767–3966,* 𝐅𝐀𝐗 *340/693–8280,* 𝐖𝐄𝐁 *www.caneelbay.com. 166 rooms. 4 restaurants, air-conditioning, 11 tennis courts, beach, dive shop, dock, snorkeling, windsurfing, boating, children's programs, meeting rooms. AE, DC, MC, V. EP, FAP, MAP.*

$$$$ 🏨 **Westin Resort, St. John.** Spread over 47 acres adjacent to Great Cruz Bay, the Westin has lushly planted gardens, a pool, a beach (the swimming is good), and enough amenities to make stepping off the grounds unnecessary. If you want to get out and about, though, taxi jaunts into Cruz Bay are a breeze. Rooms have white spreads, rattan furniture, and phones and computer ports for those who just *have* to keep in touch with the world. Many rooms have views of boats bobbing in the turquoise sea. You can keep very busy here if you like; perhaps play some tennis in the morning, go windsurfing in the afternoon, and then get a massage before heading to dinner in one of the restaurants. Younger guests will appreciate the children's program. Guests at the Westin Vacation Club, a condominium complex across the street, enjoy all the hotel amenities. ⊠ *Rte. 104 (Box 8310), Cruz Bay, 00831,* ☎ *340/693–8000 or 800/808–5020,* 𝐅𝐀𝐗 *340/693–8888,* 𝐖𝐄𝐁 *www.thewestinstjohnresort.com. 282 rooms. 3 restaurants, air-conditioning, in-room data ports, refrigerators, pool, massage, 6 tennis courts, gym, beach, dive shop, snorkeling, windsurfing, boating, fishing, shops, children's programs, meeting rooms. AE, D, DC, MC, V. EP.*

$$$ 🏨 **Garden By the Sea Bed and Breakfast.** This cozy spot is an easy walk from Cruz Bay. Its rooms are done in the hues of the sea and sky, and white spreads and curtains provide pristine counterpoints. Enjoy views of a salt pond and the sea as you enjoy your piña colada French toast on the front porch. It's perfect for folks who enjoy peace and quiet—there are no phones or TVs in the rooms, but each room does have a small tabletop fountain. (If the gurgle of water over rocks annoys you, the fountain has an off switch.) ⊠ *Enighed (Box 1469), Cruz Bay 00831,* ☎ 𝐅𝐀𝐗 *340/779–4731,* 𝐖𝐄𝐁 *www.gardenbythesea.com. 3 rooms. Fans. No credit cards. BP.*

$$$ 🏨 **Harmony.** In the tree-covered hills adjacent to the Maho Bay Camps is this Stanley Selengut ecotourism resort. The spacious two-story units have the usual amenities—decks, sliding glass doors, living-dining areas, great views. What makes this place unusual are the materials used to build it. Though you can't tell when you look at them, the carpets are made of recycled milk cartons, the pristine white walls of old newspapers. Energy for the low-wattage appliances is generated entirely by the wind and the sun, and each unit has a laptop computer programmed to monitor energy consumption. Tile floors, undyed cotton linens, and South American handicrafts create a decor that seems in keeping with the ideals. There's a water-sports outfitter on the beach. ✉ *Maho Bay (Box 310), Cruz Bay, 00830,* ☎ *340/776–6240, 212/472–9453, or 800/392–9004,* ℻ *212/861–6210,* 🌐 *www.mahobay.com. 12 units. Restaurant, beach, snorkeling, windsurfing. AE, D, MC, V. EP.*

$$$ 🏨 **Estate Concordia.** The latest brainchild of Stanley Selengut, the developer of Maho Bay Camps and Harmony, these "environmentally correct" studios and duplexes are on 51 oceanfront acres of remote Salt Pond Bay. The spacious units are constructed of recycled materials, and energy for all the appliances (even the ice makers) is wind- and solar-generated. Next door are five eco-tents, upscale camping structures made of environmentally friendly materials and equipped with solar power and composting toilets. ✉ *20–27 Estate Concordia, Coral Bay 00830,* ☎ *340/693–5855, 212/472–9453, or 800/392–9004,* ℻ *212/861–6210,* 🌐 *www.mahobay.com. 20 units. Kitchenettes, pool. AE, D, MC, V. EP.*

$$ 🏨 **St. John Inn.** Within walking distance of Cruz Bay's shops and restaurants, this inn offers not only a convenient location but also affordable accommodations with a touch of charm. You might find a four-poster bed or an antique-style armoire in rooms painted in lush hues. ✉ *Off Rte. 104 (Box 37), Cruz Bay 00831,* ☎ *340/693–86888 or 800/666–7688,* ℻ *340/693–9900,* 🌐 *www.stjohninn.com. 13 units. Kitchenettes, air-conditioning, fans, pool. AE, D, DC, MC, V. EP.*

Campgrounds

$$ ⛺ **Maho Bay Camps.** Eight mi (13 km) from Cruz Bay, this eco-camp is a lush hillside community of rustic structures. The 16×16-ft (5×5-m) tents (wooden platforms protected from the elements by canvas and screening) are linked by wooden stairs, ramps, and walkways—some of them elevated—so that you can trek around camp and down to the beach without disturbing the terrain. The tents sleep as many as four people and have beds, tables and chairs, electric lamps, propane stoves, coolers, and kitchenware and cutlery. Though all the units are surrounded by tropical greenery, some have spectacular views of the Caribbean. The camp has the chummy feel of a retreat, making it very popular; book well in advance. ✉ *Maho Bay (Box 310), Cruz Bay 00830,* ☎ *340/776–6240, 212/472–9453, or 800/392–9004;* ℻ *212/861–6210,* 🌐 *www.mahobay.com. 114 tent cottages. Restaurant, beach, snorkeling, windsurfing. AE, D, MC, V. EP.*

$ ⛺ **Cinnamon Bay Campground.** Camping here puts you in the national park, surrounded by jungle and at the edge of Cinnamon Bay Beach. The unlockable concrete "cottages" have electric lights, and the tents have propane lanterns; both come with propane camping stoves, coolers, cooking gear, and linens. Bring your own tent and supplies for the bare sites (a steal at $25 a night), which, like the cottages and tents, have a grill and a picnic table. The showers (on the cool side) and flush toilets, as well as a restaurant and a small store, are a trek down the hill. Hiking, snorkeling, swimming, and evening environmental or history programs are free and at your doorstep. Spaces for the winter months fill up far in advance (by as much as a year), so call for reservations. ✉ *Rte. 20 (Box 720), Cruz Bay, 00830-0720,* ☎ *340/776–6330 or 800/539–9998,* ℻ *340/776–6458,* 🌐 *www.cinnamonbay.com. 44 tents, 40 cottages, 26 bare sites. Restaurant, hiking, beach, snorkeling, windsurfing. AE, MC, V. EP.*

Condominiums and Cottages

Most of the island's condos are just minutes from the hustle and bustle of Cruz Bay, but you'll find cottages in more far-flung locations.

$$$$ 🏠 **Coconut Coast Villas.** Within walking distance of Cruz Bay's shops and restaurants, this small condominium complex sits so close to the water you'll fall asleep to the sound of waves. ✉ *Turner Bay (Box 618), Cruz Bay 00831,* ☎ *340/693–9100 or 800/858–7989,* FAX *340/779–4157,* WEB *www.coconutcoast.com. 9 units. Air-conditioning, kitchenettes, pool, beach. MC, V. EP.*

$$$$ 🏠 **Estate Zootenvaal.** Set at the far reaches of the island, this small complex provides modest cottages right at the water or across the street. It's a quiet spot perfect for people who like to sit in the chaise and read. ✉ *Rte. 10, Hurricane Hole, Coral Bay, 00830,* ☎ *340/776–6321,* WEB *www.usviguide.com/zootenvaal. 3 units. Fans, kitchenettes, beach. No credit cards. EP.*

$$$$ 🏠 **Gallows Point Suite Resort.** These soft-gray buildings are clustered on a peninsula south of the Cruz Bay ferry dock. The upper-level apartments have loft bedrooms and good views. There's air-conditioning only in the first-floor units; the harborside villas get better trade winds, but they're also noisier. The entranceway is bridged by Ellington's restaurant, which serves delicious contemporary cuisine. ✉ *Gallows Point (Box 58), Cruz Bay 00831,* ☎ *340/776–6434; 800/323–7229 direct to hotel,* FAX *340/776–6520,* WEB *www.gallowspointresort.com. 52 rooms. Restaurant, air-conditioning, pool, beach, snorkeling. AE, MC, V. EP.*

$$$ 🏠 **Serendip.** This complex offers modest units on lush grounds with lovely views. You definitely need a rental car if you stay here, though; it's about 1 mi (1½ km) up a killer hill out of Cruz Bay. If air-conditioning is important to you, be sure to mention it when booking, as some units have only ceiling fans. ✉ *Enighed (Box 273), Cruz Bay 00831,* ☎ *340/776–6646 or 888/800–6445,* WEB *www.stjohn.com/serendip. 10 units. Air-conditioning, fans, kitchenettes. MC, V. EP.*

Villas

Tucked here and there between Cruz Bay and Coral Bay are about 350 villas (prices range from $ to $$$$). With pools and/or hot tubs, full kitchens, and living areas, they provide a home away from home. They're perfect for couples and extended groups of families or friends. You'll need a car since most are up in the hills (very few are at the beach). Villa managers usually pick you up at the dock, arrange for your rental car, and answer questions you have upon arrival as well as during your stay.

To rent a luxury villa, contact one of the following rental agents:

Caribbean Villas and Resorts (✉ Box 458, 00831, ☎ 340/776–6152 or 800/338–0987, FAX 340/779–4044, WEB www.caribbeanvilla.com) handles condo rentals for Cruz Views, Lavender Hill, and Suite St. John as well as for private villas. **Catered To, Inc.** (✉ Box 704, 00830, ☎ 340/776–6641, FAX 340/693–8191, WEB www.cateredto.com) has luxury homes in Creat Cruz Bay and Chocolate Hole areas. **Destination St. John** (✉ Box 8306, 00831, ☎ FAX 340/779–4647 or ☎ 800/562–1901, WEB www.destinationstjohn.com) manages villas within a 10-minute drive of Cruz Bay. **Park Isle Villas** (✉ Box 1263, 00831, ☎ FAX 340/693–8261 or ☎ 800/416–1205, WEB www.batteryhill.com) handles Battery Hill and Villa Caribe condos. **Private Homes for Private Vacations** (✉ Mamey Peak, 00830, ☎ FAX 340/776–6876, WEB www.privatehomesvi.com) has homes across the island. **Star Villa** (✉ Box 599, 00830, ☎ 340/776–6704, FAX 340/776–6183, WEB starvillas.com) has cozy villas just outside Cruz Bay. **Vacation Homes** (☒ Box 272, 00831, ☎ 340/776–6094, FAX 340/693–8455, WEB vacationstjohn.com) has luxury homes from outside Cruz Bay to mid-island. **Vacation Vistas** (☒ Box 476, 00831, ☎ 340/776–6462, WEB www.vacationvistas.com) manages villas in the Chocolate Hole and Great Cruz Bay area. **Windspree** (☒ 6-2-1A Estate Carolina, 00830, ☎ 340/693–5423, FAX 340/693–5623, WEB www.windspree.com) handles villas mainly in the Coral Bay area.

Dining

The cuisine on St. John seems to get better every year, with culinary school–trained chefs vying to see who can come up with the most imaginative dishes. There are restaurants to suit every taste and budget—from the elegant establishments at Caneel Bay Resort (where men may be required to wear a jacket at dinner) to the casual in-town eateries of Cruz Bay. For quick lunches try the West Indian food stands in Cruz Bay Park and across from the post office. The cooks prepare fried chicken legs, pates (meat- and fish-filled pastries), and callaloo.

For approximate costs *see* the dining price chart *in* St. Thomas.

Bordeaux Mountain
CONTEMPORARY

$$$$ ✕ **Chateau Bordeaux.** This rustic restaurant with a to-die-for view is practically a tree house, albeit one that's made very elegant and romantic by wrought-iron chandeliers, lace tablecloths, and antiques. You might start with the ostrich stuffed with a roasted portabello mushrooms, sundried cherries, and roasted pine nuts; then segue into New Zealand rack of lamb with a honey-Dijon-pecan crust in a port wine cream sauce; or salmon crusted with black pepper and lemon zest and finished with a caviar and balsamic vinaigrette. Save room for dessert—the fresh berry cups with Chambord and caramel are to die for. The comprehensive, moderately priced wine list is predictably strong on Bordeaux reds. ☒ *Rte. 10,* ☎ *340/776–6611. AE, MC, V. No lunch.*

Coral Bay and Environs
AMERICAN

$ ✕ **Skinny Legs Bar and Restaurant.** Sailors who live aboard boats anchored just off shore and an eclectic coterie of residents gather for lunch and dinner at this funky spot. If owners Doug Sica and Moe Chabuz are around, take a gander at their gams; you'll see where the restaurant got its name. It's a great place for burgers, fish sandwiches, and watching whatever sports event is on cable TV. ☒ *Rte. 107 (near the Coral Bay dinghy dock),* ☎ *340/779–4982. AE, D, MC, V.*

CARIBBEAN

$ ✕ **Vie's Snack Shack.** Vie Mahabir conjures up what may well be the best conch fritters in all of St. John. They're crispy on the outside and creamy on the inside, with lots of conch. And they're not so spicy that you need a gallon of water to cool your throat. The coconut tarts, what mainlanders call a pie, add a sweet end to your alfresco meal. Take a swim afterward at Vie's gorgeous white strand just across the road. ☒ *Rte. 10, Hansen Bay,* ☎ *340/693–5033. No credit cards.* ☉ *Lunch only.*

ECLECTIC

$$ ✕ **Shipwreck Landing.** Start with one of the house drinks, perhaps a fresh-squeezed concoction of lime, coconut, and rum, then move on to hearty taco salads, fried shrimp, teriyaki chicken, and conch fritters. The birds keep up a lively chatter in the bougainvillea that surrounds you at this open-air restaurant, and there's live music on Wednesday and Sunday nights in season. ☒ *Rte. 107,* ☎ *340/693–5640. AE, MC, V.*

Cruz Bay

CONTEMPORARY

$$$$ ✗ **Ellington's.** This peaceful, appealing spot extends out onto the second-story veranda of the Gallows Point Suite Resort's central building. The outside tables are particularly quiet and romantic. You might start with the jumbo shrimp cooked in sweet coconut and served with mango sauce, or the seafood chowder. Entrées include sea scallops with garlic and olive oil, aïoli, Parmesan cheese, and paprika; swordfish scampi; filet mignon; and fresh lobster. For dessert the banana–chocolate chip cake or the chocolate brownie are good bets. ⊠ *Gallows Point (5-min walk from Cruz Bay),* ☎ *340/693–8490. AE, MC, V. No lunch.*

$$$ ✗ **Lime Inn.** This open-air restaurant attracts mainland transplants who call St. John home as well as visitors who come for the congenial atmosphere and good food. There are shrimp and steak dishes and such specials as pistachio chicken breasts with plantains and Thai curry cream sauce. On Wednesday night there's an all-you-can-eat shrimp feast, and fresh lobster is the specialty every night. ⊠ *Downtown, east of Chase Manhattan Bank,* ☎ *340/776–6425. AE, MC, V. Closed Sun.*

$$$ ✗ **Morgan's Mango.** A long flight of stairs leads you to this alfresco eatery, but good food awaits you. Although fish is the specialty—try the voodoo snapper topped with a many-fruit salsa—the chef also creates a vegetarian platter with black beans, fried plantains, salad, and even an ear of corn. ⊠ *Across from V.I. National Park's Visitors Center,* ☎ *340/693–8141. AE, MC, V. No lunch.*

ECLECTIC

$$$ ✗ **Paradiso.** This popular spot is on the upper level of the island's largest
★   shopping complex. The menu is a mix of everything from beef sirloin with an herb-mustard crust to garlic rosemary-basted mahimahi. You can dine indoors, in the comfort of air-conditioning, or outdoors on a small terrace that overlooks the street. ⊠ *Mongoose Junction shopping center,* ☎ *340/693–8899. AE, MC, V.*

$$$ ✗ **La Tapa.** Locals congregate here to feast on tapas and sip sangria. Although street-side tables let you watch the world go by, they're a little noisy; head inside for a quiet, bistrolike atmosphere. Owner Alex Ewald dishes up a changing menu of delicious soups, tapas as lighter fare or dinner, and yummy desserts. The buffalo mozzarella served with tomatoes and basil is made in her own tiny kitchen. ⊠ *Across from Scotia Bank on unnamed street that heads inland from ferry dock,* ☎ *340/693–7755. AE, MC, V. No lunch.*

$$ ✗ **Fish Trap.** The rooms and terraces here all open to the breezes and buzz with a mix of locals and visitors. Chef Aaron Willis conjures up such tasty appetizers as conch fritters and Fish Trap chowder (a creamy soup of snapper, white wine, paprika, and secret spices). The menu also includes an interesting pasta of the day, steak and chicken dishes, and hamburgers. ⊠ *Downtown, next to Our Lady of Mount Carmel Church,* ☎ *340/693–9994. AE, D, MC, V. No lunch. Closed Mon.*

$$ ✗ **Mongoose Restaurant.** Open to the breezes, this restaurant attracts an eclectic local crowd that tends to drop by for lunch at the bar. They aren't the only ones: tiny yellow birds peck at the wine glasses (full of sugar) that are used as feeders. For lunch there are hamburgers, sandwiches, and salads; for dinner, chicken, pork chops, and fish. ⊠ *Mongoose Junction shopping center,* ☎ *340/693–8677. AE, MC, V.*

$ ✗ **Sun Dog Cafe.** You'll find an unusual assortment of dishes at this charming restaurant tucked into a courtyard in the upper reaches of the Mongoose Junction shopping center. Kudos to the white artichoke pizza with roasted garlic, artichoke hearts, mozzarella cheese, and capers. The Jamaican jerk chicken sub or the black bean quesadilla are also good choices. ⊠ *Mongoose Junction shopping center,* ☎ *340/693–8340. AE, MC, V. ☉ Lunch only.*

FRENCH

FRENCH

$$$ ✕ **Dinner with Andre.** At night, this unassuming spot—it spends its days as Chilly Billy's sandwich joint—metamorphoses into a bistro with true French fare. If you aren't convinced, try the snails cooked in a sherry cream demi-glace or frog legs in a garlic cream sauce before moving on to the magret de canard, a breast of duck topped with Roquefort cheese and crushed walnuts. Desserts are just as rich (the profiteroles topped with Belgium chocolate sauce are yummy). ⊠ *Lumberyard Shopping Complex,* ☎ *340/693–8708. MC, V. No lunch. Closed Sun.*

ITALIAN

$$ ✕ **Café Roma.** This casual second-floor restaurant in the heart of Cruz Bay is *the* place for traditional Italian cuisine: lasagna, spaghetti and meatballs, chicken Parmesan. There is also a variety of excellent pizzas. Polenta cake with raspberry sauce is a dessert specialty. ⊠ *Downtown on Vesta Gade,* ☎ *340/776–6524. MC, V. No lunch.*

PAN-ASIAN

$$$$ ✕ **Asolare.** Contemporary Asian cuisine dominates the menu at this
★ elegant open-air eatery in an old St. John house. Come early and relax over drinks while you enjoy the sunset over the harbor. Start with an appetizer, say, pork spring rolls served with a cucumber salad. Entrées include such delights as grilled yellowfin tuna served with a sweet pepper and scallion rice cake and a bok choy and carrot salad. If you still have room for dessert, try the chocolate pyramid, a luscious cake with homemade ice cream melting in the middle. ⊠ *Caneel Hill, Rte. 20,* ☎ *340/779–4747. AE, MC, V. No lunch.*

Beaches

St. John is blessed with many beaches, and all of them fall into the good, great, and don't-tell-anyone-else-about-this-place categories. Those along the north shore are all within the national park. Some are more developed than others—and all are crowded on weekends, holidays, and in high season—but by and large they're still pristine. Beaches along the south and eastern shores are quiet and isolated.

Caneel Bay. Caneel Bay is actually a catch-all name for seven white-sand north-shore beaches, six of which can be reached only by water if you aren't a guest at the Caneel Bay Resort. (Access to beaches is a civil right in the USVI, but access to land that leads to the beaches is not.) The seventh, **Caneel Beach,** is open to the public and is easy to reach from the main entrance of the resort; just ask for directions at the gatehouse. Nonguests can also dine at the three of the hotel's four restaurants and browse in its gift shop.

Cinnamon Bay. This long, sandy beach faces beautiful cays and abuts the national park campground. The facilities are open to the public and include cool showers, toilets, a commissary, and a restaurant. You can rent water-sports equipment here—a good thing because there's excellent snorkeling off the point to the right; look for the big angelfish and large schools of purple triggerfish. Afternoons on Cinnamon Bay can be windy, so arrive early to beat the gusts. The Cinnamon Bay hiking trail begins across the road from the beach parking lot; the ruins of a sugar mill mark the trailhead. There are actually two paths here: a level nature trail (signs along it identify the flora) that loops through the woods and passes an old Danish cemetery, and a steep trail that starts where the road bends past the ruins and heads straight up to Route 10.

Hawksnest Beach. Sea-grape trees line this narrow beach, and there are rest rooms, cooking grills, and a covered shed for picnicking. It's the closest beach to town, so it's often crowded.

Lameshur Bay. This nifty beach is toward the end of a very long dirt road on the southeast coast. It offers solitude, good snorkeling, and a chance to spy on some pelicans. The ruins of the old plantation are a five-minute walk down the road past the beach.

Maho Bay. This popular beach is below the Maho Bay Camps—a wonderful hillside enclave of tents. The campground offers informal talks and slide and film presentations on nature, environmentally friendly living, and whatever else crosses the manager's mind. In spring, jazz and jungle harmonize during a music series in the outdoor pavilion.

Salt Pond Bay. If you're adventurous, this somewhat rocky beach on the scenic southeastern coast—next to Coral Bay and rugged Drunk Bay—is worth exploring. It's a short hike down a hill from the parking lot, and the only facilities are an outhouse and a few picnic tables scattered about. There are interesting tidal pools, and the snorkeling is good. Take special care to leave nothing valuable in your car; reports of thefts are common.

Trunk Bay. St. John's most-photographed beach is also the preferred spot for beginning snorkelers because of its underwater trail. (Cruise-ship passengers interested in snorkeling for a day come here, so if you're looking for seclusion, check cruise-ship schedules in *St. Thomas This Week* before heading here.) Crowded or not, this stunning beach is sure to please. There are changing rooms, a snack bar, picnic tables, a gift shop, phones, lockers, and snorkeling equipment rentals.

Outdoor Activities and Sports

BOATING AND SAILING

For a speedy trip to offshore cays and remote beaches, a powerboat is a necessity. Rates start at around $300 per day with gas and oil charges depending on how much you use. More leisurely day sails to islands not far offshore or longer sails to points east are also possibilities. If you're boatless, book with one of the island's agents. Most day sails include lunch, beverages, and at least one stop to snorkel. A full-day sail with lunch runs around $90 per person.

Adventures in Paradise (☎ 340/779–4527), across from the post office in Cruz Bay, books fishing, sailing and scuba trips on most of the island's charter boats. **Connections** (✉ Cruz Bay, a block upfrom the ferry dock and catercorner from Chase Manhattan Bank, ☎ 340/776–6922) pairs you up with the sailboat that suits you. Have simple tastes? The smiling staff can help. If luxury is more your style, they can book that, too. **Ocean Runner** (☎ 340/693–8809), on the waterfront in Cruz Bay, rents one- and two-engine boats for fast trips around the island's seas. **Proper Yachts** (☎ 340/776–6256) books day sails and longer charters on its fleet of luxury yachts that depart from Caneel Bay Resort.

FISHING

Well-kept charter boats head out to the north and south drops or troll along the inshore reefs. The captains usually provide bait, drinks, and lunch, but you'll need your hat and sunscreen. Fishing charters run around $100 per hour per person. The **Charter Boat Center** (☎ 340/775–7990), in Red Hook on St. Thomas, also arranges fishing trips for folks in St. John. **Gone Ketchin'** (☎ 340/693–8657), in St. John, arranges trips with old salt Wally Leopold. **St. John World Class Anglers** (☎ 340/779–4281) offers light-tackle shore and offshore half- and full-day trips.

HIKING

Although it's fun to go hiking with a Virgin Islands National Park guide, don't be afraid to strike out on your own. To find a hike that suits your ability, stop by the park's visitors center in Cruz Bay and pick up the free trail guide; it details points of interest, dangers, trail lengths, and estimated hiking times. Although the park staff recommends pants to protect against thorns and insects, most people hike in shorts because pants are too hot. Wear sturdy shoes or hiking boots even if you're hiking to the beach. Don't forget to bring water and insect repellent.

The **Virgin Islands National Park** (☎ 340/776–6201) maintains more than 20 trails on the north and south shores and offers guided hikes along popular routes. A full-day trip to Reef Bay is a must; it's an easy hike through lush and dry forest, past the ruins of an old plantation, and to a sugar factory adjacent to the beach. Take the public Vitran bus or a taxi to the trailhead, where you'll meet a ranger who will serve as your guide. The park provides a boat ride back to Cruz Bay for $15 to save you the walk back up the mountain. The schedule changes from season to season; call for times and reservations, which are essential.

HORSEBACK RIDING

Clip-clop along the island's byways for a slower-pace tour of St. John. **Carolina Corral** (☎ 340/693–5778) offers horseback, donkey-back, and donkey-cart rides as well as riding lessons. Rates start at $45 for a one-hour ride.

SCUBA DIVING AND SNORKELING

Although just about every beach has nice snorkeling—Trunk Bay, Cinnamon Bay, and Waterlemon Cay at Leinster Bay get the most praise—you'll need a boat to head out to the more remote snorkeling locations and the best scuba spots. Sign on with any of the island's water-sports operators to get to spots further from St. John. Their boats will take you to hot spots between St. John and St. Thomas, including the tunnels at **Thatch Cay,** the ledges at **Congo Cay,** and the wreck of the *General Rogers.* Dive off St. John at **Stephens Cay,** a short boat ride out of Cruz Bay, where fish swim around the reefs as you float downward. At **Devers Bay,** on St. John's south shore, fish dart about in colorful schools.

Count on paying $55 for a one-tank dive and $75 for a two-tank dive. Rates include equipment and a tour. **Cruz Bay Watersports** (☎ 340/776–6234) has three locations: in Cruz Bay, at the Westin Resort, and in the Palm Plaza Shopping Center. Owners Marcus and Patty Johnston offer regular reef, wreck, and night dives and USVI and BVI snorkel tours. **Low Key Watersports** (☎ 340/693–8999 or 800/835–7718), at Wharfside Village, offers PADI certification and resort courses, one- and two-tank dives, and specialty courses.

SEA KAYAKING

Poke around crystal bays and explore undersea life from a sea kayak. **Arawak Expeditions** (☎ 340/693–8312 or 800/238–8687) professional guides use traditional kayaks to ply coastal waters. Prices start at $40 for a half-day trip.

TENNIS

With hot weather the norm, tennis players take to the courts in the morning or late afternoon. The **Westin Resort, St. John** (⊠ Rte. 104, ☎ 340/693–8000), has six lighted courts. Nonguests are welcome to play here for a fee of $15 an hour. The **public courts,** near the fire station in Cruz Bay, are lit until 10 PM and are available on a first-come, first-served basis.

Steady breezes and expert instruction make learning to windsurf a snap. Try **Cinnamon Bay Campground** (✉ Rte. 20, ☎ 340/776–6330), where rentals are available for $20–$30 per hour. Lessons are available right at the waterfront; just look for the Windsurfers stacked up on the beach. The cost for a one-hour lesson is about $60.

Shopping

Areas and Malls

You'll find luxury items and handicrafts on St. John. Most shops carry a little of this and a bit of that, so it pays to poke around. The Cruz Bay shopping district runs from **Wharfside Village,** just around the corner from the ferry dock, through the streets of town to North Shore Road and **Mongoose Junction,** an inviting shopping center with stonework walls (its name is a holdover from a time when those furry island creatures gathered at a garbage bin that was here). Steps connect the two sections of the center, which has unique upscale shops. Out on Route 104, stop in at **Palm Plaza** to explore its handful of gift and crafts shops. At the island's other end, you'll find a few stores—selling clothes, jewelry, and artwork—here and there from the village of **Coral Bay** to the small complex at **Shipwreck Landing.**

Specialty Items

ART

Bajo el Sol. A cooperative gallery, Bajo el Sol features Aimee Trayser's expressionistic Caribbean scenes, Les Anderson's island scenes in oil, Kat Sowa's watercolors, and works by a handful of other artists. ✉ *Mongoose Junction,* ☎ *340/693–7070.*

Coconut Coast Studios. This waterside shop, a five-minute walk from Cruz Bay, showcases the work of Elaine Estern. She specializes in undersea scenes. ✉ *Frank Bay,* ☎ *340/776–6944.*

BOOKS

MAPes MONDe. Here you'll find a huge selection of books on the Caribbean, including the exquisite-looking publications that are the hallmark of Virgin Islands publisher MAPes MONDe. You'll also find many reproductions of old maps as well as contemporary prints and greeting cards. ✉ *Mongoose Junction,* ☎ *340/779–4545.*

National Park Headquarters. The headquarters sells several good histories of St. John, including *St. John Back Time,* by Ruth Hull Low and Rafael Lito Valls, and for linguists, Valls's *What a Pistarckle!*—an explanation of the colloquialisms that make up the local version of English (*pistarckle* is a Dutch Creole word that means "noise" or "din," which pretty much sums up the language here). ✉ *At the Creek,* ☎ *340/776–6201.*

CLOTHING

Big Planet Adventure Outfitters. You knew when you arrived that some place on St. John would cater to the outdoor enthusiasts that hike up and down the island's trails. Well, this outdoor-clothing store is where you'll find the popular Noats sandals, along with colorful and durable cotton clothing and accessories by Patagonia, the North Face, Columbia, and others. The nearby **Little Planet** sells children's clothes, often made from such unlikely materials as recycled plastic bottles. ✉ *Mongoose Junction,* ☎ *340/776–6638.*

Bougainvillea Boutique. If you want to look like you stepped out of the pages of the resort-wear spread in an upscale travel magazine, try this store. Owner Susan Stair carries *very* chic men's and women's resort wear, straw hats, leather handbags, and fine gift items. ⊠ *Mongoose Junction,* ☎ *340/693–7190.*

The Clothing Studio. Several talented artists hand-paint original designs on clothing for all members of the family. You'll find T-shirts, beach cover-ups, pants, shorts, and even bathing suits with beautiful hand-painted creations. ⊠ *Mongoose Junction,* ☎ *340/776–6585.*

Jolly Dog. Stock up on the stuff you forgot to pack at this store. Sarongs in cotton and rayon, beach towels with tropical motifs, and hats and T-shirts sporting the Jolly Dog logs fill the shelves. ⊠ *Shipwreck Landing, Coral Bay,* ☎ *340/693–5333.*

St. John Editions. Shop here for nifty cotton shifts that go from beach to dinner with a change of shoes and accessories. Owner Ann Soper also carries attractive straw hats and inexpensive jewelry. ⊠ *North Shore Rd., Cruz Bay,* ☎ *340/693–8444.*

FOODSTUFFS

If you're renting a villa, condo, or cottage and doing your own cooking, there are several good places to shop for food; just be aware that prices are much higher than those at home.

Marina Market usually has the best prices, but its selection is small. ⊠ *Rte. 104, Cruz Bay,* ☎ *340/779–4401.*

Starfish Market is the island's largest store and usually has the best selection of meat, fish and produce. ⊠ *Marketplace Shopping Center, Rte 104, Cruz Bay,* ☎ *340/779–4949.*

Tropicale has great take-out meals in addition to its rather smallish selection of groceries. ⊠ *Palm Plaza, Rte. 104, Cruz Bay,* ☎ *340/693–7474.*

GIFTS

Bamboula. Owner Jo Sterling travels the Caribbean and the world to find unusual housewares, rugs, bedspreads, accessories, shoes, and men's and women's clothes for this multicultural boutique. ⊠ *Mongoose Junction,* ☎ *340/693–8699.*

The Canvas Factory. If you're a true shopper who needs an extra bag to carry all your treasures home, this store offers every kind of tote and carrier imaginable—from simple bags to suitcases with numerous zippered compartments—all made of canvas, naturally. It also sells great canvas hats. ⊠ *Mongoose Junction,* ☎ *340/776–6196.*

Donald Schnell Pottery. In addition to pottery, this place sells unique hand-blown glass, wind chimes, kaleidoscopes, fanciful water fountains, and more. Your purchases can be shipped worldwide. ⊠ *Mongoose Junction,* ☎ *340/776–6420.*

Fabric Mill. Shop here for handmade dolls, place mats, napkins, and batik wraps. Or take home a bolt of tropical brights from the upholstery-fabric selection. ⊠ *Mongoose Junction,* ☎ *340/776–6194.*

Pink Papaya. This store is the home of longtime Virgin Islands resident M. L. Etre's well-known artwork plus a huge collection of one-of-a-kind gift items, including bright tablecloths, unusual trays, dinnerware, and unique tropical jewelry. ⊠ *Lemon Tree Mall, Cruz Bay,* ☎ *340/693–8535.*

Wicker, Wood and Shells. Shop the second floor of this store for lovely sculptures and other objects d'art, all with a tropical theme. On the first floor, you'll find the island's best selection of greeting cards, notepaper, and other interesting items to tuck in your suitcase for friends back home. ⊠ *Mongoose Junction,* ☎ *340/776–6909.*

JEWELRY

Blue Carib Gems. Here you'll find custom-made jewelry, loose gemstones, and old coins as well as a small art gallery. ☒ *Wharfside Village,* ☎ *340/693–8299.*

Caravan Gallery. Owner Radha Speer creates much of the unusual jewelry you'll find here. And the more you look, the more you see—folk art, tribal art, and masks for sale cover the walls and tables, making this a great place to browse. ☒ *Mongoose Junction,* ☎ *340/779–4566.*

Colombian Emeralds. This branch of a St. Thomas store has high-quality emeralds and also sells rubies, diamonds, and other jewels set in attractive gold and silver settings. ☒ *Mongoose Junction,* ☎ *340/ 776–6007.*

Free Bird Creations. Head here for the unique handcrafted jewelry— earrings, bracelets, pendants, chains—as well as the good selection of waterproof watches great for your excursions to the beach. ☒ *Wharfside Village,* ☎ *340/693–8625.*

R&I Patton Goldsmiths. Rudy and Irene Patton design most of the unique silver and gold jewelry in this shop. The rest comes from various jeweler friends of theirs. Sea fans (those large, lacy plants that sway with the ocean's currents) in filigreed silver, lapis set in long drops of gold, starfish and hibiscus pendants in silver or gold, and gold sand dollar–shape charms and earrings are tempting choices. ☒ *Mongoose Junction,* ☎ *340/776–6548.*

Nightlife

St. John isn't the place to go for glitter and all-night partying. Still, after-hours Cruz Bay can be a lively little village in which to dine, drink, dance, chat, or flirt. Notices posted on the bulletin board outside the Connections telephone center—up the street from the ferry dock in Cruz Bay—or listings in the island's two small newspapers (the *St. John Times* and *Tradewinds*) will keep you apprised of special events, comedy nights, movies, and the like.

After a sunset drink at **Ellington's** (☒ Gallows Point Suite Resort, ☎ 340/693–8490), up the hill from Cruz Bay, you can stroll here and there in town (much is clustered around the small waterfront park). Many of the young people from the U.S. mainland who live and work on St. John will be out sipping and socializing, too.

Outside town, **Caneel Bay Resort** (☒ Rte. 20, ☎ 340/776–6111) usually has entertainment (generally, of the quiet calypso variety) several nights a week in season. There's calypso and reggae on Wednesday and Friday at **Fred's** (☒ Cruz Bay, ☎ 340/776–6363). The **Inn at Tamarind Court** (☒ Rte. 104, ☎ 340/776–6378) serves up country rock on Friday. At Coral Bay, on the far side of the island, check out the action at **Skinny Legs Bar and Restaurant** (☒ Rte. 107, ☎ 340/779–4982). Young folks like to gather at **Woody's** (☒ Cruz Bay, ☎ 340/779–4625). Its sidewalk tables provide a close-up view of Cruz Bay's action.

Exploring St. John

St. John is an easy place to explore. One road runs along the north shore, another across the center of the mountains. There are a few roads that branch off here and there, but it's hard to get lost. Pick up a map at the visitor center before you start out, and you'll have no problems. Few residents remember the route numbers, so have your map in hand if you stop to ask for directions. Bring along a swimsuit for stops at some of the most beautiful beaches in the world. You can spend all day or just a couple of hours exploring, but be advised that the roads are narrow and wind up and down steep hills, so don't expect to get anywhere in a hurry. There are lunch spots at Cinnamon Bay and in Coral Bay, or you can do what the locals do—picnic. The grocery stores in Cruz Bay sell Styrofoam coolers just for this purpose.

If you plan to do a lot of touring, renting a car will be cheaper and will give you much more freedom than relying on taxis, which are reluctant to go anywhere until they have a full load of passengers. Although you may be tempted by an open-air Suzuki or Jeep, a conventional car can get you just about everywhere on the paved roads, and you'll be able to lock up your valuables. You may be able to share a van or open-air vehicle (called a safari bus) with other passengers on a tour of scenic mountain trails, secret coves, and eerie bush-covered ruins.

Numbers in the margin correspond to points of interest on the St. John map.

Sights to See

6 **Annaberg Plantation.** In the 18th-century sugar plantations dotted the steep hills of the USVI. Slaves and free Danes and Dutchmen toiled to harvest the cane that was used to create sugar, molasses, and rum for export. Built in the 1780s, the partially restored plantation at Leinster Bay was once an important sugar mill. Though there are no official visiting hours, the National Park Service has regular tours, and some well-informed taxi drivers will show you around. Occasionally you'll find a living-history demonstration—someone making johnny-cake or weaving baskets. For information on tours and cultural events, contact the St. John National Park Service Visitors Center. ⊠ *Leinster Bay Rd.,* ☎ *340/776–6201.* ✎ *$4.*

4 **Bordeaux Mountain.** St. John's highest peak rises to 1,277 ft (391 m). Route 10 passes near enough to the top to offer breathtaking views. Drive nearly to the end of the dirt road for spectacular views at Picture Point and for the trailhead of the hike downhill to Lameshur. Get a trail map from the park service before you start. ⊠ *Rte. 10.*

7 **Catherineberg Ruins.** At this fine example of an 18th-century sugar and rum factory, there's a storage vault beneath the windmill. Across the road, look for the round mill, which was later used to hold water. In the 1733 slave revolt, Catherineberg served as headquarters for the Amina warriors, a tribe of Africans captured into slavery. ⊠ *Rte. 10.*

5 **Coral Bay.** This laid-back community at the island's dry, eastern end is named for its shape rather than for its underwater life—the word *coral* comes from *krawl,* Danish for "corral." It's a small, quiet, neighborhoody settlement—a place to get away from it all. You'll need a Jeep if you plan to stay at this end of the island, as some of the rental houses are up unpaved roads that wind around the mountain. If you come just for lunch, a regular car will be fine.

1 **Cruz Bay.** St. John's main town may be compact (it consists of only several blocks), but it's definitely a hub: the ferries from St. Thomas and the BVI pull in here, and it's where you can get a taxi or rent a car to travel around the island. There are plenty of shops in which to browse, a number of watering holes where you can stop for a breather, many restaurants, and a grassy square with benches where you can sit back and take everything in. Look for the current edition of the handy, amusing "St. John Map" featuring Max the Mongoose.

To pick up a handy guide to St. John's hiking trails, see various large maps of the island, and find out about current park service programs, including guided walks and cultural demonstrations, stop by the **V. I.**

National Park Visitors Center. ✉ *In an area known as the Creek, near Cruz Bay bulkhead and baseball field, Cruz Bay 00831,* ☎ *340/776–6201.* WEB *www.nps.gov/viis.* ☞ *Free.* ☉ *Daily 8–4:30.*

❷ **Elaine Ione Sprauve Library and Museum.** On the hill just above Cruz Bay is the **Enighed Estate Great House,** built in 1757. *Enighed* is the Danish word for "concord" (unity or peace). The great house and its outbuildings (a sugar-production factory and horse-driven mill) were destroyed by fire and hurricanes, and the house sat in ruins until 1982. Today it houses a library and museum that contains a dusty collection of Indian pottery and colonial artifacts. ✉ *Rte. 104 (make a right past Texaco station),* ☎ *340/776–6359.* ☞ *Free.* ☉ *Weekdays 9–5.*

❽ **Peace Hill.** It's worth stopping at this spot just past the Hawksnest Bay overlook for great views of St. John, St. Thomas, and the BVI. The flat promontory features an old sugar mill. ✉ *Off Rte. 20.*

❸ **Reef Bay Trail.** Although this is one of the most interesting hikes on St. John, unless you're a rugged individualist who wants a physical challenge (and that describes a lot of people who stay on St. John), you'll probably get the most out of the trip if you join a hike led by a park service ranger, who can identify the trees and plants on the hike down, fill you in on the history of the Reef Bay Plantation, and tell you about the petroglyphs on the rocks at the bottom of the trail. If you're without a car, take a taxi or the public Vitran bus from the Cruz Bay ferry dock to the trailhead on Route 10, where you'll meet a ranger for the hike downhill. A boat will take you to Cruz Bay ($15), saving you the uphill return climb.

The **Reef Bay Plantation,** according to architectural historian Frederik C. Gjessing, is the most architecturally ambitious structure of its kind on St. John. Though gutted, the great house is largely intact, and its classical beauty is still visible. It sits on a side trail to the north, off the trail to Lameshur Bay, and the sugar works are near the beach. Reef Bay was the last working plantation on St. John when it stopped production in 1920. ✉ *Rte. 10 between Cruz Bay and Coral Bay; parking area is on the left, trail is to the right.*

U.S. VIRGIN ISLANDS A TO Z

To research prices, get advice from other travelers, and book travel arrangements, visit www.fodors.com.

AIR TRAVEL

One advantage to visiting the USVI is the abundance of nonstop and connecting flights to St. Thomas and St. Croix that can have you at the beach in three to four hours from most eastern United States departures. Small island-hopper planes and a seaplane connect St. Thomas and St. Croix, and a ferry takes you from St. Thomas to St. John.

American is the territory's major carrier with flights from Miami and New York. Continental flies from Newark. Delta flies from Atlanta. United flies from Chicago and Washington, D.C. US Airways flies from Philadelphia. American Eagle has frequent flights throughout the day from San Juan. Cape Air flies from San Juan to both St. Thomas and St. Croix. It has code-sharing arrangements with all major airlines so your luggage can transfer seamlessly. Seaborne Airlines flies between St. Thomas and St. Croix.

➤ AIRLINES AND CONTACTS: **American Airlines** (☎ 340/774–6464 or 340/778–1140); **American Eagle** (☎ 340/776–2560 or 340/778–2000); **Cape Air** (☎ 800/352–0714 or 340/774–2204); **Continental Airlines** (☎ 800/231–0856); **Delta Airlines** (☎ 340/777–4177); **Seaborne Air-**

lines (☏ 340/773–6442); **United Air Lines** (☏ 340/774–9190); **US Airways** (☏ 340/774–7885).

AIRPORTS

St. Thomas's Cyril E. King Airport sits at the western end of the island. There is no airport on St. John. St. Croix's Henry Rohlsen Airport sits outside Frederiksted, a 10-minute drive away. It takes about a half-hour to reach Christiansted from the airport.

Most hotels on St. Thomas do not have airport shuttles, but taxi vans at the airport are plentiful. From the airport, fees (set by the VI Taxi Commission) for two or more people sharing a cab are: $12 to the Ritz-Carlton, $9 to Renaissance Grand Beach Resort, $7.50 to Marriott Frenchman's Reef, and $5 to Bluebeard's Castle. Expect to be charged 50¢ per bag and to pay a higher fee if you're riding alone. During rush hour the trip to east end resorts can take up to 40 minutes, but a half hour is typical. Driving time from the airport to Charlotte Amalie is 15 minutes.

Getting from the airport to St. Croix hotels by taxi costs about $10–$13. You'll spend a half-hour getting to the hotels in the Christiansted area, but those in the Frederiksted area are only about 10 minutes away. It takes about 45 minutes to get to the hotels on the East End.

Visitors to St. John fly into St. Thomas and take a taxi to either Charlotte Amalie or Red Hook, where they catch a ferry to Cruz Bay, St. John. The ferry from Charlotte Amalie makes the 45-minute trip several times a day and costs $7 a person. From Red Hook the ferry leaves on the hour; the 20-minute trip costs $3 a person.

➤ AIRPORT INFORMATION: **St. Croix's Henry Rohlsen Airport** (☏ 340/778–0589). **St. Thomas's Cyril E. King Airport** (☏ 340/774–5100).

BOAT AND FERRY TRAVEL

Virtually every type of ship and major cruise line calls at St. Thomas; only a few call at St. Croix. Many ships that call at St. Thomas also call in St. John or offer an excursion to that island.

Ferries are a great way to travel around the islands; there's service between St. Thomas and St. John and their neighbors, the BVI. There's something special about spending a day on St. John and then joining your fellow passengers—a mix of tourists, local families, and restaurant staffers en route to work—for a peaceful, sundown ride back to St. Thomas. Sometimes one of the St. John ferry services offers a special weekend trip to Fajardo, Puerto Rico. Such junkets depart from the waterfront in St. Thomas on a Friday evening and return to the same locale on Sunday afternoon.

FARES AND SCHEDULES

Ferries to Cruz Bay, St. John, leave St. Thomas from either the Charlotte Amalie waterfront west of the U.S. Coast Guard dock or from Red Hook. From Charlotte Amalie ferries depart at 9, 11, 1, 3, 4, and 5:30. To Charlotte Amalie from Cruz Bay, they leave at 7:15, 9:15, 11:15, 1:15, 2:15, and 3:45. The one-way fare for the 45-minute ride is $7. From Red Hook, ferries to Cruz Bay leave at 6:30 AM and 7:30 AM. Starting at 8 AM, they leave hourly until midnight. Returning from Cruz Bay, they leave hourly starting at 6 AM until 11 PM. The 15- to 20-minute ferry ride is $3 one-way.

Car ferries, called barges, run every half hour between Red Hook, St. Thomas, and Cruz Bay, St. John. The ride is 20 minutes (one way) and costs $25 (round-trip). Plan to check your vehicle in 15 minutes before departure.

Reefer is the name of both of the brightly colored 26-passenger skiffs that run between the Charlotte Amalie waterfront and Marriott Frenchman's Reef hotel daily every hour from 9 to 4, returning from the Reef from 9:30 until 4:30. It's a good way to beat the traffic (and is about the same price as a taxi) to Morning Star Beach, which adjoins the Reef. And you get a great view of the harbor as you bob along in the shadow of the giant cruise ships anchored in the harbor. The captain of the *Reefer* may also be persuaded to drop you at Yacht Haven, but check first. The fare is $4 one-way, and the trip takes about 15 minutes.

There's daily service between either Charlotte Amalie or Red Hook, on St. Thomas, and West End or Road Town, Tortola, BVI, by either Smiths Ferry or Native Son, Inc., and to Virgin Gorda, BVI, by Smiths Ferry. The times and days the ferries run change, so it's best to call for schedules once you're in the islands. The fare is $22 one-way or $40 round-trip, and the trip from Charlotte Amalie takes 45 minutes to an hour to West End, up to 1½ hours to Road Town; from Red Hook the trip is only half an hour. The twice-weekly 2¼-hour trip from Charlotte Amalie to Virgin Gorda costs $28 one-way and $40 round-trip. There's also daily service between Cruz Bay, St. John, and West End, Tortola, aboard the *Sundance*. The half-hour one-way trip is $21. You'll need to present proof of citizenship upon entering the BVI; a passport is best, but a birth certificate with a raised seal in addition to a government-issued photo ID will suffice.

➤ BOAT AND FERRY INFORMATION: **Native Son, Inc.** (☎ 340/774–8685); *Reefer* (☎ 340/776–8500 Ext. 6814); **Smiths Ferry** (☎ 340/775–7292); *Sundance* (☎ 340/776–6597).

BUSINESS HOURS
BANKS
Bank hours are generally Monday–Thursday 9–3 and Friday 9–5; a handful have Saturday hours (9–noon). Walk-up windows open at 8:30 on weekdays.

POST OFFICES
Hours may vary slightly from branch to branch and island to island, but they are generally 7:30 or 8 to 4 or 5:30 weekdays and 7:30 or 8 to noon or 2:30 Saturday.

SHOPS
On St. Thomas, stores on Main Street in Charlotte Amalie are open weekdays and Saturday 9–5. The hours of the shops in the Havensight Mall (next to the cruise-ships dock) are the same, though occasionally some stay open until 9 on Friday, depending on how many cruise ships are at the dock. You may also find some shops open on Sunday if a lot of cruise ships are in port. Hotel shops are usually open evenings, as well.

St. Croix shop hours are usually Monday–Saturday 9–5, but you'll find some shops in Christiansted open in the evening. On St. John, store hours run from 9 or 10 to 5 or 6. Wharfside Village and Mongoose Junction shops in Cruz Bay are often open into the evening.

CAR RENTALS
Any U.S. driver's license is good for 90 days on the USVI, as are valid driver's licenses from other countries; the minimum age for drivers is 18, although many agencies won't rent to anyone under the age of 25. At the height of the winter season, it may be tough to find a car and occasionally, all rental companies run out of cars at once; reserve well in advance to ensure you get the vehicle of your choice.

ST. THOMAS

You can rent a car from several local and worldwide agencies.
➤ MAJOR AGENCIES: **ABC Rentals** (☎ 340/776–1222 or 800/524–2080); **Anchorage E-Z Car** (☎ 340/775–6255); **Avis** (☎ 340/774–1468 or 800/331–1084); **Budget** (☎ 340/776–5774 or 800/626–4516); **Cowpet Rent-a-Car** (☎ 340/775–7376); **Dependable Car Rental** (☎ 340/774–2253 or 800/522–3076); **Discount** (☎ 340/776–4858); **Hertz** (☎ 340/774–1879 or 800/654–3131).

ST. CROIX

Atlas is located outside Christiansted but provides pickups at hotels. Avis is located at the airport. Budget has locations at the airport and in the King Christian Hotel in Christiansted. Midwest is located outside Frederiksted, but picks up at hotels. Olympic and Thrifty are located outside Christiansted, but will pick up at hotels.
➤ CONTACTS: **Atlas** (☎ 340/773–2886 or 800/426–6009); **Avis** (☎ 340/778–9355 or 800/331–1084); **Budget** (☎ 340/778–9636 or 888/227–3359); **Midwest** (☎ 340/772–0438); **Olympic** (☎ 340/773–2208 or 888/878–4227); **Thrifty** (☎ 340/773–7200 or 800/367–2277).

ST. JOHN

Best is just outside Cruz Bay near the public library off Route 10. Cool Breeze is in Cruz Bay across from the Creek. Delbert Hill Taxi Rental Service is in Cruz Bay around the corner from the ferry dock across from Wharfside Village. Denzil Clyne is across from the Creek. O'Connor Jeep is in Cruz Bay at the Texaco Station. St. John Car Rental is at the Creek in Cruz Bay. Spencer's Jeep is across from the Creek in Cruz Bay. V.I. Miscellaneous is in Cruz Bay across from the Creek.
➤ CONTACTS: **Best** (☎ 340/693–8177); **Cool Breeze** (☎ 340/776–6588); **Delbert Hill Taxi Rental Service** (☎ 340/776–6637); **Denzil Clyne** (☎ 340/776–6715); **O'Connor Jeep** (☎ 340/776–6343); **St. John Car Rental** (☎ 340/776–6103, WEB www.st-john.com/stjohncarrental); **Spencer's Jeep** (☎ 340/693–8784 or 888/776–6628); **V.I. Miscellaneous** (☎ 340/776–6374).

CAR TRAVEL

Even at a sedate speed of 20 mph, driving can be an adventure—for example, you may find yourself in a stick-shift Jeep slogging behind a slow tourist-packed safari bus at a steep hairpin turn. Give a little beep at blind turns. Note that the general speed limit on these islands is only 25 mph to 35 mph, which will seem fast enough for you on most roads. If you don't think you'll need to lock up your valuables, a Jeep or open-air Suzuki with four-wheel drive will make it easier to navigate pot-holed dirt side roads and to get up slick hills when it rains. All main roads are paved.

GASOLINE

Gas is pricey: about $2 per gallon on St. Thomas and $2.15 on St. John, but much less so ($1.25 per gallon) on St. Croix.

ROAD CONDITIONS

In St. Thomas, traffic can get pretty bad, especially in Charlotte Amalie at rush hour (7–9 and 4:30–6). Cars often line up bumper to bumper along the waterfront. If you need to get from an east end resort to the airport during these times, find the alternate route (starting from the east end, Route 38 to 42 to 40 to 33) that goes up the mountain and then drops you back onto Veterans Highway. If you plan to explore by car, be sure to pick up the "2002 Road Map St. Thomas–St. John" that includes the route numbers *and* the names of the roads that are used by locals. It's available anywhere you find maps and guidebooks.

St. Croix, unlike St. Thomas and St. John where narrow roads wind through hillsides, is relatively flat, and it even has a four-lane highway. The speed limit on the Melvin H. Evans Highway is 55 mph and ranges from 35 mph to 40 mph elsewhere. Roads are often unmarked, so be patient—sometimes getting lost is half the fun.

In St. John, use caution. The terrain is very hilly, the roads are winding, and the blind curves numerous. You may suddenly come upon a huge safari bus careening around a corner or a couple of hikers strolling along the side of the road. Major roads are well paved, but once you get off a specific route, dirt roads filled with potholes are common. For such driving a four-wheel-drive vehicle is your best bet.

RULES OF THE ROAD
Driving is on the left side of the road (although your steering wheel will be on the left side of the car). The law requires *everyone* in a car to wear seat belts: many of the roads are narrow, and the islands are dotted with hills, so there's ample reason to put safety first.

ELECTRICITY
The USVI use the same current as the U.S. mainland—110 volts. Since power fluctuations occasionally occur, bring a heavy-duty surge protector (available at hardware stores) if you plan to use your computer.

EMERGENCIES
➤ AMBULANCE AND FIRE: Dial ☎ 911. The **Air Ambulance Network** (☎ 800/327–1966) serves the USVI area from Florida. **Medical Air Services** (☎ 340/777–8580 or 800/643–9023) has its Caribbean headquarters in St. Thomas.
➤ COAST GUARD: Call the **Marine Safety Detachment** (☎ 340/776–3497 in St. Thomas and St. John; 340/772–5557 in St. Croix) from 7 to 3:30 weekdays. If there's no answer at either number, call the **Rescue Coordination Center** (☎ 787/289–2040) in San Juan, Puerto Rico; it's open 24 hours a day.
➤ HOSPITALS ON ST. CROIX: **Gov. Juan F. Luis Hospital and Health Center** (✉ 6 Diamond Ruby, north of Sunny Isle Shopping Center on Rte. 79, Christiansted, ☎ 340/778–6311); **Frederiksted Health Center** (✉ 516 Strand St., ☎ 340/772–1992).
➤ HOSPITALS ON ST. JOHN: **Myrah Keating Smith Community Health Center** (✉ Rte. 10, about 7 mins east of Cruz Bay, ☎ 340/693–8900).
➤ HOSPITALS ON ST. THOMAS: **Roy L. Schneider Hospital & Community Health Center** (✉ Sugar Estate, 1 mi east of Charlotte Amalie, ☎ 340/776–8311).
➤ PHARMACIES ON ST. CROIX: **D&D Apothecary Hall** (✉ 501 Queen St., Frederiksted, ☎ 340/772–1890); **Kmart Pharmacy** (✉ Sunshine Mall, ☎ 340/692–2622); **People's Drug Store, Inc.,** (✉ Christiansted Wharf, ☎ 340/778–7355; ✉ Sunny Isle Shopping Center, Rte. 70, Christiansted, ☎ 340/778–5537).
➤ PHARMACIES ON ST. JOHN: **St. John Drug Center** (✉ Boulon Shopping Center, Rte. 10, Cruz Bay, ☎ 340/776–6353).
➤ PHARMACIES ON ST. THOMAS: **Havensight Pharmacy** (✉ Havensight Mall, ☎ 340/776–1235); **Kmart Pharmacy** (✉ Tutu Park Mall, ☎ 340/777–3854); **Sunrise Pharmacy** (✉ Red Hook, ☎ 340/775–6600; Vitraco Park, near Havensight Mall, ☎ 340/776–7292).
➤ POLICE: Dial ☎ 911.
➤ SCUBA-DIVING EMERGENCIES: The only hyperbaric chamber in the territory is at St. Thomas's Roy L. Schneider Hospital & Community Health Center (☎ 340/776–2686).

ETIQUETTE AND BEHAVIOR

A smile and a "good day" greeting will start any encounter off on the right foot. Dress is casual throughout the islands, but cover up when you're sightseeing or shopping in town; bare chests and bathing suit tops are frowned upon.

FESTIVALS AND SEASONAL EVENTS

ST. THOMAS

January–April sees Classics in the Garden, a chamber-music series at Tillett Gardens where young musicians from all over the world perform. Tillett Gardens hosts annual Arts Alive festivals in November, March, and August. During Easter weekend, St. Thomas Yacht Club hosts the Rolex Cup Regatta, which is part of the three-race Caribbean Ocean Racing Triangle (CORT) that pulls in yachties and their pals from all over. Carnival is a weeklong major-league blowout of parades, parties, and island-wide events. The dates change from year to year, following the Easter calendar. Marlin mania begins in May and so do the sportfishing tournaments. There are also several locally sponsored fishing events throughout summer and fall.

The St. Thomas Gamefishing Club hosts its July Open Tournament over the Fourth of July weekend. There are categories for serious marlin anglers, just-for-fun fishermen, and even kids who want to try their luck from docks and rocks. The mid-July celebration of Bastille Day—which commemorates the French Revolution—is marked by a mini-carnival in Frenchtown. During full moon in August, anglers compete for big-money prizes in the USVI Open/Atlantic Blue Marlin Tournament. September's Texas Society Chili Cook-Off is a party on Sapphire Beach—you'll find country music performances, dancing, games, and, of course, chili tasting. In November the St. Thomas–St. John Agricultural Fair showcases fresh produce, home-grown herbs, and local dishes, such as callaloo, salt fish and dumplings, and fresh fish simmered with green banana, pumpkin, and potatolike *tannia*.
➤ CONTACTS: **Arts Alive Festival** (☎ 340/775–1405); **Carnival** (☎ 340/776–3112); **Classics in the Garden** (☎ 340/775–1405); **July Open Tournament** (☎ 340/775–9144); **Rolex Cup Regatta** (☎ 340/775–6320); **St. Thomas–St. John Agricultural Fair** (☎ 340/693–1080); **Texas Society Chili Cook-Off** (☎ 340/776–3595); **USVI Open/Atlantic Blue Marlin Tournament** (☎ 340/775–9500).

ST. CROIX

The island celebrates Carnival with its Crucian Christmas Festival, which starts in late December. After weeks of beauty pageants, food fairs, and concerts, the festival wraps up with a parade in early January. In February and March the St. Croix Landmarks Society House Tours visit some of the island's most exclusive and historic homes and give you a chance to peek inside places you can usually view only from the road.

The St. Croix Half Ironman Triathlon attracts international-class athletes as well as amateurs every May for a 1-mi (2-km) swim, a 7-mi (12-km) run, and a 34-mi (55-km) bike ride; it includes a climb up The Beast, on Route 69. Serious swimmers should join island residents in early November for the Coral Reef Swim. Participants swim about 5 mi (8 km) from Buck Island to Christiansted. The event also includes an awards dinner. The International Regatta sets sail in February at the St. Croix Yacht Club. Sailors converge on Teague Bay for three days of sailing and parties.
➤ CONTACTS: **Coral Reef Swim** (☎ 340/773–2100); **International Regatta** (☎ 340/773–9531); **St. Croix Half Ironman Triathlon** (☎ 340/773–4470); **St. Croix Landmarks Society House Tours** (☎ 340/772–0598).

ST. JOHN

The island dishes up its own version of Carnival with the July 4th Celebration. Weeks of festivities—including beauty pageants and a food fair—culminate in a parade through the streets of Cruz Bay on July 4. On the two days after Thanksgiving an eclectic group of sailors takes to the waters of Coral Bay for the annual Coral Bay Thanksgiving Regatta. Some boats are "live-aboards," whose owners only pull up anchor for this one event; other boats belong to Sunday sailors; and a very few are owned by hotshot racers. If you'd like to crew, stop by Skinny Legs Bar and Restaurant.

➤ CONTACTS: **Coral Bay Thanksgiving Regatta Crew Information** (☎ 340/779–4982).

HEALTH

You should always wash produce before eating it. Also note that ciguatera, a toxin found in some reef fish (particularly kingfish), can be a problem at local restaurants.

HOLIDAYS

Public holidays, in addition to the U.S. federal holidays, for 2002 are: Three Kings Day (Jan. 6); Transfer Day (commemorates Denmark's 1917 sale of the territory to the United States, Mar. 31); Holy Thursday and Good Friday (Apr. 12–13); Emancipation Day (when slavery was abolished in the Danish West Indies in 1848, July 3); Columbus Day and USVI–Puerto Rico Friendship Day (Oct. 11); and Liberty Day (honoring Judge David Hamilton Jackson who secured freedom of the press and assembly from King Christian X of Denmark, Nov. 1).

Although the government closes down for 26 days a year, most of these holidays have no effect on shopping hours. Unless there's a cruise ship arrival, expect most stores to close for Christmas and a few other holidays in the slower summer months.

LANGUAGE

English is the official language, though island residents often speak it with a lilting Creole accent, so you might not recognize certain words at first. If you have trouble understanding someone, ask them to speak slowly.

MAIL AND SHIPPING

The main U.S. Post Office on St. Thomas is near the hospital, with branches in Charlotte Amalie, Frenchtown, Havensight, and Tutu Mall; there are post offices at Christiansted, Frederiksted, Gallows Bay, and Sunny Isle, on St. Croix, and at Cruz Bay, on St. John. The postal service offers Express Mail next-day service to major cities if you mail before noon; outlying areas may take two days. Letters to the United States are 33¢ and postcards are 20¢. Sending mail home to Canada you'll pay 46¢ for a letter and 40¢ for a postcard. To the United Kingdom and Australia, letters are 60¢, postcards 50¢.

On St. Thomas, Federal Express offers overnight service if you get your package to the office before 5 PM. Parcel Plus, across from Havensight Mall, also has express mail service. The Federal Express office on St. Croix is in Peter's Rest Commercial Center; try to drop off your packages before 5:30 PM. On St. John, Sprint Courier Service connects to all major couriers.

➤ CONTACTS: **Federal Express** (✉ Cyril E. King Airport, St. Thomas, ☎ 340/777–4140; ✉ Peter's Rest Commercial Center, Rte. 708, St. Croix, ☎ 340/778–8180); **Parcel Plus** (✉ across from Havensight Mall on Rte. 30, St. Thomas, ☎ 340/776–9134); **Sprint Courier Service** (✉ just off Rte. 104 across from the basketball court, St. John, ☎ 340/693–8130).

MONEY MATTERS

Prices quoted in this chapter are in U.S. dollars.

BANKS AND ATMS

Each of the islands has several banks. On St. Thomas, First Bank is near Market Square. There are waterfront locations for both Banco Popular and V.I. Community Bank.

St. Croix has branches of Banco Popular in Orange Grove and Sunny Isle Shopping Centers. V.I. Community Bank is located in Orange Grove Shopping Center and in downtown Christiansted. Scotia Bank has branches in Sunny Isle Frederiksted, Christiansted, and Sunshine Mall.

St. John's two banks are located near the ferry docks. Chase is one block up from the ferry dock, while Scotia Bank is located in a trailer about a block up from it.

➤ CONTACTS: **Banco Popular** (☎ 340/693–2777); **Chase Manhattan Bank** (☎ 340/775–7777); **First Bank** (☎ 340/776–9494); **Scotia Bank** (St. Croix, ☎ 340/778–5350; St. John, ☎ 340/776–6552).

CREDIT CARDS

All major credit cards and traveler's checks are generally accepted. Some places will take Discover, though it is not as widely accepted as Visa, Mastercard, and American Express.

CURRENCY

The American dollar is used throughout the territory, as well as in the neighboring BVI. If you need to exchange foreign currency, you'll need to go to the main branch of major banks.

PASSPORTS AND VISAS

If you're a U.S. or Canadian citizen, you can prove citizenship with a current or expired (but not by more than five years) passport or with a birth certificate (with a raised seal) along with a government-issued photo ID. A valid passport, however, is best. Citizens of other countries need a passport.

SAFETY

Vacationers tend to assume that normal precautions aren't necessary in paradise. They are. Though there isn't quite as much crime here as in large U.S. mainland cities, it does exist. To be safe, stick to well-lighted streets at night and use the same kind of street sense (don't wander the back alleys of Charlotte Amalie or Christiansted after five rum punches, for example) that you would in any unfamiliar territory. If you plan to carry things around, rent a car—not a Jeep—and lock possessions in the trunk. Keep your rental car locked wherever you park. Don't leave cameras, purses, and other valuables lying on the beach while you snorkel for an hour (or even for a minute), whether you're on the deserted beaches of St. John or the more crowded Magens and Coki beaches on St. Thomas. St. Croix has several remote beaches outside Frederiksted and on the east end; it's best to visit them with a group rather than on your own.

SIGHTSEEING TOURS

AIR TOURS

Air Center Helicopters, on the Charlotte Amalie waterfront (next to Tortola Wharf) on St. Thomas, has 30-minute island tours priced at $375 (for up to four passengers) per trip. You can also arrange longer flights that loop over to the neighboring BVI, as well as photography tours. Seaborne Airlines offers narrated flightseeing tours of the USVI and the BVI from its Havensight base on St. Thomas. The 30-minute "Round-the-Island" tour is $89 per person.

➤ CONTACTS: **Air Center Helicopters** (✉ Waterfront, Charlotte Amalie, St. Thomas, ☎ 340/775–7335); **Seaborne Adventures** (✉ 5305 Long Bay Rd., Charlotte Amalie, St. Thomas, ☎ 340/773–5991).

BOAT TOURS

St. Thomas's *Kon Tiki* party boat is a kick. Put your sophistication aside, climb on this big palm-thatch raft, and dip into bottomless barrels of rum punch along with a couple of hundred of your soon-to-be closest friends. Dance to the steel-drum band, sun on the roof (watch out: you'll fry), and join the limbo dancing on the way home from an afternoon of swimming and beachcombing at Honeymoon Beach on Water Island. This popular 3½-hour afternoon excursion costs $29.

Caribbean Pelican Rides offers a unique land and sea tour of Charlotte Amalie aboard an amphibious British Alvis Stalward vessel. Tours depart from the Coast Guard dock opposite Vendor's Plaza. The 55-minute excursions costs $55.

➤ CONTACTS: **Caribbean Pelican Rides** (✉ Coast Guard Dock, opposite Vendor's Plaza, Charlotte Amalie, St. Thomas, ☎ 340/774–7808); *Kon Tiki* (✉ Gregorie Channel East Dock, Frenchtown, St. Thomas, ☎ 340/775–5055).

BUS AND TAXI TOURS

V. I. Taxi Association St. Thomas City-Island Tour gives a two-hour $45 tour for two people in an open-air safari bus or enclosed van; aimed at cruise-ship passengers, this tour includes stops at Drake's Seat and Mountain Top. For just a bit more money (about $45–$50 for two) you can hire a taxi and ask the driver to take the opposite route so you'll avoid the crowds. But do see Mountain Top: the view is wonderful.

Tropic Tours offers half-day shopping and sightseeing tours of St. Thomas by bus six days a week ($25 per person). The company also has a full-day ferry tour to St. John that includes snorkeling and lunch. The cost is $70 per person.

St. Croix Safari Tours offers van tours of St. Croix. They depart from Christiansted, last about three hours, cost from $25 per person plus admission fees to attractions. St. Croix Transit offers van tours of St. Croix. They depart from Christiansted, last about three hours, cost from $25 per person plus admission fees to attractions.

In St. John, taxi drivers provide tours of the island, making stops at various sites including Trunk Bay and Annaberg Plantation. Prices run around $15 a person. The taxi drivers congregate near the ferry in Cruz Bay. The dispatcher will find you a driver for your tour.

➤ CONTACTS: **St. Croix Safari Tours** (☎ 340/773–6700); **St. Croix Transit** (☎ 340/772–3333); **Tropic Tours** (☎ 340/774–1855 or 800/524–4334); **V. I. Taxi Association St. Thomas City-Island Tour** (☎ 340/774–4550).

WALKING TOURS

The *St. Thomas–St. John Vacation Handbook,* available free at hotels and tourist centers, has an excellent self-guided walking tour of Charlotte Amalie on St. Thomas. The St. Thomas Historical Trust has published a self-guided tour of the historic district; it's available in book and souvenir shops for $1.95. A two-hour guided historic walking tour is available by reservation. It begins (at 9 AM) at the Emancipation Garden, covers all the in-town sights, and can be narrated in Spanish, Danish, German, and Japanese as well as in English. The cost is $35 per person; wear a hat and comfortable walking shoes.

Possible nature tours on St. Thomas include bird-watching, whale-watching, and waiting hidden on a beach while the magnificent hawksbill turtles come ashore to lay their eggs. Contact EAST (Environmental Association of St. Thomas–St. John.

St. Croix Heritage Tours leads walks through the historic towns of Christiansted and Frederiksted, detailing the history of the people and the buildings. Custom tours that cover the island are also available.

Along with providing trail maps and brochures about Virgin Islands National Park, the park service also gives a variety of guided tours on- and off-shore. Some are only offered during particular times of the year, and some require reservations. For more information, contact the National Park Service on St. John.

➤ CONTACTS: **EAST** (Environmental Association of St. Thomas–St. John; (✉ Box 12379, St. Thomas 00801, ☎ 340/776–1976); **St. Croix Heritage Tours** (✉ Box 7937, Sunny Isle, 00823, ☎ 340/778–6997); **St. Thomas Historical Trust** (☎ 340/776–2726); **V. I. National Park Visitors Center** (✉ at area known as the Creek; across from Cruz Bay bulkhead and adjacent to ball field, Cruz Bay, ☎ 340/776–6201; ✉ Cinnamon Bay, ☎ 340/776–6330, WEB www.nps.gov/viis).

TAXES

DEPARTURE TAX

Departure taxes ($10 for those leaving by air, $5 for those leaving by sea) are included in your ticket.

SALES TAX

There's no sales tax, but there is an 8% hotel-room tax in the USVI. The St. John Accommodations Council members ask that hotel and villa guests voluntarily pay a $1-a-day surcharge to help fund school and community projects and other good works.

TAXIS

USVI taxis don't have meters, but you needn't worry about fare gouging if you check a list of standard rates to popular destinations (required by law to be carried by each driver and often posted in hotel and airport lobbies and printed in free tourist periodicals, such as *St. Thomas This Week* and *St. Croix This Week*) and settle on the fare before you start out. Fares are per person, not per destination, but drivers taking multiple fares (which often happens, especially from the airport) will charge you a lower rate than if you're in the cab alone.

ST. THOMAS

On St. Thomas taxi vans line up along Havensight and Crown Bay docks when a cruise ship pulls in. If you booked a shore tour, the operator will lead you to a designated vehicle. Otherwise, there are plenty of air-conditioned vans and open-air safari buses to take you to Charlotte Amalie or the beach. The cab fare from Havensight to Charlotte Amalie is $2.50 per person; you can, however, make the 1½ mi- (2½ km-) walk into town in about 30 minutes along the beautiful waterfront. From Crown Bay to town the taxi fare is $2.50 per person whether you travel solo or you share; it's a 1-mi (1½-km) walk, but the route passes along a busy highway. Transportation from Havensight to Magens Bay for swimming is $6.50 per person ($4 if you share).

Additionally, taxis of all shapes and sizes are available at various ferry, shopping, resort, and airport areas, and they also respond to phone calls. There are taxi stands in Charlotte Amalie across from Emancipation Garden (in front of Little Switzerland, behind the post office) and along the waterfront. But you probably won't have to look for a stand, as taxis are plentiful and routinely cruise the streets. Walking down Main Street, you'll be asked "Back to ship?" often enough to make you never want to carry another shopping bag.

➤ CONTACTS: **East End Taxi** (☎ 340/775–6974); **Islander Taxi** (☎ 340/774–4077); **VI Taxi Association** (☎ 340/774–4550).

ST. CROIX

Taxis, generally station wagons or minivans, are a phone call away from most hotels and are available in downtown Christiansted, at the Alexander Hamilton Airport, and at the Frederiksted pier during cruise-ship arrivals.

In Frederiksted, all the shops are just a short walk away, and you can swim off the beach in Frederiksted. Most ship passengers visit Christiansted on a tour; a taxi will cost $20 for one or two people.
➤ CONTACTS: **Antilles Taxi Service** (☎ 340/773–5020); **Cruzan Taxi and Tours** (☎ 340/773–6388); **St. Croix Taxi Association** (☎ 340/778–1088).

ST. JOHN

Taxis meet ferries arriving in Cruz Bay. Most drivers use vans or open-air safari buses. You'll find them congregated at the dock and at hotel parking lots. You can also hail them anywhere on the road. You're likely to travel with other tourists en route to their destinations. It's very difficult to get taxis to respond to a phone call. If you need one to pick you up at your rental villa, ask the villa manager for suggestions on who to call or arrange a ride in advance.

Some cruise ships stop at St. John to let passengers disembark for a day. The main town of Cruz Bay is near the ship terminal. If you want to swim, the famous Trunk Bay is an $11 taxi ride (for two) from town.

TELEPHONES

On St. Thomas, AT&T has a state-of-the-art telecommunications center (it's across from the Havensight Mall) with 15 desk booths, fax and copy services, video phone, and TDD equipment (for people with hearing impairments). Islander Services and East End Secretarial Services offer long-distance dialing, copying, and fax services. Parcel Plus in St. Thomas has three computers available for accessing e-mail; the cost is $5 per half hour. Express mail service, international calling, and phone cards are also available here. On St. John, the place to go for phone or message needs is Connections.
➤ CONTACTS: **AT&T** (✉ across from Havensight Mall, Charlotte Amalie, St. Thomas, ☎ 340/777–9201); **Connections** (✉ Cruz Bay, St. John, ☎ 340/776–6922; ✉ Coral Bay, St. John,☎ 340/779–4994); **East End Secretarial Services** (✉ upstairs at Red Hook Plaza, Red Hook, St. Thomas, ☎ 340/775–5262); **Islander Services** (✉ 5302 Store Tvaer Gade, behind the Greenhouse Restaurant, Charlotte Amalie, St. Thomas, ☎ 340/774–8128); **Parcel Plus** (✉ across from Havensight Mall, Charlotte Amalie, St. Thomas, ☎ 340/776–9134).

COUNTRY AND AREA CODES

The area code for all of the USVI is 340. If you are calling from within the U.S., you need only dial 1 plus the area code and number. If you are calling from outside the U.S., dial the U.S. country code 01.

INTERNATIONAL CALLS

You can dial direct to and from the mainland U.S., and to and from Australia, Canada, New Zealand, and the United Kingdom from most phones.

LOCAL CALLS

Local calls from a public phone cost up to 35¢ for each five minutes. If you have a cell phone, you can dial 6611 for information about how to use it locally.

TIPPING

Many hotels add a 10% to 15% service charge to cover the room maid and other staff. However, some hotels may use part of that money to fund their operations, passing on only a portion of it to the staff. Check with your maid or bellboy to determine the hotel's policy. If you discover you need to tip, give bellmen and porters 50¢ to $1 per bag and maids $1 or $2 per day. Special errands or requests of hotel staff always require an additional tip. At restaurants bartenders and waiters expect a 10%–15% tip, but always check your tab to see whether service is included. Taxi drivers get a 15% tip.

TRANSPORTATION AROUND THE U.S. VIRGIN ISLANDS

AIRPLANE

American Eagle offers frequent flights daily from St. Thomas to St. Croix's Henry E. Rohlsen Airport. Cape Air flies from St. Thomas to St. Croix, beginning its flight in Puerto Rico. Seaborne Airlines also flies between St. Thomas and St. Croix several times daily as well as to Beef Island Airport on Tortola, British Virgin Islands. LIAT has service from St. Thomas and St. Croix to Caribbean islands to the south.

➤ CONTACTS: **American Airlines/American Eagle** (☎ 340/778–0589, WEB www.aa.com); **Cape Air** (☎ 340/774–2204 or 800/352–0714, WEB www.capeair.com); **LIAT** (☎ 340/774–2313, WEB www.liatairline.com); **Seaborne Airlines** (☎ 340/773–6442, WEB www.seaborneairlines.com).

BUS

On St. Thomas, the island's 20 deluxe mainland-size buses make public transportation a very comfortable—though slow—way to get from east and west to Charlotte Amalie and back (service to the north is limited). Buses run about every 30 minutes from stops that are clearly marked with VITRAN signs. Fares are $1 between outlying areas and town and 75¢ in town.

Privately owned taxi vans crisscross St. Croix regularly, providing reliable service between Frederiksted and Christiansted along Route 70. This inexpensive ($1.50 one-way) mode of transportation is favored by locals, and though the many stops on the 20-mi (32-km) drive between the two main towns make the ride slow, it's never dull. The public Vitran buses aren't the quickest way to get around the island, but they're comfortable and affordable. The fare is $1 between Christiansted to Frederiksted or to places in between.

Modern Vitran buses on St. John run from the Cruz Bay ferry dock through Coral Bay to the far eastern end of the island at Salt Pond, making numerous stops in between. The fare is $1 to any point.

VISITOR INFORMATION

➤ BEFORE YOU LEAVE: **USVI Government Tourist Office** (✉ 245 Peachtree St., Center Ave. Marquis One Tower MB-05, Atlanta, GA 30303, ☎ 404/688–0906; ✉ 500 N. Michigan Ave., Suite 2030, Chicago, IL 60611, ☎ 312/670–8784; ✉ 3460 Wilshire Blvd., Suite 412, Los Angeles, CA 90010, ☎ 213/739–0138; ✉ 2655 Le Jeune Rd., Suite 907, Coral Gables, FL 33134, ☎ 305/442–7200; ✉ 1270 Ave. of the Americas, Room 2108, New York, NY 10020, ☎ 212/332–2222; ✉ Hall of Streets, #298, 444 N. Capital St. NW, Washington, DC 20006, ☎ 202/624–3590; ✉ 60 Washington St., San Juan, Puerto Rico 00907, ☎ 787/722–8023; ✉ 703 Evans Ave. Suite 106, Toronto, Ontario, Canada M9C 5E9, ☎ 416/233–1414; ✉ Molasses House, Clove Hitch Quay, Plantation Wharf, York Place, London SW11 3TW, U.K., ☎ 020/ 7978–5262; WEB www.usvi.net).

➤ IN THE U.S. VIRGIN ISLANDS: **USVI Division of Tourism** (✉ Box 6400, Charlotte Amalie, St. Thomas 00804, ☎ 340/774–8784 or 800/372–8784; ✉ Box 4538, Christiansted, St. Croix 00822, ☎ 340/773–0495; ✉ Strand St., Frederiksted, St. Croix 00840, ☎ 340/772–0357. St. John; ✉ Box 200, Cruz Bay, St. John 00830, ☎ 340/776–6450). **V.I. National Park** (✉ at the Creek in Cruz Bay, St. John, 00831, ☎ 340/776–6201, WEB www.nps.gov/viis).

3 BRITISH VIRGIN ISLANDS

The eight-seater Cessna took off smoothly and on schedule for the 20-minute flight from St. Thomas. As it flew up the Sir Francis Drake Channel to the Beef Island/Tortola Airport, passengers gazed out at stunning views of island and channel. Suddenly everyone turned from the windows and looked at each other quizzically. They sat in stunned silence as the plane flew past the airport and headed to the little runway on nearby Virgin Gorda. After this unscheduled landing, the pilot turned around nervously and said, "Sorry. I'm late for my wedding. Nelson, my copilot, will fly you back to Tortola."

Updated by
Pamela
Acheson

T HE BRITISH VIRGIN ISLANDS (BVI) consist of about 50 islands, islets, and cays. Most are remarkably hilly, and all but Anegada are volcanic, having exploded from the depths of the sea some 25 million years ago. The BVI are serene, seductive, spectacularly beautiful, and still remarkably laid-back. At some points they lie only a mile or so from the U.S. Virgin Islands (USVI), but they remain unique and have maintained their quiet, friendly, casual character.

The pleasures here are understated: sailing around the multitude of tiny nearby islands; diving to the wreck of the RMS *Rhone*, sunk off Salt Island in 1867; snorkeling in one of hundreds of wonderful spots; walking empty beaches; taking in spectacular views from the island peaks; and settling in on a breeze-swept terrace to admire the sunset.

Several factors have enabled the BVI to retain the qualities of yesteryear's Caribbean: no building can rise higher than the surrounding palms, and there are no direct flights from the mainland United States, so the tourism tide is held back. Many visitors travel here by water, aboard their own ketches and yawls or on one of the ferries that cross the waters between St. Thomas and Tortola. Such a passage is a fine prelude to a stay in these unhurried havens.

Tortola, about 10 square mi (26 square km), is the largest and most populated of the islands; Virgin Gorda, with 8 square mi (21 square km), ranks second. The islands scattered around them include Jost Van Dyke, Great Camanoe, Norman, Peter, Salt, Cooper, Ginger, Dead Chest, and Anegada. Tortola has the most hotels, restaurants, and shops. Virgin Gorda offers a few restaurants, shops, and resorts (many are self-contained). Jost Van Dyke is a major charter-boat anchorage; little bars line the beach at Great Harbour, but there are few places to stay. The other islands are either uninhabited or have a single hotel or resort— or even just a restaurant. Many of these, such as Peter Island, offer excellent anchorages, and their bays and harbors are popular with overnighting boaters.

Sailing has always been a popular activity in the BVI. The first arrivals here were a romantic seafaring tribe, the Ciboney Indians. They were followed (circa AD 900) by the Arawaks, who sailed from South America, established settlements, and farmed and fished. Still later came the mighty Caribs.

In 1493 Christopher Columbus was the first European visitor. Impressed by the number of islands dotting the horizon, he named them *Las Once Mil Virgines*—the 11,000 Virgins—in honor of the 11,000 virgin companions of St. Ursula, martyred in the 4th century. In the ensuing years, the Spaniards passed through, fruitlessly seeking gold. Then came pirates and buccaneers, who found the islands' hidden coves and treacherous reefs ideal bases from which to prey on passing galleons crammed with gold, silver, and spices. Among the most notorious of these fellows were Blackbeard Teach, Bluebeard, Captain Kidd, and Sir Francis Drake, who lent his name to the channel that sweeps through the BVI's two main clusters. In the 17th century the colorful cutthroats were replaced by the Dutch, who, in turn, were sent packing by the British. It was the British who established a plantation economy and for the next 150 years developed the sugar industry. When slavery was abolished in 1838, the plantation economy faltered, and the majority of the white population left for Europe.

The islands dozed, a forgotten corner of the British empire, until the early 1960s. In 1966 a new constitution granting the islands greater autonomy was approved. Still appointed by the queen of England, the governor has limited powers, concentrated on external affairs and local security. The legislative council, with representatives from nine districts, administers other matters. General elections are held every four years. The arrangement seems to suit the islanders just fine: the political mood is serene. It was also in the 1960s that Laurence Rockefeller and American expatriate Charlie Cary brought tourism to the BVI. In 1965 Rockefeller set about creating the Little Dix Bay resort on Virgin Gorda. Dedicated to preserving the island's natural beauty while providing guests with unpretentious yet elegant surroundings, Little Dix set the standard that still prevails in the BVI. A few years later Cary and his wife, Ginny, established the Moorings marina complex on Tortola, and sailing in the area burgeoned.

Although offshore banking is currently the BVI's number one industry, tourism is the second major source of income. The majority of the islands' jobs are tourism-related, and there may well be even more such jobs by 2003, when the Beef Island airport expansion is slated for completion. The runway enlargement will accommodate larger prop planes and small regional jets but will still be too small for full-size jets, so there's no doubt that BVIers—who so love their unspoiled tropical home—will maintain their islands' easygoing charms for both themselves and their guests.

TORTOLA

Unwinding can easily become a full-time occupation on Tortola. Though the island offers a wealth of things to see and do, many visitors prefer just to loll about on its deserted sands or linger over lunch at one of its many delightful restaurants. Beaches are never more than a few minutes away, and the steep green hills that form Tortola's spine are fanned by gentle trade winds. The neighboring islands glimmer like emeralds in a sea of sapphire. It's a world far removed from the hustle of modern life.

Lodging

Luxury on Tortola is more a state of mind—serenity, seclusion, gentility—than state-of-the-art amenities and facilities. Hotels in Road Town don't have beaches, but they do have pools and are within walking distance of restaurants, nightspots, and shops. Accommodations outside Road Town are relatively isolated but are on beaches (some of them are exquisite; others are small or have been enlarged by bringing in sand). The BVI resorts are intimate: none are large—only four have more than 50 rooms. Visitors spend most of their time outside, so the location, size, or price of a hotel are more important than the decor of its rooms. Guests are treated as more than just room numbers, however, and many return year after year. This can make booking a room at popular resorts difficult, even off-season, despite the fact that more than half the island's visitors stay aboard their own or chartered boats.

Throughout the BVI a few hotels lack air-conditioning, relying instead on ceiling fans to capture the almost constant trade winds. Nights are cool and breezy, even in midsummer, and never reach the temperatures or humidity levels that are common in much of the United States during the summer.

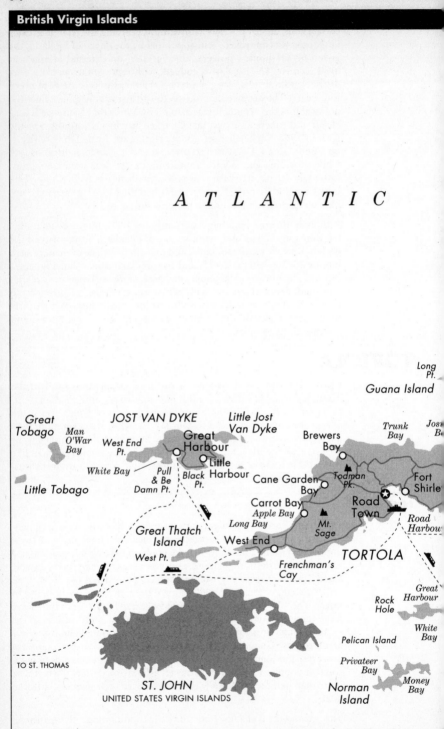

ATLANTIC

Long Pt.

Guana Island

Great Tobago

Man O'War Bay

JOST VAN DYKE

Little Jost Van Dyke

West End Pt.

Great Harbour

White Bay

Little Harbour

Pull & Be Damn Pt.

Black Pt.

Brewers Bay

Trunk Bay

Jos' B.

Little Tobago

Cane Garden Bay

Todman Pk.

Fort Shirle

Carrot Bay

Apple Bay

Road Town

Long Bay

Mt. Sage

Road Harbour

Great Thatch Island

West End

TORTOLA

West Pt.

Frenchman's Cay

Great Harbour

Rock Hole

White Bay

Pelican Island

TO ST. THOMAS

Privateer Bay

Money Bay

ST. JOHN
UNITED STATES VIRGIN ISLANDS

Norman Island

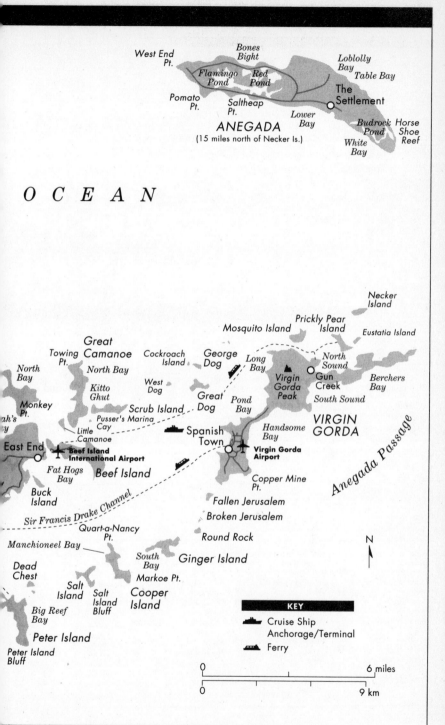

West End
Pt.

Bones
Bight

Loblolly
Bay

Table Bay

Flamingo
Pond

Red
Pond

The
Settlement

Pomato
Pt.

Saltheap
Pt.

Lower
Bay

ANEGADA
(15 miles north of Necker Is.)

Budrock
Pond

Horse
Shoe
Reef

White
Bay

O C E A N

Necker
Island

Prickly Pear
Island

Mosquito Island

Eustatia Island

Great
Camanoe

Towing
Pt.

North Bay

Cockroach
Island

George
Dog

Long
Bay

North
Sound

Gun
Creek

Berchers
Bay

North
Bay

West
Dog

Virgin
Gorda
Peak

Kitto
Ghut

South Sound

Monkey
Pt.

Scrub Island

Great
Dog

Pond
Bay

VIRGIN
GORDA

Pusser's Marina

ah's
y

Little
Camanoe

Cay

Spanish
Town

Handsome
Bay

East End

Beef Island
International Airport

Virgin Gorda
Airport

Anegada Passage

Fat Hogs
Bay

Beef Island

Copper Mine
Pt.

Buck
Island

Sir Francis Drake Channel

Fallen Jerusalem

Broken Jerusalem

Quart-a-Nancy
Pt.

Round Rock

N

Manchioneel Bay

South
Bay

Ginger Island

Dead
Chest

Markoe Pt.

Salt
Island

Salt
Island
Bluff

Cooper
Island

Big Reef
Bay

Peter Island

KEY

Cruise Ship
Anchorage/Terminal

Peter Island
Bluff

Ferry

0   6 miles

0   9 km

Tortola

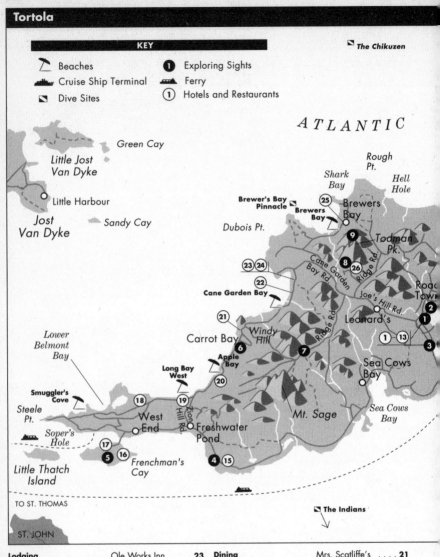

KEY

🏖 Beaches
🚢 Cruise Ship Terminal
◣ Dive Sites
1 Exploring Sights
⛴ Ferry
① Hotels and Restaurants

◥ The Chikuzen

ATLANTIC

Green Cay

Little Jost
Van Dyke

○ Little Harbour

Jost
Van Dyke

Sandy Cay

Rough
Pt.

Shark
Bay

Hell
Hole

**Brewer's Bay
Pinnacle** ◣

25

Brewers
Bay

**Brewers
Bay**

Dubois Pt.

9

Todman
Pk.

23 24

8 26

Cane Garden Bay

22

21

Cane Garden Bay

Joe's Hill Rd.

Road
Tow

Leonard's

2

1

① 13

3

Sea Cows
Bay

Carrot Bay

6

Windy
Hill

7

**Apple
Bay**

Lower
Belmont
Bay

**Long Bay
West**

20

Smuggler's
Cove

18

19

Sea Cows
Bay

Steele
Pt.

Soper's
Hole

17

West
End

○

Freshwater
Pond

Mt. Sage

16

5

Frenchman's
Cay

4 15

Little Thatch
Island

TO ST. THOMAS

◣ The Indians

ST. JOHN

Lodging

Brewers Bay
Campground **25**
Frenchman's Cay
Hotel **16**
Hotel Castle
Maria **10**
Lambert Beach
Resort **27**
Long Bay Beach
Resort **18**
Maria's Hotel
by the Sea **5**
Moorings-Mariner
Inn **11**

Ole Works Inn **23**
Pusser's Fort
Burt Hotel **14**
Sebastian's on the
Beach **19**
Sugar Mill Hotel . . . **20**
Village Cay Resort
and Marina **2**
The Villas of Fort
Recovery Estates . . . **15**

Dining

Brandywine Bay . . . **30**
C and F
Restaurant **8**
Capriccio di Mare . . **4**
The Captain's
Table **13**
Eclipse **28**
Garden
Restaurant **18**
The Last Resort . . . **29**
Le Cabanon **7**
Lime 'n' Mango **12**

Mrs. Scatliffe's **21**
Myett's **22**
The Pub **9**
Pusser's Landing . . . **17**
Pusser's
Road Town Pub **3**
Quito's Gazebo . . . **24**
Skyworld **26**
Spaghetti
Junction **6**
Sugar Mill
Restaurant **20**
Virgin Queen **1**

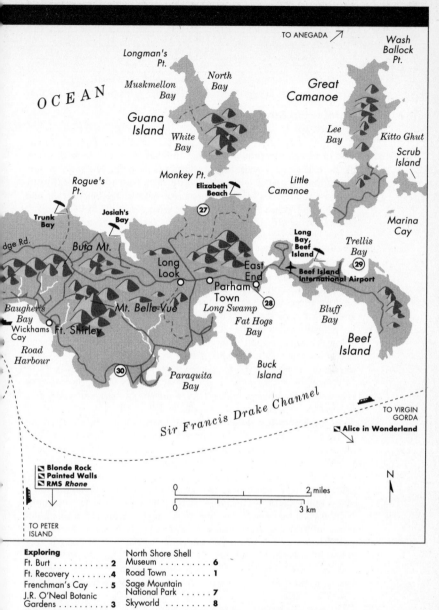

Exploring

Ft. Burt **2**
Ft. Recovery **4**
Frenchman's Cay . . . **5**
J.R. O'Neal Botanic
Gardens **3**
Mt. Healthy
National Park **9**
North Shore Shell
Museum **6**
Road Town **1**
Sage Mountain
National Park **7**
Skyworld **8**

CATEGORY	COST*
$$$$	over $225
$$$	$150–$225
$$	$75–$150
$	under $75

All prices are for a standard double room in high season, excluding 7% hotel tax and 10% (5%–15% on Virgin Gorda) service charge.

Hotels and Inns

ROAD TOWN

$$$ 🏨 **Maria's Hotel by the Sea.** Perched on the edge of Road Harbour, next to a large government building and the cruise ship dock, this simple hotel is an easy walk from restaurants in town. The small rooms are minimally decorated, with white rattan furniture, floral-print spreads, and murals by local artists. All rooms have balconies, some with harbor views. ⊠ *Waterfront Dr. (Box 206),* ☎ *284/494–2595,* FAX *284/494–2420. 38 rooms. Restaurant, bar, air-conditioning, kitchenettes, pool. AE, MC, V. EP.*

$$$ 🏨 **Moorings-Mariner Inn.** This two-story inn is also the headquarters for the Moorings Charter operation. It's popular with both yachting folk—who find its facilities convenient and the companionship of fellow "boaties" congenial—and landlubbers who are happy with simple furnishings and want to be within walking distance of town. The atmosphere is laid-back *and* lively. The pale peach color scheme is picked up in the floor tiles, and tropical-print fabrics add splashes of contrasting color. All units are on the large side and have small kitchenettes and balconies, and you'll face the marina in all but the eight rooms that overlook the pool or the tennis court. ⊠ *Waterfront Dr. (Box 139),* ☎ *284/494–2332 or 800/535–7289,* FAX *284/494–2226. 38 rooms, 4 suites. Air-conditioning, kitchenettes, pool, tennis court, volleyball, dive shop, dock, marina, shops. AE, MC, V. EP.*

$$$ 🏨 **Pusser's Fort Burt Hotel.** Originally a fort built by the Dutch in the 17th century, this hillside landmark is at the edge of town and—like all good Caribbean forts and hotels—overlooks the harbor; some rooms have stunning views. The exterior is primarily handsome island stonework. Rooms are painted in pale pastels, cushions and bedspread fabrics are floral prints, and balconies are private. You could also go all out and book one of the two suites that have their own private pools. Now owned by Pusser's, of Pusser's Company Store fame, this hotel is a comfortable choice if you want to be close to town. Two-line data port telephones and printer/fax machines in every room make it Tortola's only true business hotel. ⊠ *Waterfront Dr. (Box 3380),* ☎ *284/494–2587,* FAX *284/494–2002,* WEB *www.pussers.com. 12 rooms, 5 suites. Restaurant, bar, air-conditioning, in-room data ports, pool. AE, MC, V. EP.*

$$$ 🏨 **Village Cay Resort and Marina.** Right in town, this pleasant, compact hotel looks out on Road Harbour and several marinas. It's popular with yachters and those who love to shop and dine. Rooms have natural rattan furniture and pastel prints. Some units have cathedral ceilings and harbor views; others are quite small. After shopping in town, you can have a swim in the tiny pool and then head for the bar. ⊠ *Wickham's Cay I (Box 145),* ☎ *284/494–2771,* FAX *284/494–2773,* WEB *www.villagecay.com. 19 rooms. Restaurant, bar, air-conditioning, pool, marina. AE, MC, V. EP.*

$$ 🏨 **Hotel Castle Maria.** You can spend all the money you save here at the nearby in-town attractions. And these very simple accommodations have everything most folks need: a refrigerator and cable TV; some rooms also have full kitchenettes, balconies, and air-conditioning. Refresh yourself either in the bar or the freshwater pool. ⊠ *Waterfront Dr. (Box*

206), ☎ *284/494–2553,* FAX *284/494–2111. 30 rooms. Bar, air-conditioning (some), refrigerators, kitchenettes (some), pool. AE, MC, V. EP.*

$$$$ 🏨 **Frenchman's Cay Hotel.** This small, casual collection of one- and two-bedroom condos overlooks Drake's Channel. Each unit includes a full kitchen, a dining area, and a sitting room—ideal for families or couples who want the convenience of an apartmentlike setting. Rooms are done in neutral colors, with cream-color curtains and bedspreads and tile floors. Ceiling fans and breezes keep things cool. There are a small pool and a modest-size artificial beach that's sandy to the water's edge but rocky offshore (snorkelers will enjoy the reef here). The alfresco bar and dining room are breeze-swept and offer simple fare. ✉ *Frenchman's Cay (Box 1054), West End,* ☎ *284/495–4844 or 800/ 235–4077 (direct to hotel),* FAX *284/495–4056,* WEB *www.frenchmans.com. 9 units. Restaurant, bar, fans, kitchenettes, pool, tennis court, beach, snorkeling. AE, MC, V. EP.*

$$$$ 🏨 **Long Bay Beach Resort.** Spectacularly set on a 1-mi-long (1½-km-
★ long) arc of white sand, this resort is one of Tortola's best. Beachfront accommodations include tropical hideaways set on stilts within feet of the water's edge, spacious deluxe units with marble-top wet bars and showers, and roomy dressing areas with Italian tiles. Hillside choices have balconies or decks and dramatic views of distant islands. Some look out over the pool and some have comfortable seating areas and in-room whirlpools. In addition, spacious one- and two-bedroom hillside villas with full kitchens are available. Floral prints and rattan furniture are used throughout. The casual Beach restaurant offers all-day dining inside and around the beachside pool and is the spot for twice-weekly West Indian barbecues. The Garden Restaurant serves romantic gourmet dinners by candlelight five nights a week. The new spa and fitness center offers a full array of massage, facials, and body scrubs, as well as state-of-the-art exercise equipment. The tennis program is run by Peter Burwash International. A rustic 9-hole, par-3 pitch-and-putt golf course completes the complex. ✉ *Long Bay (Box 433, Road Town),* ☎ *284/495–4252 or 800/729–9599,* FAX *284/495–4677,* WEB *www.longbay.com. 78 rooms, 12 suites, 26 villas. 2 restaurants, 2 bars, air-conditioning, kitchenettes, 2 pools, massage, spa, 3 tennis courts, gym, beach, snorkeling, shops, meeting rooms. AE, MC, V. EP, MAP.*

$$$$ 🏨 **Sugar Mill Hotel.** The owners of this small, out-of-the-way hotel know
★ what they're doing—they were food and travel writers before they opened the Sugar Mill more than two decades ago. Their savvy has paid off: many visitors return year after year. The reception area, bar, and restaurant are in the ruins of an old sugar mill, and the walls throughout are hung with bright Haitian artwork. Guest houses are scattered up a hill; rooms are simply decorated in soft pastels and have rattan furnishings. A small circular pool is set into the hillside, and lunches and dinners (in season) are served on a terrace at the tiny beach. The Sugar Mill Restaurant is well known on the island. ✉ *Apple Bay (Box 425, Road Town),* ☎ *284/495–4355,* FAX *284/495–4696,* WEB *www.sugarmillhotel.com. 16 rooms, 4 suites, 2 villas. 2 restaurants, 2 bars, air-conditioning, pool, beach, snorkeling. AE, MC, V. EP, MAP.*

$$$$ 🏨 **The Villas of Fort Recovery Estates.** This complex has all the ingre-
★ dients for a good Caribbean vacation: grounds full of flowers; a remote beachside setting around the remnants of a Dutch fort; and friendly, helpful management. All the suites and the four-bedroom villa have excellent views (sliding glass doors open onto patios or balconies that face Drake's Channel and the beach) and fully equipped kitchens. Living rooms (not air-conditioned) can be used as a bedroom. A gourmet kitchen provides room-service dinners, served course by course

and accompanied by candlelight. There are exercise and yoga classes, massages, and VCRs and videos for rent. ⊠ *Waterfront Dr. (Box 239, Road Town),* ☎ *284/495–4354 or 800/367–8455 (direct to hotel),* FAX *284/495–4036,* WEB *www.fortrecovery.com. 14 suites, 1 villa. Kitchenettes, pool, massage, beach, snorkeling, baby-sitting. AE, MC, V. EP.*

$$$ ⌂ **Lambert Beach Resort.** On the somewhat remote north shore, this Mediterranean-style cottage complex has rooms in eight one-story buildings with red-tile roofs and white stucco exteriors. Two two-bedroom villas on a hillside have full kitchens. Rooms face the beach or look out on tropical gardens and have bold, colorful prints and blond rattan furniture. It's a very short walk to the stunning beach or the remarkably large pool. The restaurant offers alfresco breakfasts, lunches, and dinners. ⊠ *Lambert Bay (Box 534), East End,* ☎ *284/495–2877,* FAX *284/495–2876,* WEB *www.pussers.com. 34 rooms, 2 villas. Restaurant, bar, air-conditioning, kitchenettes (some), pool, tennis court, beach, snorkeling, windsurfing, shop. AE, MC, V. EP.*

$$$ ⌂ **Sebastian's on the Beach.** The best rooms here are the eight small rooms that open onto the beach. Although compact, they're airy and white, very simply decorated with floral-print curtains and bedspreads, and have terraces or balconies and great breezes and views (the ocean lulls you to sleep). Tiny bathrooms have only stall showers. The other 18 rooms are very basic, lack views, and can be noisy, but these are all air-conditioned. Some of these are across the street and are considerably cheaper than the beach rooms. The casual restaurant looks out over the water; at lunch you can order fresh salads, grilled vegetables, or soups and sandwiches; the dinner menu includes grilled fish, lobster, and steak. ⊠ *Apple Bay (Box 441, Road Town),* ☎ *284/495–4212 or 800/336–4870,* FAX *284/495–4466,* WEB *www.sebastiansbvi.com. 26 rooms. Restaurant, bar, snack bar, air-conditioning (some), fans, beach. AE. EP.*

$$ ⌂ **Ole Works Inn.** Tucked against a hill and across the road from a beautiful beach is this rustic, appealing inn—owned by local recording star Quito Rhymer. A steeply pitched roof along with wood and stonework add contemporary flair to what was once an old sugar mill that dates from the 18th century. Rooms are simply decorated, but some have private balconies and kitchenettes, and you can't beat the Cane Garden Bay location. The Honeymoon Suite has an indoor swing for two. ⊠ *Cane Garden Bay (Box 560, Road Town),* ☎ *284/495–4837,* FAX *284/495–9618. 15 rooms, 3 suites. Air-conditioning, fans, refrigerators. MC, V. EP.*

Private Homes and Villas

Areana Villas (⊠ Box 263, Road Town, ☎ 284/494–5864, FAX 284/494–7626, WEB www.areanavillas.com) represents top-of-the-line properties. Homes offer accommodations for 2 to 10 people in one- to five-bedroom villas decorated in soothing pastels. Many have pools, Jacuzzis, and glazed terra-cotta courtyards. On Long Bay, Areana represents Sunset House and Villas, an exquisite hideaway whose first guest was Britain's Princess Alexandra (but you needn't be royalty to receive the royal treatment here). The company also works with Equinox House, also on Long Bay, a handsome three-bedroom estate set amid lavish tumbling gardens. Rates range from expensive ($$$) to very expensive ($$$$) in season. **Lambert Beach Villas** (⊠ Lambert Estate Box 534, East End, ☎ 284/495–2877, FAX 284/495–2876) rents two- and three-bedroom villas on the hills overlooking Elizabeth Beach.

Campground

$ ⌂ **Brewers Bay Campground.** Both prepared and bare sites are on Brewers Bay, one of Tortola's prime snorkeling spots. Check out the ruins of the distillery that gave the bay its name. You'll find a small commissary and public bathrooms but no showers. ✉ *Brewers Bay (Box 185, Road Town),* ☎ *284/494–3463. 28 sites. Restaurant, bar, beach, windsurfing, baby-sitting. No credit cards.*

Dining

On Tortola local seafood is plentiful, and although other fresh ingredients are scarce, the island's chefs are a creative lot, who apply genius to whatever the weekly supply boat delivers. Contemporary American dishes prepared with a Caribbean influence are very popular. The fancier, more expensive restaurants have dress codes: long pants and collared shirts for men, and elegant, casual resort wear for women.

CATEGORY	COST*
$$$$	over $35
$$$	$25–$35
$$	$15–$25
$	under $15

per person for a main course at dinner

Road Town
AMERICAN/CASUAL

$$ ✕ **The Pub.** At this lively waterfront spot, tables are arranged along a terrace facing a small marina and the Road Town harbor. Hamburgers, salads, and sandwiches are typical lunch offerings. In the evening you can also choose grilled fish, steak, chicken, sautéed conch, or barbecued ribs. In fact, head here on Saturday night for all-you-can-eat ribs. There's entertainment on weekends, and locals gather here nightly for spirited dart games. ✉ *Waterfront Dr.,* ☎ *284/494–2608. Reservations not accepted. AE, DC, MC, V. No lunch Sun.*

$ ✕ **Pusser's Road Town Pub.** Almost everyone who visits Tortola stops here at least once to have a bite to eat and to sample the famous Pusser's Rum Painkiller (fruit juices and rum). The menu includes cheesy pizza, shepherd's pie, fish-and-chips, and deli sandwiches. Dine inside in air-conditioned comfort or outside on the veranda, which looks out on the harbor. Stop by on Friday for nickel beer night. ✉ *Waterfront Dr.,* ☎ *284/494–3897. AE, MC, V.*

CARIBBEAN

$$ ✕ **C and F Restaurant.** Crowds head to this casual spot for the best
★ barbecue in town (chicken, fish, and ribs), fresh local fish prepared your way, and excellent curries. Sometimes there's a wait for a table, but it's worth it. The restaurant is just outside Road Town, on a side street past the Moorings and Riteway. ✉ *Purcell Estate,* ☎ *284/494–4941. Reservations not accepted. AE, MC, V. No lunch.*

ECLECTIC

$$ ✕ **Virgin Queen.** The sailing and rugby crowds head here to play
★ darts, drink beer, and eat Queen's Pizza—a crusty, cheesy pie topped with sausage, onions, green peppers, and mushrooms. Also on the menu is excellent West Indian and English fare: salt fish, barbecued ribs with beans and rice, bangers and mash, shepherd's pie, chili, and grilled sirloin steak. ✉ *Fleming St.,* ☎ *284/494–2310. Reservations not accepted. No credit cards. Closed Sept. and Sun.*

FRENCH

$$ ✕ **Le Cabanon.** Birds and bougainvillea brighten the patio setting of this breezy French restaurant and bar, a popular gathering place for locals and visitors alike. Fresh oysters or fried mozzarella with tomatoes is a good appetizer choice. Then move on to the rack of lamb, the grilled salmon, or the rib-eye steak. Or try the shepherd's pie made with a French twist—duck instead of ground beef. Save room for such tasty dessert offerings as chocolate mousse, coconut mousse, apple tart, and a platter of French cheeses. ⊠ *Waterfront Dr.,* ☎ *284/494–8660. MC, V. Closed Sun.*

ITALIAN

\$\$ ✕ **Spaghetti Junction.** Popular with the boating crowd, this well-
★ known island favorite moved to new and roomier upstairs digs near the cruise ship dock. Join the crowd outside on the deck overlooking the marina or inside, where it's bustling. The expanded menu includes more fresh seafood and more nightly specials but still features house specialties such as penne with a spicy tomato sauce, spinach-mushroom lasagna, *cappellini* (very thin spaghetti) with shellfish, and jambalaya pasta. ⊠ *Inner Harbour Marina,* ☎ *284/494–4880. MC, V. Closed Sun. No lunch.*

\$ ✕ **Capriccio di Mare.** The owners of the well-known Brandywine Bay
★ restaurant also run this authentic little Italian outdoor café. People stop by in the morning for an espresso and fresh pastry and all day long for a cappuccino or a tiramisù, delicious toast Italiano (a grilled ham and Swiss cheese sandwich), a fresh salad, a bowl of perfectly cooked linguine or penne with a variety of sauces, or a crispy tomato and mozzarella pizza. Drink specialties include the Mango Bellini, an adaptation of the famous Bellini cocktail served by Harry's Bar in Venice. ⊠ *Waterfront Dr.,* ☎ *284/494–5369. Reservations not accepted. No credit cards. Closed Sun.*

MEXICAN

\$\$ ✕ **Lime 'n' Mango.** A long veranda is the romantic setting for this popular restaurant in the Treasure Isle Hotel. The menu features local specialties and surprisingly authentic Mexican cuisine. Try the conch fritters, salt fish cakes, or Jamaican calamari for an appetizer. The fajitas—chicken, beef, or vegetarian—are the best Mexican entrée; they arrive at your table sizzling in a hot iron frying pan, with a side of warm tortillas. The coconut shrimp is also popular. Saturday night crowds form here to enjoy the popular West Indian barbecue. ⊠ *Waterfront Dr.,* ☎ *284/494–2501. AE, MC, V.*

SEAFOOD

\$\$\$ ✕ **The Captain's Table.** Select the lobster you want from the pool here, and be careful not to fall in—it's in the floor right in the middle of the dining room. The menu also includes traditional escargots, fresh local fish, filet mignon with béarnaise sauce, duckling with berry sauce, and creative daily specials. Ceiling fans keep the dining room cool, but there are also tables on a breezy terrace overlooking the harbor. ⊠ *Columbus Centre, Wickham's Cay I,* ☎ *284/494–3885. AE, MC, V. No lunch Sat.*

Outside Road Town

AMERICAN/CASUAL

\$\$ ✕ **Pusser's Landing.** Yachters flock to this waterfront restaurant. Downstairs, from late morning to well into the evening, belly up to the outdoor mahogany bar or choose a waterside table for drinks, sandwiches, rotis, fish and chips, and pizzas. At dinnertime head upstairs for a harbor view and a quiet alfresco meal of grilled steak or local fish. ⊠ *Soper's Hole,* ☎ *284/495–4554. AE, MC, V.*

CARIBBEAN

\$\$ ✕ **Mrs. Scatliffe's.** The island's best West Indian cooking is here, according to many Tortolans (though some bemoan, "She's gone Continental"). Lunch and dinner are served on the upstairs terrace of Mrs. Scatliffe's home. The food is freshly prepared (vegetables come from the family garden); the baked chicken in coconut is meltingly tender. If you're lucky, after dinner you'll be treated to a lively *fungi* (bands that make music using household items—washboards, spoons, and the like—as instruments) performance by members of Mrs. Scatliffe's family. ⊠ *Carrot Bay,* ☎ *284/495–4556. Reservations essential. No credit cards.*

$$ ✕ **Quito's Gazebo.** This rustic beachside bar and restaurant is owned and operated by Quito Rhymer, a multitalented BVI recording star who plays the guitar and sings Calypso ballads and love songs Tuesday, Thursday, Friday, and Sunday; a reggae band performs Saturday. The menu is Caribbean with an emphasis on fresh fish. Try the conch stew or the curried chicken. A Caribbean buffet is featured on Sunday night, and Friday is fish-fry night. The atmosphere is so convivial that by the time you finish dinner you may find yourself swapping yarns with some colorful local personalities. ⊠ *Cane Garden Bay,* ☎ *284/495–4837. MC, V. Closed Mon.*

$ ✕ **Myett's.** Right on the beach, this bi-level restaurant-bar is hopping
★ day and night. Chowder made with fresh Anegada lobsters is the specialty, though the menu includes everything from hamburgers to fruit platters and vegetarian dishes to grilled shrimp, steak, and tuna. There's live entertainment on Saturday, Sunday, and Monday nights. ⊠ *Cane Garden Bay,* ☎ *284/495–9649. Reservations not accepted. AE, MC, V.*

CONTEMPORARY

$$$ ✕ **Eclipse.** Dine under a canopy of stars at this popular spot that isn't
★ much more than an outdoor terrace filled with tables. The menu is a mixture of fusion and Caribbean cuisine. Spend the evening sampling one dish after another—cracked conch, baked chevre, tuna carpaccio— as you order off the two-page grazing menu, or dig into the spicy curries, fusion chicken, fresh grilled Anegada swordfish, and vegetarian dishes on the regular menu. ⊠ *Fat Hog's Bay, East End,* ☎ *284/495– 1646. AE, MC, V. No lunch Aug.*

$$$ ✕ **Skyworld.** Come to this mountaintop aerie at sunset and watch the
★ western horizon go ablaze with color, then settle back in the casually elegant dining room to feast. The superbly cooked filet mignon with port wine and mushroom sauce is truly exceptional. Other specialties include the smoked salmon in whiskey sauce appetizer, grilled local fish, roast duck, cinnamon roast pork loin with pears and rosemary, and key lime pie. The very simple lunch menu features hamburgers and sandwiches, though the restaurant can be crowded at this time when a cruise ship docks. ⊠ *Ridge Rd.,* ☎ *284/494–3567. AE, MC, V.*

$$$ ✕ **Sugar Mill Restaurant.** Candles gleam, and the background music is peaceful in this romantic restaurant. Inside a 360-year-old mill that's part of their Sugar Mill Hotel, owners Jeff and Jinx Morgan never disappoint. Well-prepared selections on the à la carte menu, which changes nightly, include pasta and vegetarian entrées. Crab bisque with crab rolls or Caribbean sweet-potato soup are good starters. House favorite entrées include the Jamaican jerk pork roast, the regimental beef curry with *poppadoms* (Indian popovers), marinated roast duck, and fresh fish with spicy creole sauce. ⊠ *Apple Bay,* ☎ *284/495–4355. AE, MC, V. No lunch.*

$$ ✕ **Garden Restaurant.** Relax over dinner in this dimly lit, open-air restau-
★ rant at Long Bay Beach Resort. Tables are well-spaced on several levels, and the atmosphere is intimate. The extensive menu changes daily. Appetizers might include escargots and Portobello mushrooms in pastry, curried cauliflower soup, or shrimp fritters; the list of entrées could feature grilled Anegada swordfish steak with avocado hollandaise, pan-roasted duck with Portobello mushrooms, or a filet mignon served with artichoke duxelle. There are always at least five desserts to choose from, such as Belgian chocolate mousse, cherry cheesecake, and carrot cake. ⊠ *Long Bay,* ☎ *284/495–4252. AE, MC, V. No lunch.*

ENGLISH

$$ ✕ **The Last Resort.** Actually on Bellamy Cay, just off Beef Island (free ferry service is provided to and from Trellis Bay/Beef Island), this spot features an English buffet, complete with pumpkin soup, prime rib, and Yorkshire pudding, as well as vegetarian selections. This is also the site of the longest-running show in the BVI. For nearly 30 years, guests have been laughing at the inimitable cabaret humor and ribald ditties of owner Tony Snell, the BVI's answer to Benny Hill. He performs nightly at 9:30. ⊠ *Bellamy Cay,* ☎ *284/495–2520. AE, MC, V.*

ITALIAN

$$$ ✕ **Brandywine Bay.** Here, candlelit outdoor tables have sweeping
★ views of neighboring islands, and owner-chef Davide Pugliese prepares foods the Tuscan way: grilled with lots of fresh herbs. The remarkable menu can include homemade mozzarella, foie gras, grilled local wahoo, and grilled veal chop with ricotta and sun-dried tomatoes; it always includes duck with an exotic fruit sauce. The wine list is excellent, and the lemon tart and the tiramisu are irresistible. ⊠ *Sir Francis Drake Hwy., east of Road Town,* ☎ *284/495–2301. Reservations essential. AE, MC, V. No lunch. Closed Sun.*

Beaches

Beaches in the BVI are less developed than those on St. Thomas or St. Croix. Try to get out on a dive-snorkeling boat or a day-trip sailing vessel at least once. This is often the best way to reach the most virgin Virgin beaches, which are on deserted islands. Tortola's north side has several perfect palm-fringed white-sand beaches that curl around turquoise bays and coves. Nearly all are accessible by car (preferably one with four-wheel-drive), albeit down bumpy roads that corkscrew precipitously. Facilities run the gamut, from absolutely none to a number of beachside bars and restaurants as well as places to rent watersports equipment.

If you want to surf, the area of **Apple Bay** (⊠ North Shore Rd.), which includes Little Apple Bay and Capoon's Bay, is the spot—although the beach itself is pretty narrow. Sebastian's, the very casual hotel here, caters to those in search of the perfect wave. Good surf is never a sure thing, but you're more apt to find it in January and February.

The water at **Brewers Bay** (⊠ Brewers Bay Rd. W or Brewers Bay Rd. E) is good for snorkeling, and there are a campground and beach bar here. The beach and its old sugar mill and rum-distillery ruins are just north of Cane Garden Bay, just past Luck Hill. There's another entrance just east of the Skyworld restaurant.

The enticing **Cane Garden Bay** (⊠ Cane Garden Bay Rd.) has exceptionally calm, crystalline waters and a silky stretch of sand. It's the closest beach to Road Town—one steep uphill and downhill drive—and is one of the BVI's best-known anchorages (unfortunately, it can be very crowded when cruise ships are in town). You can rent sailboards and such, stargaze from the bow of a boat, and nosh or sip at a variety of places, including Quito's Gazebo.

Lined with palm trees, wide, sandy **Elizabeth Beach** (⊠ Ridge Rd.) is accessible by walking down a private road. However, the undertow can be severe here in winter. The oft-deserted **Josiah's Bay** (⊠ Ridge Rd.) is a favored place to picnic or to hang ten, although in winter the undertow is often strong.

The scenery at **Long Bay, Beef Island** (⊠ Beef Island Rd.) draws superlatives: you can catch a glimpse of Little Camanoe and Great Camanoe islands, and if you walk around the bend to the right, you can see little Marina Cay and Scrub Island. Long Bay is also a good place to find seashells. Take the Queen Elizabeth II Bridge to Beef Island and watch for a small dirt turnoff on the left before the airport. Follow the road that curves along the east side of the dried-up marsh flat; don't drive directly across the flat as you can damage it.

Long Bay West (⊠ Long Bay Rd.) is a stunning 1-mi (1½-km) stretch of white sand. Have your camera ready for snapping the breathtaking approach. Although Long Bay Resort sprawls along part of it, the entire beach is open to the public. The water isn't as calm here as at Cane Garden or Brewers Bay, but it's still swimmable.

After bouncing your way to the beautiful **Smuggler's Cove** (⊠ Belmont Rd.), you'll feel as if you've found a hidden piece of the island, although you probably won't be alone on weekends. There's a fine view of Jost Van Dyke Island, and the snorkeling is good.

About the only thing you'll find moving at **Trunk Bay** (⊠ Ridge Rd.) is the surf. It's directly north of Road Town, midway between Cane Garden Bay and Beef Island, and to reach it you have to hike down a *ghut* (gully) from Ridge Road.

Outdoor Activities and Sports

Participant Sports

FISHING

The deep-sea fishing here is so good that tournaments draw competitors from around the world for the largest bluefish, wahoo, and shark. You can bring a catch back to your hotel's restaurant, and the staff will prepare it for you for dinner. A half-day of deep-sea fishing runs $300–$350, a full day $500–$600. For a few hours of reel fun, try **Persistence** (⊠ Towers, West End, ☎ 284/495–4122). If bone fishing is your cup of tea, call **Caribbean Fly Fishing** (⊠ Nanny Cay, ☎ 284/499–1590).

HORSEBACK RIDING

If you've ever wanted to ride a horse along a deserted beach, now's your chance. Or you can head up to Tortola's ridges for spectacular views. **Shadow Stables** (⊠ Ridge Rd., ☎ 284/494–2262) offers small group rides for $20 per person per hour.

SAILING

The BVI are among the world's most popular sailing destinations. They're close together and surrounded by calm waters, so it's fairly easy to sail from one anchorage to the next. If you know how to sail, you can charter a bare boat (perhaps for your entire vacation); if you're unschooled, you can hire a boat with a captain or learn to sail. Prices vary quite broadly depending on the type and size of the boat you wish to charter. In season, a weekly charter runs $1,500–$35,000.

BVI Yacht Charters (⊠ Inner Harbour Marina, Road Town, ☎ 284/494–4289) offers 38-ft to 51-ft sailboats for charter—with or without a captain, whichever you prefer. **Catamaran Charters** (⊠ Nanny Cay Marina, Nanny Cay, ☎ 284/495–6661) charters catamarans with or without captains. **Full Sail Sailing School** (⊠ Seabreeze Marina, East End, ☎ 284/494–0512) offers beginner and advanced sailing lessons. **The Moorings** (⊠ Wickham's Cay II, Road Town, ☎ 284/494–2501 or 800/535–7289), considered one of the best bareboat operations in the world, has a large fleet of well-maintained, mostly Beneteau yachts. Hire a captain or sail the boat yourself. If you prefer a powerboat, call **Regency Yacht Vacations** (⊠ Hodge's Creek, ☎ 284/495–1970) for both bareboat and captained charters.

SCUBA DIVING AND SNORKELING

Clear waters and numerous reefs afford some wonderful opportunities for underwater exploration. **Alice in Wonderland** is a deep dive south of Ginger Island with a wall that slopes gently from 15 ft (5 m) to 100 ft (30 m). It features huge mushroom-shape coral, hence its name.

Crabs, lobsters, and shimmering fan corals make their home in the tunnels, ledges, and overhangs of **Blonde Rock,** a pinnacle that goes from just 15 ft (5 m) below the surface to 60 ft (18 m) deep. It's between Dead Chest and Salt Island.

When the currents aren't too strong, **Brewer's Bay Pinnacle** (20–90 ft/6–27 m down) teems with sea life.

The *Chikuzen,* sunk northwest of Brewer's Bay in 1981, is a 246-ft vessel in 75 ft (23 m) of water; it's home to thousands of fish, colorful corals, and big rays.

At **The Indians,** near Pelican Island, colorful corals decorate canyons and grottoes created by four large, jagged pinnacles that rise 50 ft (15 m) from the ocean floor.

In 1867 the RMS *Rhone,* a 310-ft-long royal mail steamer, split in two when it sank in a devastating hurricane. It's so well preserved that it was used in the movie *The Deep*. You can see the crow's nest and bowsprit, the cargo hold in the bow, and the engine and enormous propeller shaft in the stern. Its four parts are at various depths from 30 to 80 ft (9 to 24 m; nearby Rhone Reef is only 20–50 ft/6–15 m down). Get yourself some snorkeling gear and hop a dive boat to this wreck, off Salt Island (across the channel from Road Town) and part of the BVI National Parks Trust. Every dive outfit in the BVI runs superlative scuba and snorkel tours here.

The **Painted Walls** is a shallow dive site where corals and sponges create a kaleidoscope of colors on the walls of four long gullies. It's northeast of Dead Chest.

Baskin' in the Sun (⊠ Prospect Reef, ☎ 284/494–2858) offers beginner and advanced diving courses and daily trips. Trainers teach open-water, rescue, advanced diving, and resort courses. The resort course costs $96; a one-tank dive is $76 and a two-tank dive is $96, including equipment.

Blue Waters Divers (⊠ Nanny Cay, ☎ 284/494–2847) teaches resort, open-water, rescue, and advanced diving courses and also makes daily trips. Resort courses cost $90, one-tank dives run $70, two-tank dives cost $90, including equipment.

Underwater Safaris (⊠ The Moorings, ☎ 284/494–3235) has resort and advanced diving courses, including rescue and open water, and scheduled day and night dives. The resort course fee is $101; one-tank dives are $68 with your own equipment, $78 including equipment. Two-tank dives cost $84 with your own equipment, $94 including equipment.

TENNIS

Tortola's tennis options range from simple, untended, concrete courts to professionally maintained facilities that host organized tournaments. The courts listed below are all open to the public; some have restrictions for nonguests.

Frenchman's Cay Hotel (⊠ West End, ☎ 284/495–4844) has an artificial-grass court with a pretty view of Sir Francis Drake Channel. Patrons of the hotel or restaurant can use the court free of charge; for others there's an hourly fee of $5. Although the court is night-lit, there's no pro available to be your guiding light, so to speak.

Long Bay Beach Resort (✉ Long Bay, ☎ 284/495–4252) features two courts and a tennis program run by Peter Burwash International. Private lessons are $55 per hour. Nonguests may rent a court for $10 an hour. Tennis rackets can be rented for $7 an hour.

Moorings-Mariner Inn (✉ Waterfront Dr., Road Town, ☎ 284/494–2332) has one all-weather hard court to which inn, marina, and Treasure Isle Hotel guests have free access; if it's empty, nonguests can use it at no charge. The lack of lights and a pro staffer may leave you in the dark, though.

Prospect Reef Resort (✉ Waterfront Dr., Road Town, ☎ 284/494–3311) guests can play free by day (there's a fee for lights) on any of six hard-surface courts; nonguests pay $7 an hour. You can make an appointment for lessons ($40 an hour) with the island's most famous pro, Mike Adamson.

WINDSURFING
The winds are so steady here that some locals use sailboards to get from island to island. Three of the best spots for sailboarding are Nanny Cay, Slaney Point, and Trellis Bay on Beef Island.

Boardsailing BVI (✉ Nanny Cay, ☎ 284/495–0422; ✉ Trellis Bay, Beef Island, ☎ 284/495–2447) rents equipment for $30 a half-day and offers private and group lessons.

With **HIHO** (✉ Prospect Reef Resort, Waterfront Dr., Road Town, ☎ 284/494–0337) you can take private or group lessons or rent equipment for $30 a half-day.

Spectator Sports
BASKETBALL
The NBA games are a national passion and folks also play pretty good basketball here. Diehard fans can catch games at the New Recreation Grounds on Monday, Wednesday, Friday, or Saturday between May and August.

CRICKET
Fans of this sport are fiercely loyal and exuberant. Matches are held at the New Recreation Grounds, next to the J. R. O'Neal Botanic Gardens weekends February–April.

SOFTBALL
If you enjoy watching softball, you can catch local games on weekend evenings at the Old Recreation Grounds between Long Bush Road and Lower Estate Road. The season runs February–August.

Shopping

The BVI aren't really a shopper's delight, but there are many shops showcasing original items—from jams and spices to resort wear to excellent artwork. Don't be put off by an informal shop entrance; some of the best finds in the BVI lie behind shabby doors.

Areas
Many shops and boutiques are clustered along and just off Road Town's **Main Street.** You can shop in Road Town's **Wickham's Cay** area adjacent to the marina. There's an ever-growing number of art and clothing stores at **Soper's Hole,** in West End.

Specialty Items
ART
Caribbean Fine Arts Ltd. (✉ Main St., Road Town, ☎ 284/494–4240) carries a wide range of Caribbean art, including original watercolors,

oils, and acrylics, as well as signed prints, limited-edition serigraphs, and turn-of-the-20th-century sepia photographs. **Fluke's** (⊠ Trellis Bay, East End, ☎ no phone) is the place to come for unique island maps, appealing prints, and colorful T-shirts. **Sunny Caribbee Art Gallery** (⊠ Main St., Road Town, ☎ 284/494–2178) has many paintings, prints, and watercolors by artists from throughout the Caribbean.

CLOTHES AND TEXTILES

Arawak (⊠ on the dock at Nanny Cay, ☎ 284/494–5240) carries gifts, batik sundresses, sportswear and resort wear for men and women, accessories, and children's clothing. **Caribbean Handprints** (⊠ Main St., Road Town, ☎ 284/494–3717) creates Caribbean-theme silk-screened fabric and sells it by the yard or in all forms of clothing and beach bags. **Latitude 18°** (⊠ Main St., Road Town, ☎ 284/494–7807; ⊠ Soper's Hole Marina, ☎ 284/495–4347) sells Maui Jim, Smith, Oakley, and Revo sunglasses; Freestyle, Quiksilver, and Roxy watches; and a fine collection of sandals, beach towels, sundresses, and sarongs. **Pusser's Company Store** (⊠ Main St. and Waterfront Rd., Road Town, ☎ 284/494–2467; ⊠ Soper's Hole Marina, ☎ 284/495–4603) features nautical memorabilia, ship models, marine paintings, an entire line of clothes and gift items bearing the Pusser's logo, handsome decorator bottles of Pusser's rum, Caribbean books, and luggage. **Sea Urchin** (⊠ Waterfront, Columbus Centre, Road Town, ☎ 284/494–2044; ⊠ Mill Mall, Road Town, ☎ 284/494–4108; ⊠ Soper's Hole Marina, ☎ 284/495–4850) is the source for local books, island jewelry, sunglasses, and resort wear—print shirts and shorts, colorful swimsuits, cover-ups, sandals, T-shirts—for the whole family. **Serendipity/Domino** (⊠ Main St., Road Town, ☎ 284/494–5879) showcases a colorful array of comfortable, light cotton clothing—including selections from Indonesia—as well as island jewelry and gift items. **Turtle Dove Boutique** (⊠ Flemming St., Road Town, ☎ 284/494–3611) is one of the best shops in the BVI for swimwear, silk and linen dresses, and gifts and accessories for the home. **Violet's** (⊠ Wickham's Cay I, ☎ 284/494–6398) features a collection of beautiful silk lingerie and a small line of designer dresses. **Zenaida's of West End** (⊠ Frenchman's Cay, ☎ 284/495–4867) displays the fabric finds of Argentine Vivian Jenik Helm, who travels through South America, Africa, and India in search of batiks, hand-painted and hand-blocked fabrics, and interesting weaves that can be made into pareos (women's wraps) or wall hangings. The shop also sells unusual bags, belts, sarongs, scarves, and ethnic jewelry.

FOODSTUFFS

Ample Hamper (⊠ Village Cay Marina, Wickham's Cay I, ☎ 284/494–2494; ⊠ Soper's Hole Marina, ☎ 284/495–4684) has cheeses, wines, fresh fruits, and canned goods from the United Kingdom and the United States. You can have the management here provision your yacht or rental villa. **Gourmet Galley** (⊠ Wickham's Cay II, Road Town, ☎ 284/494–6999) sells wines, cheeses, fresh produce, and provides full provisioning for yachtspeople and villa renters.

GIFTS

Buccaneer's Bounty (⊠ Main St., Road Town, ☎ 284/494–7510) purveys greeting cards, pirate memorabilia, nautical and tropical artwork, books on seashells and the islands, and Christmas ornaments. **Caribbean Corner Spice House** (⊠ Soper's Hole, ☎ 284/495–4498) sells exotic herbs and spices and homemade jams, jellies, hot sauces, and natural soaps. You'll find Cuban cigars here, too. **J. R. O'Neal, Ltd.** (⊠ Main St., Road Town, ☎ 284/494–2292) stocks the shelves of its somewhat hidden shop with fine crystal, Royal Worcester china, hand-painted Italian dishes, handblown Mexican glassware, Spanish ceramics, and Indian woven rugs and tablecloths. **Sunny Caribbee Herb and Spice**

Company (⊠ Main St., Road Town, ☎ 284/494–2178), in a brightly painted West Indian house, packages its own herbs, teas, coffees, vinegars, hot sauces, soaps, skin and suntan lotions, and exotic concoctions—Arawak Love Potion and Island Hangover Cure, for example. You'll also find Caribbean books and art as well as hand-painted decorative accessories.

JEWELRY

Columbian Emeralds International (⊠ Wickham's Cay I, Road Town, ☎ 284/494–7477), a Caribbean chain catering to the cruise-ship crowd, is the source for duty-free emeralds plus other gems, gold jewelry, crystal, and china. **Samarkand** (⊠ Main St., Road Town, ☎ 284/494–6415) crafts charming gold and silver pendants, earrings, bracelets, and pins—many with an island theme: seashells, lizards, pelicans, palm trees. You'll also find genuine Spanish pieces of eight (coins—old Spanish pesos worth eight reals—from sunken galleons).

PERFUMES AND COSMETICS

Flamboyance (⊠ Main St., Road Town, ☎ 284/494–4099; ⊠ Soper's Hole Marina, ☎ 284/495–5946) carries designer fragrances and upscale cosmetics.

Nightlife and the Arts

Nightlife

Like any good sailing destination, Tortola has watering holes that are popular with salty and not-so-salty dogs. Many offer entertainment; check the weekly *Limin' Times* for schedules. The local beverage is the painkiller, an innocent-tasting mixture of fruit juices and rums. It goes down smoothly but packs quite a punch, so give yourself a moment before you order another.

Bing's Drop In Bar. This rollicking local hangout has a DJ nightly in season. ⊠ *Fat Hog's Bay, East End,* ☎ *284/495–2627.*

Bomba's Surfside Shack. By day this little shack—covered with everything from crepe-paper leis to license plates to colorful graffiti—looks like a pile of junk; by night it's one of Tortola's liveliest spots and one of the Caribbean's most famous beach bars. Sunday at 4 there's always some sort of live music, and Wednesday at 8 the locally famous Blue Haze Combo shows up to play everything from reggae to Top 40 tunes. Every full moon, bands play all night long and people flock here from all over. ⊠ *Apple Bay,* ☎ *284/495–4148.*

Ceta's Place. Every Thursday night there's a fish fry and a live band at this informal spot. ⊠ *Capoon's Bay,* ☎ *no phone.*

Jolly Roger. An ever-changing array of local, U.S., and down-island bands plays everything from rhythm and blues to reggae to country to good old rock and roll Friday and Saturday—and sometimes Sunday—starting at 8. ⊠ *West End,* ☎ *284/495–4559.*

Myett's. Local bands play here Saturday, Sunday, and Monday evenings, and there's usually a lively dance crowd. ⊠ *Cane Garden Bay,* ☎ *284/495–9543.*

The Pub. Here you'll find an all-day happy hour on Friday, and Ruben Chinnery on the guitar Friday and Saturday evenings from 6 to 9. ⊠ *Waterfront St., Road Town,* ☎ *284/494–2608.*

Pusser's Deli. Thursday is nickel-beer night, and crowds gather here for courage (John Courage, that is) by the pint. Other nights try Pusser's famous mixed drinks—painkillers—and snack on the excellent pizza. ⊠ *Waterfront St., Road Town,* ☎ *284/494–4199.*

Pusser's Landing. The schedule varies nightly, but you can usually count on some kind of live music (it could be reggae, rock, or a steel band) on Friday and Saturday evenings and Sunday afternoon. ⊠ *Soper's Hole, West End,* ☏ *284/495–4554.*

Quito's Gazebo. BVI recording star Quito Rhymer sings island ballads and love songs, accompanied by the guitar at this rustic beachside bar-restaurant. Solo shows are on Sunday, Tuesday, and Thursday nights at 8:30; Friday and Saturday, Quito and the band—The Edge—pump out a variety of tunes. ⊠ *Cane Garden Bay,* ☏ *284/495–4837.*

Sebastian's. There's often live music here on Saturday and Sunday, and you can dance under the stars. ⊠ *Apple Bay,* ☏ *284/495–4214.*

The Arts
Classics in the Atrium. Musicians from around the world perform here October–February each year. Past artists have included Britain's premier a cappella group, Black Voices; New Orleans jazz pianist Ellis Marsalis; and Keith Lockhart and the Serenac Quartet (from the Boston Pops Symphony). ⊠ *The Atrium at the H. Lavity Stoutt Community College, Paraquita Bay,* ☏ *284/494–4994.*

Exploring Tortola

Tortola doesn't have many historical sights, but it does have lots of beautiful natural scenery. Although you could explore the island's 10 square mi (26 square km) in a few hours, opting for such a whirlwind tour would be a mistake. Life in the fast lane has no place amid some of the Caribbean's most breathtaking panoramas and beaches. Also the roads are extraordinarily steep and twisting, making driving demanding. The best strategy is to explore a bit of the island at a time. For example, you might try Road Town (the island's main town) one morning and a drive to Cane Garden Bay and West End (a little town on, of course, the island's west end) the next afternoon. Or consider a visit to East End, a *very* tiny town located exactly where its name suggests. The north shore is where you'll find all the best beaches.

Numbers in the margin correspond to points of interest on the Tortola map.

Sights to See
❷ Ft. Burt. The most intact historic ruin on Tortola was built by the Dutch in the early 17th century to safeguard Road Harbour. It sits on a hill at the western edge of Road Town and is now the site of a small hotel and restaurant. The foundations and magazine remain, and the structure offers a commanding view of the harbor. ⊠ *Waterfront Dr.,* ☏ *no phone.* 🖼 *Free.* ☼ *Daily dawn–dusk.*

❹ Ft. Recovery. The unrestored ruins of a 17th-century Dutch fort, 30 ft in diameter, sit amid a profusion of tropical greenery on the Villas of Fort Recovery Estates grounds. There's not much to see here, and there are no guided tours, but you're welcome to stop by and poke around. ⊠ *Waterfront Dr.,* ☏ *284/485–4467.* 🖼 *Free.*

❺ Frenchman's Cay. On this little island connected by a causeway to Tortola's western end, there are a marina and a captivating complex of pastel West Indian–style buildings with shady balconies, shuttered windows, and gingerbread trim that house art galleries, boutiques, and restaurants. Pusser's Landing here is a lively place to stop for a cold drink (many are made with Pusser's famous rum) and a sandwich and watch the boats in harbor.

❸ J. R. O'Neal Botanic Gardens. Take a walk through this 4-acre show-case of lush plant life. There are sections devoted to prickly cacti and succulents, hothouses for ferns and orchids, gardens of medicinal herbs, and plants and trees indigenous to the seashore. From the tourist board office in Road Town, cross Waterfront Drive and walk one block over to Main Street and turn right. Keep walking until you see the high school. The gardens are on your left. ⊠ *Botanic Station,* ☎ *no phone.* 💷 *Free.* ⊙ *Mon.–Sat. 9–4:30.*

❾ **Mt. Healthy National Park.** The remains of an 18th-century sugar plantation are here. The windmill structure has been restored, and you can see the ruins of a mill, a factory with boiling houses, storage areas, stables, a hospital, and many dwellings. This is a nice place to picnic. ⊠ *Ridge Rd.,* ☎ *no phone.* 💷 *Free.* ⊙ *Daily dawn–dusk.*

❻ **North Shore Shell Museum.** On Tortola's north shore, this casual museum has a very informal exhibit of shells, unusually shaped driftwood, fish traps, and traditional wooden boats. ⊠ *North Shore Rd.,* ☎ *284/ 495–4714.* 💷 *Free.* ⊙ *Daily dawn–dusk.*

❶ **Road Town.** The laid-back capital of the BVI looks out over Road Harbour. It takes only an hour or so to stroll down Main Street and along the waterfront, checking out the traditional West Indian buildings, painted in pastel colors and with high-pitched, corrugated-tin roofs; bright shutters; and delicate fretwork trim. For hotel and sightseeing brochures and the latest information on everything from taxi rates to ferry-boat schedules, stop in the BVI Tourist Board office. Or just choose a seat on one of the benches in Sir Olva Georges Square, on Waterfront Drive, and watch the people come and go from the ferry dock and customs office across the street.

❼ **Sage Mountain National Park.** At 1,716 ft (525 m) Sage Mountain is the highest peak in the BVI. From the parking area a trail leads you in a loop not only to the peak itself (and extraordinary views) but also to a small rain forest, sometimes shrouded in mist. Most of the forest was cut down over the centuries to clear land for sugarcane, cotton, and other crops; to create pastureland; or to simply utilize the stands of timber; in 1964 this park was established to preserve what rain forest remained. Up here you can see mahogany trees, white cedars, mountain guavas, elephant-ear vines, mamey trees, and giant bullet woods, to say nothing of such birds as mountain doves and thrushes. Take a taxi from Road Town or drive up Joe's Hill Road and make a left onto Ridge Road toward Chalwell and Doty villages. The road dead-ends at the park. ⊠ *Ridge Rd.,* ☎ *no phone.* 💷 *Free.*

★ ❽ **Skyworld.** Drive up here and climb the observation tower for a stunning, 360-degree view of numerous islands and cays. On a clear day you can even see St. Croix (40 mi/64½ km away) and Anegada (20 mi/32 km away). ⊠ *Ridge Rd.,* ☎ *no phone.* 💷 *Free.*

VIRGIN GORDA

Virgin Gorda, with its mountainous central portion connected by skinny necks of land to southern and northern appendages—on a map it looks like the slightest breeze would cause the whole island to splinter apart—is quite different from Tortola. The pace is even slower here, and Virgin Gorda receives less rain, so some areas are more arid and home to scrub brush and cactus. Goats and cattle own the right of way, and the unpretentious friendliness of the people is winning.

Lodging

Virgin Gorda's charming hostelries appeal to a select, appreciative clientele; repeat business is extremely high. Visitors who prefer Sher-

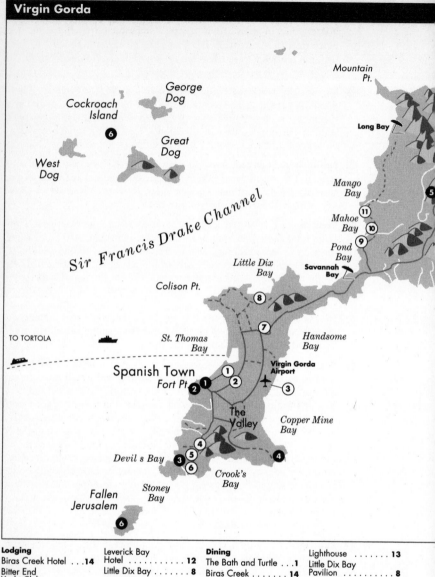

Lodging

Biras Creek Hotel ...**14**
Bitter End
Yacht Club
and Marina **15**
Drake's
Anchorage **16**
Guavaberry
Spring Bay
Vacation Homes **4**

Leverick Bay
Hotel **12**
Little Dix Bay **8**
Mango Bay
Resort **10**
Olde Yard Inn **7**
Paradise Beach
Resort **11**
Virgin Gorda
Villa Rentals **13**

Dining

The Bath and Turtle ...**1**
Biras Creek **14**
Chez Bamboo **2**
The Clubhouse **15**
Drake's Anchorage ...**16**
The Flying Iguana ...**3**
Giorgio's Table **9**

Lighthouse **13**
Little Dix Bay
Pavilion **8**
Mad Dog's **5**
Olde Yard Inn **7**
Sip and Dip Grill **7**
Top of the Baths **6**

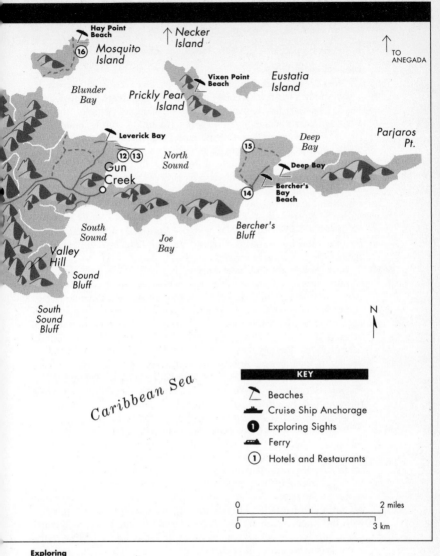

Exploring

The Baths 3
Coastal Islands 6
Copper Mine
Point 4
Little Fort
National Park 2
Spanish Town 1
Virgin Gorda Peak
National Park 5

atons, Marriotts, and the like may feel they get more for their money on other islands, but the peace and pampering offered on Virgin Gorda are priceless to the discriminating traveler.

For approximate costs, *see* the lodging price chart *in* Tortola.

Hotels and Inns

$$$$ **Biras Creek Hotel.** A long-time guest purchased this 140-acre hide-
★ away and has made it so classy that it's accepted by the exclusive Re-lais & Chateaux family of hotels. Units are in duplex cottages, and each has a bedroom and a living room with terra-cotta floor tiles and a decor of soft Caribbean colors. Off the bath is an enclosed garden shower that's open to the sky. Although entrances are hidden among the trees, many cottages are feet from the water's edge. Bike paths and trails lead to the beaches and the outstanding Biras Creek restaurant. On a hilltop affording stunning views of North Sound is the open-air stonework bar-restaurant area. A sailaway package includes two nights on a private yacht. ⊠ *North Sound (Box 54),* ☎ *284/494–3555 or 800/223–1108,* FAX *284/494–3557,* WEB *www.biras.com. 33 suites, 2 villas. 3 restaurants, bar, air-conditioning, pool, 2 tennis courts, hiking, beach, snorkeling, windsurfing, boating, bicycles, shops. AE, MC, V. FAP.*

$$$$ **Bitter End Yacht Club and Marina.** This family-oriented, convivial resort-cum-marina is accessible only by boat. Accommodations range from comfortable hillside or beachfront rooms with spacious bal-conies to live-aboard yachts. Your day can include snorkeling and div-ing trips to nearby reefs, cruises, windsurfing lessons, excursions to local attractions, and lessons at the well-regarded Nick Trotter Sailing School. When the sun goes down, the festivities continue at The Club-house, an open-air restaurant-bar overlooking North Sound. ⊠ *North Sound (Box 46),* ☎ *284/494–2746 or 800/872–2392,* FAX *284/494–4756,* WEB *www.beyc.com. 95 rooms. 2 restaurants, bar, air-conditioning (some), pool, beach, dive shop, snorkeling, windsurfing, boating, wa-terskiing, children's programs. AE, MC, V. EP, FAP.*

$$$$ **Drake's Anchorage Resort Inn.** Set on the edge of its own, very hilly,
★ 125-acre island (on the northwest side of North Sound), this tiny, se-cluded, and delightful getaway provides the true privacy of an elegant resort, but without the pampering or the formality. Dinner attire here means changing from bathing suit to comfortable cottons. Three West Indian–style waterfront bungalows contain 4 rooms and 5 suites that are simply furnished in rattan, wicker, and pastel prints. Three villas with full kitchens are also available. The appealing Drake's Anchor-age Resort Inn restaurant is an elegant stop for all meals. Hiking trails, water-sports facilities, four delightful beaches, and hammocks here and there make this a place you never want to leave. In 2000, rooms and suites and the restaurant were completely refurbished and it shows. ⊠ *North Sound (Box 2510),* ☎ *284/494–2254 or 800/624–6651 (direct to hotel),* FAX *284/495–2254,* WEB *www.drakesanchorage.com. 4 rooms, 5 suites, 3 villas. Restaurant, bar, hiking, beach, snorkeling, boating. AE, MC, V. MAP.*

$$$$ **Little Dix Bay.** Relaxed elegance is the hallmark here. The resort sits
★ amid the mangroves, along a curving beach. Duplexes with hexago-nal units and quadraplex cottages are tucked among the trees and on a little hill. Interiors have handsome fieldstone walls and are decorated in Caribbean prints. About half the rooms are air-conditioned. Lawns are beautifully manicured; the reef-protected beach is long and silken; and the candlelight dining in an open, peak-roof pavilion is memorable. This resort is popular with honeymooners and older couples who have been coming for years. The Little Dix Bay Pavilion is an unforgettable setting for any meal. ⊠ *Little Dix Bay (Box 70),* ☎ *284/495–5555,*

FAX *284/495–5661,* WEB *www.littledixbay.com. 94 rooms, 4 suites. 3 restaurants, 2 bars, air-conditioning, 7 tennis courts, beach, snorkeling, windsurfing, library, children's programs. AE, MC, V. EP, MAP.*

$$$ 🏠 **Olde Yard Inn.** Owners Charlie Williams and Carol Kaufman have ★ cultivated a friendly, refreshing atmosphere at this quiet retreat outside Spanish Town. Classical music plays in the bar, and books line the walls of the octagonal library cottage. Rooms are cozy and simply furnished (in warmer months request a room with air-conditioning). You can make arrangements for day sails and scuba excursions, and you can swim in the large pool, work out, or get a massage in the health club. There are two excellent restaurants: the Olde Yard Inn, for French-accented dinners, and the Sip and Dip Grill, for poolside lunches. The inn isn't on the beach, but free transportation is provided to nearby Savannah Bay. ⊠ *The Valley (Box 26),* ☎ *284/495–5544; 800/653–9273 direct to hotel,* FAX *284/495–5986,* WEB *www.olde-yardinn.com. 14 rooms, 1 suite. 2 restaurants, bar, air-conditioning, pool, health club, croquet, shops, library. AE, MC, V. EP.*

$$ 🏠 **Leverick Bay Hotel.** The small hillside rooms at this hotel are decorated in pastels and original artwork. All have refrigerators, balconies, and views of North Sound; four two-bedroom condos are also available. Down the hill, a Spanish colonial-style main building houses the Lighthouse restaurant and a store (operated by Pusser's of Tortola). The resort's office has games that you can borrow. Several shops, a pool, a beauty salon, a tiny beach, a dive shop, a coin-operated laundry, and a market are just down the hill. ⊠ *Leverick Bay (Box 63),* ☎ *284/495–7421,* FAX *284/495–7367,* WEB *www.virgingordabvi.com. 16 rooms, 4 condos. Ceiling fans, refrigerators. AE, D, MC, V. EP.*

Private Homes and Villas

Those craving seclusion would do well at a villa or even a private home. Both offer comfortable lodgings with full kitchens and maid service.

$$$$ 🏠 **Mango Bay Resort.** Sparkling white villas framed by morning glories and frangipanis, handsome contemporary Italian decor, and a gorgeous ribbon of golden sand that all but vanishes at high tide make this an idyllic family retreat. Even for Virgin Gorda it's a study in isolation. ⊠ *Mahoe Bay (Box 1062),* ☎ *284/495–5672,* FAX *284/495–5674,* WEB *www.mangobayresort.com. 5 villas. Beach. No credit cards.*

$$$$ 🏠 **Paradise Beach Resort.** These one-, two-, and three-bedroom beachfront suites and villas have a handsome Caribbean-style decor, pastel color schemes, and outdoor showers. Four-wheel-drive vehicles are included in the daily rate. ⊠ *Mahoe Bay (Box 534),* ☎ *284/495–5871,* FAX *284/495–5872,* WEB *www.paradisebeachresort.com. 9 units. Beach. No credit cards.*

$$$$ 🏠 **Virgin Gorda Villa Rentals.** This company manages many properties that are near Leverick Bay Hotel, so it's perfect for those who want to be close to some activity. Many villas have private swimming pools; all are well maintained and have spectacular views. ⊠ *Leverick Bay (Box 63),* ☎ *284/495–7421. 26 villas, from studios to 3-bedrooms. AE, MC, V.*

$$$ 🏠 **Guavaberry Spring Bay Vacation Homes.** It's hard to say what's more unusual about these one- and two-bedroom units: their shape (hexagonal) or their location (perched on stilts and scattered about a hillside). Regardless, you're so close to chirping birds and breezes through leaves, you feel as if you're in a tree house. It's just a short walk from the cottages down to the tamarind-shaded beach and not far from the mammoth boulders and cool basins of the famed Baths, which adjoin this property. Eleven private houses are also available. ⊠ *The Valley (Box 20),* ☎ *284/495–5227,* WEB *www.guavaberryspringbay.com. 12 1-bedroom units, 9 2-bedroom units. Beach. No credit cards.*

Dining

Restaurants range from simple to elegant. Hotels that are accessible only by boat will arrange transport in advance upon request for nonguests who wish to dine at their restaurants. It's wise to make dinner reservations almost everywhere except really casual spots.

For approximate costs, *see* the dining price chart *in* Tortola.

AMERICAN/CASUAL

$$ ✕ **The Flying Iguana.** In this charming restaurant's comfortable lounge, lifelike stuffed or colorfully painted wooden iguanas are perched in the plants, and local artwork is displayed. The open-air dining room looks out over Virgin Gorda's tiny airport to the sea. Sandwiches and thick, juicy hamburgers are served for lunch. The dinner menu includes a pasta special, grilled chicken, and steaks. ⊠ *The Valley, at the airport,* ☎ *284/495–5277. AE, MC, V.*

$$ ✕ **Lighthouse.** This bi-level restaurant at the Leverick Bay Hotel looks out over North Sound. The upstairs is slightly less casual but definitely more expensive, with a menu that includes grilled steak, chops, and chicken dishes. Below, the Beach Bar offers light fare all day—starting with breakfast and moving on to hamburgers, salads, and pizzas until well into the evening. ⊠ *Leverick Bay,* ☎ *284/495–7369. AE, MC, V.*

$$ ✕ **Top of The Baths.** At the entrance to The Baths, this popular restaurant starts serving at 8 AM. Tables are outside on a terrace or in an open-air pavilion; all have stunning views of the Sir Francis Drake Channel. Hamburgers, salads, and sandwiches are offered at lunch. Conch seviche and lentil soup are among the dinner appetizers. Entrées include Cornish hen with wild rice, grilled swordfish with fresh rosemary sauce, and local lobster. For dessert you can choose from such delectables as chocolate cheesecake or pecan pie. ⊠ *The Valley,* ☎ *284/495–5497. AE, MC, V.*

$ ✕ **The Bath and Turtle.** You can really sit back and relax at this infor-
★ mal patio tavern with a friendly staff—although the TV noise can be a bit much. Burgers, well-stuffed sandwiches, pizzas, pasta dishes, and daily specials round out the casual menu. Live entertainers perform Wednesday and Sunday nights. ⊠ *Virgin Gorda Yacht Harbour,* ☎ *284/495–5239. MC, V.*

$ ✕ **Mad Dog's.** Piña coladas are *the* thing at this breezy bar just outside The Baths. The menu includes great BLTs, hot dogs, and burgers. ⊠ *The Valley, at the entrance to The Baths,* ☎ *284/495–5830. Reservations not accepted. MC, V. No dinner.*

$ ✕ **Sip and Dip Grill.** The pool at the Olde Yard Inn is the setting for
★ this pleasant, informal lunch spot. Come for the grilled fish, pasta salads, chilled soups, and ice cream. Sunday evening there's a barbecue with live entertainment. ⊠ *The Valley,* ☎ *284/495–5544. Reservations not accepted. AE, MC, V. No dinner Mon.–Sat.*

CAJUN/CREOLE

$$ **Chez Bamboo.** This pleasant little hideaway isn't really that hard to find: look for the building with the purple and green latticework. Candles on the dining room tables and the patio create a mellow atmosphere in which to enjoy such dishes as conch gumbo, Chez B's bouillabaisse, and steak New Orleans. For dessert try the chocolate bourbon mint cake. Stop by Friday night for live jazz. ⊠ *Across from and a little north of Virgin Gorda Yacht Harbour,* ☎ *284/495–5752. Reservations not accepted. AE, MC, V. Closed Mon. No lunch.*

CONTEMPORARY

$$$$ ✕ **Biras Creek.** This hilltop restaurant at the Biras Creek Hotel is stun-
★ ning: broad steps lead up to an open-air lounge and restaurant with beautiful views of North Sound. The three-course prix-fixe menu

changes daily and includes several choices per course: appetizers might be chilled yellow-pepper soup, conch fritters with papaya sauce, or avocado and lobster salad. Roast duck breast with plum sauce, grilled swordfish with bacon and caper sauce, pan-seared snapper with a ginger beurre blanc, and a roast breast of pheasant are some of the enticing entrées. Delightful desserts include key lime pie with raspberry sauce and a rich chocolate brownie with chocolate sauce. Dinner ends with Biras Creek's signature offering of Stilton and port. ⊠ *North Sound,* ☎ *284/494–3555. Reservations essential. AE, MC, V.*

$$$$ ✕ **Drake's Anchorage.** Waves lap almost within reach at tables strung
★ along the front of this waterside, open-air restaurant at Drake's Anchorage Resort Inn. At sunset you can see stunning North Sound and the surrounding hills, and at night the lights of neighboring resorts twinkle and shimmer. Dinner is an elegant four-course affair. The evening begins with an exceptional soup of the evening. Next comes a salad, then the entrée you chose, such as boneless breast of duck with orange-pineapple sauce, roasted rack of lamb with Caribbean-spiced mustard sauce, fillet of local red snapper, or a filet mignon with brandy cream sauce. Dessert choices change but are always tempting. ⊠ *North Sound,* ☎ *284/494–3555. Reservations essential. AE, MC, V. No lunch.*

$$$$ ✕ **Little Dix Bay Pavilion.** For an elegant evening at the Little Dix Bay
★ resort, you can't do better than this—the candlelight in the main open-air pavilion is enchanting, the menu sophisticated, the service attentive. The dinner menu changes daily, but there's always a fine selection of superbly prepared seafood, meat, and vegetarian entrées—gingered duck breast with Pacific Rim vegetables, black Angus rib eye with horseradish and mustard sauce, pan-seared snapper with christophene ratatouille. The breakfast and lunch buffets shine. ⊠ *Spanish Town,* ☎ *284/495–5555 Ext. 174. AE, MC, V.*

$$$ ✕ **Olde Yard Inn.** The intimate dining room is suffused with gentle,
★ classical melodies and the scent of herbs; a cedar roof covers the breezy space, which is decorated with old-style Caribbean charm. The French-accented cuisine includes lamb chops with mango chutney, chicken breast in a rum cream sauce, grilled fish, steaks, and lobster. Chocolate mousse, cheesecake, and Key lime pie are sweet endings. ⊠ *The Valley, north of the marina,* ☎ *284/495–5544. AE, MC, V.*

ITALIAN

$$ ✕ **Giorgio's Table.** Gaze out at the stars and the lights of Tortola and listen to the water lap against the shore while dining on veal scallopini, filet mignon with mushrooms, fresh local fish, or penne with garlic and tomatoes. Lunch fare at this casual establishment includes pizzas and sandwiches. ⊠ *Mahoe Bay,* ☎ *284/495–5684. MC, V.*

SEAFOOD

$$ ✕ **The Clubhouse.** The Bitter End Yacht Club's open-air waterfront restaurant is a favorite rendezvous for the sailing set—busy day and night. At the lavish buffets you get your choice of an entrée for breakfast, lunch, and dinner. Dinner selections include grilled swordfish or tuna, chopped sirloin, scallops, and shrimp. ⊠ *Bitter End Yacht Club, North Sound,* ☎ *284/494–2746. AE, MC, V.*

Beaches

The best beaches are easily reached by water, although they're also accessible on foot, usually after a moderately strenuous 10- to 15-minute hike. Either way, your persistence is rewarded. Anybody going to Virgin Gorda must experience swimming or snorkeling among its unique boulder formations, which can be visited at several beaches along Lee Road. **The Baths** feature the most outstanding grouping of boulders but is usually quite crowded. From The Baths you can walk on Lee

Road or swim north to less-populated **Spring Bay Beach,** which is a gem. Swim or walk north from **Spring Bay Beach** to reach **The Crawl,** a small and appealing beach.

From Biras Creek or Bitter End on the north shore, you can walk to **Bercher's Bay Beach** and along the windswept surf. Footpaths from Bitter End and foot and bike paths from Biras Creek also lead to **Deep Bay,** a calm, well-protected swimming beach. Mosquito Island's **Hay Point Beach** is a broad band of white sand accessible only by boat or by a path from a little dock on the island's east side.

Leverick Bay (⊠ Leverick Bay Rd.) is a tiny, busy beach-cum-marina that fronts a resort restaurant and pool. Come here if you want a break from the island's serenity. The view of Prickly Pear Island is a plus, and the dive facility here can arrange to motor you out to beautiful Eustatia Reef, just across North Sound.

It's worth heading out to **Long Bay** (⊠ Plum Tree Bay Rd., near Virgin Gorda's northern tip, past the Diamond Beach Club), for the snorkeling (Little Dix Bay resort has outings here). The drive takes about half an hour after the turnoff from North Sound Road, and a dirt road makes up part of the route.

For a wonderfully private beach close to Spanish Town, try **Savannah Bay** (⊠ North Sound Rd.). It may not always be completely deserted, but it's a lovely long stretch of white sand. Prickly Pear Island has a calm swimming beach at **Vixen Point Beach.**

Outdoor Activities and Sports

Participant Sports

FISHING

The sportfishing here is so good that anglers from around the world fly in for the annual tournaments. **Walford Ferrington** (⊠ Leverick Bay, North Sound, ☎ 284/495–7612) will pick you up almost anywhere on Virgin Gorda and take you out on his 24-ft speedboat for half- or full-day fishing jaunts. Plan to spend $250–$600.

SAILING

The BVI waters are calm and, hence, are terrific places to learn to sail. The **Nick Trotter Sailing School** (⊠ Bitter End Yacht Club, North Sound, ☎ 284/494–2745) offers beginner and advanced courses. Private lessons are $40 per hour.

SCUBA DIVING AND SNORKELING

Many of the breathtaking sites off Tortola can also be reached easily from Virgin Gorda. Also, note that the North Sound has some terrific snorkeling spots. The **Bitter End Yacht Club** (⊠ North Sound, ☎ 284/494–2746) offers a number of snorkeling trips day and night. Costs range from $5 per person to $55 per person depending on the length and type of trip. Contact **Dive BVI** (⊠ Virgin Gorda Yacht Harbour, ☎ 284/495–5513) for expert instruction, certification, and day trips. It costs $101 for a resort course, $85 for a two-tank dive, and $65 for a one-tank dive; equipment rental is an additional $15. **Kilbride's** (⊠ Bitter End, North Sound, ☎ 284/495–9638) offers resort, advanced, and rescue courses. The fee for a resort course is $95. One-tank dives run $60; two-tank dives, $85. Equipment rental is an additional $15.

WINDSURFING

The North Sound is a good place to learn to windsurf: it's protected, so you can't be easily blown out to sea. The **Bitter End Yacht Club** (⊠ North Sound, ☎ 284/494–2746) gives lessons and rents equipment for $20 per hour.

Spectator Sports

CRICKET

You can catch a match at the **Recreation Grounds** in Spanish Town February–April. The Virgin Gorda BVI Tourist Board office can give you information on game dates and times.

Shopping

Most boutiques are within hotel complexes. Two of the best are at Biras Creek and Little Dix Bay. Other properties—the Bitter End, Leverick Bay, and the Olde Yard Inn—have small but equally select boutiques, and there's a respectable and diverse scattering of shops in the bustling yacht harbor complex in Spanish Town.

CLOTHING

Dive BVI (⊠ Virgin Gorda Yacht Harbour, ☎ 284/495–5513) sells books about the islands as well as sportswear, sunglasses, and beach bags. **Island Silhouette in Flax Plaza** (⊠ Near Fischer's Cove Beach Hotel, ☎ no phone) is the place to go for resort wear hand-painted by Virgin Gorda artists and for locally made tie-dyed T-shirts. **Next Wave** (⊠ Virgin Gorda Yacht Harbour, ☎ 284/495–5623) sells bathing suits, T-shirts, canvas tote bags, and locally made jewelry. **Pavilion Gift Shop** (⊠ Little Dix Bay Hotel, ☎ 284/495–5555) has the latest in resort wear for men and women, as well as jewelry, books, housewares, and expensive T-shirts. **Pelican's Pouch Boutique** (⊠ Virgin Gorda Yacht Harbour, ☎ 284/495–5477) is where you'll find a large selection of swimsuits plus cover-ups, T-shirts, and accessories. **Pusser's Company Store** (⊠ Leverick Bay, ☎ 284/495–7369) has a trademark line of sportswear, rum products, and gift items.

FOODSTUFFS

Bitter End's Emporium (⊠ North Sound, ☎ 284/494–2745) is the place for such edible treats as local fruits, cheeses, and baked goods. **Commissary and Ship Store** (⊠ The Valley, ☎ 284/495–5555) offers daily specials prepared by Little Dix Resort chefs, as well as assorted cheeses, canned goods, wines, and gourmet items. **Wine Cellar and Bakery** (⊠ Virgin Gorda Yacht Harbour, ☎ 284/495–5250) bakes bread, rolls, muffins, and cookies and has sandwiches and sodas to go.

GIFTS

Palm Tree Gallery (⊠ Leverick Bay, ☎ 284/495–7479) sells attractive handcrafted jewelry, paintings, and one-of-a-kind gift items, as well as games and books about the Caribbean. **Thee Artistic Gallery** (⊠ Virgin Gorda Yacht Harbour, ☎ 284/495–5104) features Caribbean jewelry, 14-karat-gold nautical jewelry, maps, collectible coins, and crystal. **The Reeftique** (⊠ Bitter End, North Sound, ☎ 284/494–2745) carries island crafts and jewelry, clothing, and nautical odds and ends with the Bitter End logo.

HANDICRAFTS

Virgin Gorda Craft Shop (⊠ Virgin Gorda Yacht Harbour, ☎ 284/495–5137) features the work of island artisans, and carries West Indian jewelry and crafts styled from straw, shells, and other local materials. It also stocks clothing and paintings by Caribbean artists.

Nightlife

The Bath and Turtle (⊠ Virgin Gorda Yacht Harbour, ☎ 284/495–5239), one of the liveliest spots on Virgin Gorda, hosts island bands on Wednesday from 8 PM until midnight. **Bitter End Yacht Club** (⊠ North Sound, ☎ 284/494–2746) features local bands most nights in season. Call for schedules. **Chez Bamboo** (⊠ across from Virgin Gorda Yacht

Harbour, ☎ 284/495–5752) is the place for jazz on Friday night and a live band Sunday night. The **Lighthouse** (✉ Leverick Bay, ☎ 284/495–7370) has live bands on Saturday night and Sunday afternoon in season. **Little Dix Bay** (✉ Little Dix Bay, ☎ 284/495–5555) presents elegant live entertainment several nights a week in season. **Rock Café** (✉ The Valley, ☎ 284/495–5672) has live bands Friday, Saturday, and Sunday nights. **Sip and Dip Grill** (✉ Olde Yard Inn, ☎ 284/495–5544) has a live local band at their Sunday night barbecue.

Exploring Virgin Gorda

One of the most efficient ways to see Virgin Gorda is by sailboat. There are few roads, and most byways don't follow the scalloped shoreline. The main route sticks resolutely to the center of the island, linking The Baths at the tip of the southern extremity with Gun Creek and Leverick Bay at North Sound and providing exhilarating views. The craggy coast, scissored with grottoes and fringed by palms and boulders, has a primitive beauty. If you drive, you can hit all the sights in one day. The best plan is to explore the area near your hotel (either The Valley or North Sound) first, then take a day to drive to the other end. Stop to climb Gorda Peak, in the island's center.

Numbers in the margin correspond to points of interest on the Virgin Gorda map.

Sights to See

❸ The Baths. At Virgin Gorda's most celebrated sight, giant boulders are scattered about the beach and in the water. Some are almost as large as houses and form remarkable grottoes. Climb between these rocks to swim in the many pools. Early morning and late afternoon are the best times to visit if you want to avoid crowds. (If it's privacy you crave, follow the shore northward to quieter bays—Spring, the Crawl, Little Trunk, and Valley Trunk—or head south to Devil's Bay.) ✉ *Lee Rd.,* ☎ *no phone.* 🆓 *Free.*

❻ Coastal Islands. You can easily reach the quaintly named Fallen Jerusalem Island and the Dog Islands by boat. They're all part of the BVI National Parks Trust, and their seductive beaches and unparalleled snorkeling opportunities display the BVI at their beachcombing, hedonistic best. ☎ *No phone.* 🆓 *Free.*

❹ Copper Mine Point. Here you'll see a tall, stone shaft silhouetted against the sky and a small stone structure that overlooks the sea. These are the ruins of a copper mine established 400 years ago and worked first by the Spanish, then by the English, until the early 20th century. ✉ *Copper Mine Rd.,* ☎ *no phone.* 🆓 *Free.*

❷ Little Fort National Park. This 36-acre wildlife sanctuary has the ruins of an old fort. Giant boulders like those at The Baths are scattered throughout the park. ✉ *Spanish Town Rd.,* ☎ *no phone.* 🆓 *Free.*

❶ Spanish Town. Virgin Gorda's peaceful main settlement, on the island's southern wing, is so tiny that it barely qualifies as a town at all. Also known as The Valley, Spanish Town is home to a marina, some shops, and a couple of car-rental agencies. Just north of town is the ferry slip. At the **Virgin Gorda Yacht Harbour** you can stroll along the dock and do a little shopping.

❺ Virgin Gorda Peak National Park. There are two trails at this 265-acre park, which contains the island's highest point, at 1,359 ft (414 m). Small signs on North Sound Road mark both entrances; sometimes, however, the signs are missing, so keep your eyes open for a set of stairs that disappears into the trees. It's about a 15-minute hike from either entrance up to a small clearing, where you can climb a ladder to the platform of a wooden observation tower and a spectacular 360-degree view. ⊠ *North Sound Rd.,* ☎ *no phone.* 🎟 *Free.*

JOST VAN DYKE

Named after an early Dutch settler, Jost Van Dyke is a small island northwest of Tortola and is *truly* a place to get away from it all. Mountainous and lush, the 4-mi-long (6½-km-long) island—home to only about 140 people—has one tiny resort, some rental houses, a campground, a handful of cars, and a single road. This is one of the Caribbean's most popular anchorages, and there's a disproportionately large number of informal bars and restaurants, which have helped earn Jost its reputation as the "party island" of the BVI.

Lodging

For approximate costs, *see* the lodging price chart *in* Tortola.

$$$ 🏨 **Sandcastle.** This six-cottage hideaway is on a ½-mi (¾-km) stretch of white-sand beach at remote White Bay. There's "nothing" to do here, except relax in a hammock, read, walk, swim, and enjoy sophisticated cuisine by candlelight in the Sandcastle restaurant. You can also make arrangements for diving, sailing, and sportfishing trips. ⊠ *White Bay,* ☎ *284/495–9888,* 𝖥𝖠𝖷 *284/495–9999,* 𝖶𝖤𝖡 *www.sandcastle-bvi.com. 6 cottages. Restaurant, bar, beach, shops. MC, V. EP.*

$$$ 🏨 **Sandy Ground Estates.** The eight privately owned one- and two-bedroom houses here are tucked into the foliage along the edge of a beach at the island's east end. Each house is architecturally different, and interiors range from spartan to stylish. The fully equipped kitchens can be pre-stocked if you supply a list of groceries (a good idea, as supplies are limited on the island), and there are four very casual restaurants on the other side of the hill—a long walk away. ⊠ *Sandy Ground,* ☎ *284/494–3391,* 𝖶𝖤𝖡 *www.sandyground.com. 8 houses. Beach. AE, MC, V. EP.*

$ 🏕 **White Bay Campground.** On the east end of White Bay Beach, this simple campground has bare sites, equipped tent sites (with electricity and a lamp), and screened cabins. The owners will take you on nature walks and can arrange island tours and sailing and diving trips. ⊠ *White Bay,* ☎ *284/495–9312. 12 sites, 4 cabins. Restaurant, bar, beach. No credit cards.*

Dining

Restaurants on Jost Van Dyke are informal (some serve meals family style at long tables) but charming. The island is a favorite charter stop, and you're bound to hear people exchanging stories about the previous night's anchoring adventures. Most restaurants don't take reservations, and in all cases dress is casual.

For approximate costs, *see* the dining price chart *in* Tortola.

ECLECTIC

$$$ ✕ **Sandcastle.** Candlelit dinners in the tiny beachfront dining room of the sandcastle cottage complex are four-course prix-fixe affairs with seating at 7 PM. The menu changes but can include a West Indian pumpkin or curried-apple soup; curried shrimp or three-mustard chicken; and for dessert, rum bananas or Key lime pie. Reservations are requested by 4 PM. Sandwiches are served at lunch at the Soggy Dollar Bar, famous as the purported birthplace of the lethal painkiller drink. ⊠ *White Bay,* ☎ *284/495–9888. Reservations essential. MC, V.*

$$ ✕ **Abe's Little Harbour.** Specialties at this informal, popular spot include fresh lobster, conch, and spareribs. During most of the winter season there's a pig roast every Wednesday night. ⊠ *Little Harbour,* ☎ *no phone (boaters can use VHF Channel 16). No credit cards.*

$$ ✕ **Club Paradise.** The dinner menu at this casual beachfront establishment includes grilled local fish such as mahimahi, red snapper, and grouper, grilled steak, and barbecued chicken and ribs. Hamburgers, West Indian conch stew, and curried chicken are the luncheon fare. ⊠ *Great Harbour,* ☎ *284/495–9267. No credit cards.*

$$ ✕ **Foxy's Tamarind.** One of the true hot spots in the BVI—and a must-
★ stop for yachters from the world over—Foxy's hosts the madcap Wooden Boat Race every May and throws big parties on New Year's Eve, April Fools' Day, and Halloween. This lively place serves local dishes and terrific barbecue, and it makes a rum punch that's all its own. Foxy plays the guitar and creates calypso ditties about his guests. Next door is Foxy's Store, which sells clothing, sundries, souvenirs, and cassettes of Foxy performing. ⊠ *Great Harbour,* ☎ *284/495–9258. AE, MC, V. No lunch weekends.*

$$ ✕ **Harris' Place.** Owner Harris Jones is famous for his pig-roast buffets and Monday night Lobstermania. Harris' Place is a great spot to rub elbows with locals and the charter-boat crowd. ⊠ *Little Harbour,* ☎ *284/495–9302. AE, MC, V.*

$$ ✕ **Sydney's Peace and Love.** Here you'll find great lobster, barbecue, and a sensational (for the BVI) jukebox. The cognoscenti sail here for dinner since there's no beach—meaning no irksome sand fleas. ⊠ *Little Harbour,* ☎ *284/495–9271. No credit cards.*

$ ✕ **Happy Laurry.** Hamburgers, cheeseburgers, and honey-dipped fried chicken are the specialties at this beachfront spot. ⊠ *Great Harbour,* ☎ *284/495–9259. No credit cards.*

Beaches

White Bay, on the south shore, west of Great Harbour, has a long stretch of white sand. Just offshore, the little islet known as **Sandy Cay** is a gleaming scimitar of white sand, with marvelous snorkeling.

PETER ISLAND

Dramatic, hilly, and with wonderful anchorages and beautiful beaches, privately owned Peter Island is about 5 mi (8 km) directly south across the Sir Francis Drake Channel from Road Town, Tortola. Set amid the string of islets that stream from the southern tip of Virgin Gorda, the island is an idyllic hideaway replete with white sand beaches, stunning views, and the Peter Island Resort. You can sail here on your own craft or take a launch from the Peter Island dock east of Road Town, Tortola ($15 each way or free if you're coming for dinner; just mention that you have a reservation). Note that the resort discourages nonguests from using hotel facilities other than the restaurants.

Lodging

For approximate costs, *see* the lodging price chart *in* Tortola.

$$$$ ⊡ **Peter Island Resort and Yacht Harbour.** This casually elegant retreat
★ has recently undergone a major renovation, and it sparkles. Fifty-two guest rooms, in four-unit cottages tucked amid beds of radiant flowers, are either at the far end of the main beach or clustered near the main building. Beachfront Junior Suites are beautiful stone-and-wood structures with French doors that open onto balconies or patios, a few steps from a lovely stretch of sand. The less expensive, second-floor

Ocean View units, and more spacious first-floor Garden Terrace rooms, look across the pool and gardens toward the hills of Tortola. A spectacular hilltop villa, the Crow's Nest, has four bedrooms, a living room, a state-of-the-art kitchen, a dining room, a huge terrace with panoramic views, an inner courtyard, an entertainment system, domestic help, vehicles, and a private pool. There's lots to do here: facilities include a tennis program run by Peter Burwash, a water sports center, a beachfront spa, mountain bicycles, a 20-station fitness trail, and a 5-star PADI dive facility. After dinner in the Tradewinds Restaurant, you can often dance under the stars. If you seek seclusion, take note: some of the resort's beaches are on bays that are popular charter-boat anchorages, and although no longer owned and run by Amway Hotel Corporation, this property is still used for Amway incentive trips. ⊠ *Sprat Bay (Box 211, Road Town, Tortola)*, ☎ *284/495–2000 or 800/346–4451*, FAX *284/495–2500*, WEB *www.peterisland.com. 52 rooms, 3 villas. 2 restaurants, 2 bars, pool, spa, 4 tennis courts, basketball, gym, beach, dive shop, windsurfing, mountain bikes, laundry service, helipad. AE, MC, V. FAP.*

Dining

For approximate costs, *see* the dining price chart *in* Tortola.

ECLECTIC

$$$$ ✕ **Tradewinds Restaurant.** The Peter Island Resort's air-conditioned dining room overlooks the Sir Francis Drake Channel and is an enchanting dinner setting. The à la carte menu offers mostly Continental selections with subtle Caribbean touches; Saturday night is buffet night. After dinner, dance under the stars to soft, rhythmic tunes performed by local musicians three or four nights a week in season. ⊠ *Sprat Bay*, ☎ *284/495–2000. Reservations essential. AE, MC, V. No lunch.*

$$$ ✕ **Deadman's Bay Bar and Grill.** This casual beach grill serves lunches of thick and juicy burgers, grilled fish, light salads, and individual pizzas freshly made in the new pizza oven. Sunday lunch features a lavish West Indian buffet and a steel band. A dinner with a choice of grilled local fish, steak, or chicken is served most evenings. Try one of the many delicious frozen tropical drinks. ⊠ *Sprat Bay*, ☎ *284/495–2000. Reservations essential. AE, MC, V.*

Beaches

Palm-fringed **Dead Man's Bay,** considered by many to be one of the world's 10 most romantic beaches, is a short hike from the dock. Snorkeling is good at both ends of the beach, and you'll find a bar and restaurant for lunch. If you feel like taking a hike instead of heading down to Dead Man's Bay, follow the road up, and when it levels off, bear right and head down to the other side of the island and secluded **White Bay.**

ANEGADA

Anegada lies low on the horizon about 14 mi (22½ km) north of Virgin Gorda. Unlike the hilly volcanic islands in the chain, this is a flat coral and limestone atoll. Nine miles (14 km) long and 2 mi (3 km) wide, the island rises no more than 28 ft (9 m) above sea level. In fact, by the time you're able to see it, you may have run your boat onto a reef. (More than 300 captains unfamiliar with the waters have done so since exploration days; note that bareboat charters don't allow their vessels to head here without a trained skipper.) Although the reefs are a sailor's nightmare, they (and the shipwrecks they've caused) are a scuba diver's dream. Snorkeling, especially in the waters around Loblolly Bay on the north shore, is also a transcendent experience. You can float in shallow, calm, reef-protected water just a few feet from shore and see one coral formation after another, each shimmering with a rainbow of colorful fish. Such watery pleasures are complemented by ever-so-fine, ever-so-white sand (the northern and western shores have long stretches of the stuff) and the occasional beach bar (stop in for burgers, Anegada lobster, or a frosty beer). The island's population of about 150 lives primarily in a small south-side village called The Settlement. Many local fisherfolk are happy to take visitors out bonefishing.

Lodging

For approximate costs, *see* the lodging price chart *in* Tortola.

$$$$ 🏨 **Anegada Reef Hotel.** If you favor laid-back living (meaning, among other things, absolutely no schedules), this is the spot for you. Pack a bathing suit and a few warmer garments for the evening, and you're good to go. The hotel's simply furnished rooms are laid out in motel fashion. It has its own narrow strip of beach, but beach lovers will want to spend their days on the deserted strands at the other side of the island; you can ask to be dropped off with a picnic lunch or be picked up and returned to the hotel for lunch. Snorkeling and diving are popular activities, as are deep-sea fishing or bonefishing in the flats. Cool down with a drink in the outdoor bar, and be sure to try the island's famous lobster—freshly grilled in the Anegada Reef restaurant. ⊠ *Setting Point,* ☎ *284/495–8002,* FAX *284/495–9362,* WEB *www.anegadareef.com. 16 rooms. Restaurant, bar, beach. MC, V. FAP.*

$$ 🏨 **Neptune's Treasure.** This little guest house offers simple double and single rooms that are very basically furnished. However, all have private baths. You'll find a restaurant, Neptune's Treasure, and a little gift shop on the premises. ⊠ *Between Pomato and Saltheap points,* ☎ *284/495–9439. 4 rooms. Restaurant, beach. AE, MC, V. EP.*

$ ⛺ **Anegada Beach Campground.** The tents (8×10 ft or 10×12 ft/2×3 m or 3×4 m) here are pitched in a marvelously serene setting. Bare sites cost $7 per person, per night; equipped sites are $20 per person. ⊠ *The Settlement,* ☎ *284/495–9466. 18 sites. Restaurant, bar, beach. No credit cards.*

Dining

There are between 6 and 10 restaurants open at any one time, depending on the season and also on whim. Check when you're on the island.

For approximate costs, *see* the dining price chart *in* Tortola.

SEAFOOD

$$$ ✕ **Anegada Reef Hotel.** Seasoned yachters gather nightly at the Anegada Reef Hotel's bar-restaurant to converse and dine with hotel guests. Dinner is by candlelight and always includes famous Anegada lobster, steaks, and chicken—all prepared on the large grill by the little open-air bar. ⊠ *Setting Point,* ☎ *284/495–8002. Reservations essential. No credit cards.*

$$ ✕ **Big Bamboo.** Ice-cold beer, island drinks, burgers, and grilled lobster entice a steady stream of barefoot diners to this beach bar for lunch. Dinner is by request. ⊠ *Loblolly Bay,* ☎ *284/495–2019. AE.*

$$ ✕ **Neptune's Treasure.** The owners catch, cook, and serve the seafood (lobster is a specialty) at this casual bar and restaurant in the Neptune's Treasure guest house. ⊠ *Between Pomato and Saltheap points,* ☎ *284/ 495–9439. AE.*

$$ ✕ **Pomato Point.** This relaxed restaurant-bar is on a narrow beach, a short walk from the Anegada Reef Hotel. Entrées include steak, chicken, lobster, and fresh-caught seafood. Owner Wilfred Creque displays various island artifacts, including shards of Arawak pottery and 17th-century coins, cannonballs, and bottles. ⊠ *Pomato Point,* ☎ *284/495–8038. Reservations essential. No credit cards.*

Shopping

Anegada Reef Hotel Boutique (⊠ Setting Point, ☎ 284/495–8002) has a bit of everything: resort wear, hand-painted T-shirts, locally made jewelry, books, and one-of-a-kind gifts. **Pat's Pottery** (⊠ Nutmeg Point, ☎ 284/495–8031) sells bowls, plates, cups, candlestick holders, original watercolors, and more.

OTHER BRITISH VIRGIN ISLANDS

Cooper Island

This small hilly island on the south side of the Sir Francis Drake Channel, about 8 mi (13 km) from Road Town, Tortola, is popular with the charter-boat crowd. There are no roads (which doesn't really matter because there aren't any cars), but you will find a beach restaurant, a casual little hotel, a few houses (some are available for rent), and great snorkeling at the south end of Manchioneel Bay.

Dining and Lodging

For approximate costs, *see* the dining and lodging price charts *in* Tortola.

$$$ ✕🏠 **Cooper Island Beach Club.** Six West Indian–style cottages—set back from the beach among the palm trees—house 12 no-frills units, each with a living area, a small but complete kitchen, and a balcony. A stay here takes you back to the basics: you use rainwater that has been collected in a cistern, and you can't use any appliances because electricity is so limited (who needs pressed clothes and blow-dried hair anyway?). There's plenty of "civilization," however, at the on-site bar, which fills nightly with boaters. The restaurant is also popular with the boating crowd (if you don't have your own vessel, note that ferry service from Road Town is available only to hotel guests). The restaurant serves great ratatouille (it's a main course at lunch, an appetizer at dinner); grilled fish, chicken and vegetable rotis, penne pasta, steak, and conch creole. For lunch there are hamburgers, conch fritters, sandwiches, and pasta salad. Reservations are essential. ⊠ *Manchioneel Bay (Box 859, Road Town, Tortola),* ☎ *413/659–2602 or 800/542–4624,* WEB *www.cooper-island.com; no phone to restaurant (boaters can use VHF Channel 16). 12 rooms. Restaurant, fans, beach, dive shop. AE, MC, V. EP.*

Guana Island

Guana Island is very quiet and because the whole island is owned by the resort, *very* private. There are *no* public amenities, and access is limited (the hotel sends a private launch to pick up its guests on Beef Island). If you arrive on your own boat, the only place you're allowed is on the beach.

Lodging

For approximate costs, *see* the lodging price chart *in* Tortola.

$$$$ 🏠 **Guana Island.** The hotel complex is atop a hill, a 10-minute walk from the beach, and views of neighboring islands are stunning. The 15 comfortable rooms are in seven houses scattered throughout the grounds. The houses are decorated in Caribbean style, with rattan furniture, and each has its own porch. You can observe more than 50 species of birds on this island, and the terrain is a verdant collection of plants ringed by six deserted beaches. Guests mingle during cocktail hour and often dine together at several large tables in the main house, but there are small tables if you prefer a more intimate meal. Daily rates include three meals, afternoon tea, and house wine with lunch and dinner. ⊠ *Hilltop (Box 32, Road Town, Tortola),* ☎ *284/494–2354 or 914/ 967–6050,* 𝖥𝖠𝖷 *284/495–2900,* 𝖶𝖤𝖡 *www.guana.com. 15 rooms. Restaurant, fans, tennis court, croquet, hiking. No credit cards. FAP.*

Little Thatch Island

Just west of Tortola is Little Thatch Island, a petite private island with an elegant hideaway.

Lodging

For approximate costs, *see* the lodging price chart *in* Tortola.

$$$$ ⌂ **Little Thatch Island.** When you want to be pampered and don't care about the price (the cost per day is $10,450 for 1–4 guests and $11,755 for 5–10 guests), this stunning hilltop hideaway can be all yours. The four octagonal one-bedroom cottages have Douglas fir roofs and broad terraces. Three of the four have handsome outdoor (but exceedingly private) stonework showers. Rattan furnishings are of the highest quality and are extremely comfortable. Views from the open-air living room, the dining room, and the pool are breathtaking. A gourmet chef prepares all your meals, and unobtrusive staff members provide impeccable service, seeing to your every need. ⊠ *Box 861, Road Town, Tortola,* ☎ *284/495–9227,* 𝖥𝖠𝖷 *284/495–9212,* 𝖶𝖤𝖡 *www.littlethatchisland.com. Pool, beach, windsurfing, boating. AE, MC, V. FAP. Closed Aug.–Oct.*

Necker Island

Necker Island, just north of Virgin Gorda, is yet another private isle. Accommodations here are luxurious, but you can only stay if you rent the whole island.

Lodging

For approximate costs, *see* the lodging price chart *in* Tortola.

$$$$ ⌂ **Necker Island.** You and as many as 25 friends can lease the whole island, including its five beaches, many walks, tennis courts, luxurious villa with 10 spacious guest rooms, and two Balinese cottages. The common living area is anything but common: the huge room is lined with doors that open to the breezes. Here and there are oversize couches and chairs, surrounded by potted plants, artwork, and sculptures. Bedrooms have slate floors, stonework walls, and stunning views. A chef prepares gourmet meals for you in the state-of-the-art kitchen; a full staff takes care of everything else. ⊠ *Box 1091, The Valley, Virgin Gorda,* ☎ *284/494–2757,* 𝖥𝖠𝖷 *284/494–4396,* 𝖶𝖤𝖡 *www.virgin.com/limitededition. 2 pools, 2 tennis courts, gym, beach, windsurfing, boating. AE, MC, V.*

Marina Cay

Beautiful little Marina Cay is in Trellis Bay, not far from Beef Island. Sometimes you can see it and its large J-shape coral reefs—a most dramatic sight—from the air soon after takeoff from the airport on Beef Island. With only 6 acres, this islet is considered small even by BVI standards. You'll find a restaurant, Pusser's Store, and a six-unit hotel here. Ferry service is free from the dock on Beef Island.

Lodging

For approximate costs, *see* the lodging price chart *in* Tortola.

$$$ ⚓ **Pusser's Marina Cay Hotel and Restaurant.** The tiny island's only hotel has four rooms and two villas, all with lovely views of the water and neighboring islands. Each has its own porch. The restaurant's menu ranges from fish and lobster to steak, chicken, and barbecued ribs. Pusser's Painkiller Punch is the house specialty. There's free ferry service from the Beef Island dock for anyone visiting the island (call for ferry times, which vary with the season). ✉ *West side of Marina Cay (Box 76, Road Town, Tortola),* ☎ *284/494–2174,* ℻ *284/494–4775,* WEB *www.pussers.com. 4 rooms, 2 villas. Restaurant, bar, beach. AE, DC, MC, V. EP.*

BRITISH VIRGIN ISLANDS A TO Z

To research prices, get advice from other travelers, and book travel arrangements, visit www.fodors.com.

AIR TRAVEL

Both the Beef Island/Tortola and Virgin Gorda airports are classic Caribbean—almost always sleepy. However, the Beef Island terminal can get crowded when several departures are scheduled close together, and lines at service desks move slowly when this happens; give yourself at least an hour. There's no nonstop service from the continental United States to the BVI; connections are usually made through San Juan, Puerto Rico, or St. Thomas, USVI. Several airlines serve either San Juan and St. Thomas or both. Air St. Thomas flies between St. Thomas and San Juan and Virgin Gorda. Air Sunshine flies back and forth from St. Thomas and San Juan to Beef Island/Tortola and Virgin Gorda. American Eagle flies between St. Thomas and Beef Island/Tortola, and between San Juan and Beef Island/Tortola. Cape Air flies to both San Juan and St. Thomas from Beef Island/Tortola. Clair Aero Services flies back and forth to St. Thomas from Beef Island/Tortola. Continental flies between San Juan and Beef Island/Tortola.

Regularly scheduled flights between the BVI and most other Caribbean islands are provided by LIAT. Many Caribbean islands can also be reached through Fly BVI, a charter service on Virgin Gorda.

➤ AIRLINES AND CONTACTS: **Air St. Thomas** (☎ 284/495–5935); **Air Sunshine** (☎ 284/495–8900); **American Eagle** (☎ 284/495–1122); **Cape Air** (☎ 284/495–2100); **Clair Aero Services** (☎ 284/495–2271); **Continental** (☎ 340/777–8190); **Fly BVI** (☎ 284/495–1747); **LIAT** (☎ 284/495–2577).

AIRPORTS

At the Beef Island/Tortola Airport, taxis hover at the exit from customs. Fares are officially set; they're not negotiable and are lower per person when there are several passengers. Figure about $15 for up to three people and $5 for each additional passenger for the 20-minute ride to Road Town and about $20–$30 for the 45-minute ride to West End. Expect to share your taxi, and be patient if your driver searches for people to fill his cab—only a few flights land each day, and this could be your driver's only run. You can also call the BVI Taxi Association.

On Virgin Gorda call Mahogany Rentals and Taxi Service. If you are staying on North Sound, a taxi will take you from the airport to the dock where your hotel launch will meet you, but be sure to make launch arrangements with your hotel before your arrival. If your destination is Leverick Bay, your land taxi will take you there directly. Note that if your destination is Virgin Gorda you can also fly to Beef Island/Tortola and catch the nearby North Sound Express, which will take you to Spanish Town or North Sound.

➤ AIRPORT INFORMATION: **BVI Taxi Association** (☎ 284/495–1982); **Mahogany Rentals and Taxi Service** (✉ The Valley, ☎ 284/495–5469).

BOAT AND FERRY TRAVEL

FARES AND SCHEDULES

Ferries connect St. Thomas, USVI, with Tortola and Virgin Gorda. Inter-Island Boat Services' *Sundance II* connects St. John and West End, Tortola, daily. Native Son, Inc. operates three ferries (*Native Son, Oriole,* and *Voyager Eagle*) and has daily service between St. Thomas and Tortola (West End and Road Town). The *Nubian Princess* operates between Red Hook, St. Thomas; Cruz Bay, St. John; and West End, Tortola, daily. Smiths Ferry Services operates between downtown St. Thomas and Road Town and West End daily. Speedy's Ferries runs between Virgin Gorda, Tortola, and St. Thomas on Tuesday, Thursday, and Saturday, and its *Speedy's Fantasy* runs between Road Town, Tortola, and Spanish Town, Virgin Gorda, daily.

North Sound Express boats run daily between Virgin Gorda's North Sound and Spanish Town and Beef Island/Tortola. The Peter Island Ferry runs daily between Peter Island's private dock on Tortola (just east of Road Town) and Peter Island. Jost Van Dyke Ferry Service makes the Jost Van Dyke–Tortola run several times daily. New Horizon Ferry Service makes the Jost Van Dyke–Tortola trip a number of times each day.

➤ BOAT AND FERRY INFORMATION: **Inter-Island Boat Services** (☎ 284/495–4166); **Jost Van Dyke Ferry Service** (☎ 284/494–2997); **Native Son, Inc.** (☎ 284/495–4617);**New Horizon Ferry Service** (☎ 284/495–9477); **North Sound Express** (☎ 284/495–2271); *Nubian Princess* (☎ 284/495–4999); **Peter Island Ferry** (☎ 284/495–2000); **Smiths Ferry Services** (☎ 284/495–4495); **Speedy's Ferries** (☎ 284/495–5240).

BUSINESS HOURS

BANKS

Banks usually have hours Monday–Thursday 9–2:30 and Friday 9–2:30 and 4:30–6.

POST OFFICES

Post offices are open weekdays 9–5 and Saturday 9–1.

SHOPS

Stores are generally open Monday–Saturday 9–5. You may find some open on Sunday.

CAR RENTALS

You'll need a temporary BVI license, available at the rental car company for $10 with a valid license from another country. Most agencies offer both four-wheel-drive vehicles and cars (often compacts).

On Tortola try Avis, Hertz, or Itgo Car Rental. On Virgin Gorda contact Mahogany Rentals and Taxi Service or L&S Jeep Rental.

➤ MAJOR AGENCIES: **Avis** (✉ Botanic Gardens, Road Town,Tortola, ☎ 284/494–3322); **Hertz** (✉ West End, Tortola, ☎ 284/495–4405); **Itgo Car Rental** (✉ Wickham's Cay I, Road Town, Tortola, ☎ 284/494–2639); **L&S Jeep Rental** (✉ Spanish Town, Virgin Gorda, ☎ 284/495–5297); **Mahogany Rentals and Taxi Service** (✉ Spanish Town, Virgin Gorda, ☎ 284/495–5469).

CAR TRAVEL

Both Tortola and Virgin Gorda have a number of car rental agencies. Although taxi service is good on these two islands, many people who want to explore the islands and try a different beach every day opt for renting a vehicle. On Anegada it is possible to rent a car, but most visitors rely on taxis for transportation. Jost Van Dyke has a single road, and visitors travel by foot or local taxi. On the other islands there are no roads.

GASOLINE
Gas costs about $2.50 a gallon.

ROAD CONDITIONS
Tortola's main roads are, for the most part, well paved, but there are exceptionally steep hills and sharp curves; driving demands your complete attention. A main road encircles the island and several roads cross it, almost always through mountainous terrain. Virgin Gorda has a smaller road system, and a single, very steep road links the north and south ends of the island.

RULES OF THE ROAD
Driving in the BVI is on the left side of the road. Speed limits (rarely enforced) are 20 mph in town and 40 mph outside town.

ELECTRICITY
Electricity is 110 volts, the same as in North America, so European appliances will require adaptors. The electricity is quite reliable.

EMERGENCIES
➤ AMBULANCE AND FIRE: For general emergencies, dial ☎ 999.
➤ HOSPITALS: **Medicure Health Center** (✉ Spanish Town, Virgin Gorda, ☎ 284/495–5479); **Peebles Hospital** (✉ Road Town, Tortola, ☎ 284/494–3497).
➤ PHARMACIES: In Road Town, Tortola: **Cay Pharmacy** (✉ Road Town, Tortola, ☎ 284/494–8128); **J. R. O'Neal Drug Store** (✉ Road Town, Tortola, ☎ 284/494–2292); **Island Drug Centre** (✉ Spanish Town, Virgin Gorda, ☎ 284/495–5449); **Medicure** (✉ Spanish Town, Virgin Gorda, ☎ 284/495–5479).
➤ POLICE: For general emergencies, dial ☎ 999.

ETIQUETTE AND BEHAVIOR
Islanders are religious, and churches fill up on Sunday. You're welcome to attend services, but be sure to dress up. If you encounter any rudeness, you probably didn't begin the conversation properly: only after courteous exchanges ("Hello, how are you today?" and "Not too bad, and how are you?") should you get down to the business of buying groceries, ordering lunch, or hiring a taxi.

FESTIVALS AND SEASONAL EVENTS
In March catch the breathtaking displays of local foliage at the Horticultural Society Show at the botanical gardens; also in March, gather together with locals and yachties at Foxy's Annual St. Patrick's Celebration on Jost Van Dyke. In April, join the fun at the Virgin Gorda Festival, which culminates with a parade on Easter Sunday; also in April, glimpse the colorful spinnakers as sailing enthusiasts gather for the internationally known BVI Spring Regatta. May is the time for partying at Foxy's Wooden Boat Regatta, on Jost Van Dyke. In August try your hand at sportfishing as anglers compete to land the largest catch at the BVI Sportfishing Tournament; August sees two weeks of joyful revelry during Tortola's BVI Emancipation Festival Celebrations. If you've always wanted to escape to the islands and live on a boat, then the November BVI Boat Show is for you. To compete in sailing races and games, drop in on Virgin Gorda's North Sound during the last six weeks of the year for the Bitter End Yacht Club's Competition Series, including

the Invitational Regatta. For the best in local *fungi* bands (bands that make music using household items as instruments), stop by the Scratch/Fungi Band Fiesta in December.

HEALTH

The manchineel tree's fruit, which resembles small green apples, is poisonous, and the tree's sap can blister skin badly. These trees are found all over the Caribbean, and trees on resort property or trails are usually marked. No-see-ums (fleas) can be a bother at twilight, especially along the beaches. Use insect repellent if there's no wind to blow them away. Underwater, watch out for those black spiny-looking things you see around rocks. They're called sea urchins and have a powerful sting.

HOLIDAYS

Public holidays for 2002 are: New Year's Day, Commonwealth Day (Mar. 14), Good Friday (Mar. 29), Easter Monday (Apr. 1), Whit Monday (May 22), Sovereign's Birthday (June 16), Territory Day (July 1), BVI August Festival Days (July 26–Aug. 7), St. Ursula's Day (Oct. 21), Christmas, and Boxing Day (Dec. 26).

LANGUAGE

English is the official language, and it's often spoken with a West Indian accent and with a few idiomatic expressions. If someone says he's just limin', it means he's hanging out. If you ask for an item in a store, and the shopkeeper replies, "It's finished," then the shop has temporarily run out.

MAIL AND SHIPPING

There are post offices in Road Town on Tortola and in Spanish Town on Virgin Gorda (note that postal service in the BVI isn't very efficient). Postage for a first-class letter to the United States, Canada, Australia, New Zealand, or the United Kingdom is 55¢; for a postcard, 35¢. For a small fee Rush It, in Road Town and in Spanish Town, offers most U.S. mail and UPS services (via St. Thomas the next day). If you wish to write to an establishment in the BVI, be sure to include the specific island in the address; there are no postal codes.

➤ CONTACTS: **Rush It** (✉ Road Town, Tortola, ☎ 284/494–4421; ✉ Spanish Town, Virgin Gorda, ☎ 284/495–5822).

MONEY MATTERS

BANKS AND ATMS

On Tortola you'll find a Barclays Bank near the waterfront in Road Town. The Chase Manhattan Bank is also near Road Town's waterfront and has an ATM machine. On Virgin Gorda, Barclays Bank isn't far from the ferry dock in Spanish Town.

➤ CONTACTS: **Barclays Bank** (✉ Wickham's Cay I, Road Town, Tortola, ☎ 284/494–2171; ✉ Virgin Gorda Yacht Harbour, Spanish Town, Virgin Gorda, ☎ 284/495–5271). **Chase Manhattan Bank** (✉ Wickham's Cay I, Road Town, Tortola, ☎ 284/494–2662).

CREDIT CARDS

Most hotels and restaurants in the BVI accept MasterCard and Visa, and some also accept American Express, Diner's Club, and Discover. Beware that a few accept only cash or traveler's checks.

CURRENCY

The currency is the U.S. dollar. Any other currency must be exchanged at a bank.

PASSPORTS AND VISAS

U.S. and Canadian citizens need a valid passport, or a birth certificate with a raised seal along with a government-issued photo ID. Visitors from all other countries need a valid passport.

SAFETY

Although crime is almost nonexistent, use common sense: don't leave your camera on the beach while you take a dip or your wallet on a hotel dresser when you go for a walk.

SIGHTSEEING TOURS

Travel Plan Tours can arrange island tours, boat tours, and yacht charters from its Tortola base. Or you can just rent a taxi (minimum of three people) on either Tortola or Virgin Gorda.
➤ CONTACTS: **Travel Plan Tours** (☎ 284/494–2872).

TAXES

DEPARTURE TAX

The departure tax is $5 by boat and $10 by plane. There is a separate booth at the airport to collect this tax.

SALES TAX

There's no sales tax in the BVI. However, there's a 7% government tax on hotel rooms; hotel service charges range from 5% to 15%.

TAXIS

Your hotel staff will be happy to summon a taxi for you. Rates aren't published, so you should negotiate the fare with your driver before you start your trip. It's cheaper to travel in groups because there's a minimum fare to each destination, which is the same whether you are one, two, or three people. The taxi number is also the license plate number. On Tortola, there are BVI Taxi Association stands in Road Town near the ferry dock, at Wickham's Cay I, and at the Beef Island/Tortola airport. You can also usually find a taxi at the ferry dock at Soper's Hole, West End, where ferries arrive from St. Thomas.

Andy's Taxi and Jeep Rental offers service from one end of Virgin Gorda to the other. Mahogany Rentals and Taxi Service provides taxi service all over Virgin Gorda.
➤ CONTACTS: **Andy's Taxi and Jeep Rental** (⌂ The Valley, Tortola, ☎ 284/495–5511); **BVI Taxi Association** (⌂ near the ferry dock, Road Town, Tortola, ☎ 284/494–7519; ⌂ Wickham's Cay I, Road Town, Tortola, ☎ 284/494–2322; ⌂ Beef Island Airport, Tortola, ☎ 284/495–1982); **Mahogany Rentals and Taxi Service** (⌂ The Valley, Virgin Gorda, ☎ 284/495–5469).

TELEPHONES

COUNTRY AND AREA CODES

The area code for the BVI is 284; when you make calls from North America, you need only dial the area code and the number. From the United Kingdom you must dial 001 and then the area code and the number. From Australia and New Zealand you must dial 0011 followed by 1, the area code, and the number.

INTERNATIONAL CALLS

For credit card or collect long-distance calls to the United States, use a phone-card telephone or look for special USADirect phones, which are linked directly to an AT&T operator. For access dial 800/872–2881, or dial 111 from a pay phone and charge the call to your MasterCard or Visa. USADirect and pay phones can be found at most hotels and in towns.

LOCAL CALLS

To call anywhere in the BVI once you've arrived, dial all seven digits. A local call from a pay phone costs 25¢, but such phones are sometimes on the blink. An alternative is a Caribbean phone card, available in $5, $10, and $20 denominations. It's sold at most major hotels and many stores and can be used to call within the BVI as well as all over the Caribbean and to access USADirect from special phone-card phones.

TIPPING

Tip porters and bellhops $1 per bag. Sometimes a service charge (10%) is included on restaurant bills; it's customary to leave another 5% if you liked the service. If no charge is added, 15% is the norm. Cabbies normally aren't tipped because most own their cabs; add 10%–15% if they exceed their duties.

TRANSPORTATION AROUND THE BRITISH VIRGIN ISLANDS

There's limited bus service on Tortola. For information about schedules, call Wheatley's Bus Service. The bus runs in a loop from East End on Beef Island to Road Town along Blackburn Highway and then back to East End via Ridge Road. The fare is $1.

Speedy's Ferries runs between Road Town, Tortola, and Spanish Town, Virgin Gorda, daily. North Sound Express boats run daily between Virgin Gorda's North Sound and Spanish Town and Beef Island/Tortola. The Peter Island Ferry runs daily between Peter Island's private dock on Tortola (just east of Road Town) and Peter Island. Jost Van Dyke Ferry Service makes the Jost Van Dyke–Tortola run several times daily. New Horizon Ferry Service makes the Jost Van Dyke–Tortola trip a number of times each day.

Clair Aero Services flies between Tortola and Anegada on Monday, Wednesday, Friday, and Sunday.
➤ CONTACTS: **Clair Aero Services** (☎ 284/495–2271); **Jost Van Dyke Ferry Service** (☎ 284/494–2997); **New Horizon Ferry Service** (☎ 284/495–9477); **North Sound Express** (☎ 284/495–2271); **Peter Island Ferry** (☎ 284/495–2000); **Speedy's Ferries** (☎ 284/495–5240); **Wheatley's Bus Service** (☎ 284/495–2421).

VISITOR INFORMATION

➤ BEFORE YOU LEAVE: **BVI Tourist Board (U.S.)** (✉ 370 Lexington Ave., Suite 1605, New York, NY 10017, ☎ 212/696–0400 or 800/835–8530; ✉ 3450 Wilshire Blvd., Suite 1202 Los Angeles, CA 90010, ☎ 213/736–8931; ✉ 3390 Peachtree Rd. NE, Suite 1000, Atlanta, GA 30326, ☎ 404/240–8018); **BVI Tourist Board (U.K.)** (✉ 55 Newman St., London W1P 3PG, U.K., ☎ 011–44–207–947–8200).
➤ IN THE BRITISH VIRGIN ISLANDS: **BVI Tourist Board** (✉ Box 134, Road Town, Tortola, ☎ 284/494–3134); **Virgin Gorda BVI Tourist Board** (✉ Virgin Gorda Yacht Harbor, Spanish Town, Virgin Gorda, ☎ 284/495–5181).

4 PORTRAITS OF THE VIRGIN ISLANDS

Beach Picnic

Me? The Dad? On a Spring-Break Cruise?

Exploring the Waters of the USBVI

Map of United States Virgin Islands Anchorages

Map of British Virgin Islands Anchorages

Map of United States Virgin Islands Dive and Snorkel Sites

Map of British Virgin Islands Dive and Snorkel Sites

Further Reading

BEACH PICNIC

A S THE BOAT from St. Thomas neared St. John, it occurred to me again that I might have made a serious mistake leaving behind my ham. You could say, after all, that our entire trip had been based on that ham. In our family, the possibility of renting a house for a week on St. John had been kicking around for years; Abigail and Sarah were so strongly for it that I sometimes referred to them as "the St. John lobby." We had been on St. John briefly during the week we'd spent on St. Thomas, only a short ferry ride away. St. Thomas is known mainly for recreational shopping—its principal town, Charlotte Amalie, had already been a tax-free port for a century and a half when the United States bought St. Thomas and St. John and St. Croix from Denmark toward the end of the five or six thousand years of human history now thought of as the pre-credit-card era—and what I remember most vividly about our week there was trying to explain to Abigail and Sarah that the mere existence of a customs exemption of $800 per person does not mean that each person is actually required to spend $800. ("I happen to know of a man who was permitted to leave even though he had purchased only $68.50 worth of goods. He is now living happily in Metuchen, New Jersey.") I was rather intent on getting the point across because according to what I could see from the shopping patterns on St. Thomas, our family would ordinarily have been expected to buy $3,200 worth of perfume—enough perfume, I figured, to neutralize the aroma of a fair-sized cattle feedlot.

What Abigail and Sarah remembered most vividly were rumless piña coladas—it was their first crack at rumless piña coladas—and the spectacular beaches on St. John. The beaches are accessible to everyone through inclusion in the Virgin Islands National Park, which covers nearly three quarters of the island, and, just as important, going to the beach is pretty much all there is to do—a state of affairs that Abigail and Sarah would think of as what ham purveyors call Hog Heaven. We had talked about it a lot, but the conversation usually ended with a simple question: What would we eat?

The question went beyond the dismal food we had come to expect in Virgin Islands restaurants. (On St. Thomas, the restaurants had seemed to specialize in that old Caribbean standby, Miami frozen fish covered with Number 22 sunblock, and my attempts to find some native cooking had resulted mainly in the discovery of bullfoot soup.) In a house on St. John, we would presumably have our own kitchen, but we'd be dependent on the ingredients available in the island stores. Our only previous experience in that line—in the British Virgin Islands, where we had once rented a house when Abigail was a baby—had produced the shopping incident that I have alluded to ever since when the subject of Caribbean eating comes up. On a shopping trip to Roadtown, the capital, Alice ordered a chicken and asked that it be cut up. When we returned from our other errands, we found that the butcher had taken a frozen chicken and run it through a band saw, producing what looked like some grotesque new form of lunch meat.

The memory of that chicken caused a lot of conversations about St. John rentals to fizzle and die. Then, during one of the conversations, my eye happened to fall on a country ham that was hanging in our living room. Maybe I'd better explain the presence of a ham in our living room; Abigail and Sarah seem to think it requires an explanation whenever they bring friends home for the first time. Now and then, we have arranged to buy a country ham from Kentucky. The ham often arrives with a wire attached to it, and since we have a couple of stalking cats, I put the ham out of their reach by attaching the wire to a living room beam in what seems to be a natural hanging place—a spot where we once briefly considered hanging a philodendron. The first time I hung a

---

The individual customs exemption has been increased from $800 to $1,200.

ham in the living room, Alice pointed out that some of the people expected at a sort of PTA gathering about to be held at our house didn't know us well enough to see the clear logic involved in the ham's presence, so I put a three-by-five card of the sort used in art galleries on a post next to the ham. The card said, "Country ham. 1983. J. T. Mitchum. Meat and wire composition." Since then, I've found that even without the card many guests tend to take the country ham as a work of art, which, at least in the view of people who have eaten one of Mr. Mitchum's, it is.

Contemplating that ham, I found my resistance to renting a house in St. John melting away. We could take the ham along to sustain us, in the way a band of Plains Indians, living in happier times, would have brought their newly killed buffalo to the next camp site. We would bring other provisions from the neighborhood. We would not be dependent on frozen chicken lunch meat. We made arrangements to rent a house for a week on St. John.

Then I left the ham at home. Not because it slipped my mind. A country ham is not the sort of thing you simply forget. Alice had argued that it was terribly heavy, that it was more than we needed, that she didn't feel like making biscuits on St. John (because the American Virgin Islands are U.S. territory, the federal law against eating country ham without biscuits applies). I finally agreed, although I couldn't resist pointing out that the remark about its being more than we needed was directly contradicted by the number of times I've heard people who have just finished off a plateful of country ham and biscuits say, "That's exactly what I needed."

I don't mean we arrived in St. John empty-handed. I had brought along an extra suitcase full of provisions. There were some breakfast necessities—tea and the seven-grain bread that Alice likes in the mornings and, of course, a dozen New York bagels. We also had smoked chicken breasts, a package of a Tuscan grain called farro, a couple of packages of spaghetti, sun-dried tomatoes, a package of pignoli nuts, an Italian salami, several slices of the flat Italian bread called focaccia that a man near our house makes every morning, a jar of olive paste, and what Alice usually refers to as her risotto kit—arborio

rice, fresh Parmesan cheese, olive oil, wild mushrooms, a head of garlic, a large onion, and a can of chicken broth. Better safe than sorry.

F INDING A PLACE to rent had turned out to be relatively simple. St. John is organized on the premise that a lot of visitors will want to rent a house. The only hotels of any size on the island are Caneel Bay, one of the first of the resorts that the Rockefellers built for those who feel the need of being cosseted for a few days in reassuringly conventional luxury, and a new resort called the Virgin Grand, a touch of flash that is always mentioned in the first 30 seconds of any discussion about whether the island is in danger of being ruined by development.

The de facto concierges of St. John are a dozen or so property managers, each of whom presides over a small array of houses that seem to have been built with renting in mind—which is to say that you can usually count on your towels being of a uniform color and you don't have to toss somebody else's teddy bears off the bed to go to sleep. Most of the houses are tacked onto the side of a hill—the side of a hill is about the only place to build a house on St. John, which has so many ups and downs that its old Indian name was probably Place Where You're Always in First Gear—and have decks whose expansive views are measured by how many bays are visible. Our house was a simple but cheery two-bedroom place with what I would call a one-and-a-sliver-bay view. It had a kitchen more than adequate for the preparation of an arrival supper of grilled smoked-chicken sandwiches on focaccia. As I ate one, I tried to keep in mind that out there in the dark somewhere people were probably eating Miami frozen fish with sunblock. We weren't safe yet.

I think it was the phrase "fresh fish" that gave me the first hint that sustaining life on St. John might be easier than I had anticipated. For years, the American Virgin Islands have been known for being surrounded by fish that never seem to make it onto a plate. The first sunny news about fresh fish came accompanied by a small black cloud: local fishermen, I was told, showed up on Tuesday and Thursday mornings on a dock behind the customs shed in Cruz Bay, the one place on St. John that more or less passes as a town, but some of the coral-feeding fish they catch had lately been carrying a disease called ciguatera, which attacks your central nervous system. There was conflicting information around on the subject of ciguatera. I met people in St. John who said that they don't hesitate to eat coral-feeders, and I met someone who said she had been horribly ill from eating one kingfish. I met someone who said that in Japan ciguatera, which isn't detectable by taste or smell, is avoided by putting the fish in a bucket of water with a quarter and discarding it if the quarter tarnishes. I decided to pass. The phrase "attacks your central nervous system" tends to dull my appetite; also, I kept wondering what all those American quarters were doing in Japan.

I**T TURNED OUT,** though, that a store in Cruz Bay called Caribbean Natural Foods sold such fresh deep-water fish as tuna—not to speak of soy sauce and rice wine and sesame oil for the marinade. Caribbean Natural Foods was one of two or three small but ambitious food stores that had opened since our previous visit to St. John, and among them the island had available California wine and Tsingtao beer and Silver Palate chocolate sauce and Ben & Jerry's ice cream (including my daughters' favorite flavor, Dastardly Mash) and New York bagels and real pastrami and a salad identified as "tortellini with walnut pesto sauce and sour cream." I suppose there are old St. John hands who grumble that the world of exotic beers and gourmet ice cream was what they were trying to get away from, but there must be a lot of regular visitors who feel like celebrating the expansion of available foodstuffs with an appropriately catered parade.

Leading the parade would be people serious about picnics. On St. John, the pleasantness of beaches tends to vary roughly in direct proportion to how hard it is to get there. Anyone who chooses a beach on St. John because it has a convenient parking lot or a commissary or a marked underwater trail or plenty of changing rooms may find himself thinking at some point in the afternoon that he should have paid more attention to what his mother said

about the rewards that come to those willing to make a little extra effort. (A difficult road, though, is not an absolute guarantee of peacefulness: someone who has been reading a novel on what seemed like an out-of-the-way beach may look up from his book and find that 20 boats of one sort or another have materialized in a line across the bay, prepared to disgorge a small but expensively outfitted invasion force.) Once you're settled in at the beach, the prospect of going back to Cruz Bay for lunch can provoke the great bicultural moan: *"Quel schlep!"* I don't know what people used to do about lunch at a beach like Francis Bay, where a beach-lounger can watch pelicans as they have a go at the flying fish and a snorkeler with a little patience can usually spot a giant sea turtle. By the time we got there, you could reach into the ice chest for a seafood-salad sandwich and a bottle of Dos Equis.

At Salt Pond, a spectacular beach on the more remote eastern end of the island, we did leave for lunch one day in order to go to Hazel's, where Hazel Eugene, whose wanderings after she left St. Lucia included New Orleans, was said to serve what she sometimes called Caribbean Creole cooking. Hazel's turned out to be on the ground floor of a sort of aqua house that had goats wandering around the back and a neighbor who seemed to be the island's leading collector of auto bodies. Its signs identified it as SEABREEZE: GROCERY, RESTAURANT, BAR, and while we were there Hazel would occasionally leave the kitchen to pour a couple of shots or to fill a shopping list that might consist of a box of Kraft Macaroni & Cheese dinner, a bottle of rum, and a beer for the ride home. She also waited on tables, and in that role she began a lot of sentences with "I could do you . . ." as in "I could do you some of my fried chicken with cottage fries" or "I could do you some codfish fritters and some of my special pumpkin soup to start." Hazel did us all of that, plus some blackened shark and some seafood creole and some puffed shrimp and some chicken curry and a plate of assorted root vegetables that tasted an awful lot better than they sounded or looked. When it was over, I was just about ready to admit that I might have sold St. John short.

I don't mean I regretted bringing along the extra suitcase. Hazel's was too far to drive at night. Places to eat dinner were limited, although at least one restaurant in Cruz Bay, the Lime Inn, had fish from the Caribbean, of all places, and served it grilled, without even a dash of sunblock on the side. And, of course, we had one dress-up evening in the main dining room at Caneel Bay. What was being sold there, I realized, was simulation of membership in the most prominent country club in town—at a cost that might seem considerable but is, I assume, nothing compared to the kick of the real club's annual dues. The food is of the sort that is described by the most enthusiastic members as "not highly seasoned," and the waiters, playing the role of old club retainers, serve it in a manner so true to the rituals of the upper-middle-class past that you even get a little tray of olives and carrot sticks to nibble on while you're waiting for your shrimp cocktail. The night we were there, the menu offered a marinated conch appetizer as the single reminder that we were on an island rather than in one of the better suburbs, and it listed some California wines as the single reminder that we hadn't found ourselves, willy-nilly, in 1954.

All of which means that we often ate dinner at the place with a one-and-a-sliver-bay view—grilled tuna with some pasta on the side; a great meal of spaghetti with garlic and oil and sun-dried tomatoes; and, finally, the fruits of Alice's risotto kit. It occurred to me, as we ate the risotto and talked about risotto in Milan, that behind our shopping there may have been an unconscious desire to create the Italian West Indies. In fact, I informed those at the table, it hadn't been a bad try—although it might have been improved by bringing along a little more focaccia for the picnics.

Back home, we decided that surviving on St. John had been easy enough to merit a return engagement. A few months later we heard that Hazel had closed her restaurant and taken her talent for Caribbean Creole cooking elsewhere. It was a blow, but not a blow severe enough to change our minds about going back. After all, we still had the country ham.

—Calvin Trillin

ME? THE DAD? ON A SPRING-BREAK CRUISE?

ON A PERFECT MORNING in the British Virgin Islands, I am sitting alone in the cockpit when two young fellows, who are rowing by not quite as accidentally as they would like it to appear, rest on their oars long enough to ask me where my crew and I are headed.

"Norman Island," I answer pleasantly, albeit untruthfully.

Our actual destination is Trellis Bay, at the other end of the BVI from Norman Island. But over the past few days I've learned that evasive tactics are sometimes necessary when you are cruising with a college-age daughter and a few of her girlfriends. I've learned that if I were to be truthful to all the young men who have taken an interest in where we were going to anchor each night, there wouldn't be any room for us to anchor.

Besides, even though the girls had been polite to these particular two young fellows when we'd talked to them ashore on the preceding evening, I'd seen Kris roll her eyes in that meaningful way I'd come to understand means "total dweebs." And I'd heard one of the other girls label them with an even more damning epithet: "high school boys."

The idea for a spring-break cruise with my daughter had been mine. I wanted to share with her one of the things I enjoy most—visiting tropical waters aboard a sailboat when everyone at home is complaining about how cold the weather is. I wanted to do it in a way that would make her feel she was the focus of our adventure, not just tagging along. And I wanted some time to get caught up with how her life was going—not, of course, by asking her, which, as most parents know, is a singularly unenlightening method of intelligence gathering, but by taking advantage of the small confines of a boat to listening in on her conversations with her friends.

Even though the idea had been mine, Kris was keen on it from the start. That's one of the reasons I was so looking forward to it. She was finally beyond the age when kids consider the ideal distance between parent and offspring on vacation to be two or three states. Either that, or she was wise enough to see that spring break in the Virgin Islands is worth a certain amount of sacrifice.

But she did have one concern. After I explained that I'd pay all expenses except her friends' airfare, she said she feared that most of her friends, who were "poor college students," probably would not be able to afford the price of a ticket to the Caribbean. That fear lasted about 24 hours, after which she called me and asked, "How many people did you say was the maximum I could bring?"

We finally signed on two: Carol, whose enrollment in a sailing course at school left me in constant fear that she would ask me to demonstrate a knot I would not remember how to tie; and Missy, who, apparently somewhat dubious about details of the cruise ending up in print, throughout the week made such statements as "Don't quote me on this, but has anybody seen my eyeliner?"

The boat I chartered was a Bénéteau 41S, from Sunsail, which is based at Soper's Hole, at the west end of Tortola. With three double cabins plus the main saloon, the beamy French design could have accommodated more. In fact, based on charters by college-age groups I've seen over the years, the typical number aboard a 41-ft boat is about a dozen—with the crew sleeping all over the deck and, in at least one instance I remember, in the dinghy. But I was glad we were only four, because knowing that my crew had little sailing experience and not knowing how enthusiastic they would be about galley chores, I'd hired a paid captain for a few days, to be followed for a few days after that by a paid cook.

The captain, a young local named David, worked out well. He had what seems to me the most important quality of a paid hand—the ability to get along pleasantly with strangers on a small boat (although he himself admitted that with our crew he didn't find it a particularly tough assignment).

He ably handled the girls' sailing instruction for the first few days and was also handy to have aboard whenever I had a question about the boat's systems. His knowledge actually added a half-day to the time we could spend cruising, because we didn't have to be checked out before Sunsail let us go off on our own. David checked us out while we were under way. And his presence allowed us to solve a few small problems that might otherwise have required me to spend more of the cruise than I cared to reading service manuals.

He had local knowledge that we benefited from immediately. He showed us, almost within sight of the dock, a great day anchorage on Little Thatch Island, which he said most people overlooked because they were in a hurry to get either into or away from Soper's Hole. As the less fortunate waited for their pre-cruise briefings, we let the chain rattle out over a white sand bottom that proved an excellent spot for introducing the girls to snorkeling; windsurfing; and, eventually, lunch as prepared by "The Dad," as I was to overhear various young men call me throughout the week.

And, as we motored into The Bight at Norman Sound just before sunset on that first day, and David said, "Look at how those boats are turned every which way; I'm going to be poppin' my head out the hatch all night," his presence allowed me the pleasant realization that I just might be sleeping better than I usually do on a charter.

At Gorda Sound, on Virgin Gorda, the ferry service that runs between the Bitter End Resort and Tortola made it simple for us to get David back home and pick up the cook whom Sunsail had assigned to us. She was an Englishwoman named Val, whom, to my great relief, the girls got along with splendidly, and not just, as they hinted, because it meant that I would no longer be cooking.

Again, Val's ability to get along with strangers was her best quality. Not counting, of course, her willingness to do all the dishwashing. None of our crew were gourmets, and none of us had spent a lifetime being the one expected to cook, so I can't really judge those aspects of having a professional aboard, which my wife and about half the human race have told me can make the difference between a true vacation and simply moving the work load to a new venue. But I do know that at the end of the time we had planned to keep her, our crew decided we needed to convince Val to stay until the end of the cruise.

The crew, I am happy to report, were themselves a joy to have aboard. As I've said, they arrived with little experience, but they set about everything they did—learning how to steer a course, set a sail, handle the dinghy, wash their hair in a rainsquall—with nearly as much enthusiasm as they exhibited when getting ready to go ashore on the evenings when young men were likely to be present.

Of course, we did have our small differences. My inability to appreciate some of their music left me with the uncomfortable feeling that I might be—well, getting old. And they didn't care much for some of my music either. Not even what they called the classical stuff, such as Jimmy Buffett. But mostly what we had was one of the most pleasant cruises I can remember.

I T WAS PLEASANT introducing my daughter and her friends to places I'd visited and enjoyed a dozen times before: the sea caves on Norman Island, where rumors still persist of buried treasure; The Baths, on Virgin Gorda, where cathedral light and the ocean's swell bounce gently back and forth beneath church-size rocks; Cane Garden Bay, on Tortola, where the evening sun turned the palm trees golden: Sandy Cay, which has a beach as beautifully white as the image its name conjures up; the Bitter End Yacht Club in North Sound, on Virgin Gorda, where (I'd never really noticed before) the boys are; and Foxy's Tamarind Bar, on Jost Van Dyke, where in the afternoon, while we were picking out lobsters for our end-of-the-cruise evening meal ashore, Foxy himself played his guitar for us and told us how he had planned to travel to America and become a big star—and would have, too, he said, if he hadn't learned at the last moment that in order to board the airplane he would be required to wear shoes.

It was pleasant sailing with a crew whose neophyte's enthusiasm helped me remember what it was like to feel a boat come alive in my hands for the first time. Yet a crew so unafraid that they delighted in taking turns at the wheel when the wind attempted to put us on our ear during a beat up Sir Francis Drake Channel. And a crew that by the end of the week, as we reached across a gentle blue sea from Jost Van Dyke to Little Thatch for one more quick swim and a tidying up before heading back into Soper's Hole, had become so competent that I had nothing to do but what I fancy myself as doing best—serving in a supervisory capacity.

Most of all, it was pleasant to think that if Kris and her friends were still as enthusiastic about their spring-break cruise when they got back to school as they were when I saw them off at the airport, she might occasionally remember it was an adventure she had shared with her dad.

Oh, and if those guys from the sailing team who sat up in our cockpit half the night are still looking for the steering wheel that somebody removed from their boat, I don't know anything about it.

–Bob Payne

EXPLORING THE WATERS OF THE USBVI

THERE ARE MOMENTS in a person's life when things seem to change forever. One such moment occurred 20 years ago, when I first arrived in the Virgin Islands and immediately shoved off from St. Thomas to "fetch Tortola" on a small, ketch-rigged sailboat. I still remember that sun-kissed passage as if it happened yesterday: tacking up through the Narrows, the sweet trades rustling my hair, I sensed the boat dip and curtsy in the Caribbean Sea and found myself grinning like a child. The palm-fringed islands seemed to wave in welcome, and I realized that a part of me would never be the same.

Of course, such memories can be dangerous. Father Time tends to burnish them into a romantic brilliance they don't deserve. So I recently bareboated a 44-ft Oceanis sloop with some snow-weary friends to see if the magic was still there. It was. On the second evening I saw it clearly reflected on the smiling face of Russ Tate, an old landlubbing friend of mine from Massachusetts. He had been totally bewitched by the day's sail. We'd seen porpoises and flying fish—even a huge manta ray just astern of our transom. We had briskly sailed past colorful sunbathers, blowing snorkelers, bubbling scuba divers and streaking windsurfers. But what most impressed Russ was our final tranquil anchorage on Tortola's northeast tip. It was as if we had sailed onto a tropical movie set. Seagulls wheeled and cackled above. Pelicans humorously dive-bombed for their small silvery prey at the harbor entrance. Ashore, an exuberant rooster crowed. The smell of frangipani, wood smoke, and coconut oil wafted gently across the water.

The next morning, Russ was already sitting in the cockpit when I arose at first light. "Tell me about it, Gary," he said, a strange light of intense interest in his eyes. "Tell me about this boat, that reef, and every single thing in between." "Okay," I said with a smile, "The first thing you should know is . . ."

Riding the Waves

With a sailing fleet of several hundred boats, based mostly on St. Thomas, Tortola, and Virgin Gorda, access to Virgin Island attractions is remarkably easy—year-round and from all directions. You can sail independently on a bareboat charter or aboard a fully crewed boat with an experienced captain and cook. The Virgin Islands can match every sailor's wish list: sunny days in the 70°F to 80°F range; dependable trade winds of 12 to 20 knots from the east–southeast; varied, exotic scenery; protected anchorages that are free and slip and mooring rentals that are affordable; tides of less than 2 ft and generally predictable currents; short passages between islands; and easy access to on-shore sights. (Note that St. Croix is an exception because it sits alone, 40 mi south of the group.)

A bareboat, no matter how luxurious, is bare of crew. You have to sail it yourself, just like you have to drive a rental car yourself. For the duration of the charter, the boat is your responsibility. A crewed charter is similar to renting a chauffeur-driven limousine. The captain and crew cater to your every whim and do all the heavy lifting. Your sole responsibility is to relax. Bare-boating offers skilled sailors a lot of freedom, but it carries with it serious responsibility and considerable physical effort. A crewed charter, on the other hand, is like having your own ocean-going resort. It is, however, less private and more expensive than bareboating, and, although the captain will make every effort to carry out your requests, the ship's navigation and routing are his sole right and responsibility.

Bareboat Charters

If you're an experienced sailor and are on a budget, bareboating is the way to go. If you don't have the experience to handle a boat, don't try to fake it. Each company has a "check out" orientation during which they carefully determine your competence.

Most sailors select a boat and make reservations at least six months in advance for high-season charters (earlier to guarantee holiday dates). Cruising in style costs about the same as staying in a mid-range resort. Prices vary depending on how many people you have to share the costs, whether or not you do some of your own provisioning, the kinds of activities (fishing, shopping, diving) you include, what type of optional equipment (e.g., refrigeration) the boat has, and the boat's age or reputation.

You can charter an older (note that it's prudent to ask for a boat in charter service for less than five years), smaller boat for less than $2,000 a week or you can pay more than $6,000 for a fully outfitted 50 footer that can accommodate a crowd. The most popular size is 42 ft. Remember: Mother Ocean will be just as awe-inspiring from the deck of a modest boat as from a mega-yacht.

Crewed Charters

Deciding on which boat to charter isn't as important as deciding on a captain and crew with whom to charter. Some crews love kids; others won't allow them aboard. Some vessels specialize in gourmet cooking, others in rail-down competitive sailing. Still others cater to scuba divers, retired couples, or gay and lesbian passengers. It's best to seek out the assistance of a charter yacht broker, a sea-going travel agent who specializes in fully crewed chartering.

How do you find a good broker? Well, a good broker always attendsthe annual Caribbean yacht "viewing" shows on St. Thomas and Tortola and has been aboard the vessels he or she represents. The very best brokers are on a first-name basis with their captains. Good brokers are also interested in ensuring that you have the vacation of a lifetime, so you'll rebook with them next year; bad brokers are interested primarily in selling you on any boat so that they can collect their commission.

Brokers' services include an interview to determine your vacation expectations, budget, and other pertinent information. This is generally followed by a mailing of brochures on recommended boats and another conversation with the broker to help you narrow the selection. Brokers can be adept at matching a crew's personalities with your needs and at helping with island travel arrangements, including air and hotel. They also coordinate with the crew all the details of the actual charter contract: special food and beverage preferences, any special occasions to be celebrated during the voyage, etc.

U.S.-flagged vessels and U.S. captains operating in the USVI (or picking up passengers from U.S. ports) must be licensed by the U.S. Coast Guard. Crewed charters in the BVI are usually (but not always) operated by people with British Yacht Masters' Tickets. In either case, besides confirming the boat's and crew's status with a broker, you can verify their good standing by contacting voluntary associations in both U.S. and British territories (e.g., the Virgin Islands Charteryacht League or the Charter Yacht Society of the BVI).

Like bareboat charters, the costs for a crewed charter depend on the type and size of vessel; the level of crew service is another factor. One mega-yacht on St. Thomas charges $26,000 per day. However, for a party of six on a well-found 50-ft sloop, figure on $1,200 to $1,800 per person per week. A couple can expect to pay between $1,600 and $2,300 each for a top-of-the-line 41 footer—not bad considering that you're getting the most private, most exclusive, catered vacation in the world. (A 15% tip is appreciated for captain and crew.)

Day-Sails

The easiest, cheapest, and least complicated way to get to sea is on a multi-passenger day-sail boat. Most charter for around $75 per person for a full day (including snorkel gear, lunch, snacks, and beverages). You can also find cheaper half-day or sunset cruises. There are two main types of boats: private "six-pack" yachts that carry as many as six passengers, and multi-passenger vessels that can take up to 100 people.

The advantage of a six-pack vessel is one of intimacy. If you charter it with several friends, chances are you'll have it all to yourself, so it's like having your own private yacht for a day. The captain and crew are often highly interesting Caribbean sea gypsies, and at the end of the day you may feel as if you've evolved from paying guest to new-found friend. Of course, there's no denying that the enthusiasm of a large group of sun-drenched mariners is infectious on multi-passenger boats. If, however, you hate crowds, loud music, and boisterous sing-alongs, perhaps a more laid-back six-pack boat would be the best choice.

United States Virgin Islands Anchorages

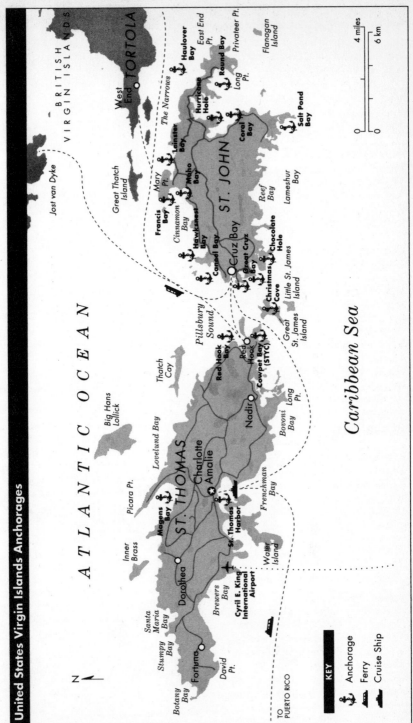

KEY

⚓ Anchorage

⛴ Ferry

🚢 Cruise Ship

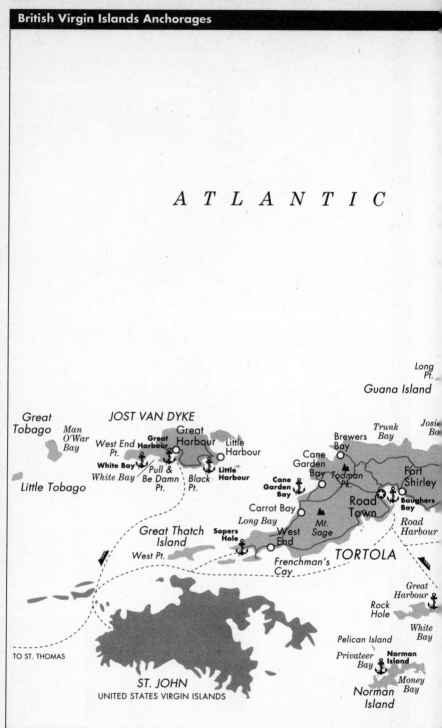

ATLANTIC

Long Pt.

Guana Island

Great Tobago

Man O'War Bay

JOST VAN DYKE

West End Pt.

Great Harbour

Great Harbour

Little Harbour

Trunk Bay

Brewers Bay

Josi Ba

White Bay

White Bay

Pull & Be Damn Pt.

Black Pt.

Little Harbour

Cane Garden Bay

Cane Garden Bay

Todman Pk.

Fort Shirley

Little Tobago

Carrot Bay

West End

Mt. Sage

Baughers Bay

Road Town

Long Bay

Sopers Hole

TORTOLA

Road Harbour

Great Thatch Island

West Pt.

Frenchman's Cay

Great Harbour

Rock Hole

TO ST. THOMAS

Pelican Island

Privateer Bay

Norman Island

White Bay

Money Bay

ST. JOHN
UNITED STATES VIRGIN ISLANDS

Norman Island

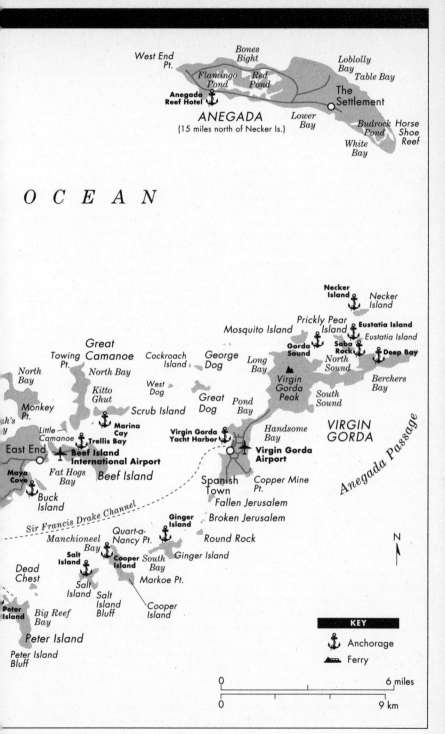

West End
Pt.

Bones
Bight

Loblolly
Bay

Table Bay

Flamingo
Pond

Red
Pond

**Anegada
Reef Hotel** ⚓

The
Settlement

ANEGADA
(15 miles north of Necker Is.)

Lower
Bay

Budrock
Pond

Horse
Shoe
Reef

White
Bay

O C E A N

**Necker
Island** ⚓

Necker
Island

Prickly Pear
Island

Mosquito Island

Eustatia Island ⚓

Eustatia Island

Gorda
Sound

**Saba
Rock** ⚓

Deep Bay ⚓

Great
Camanoe

Towing
Pt.

North Bay

Cockroach
Island

George
Dog

Long
Bay

North
Sound

Berchers
Bay

North
Bay

Virgin
Gorda
Peak ▲

South
Sound

**VIRGIN
GORDA**

Monkey
Pt.

Kitto
Ghut

West
Dog

Great
Dog

Pond
Bay

*h's
y*

Little
Camanoe

⚓ **Marina
Cay**

Scrub Island

**Virgin Gorda
Yacht Harbor** ⚓

Handsome
Bay

East End

Trellis Bay

**Beef Island
International Airport**

**Virgin Gorda
Airport** ✈

Anegada Passage

Maya
Cove ⚓

Fat Hogs
Bay

Beef Island

Spanish
Town

Copper Mine
Pt.

Buck
Island

Fallen Jerusalem

Sir Francis Drake Channel

**Ginger
Island** ⚓

Broken Jerusalem

Manchioneel
Bay

Quart-a-
Nancy Pt.

Round Rock

**Salt
Island** ⚓

**Cooper
Island**

South
Bay

Ginger Island

Dead
Chest

Salt
Island

Salt
Island
Bluff

Markoe Pt.

Cooper
Island

**Peter
Island**

Big Reef
Bay

Peter Island

Peter Island
Bluff

N

KEY	
⚓	Anchorage
⛴	Ferry

0 — 6 miles

0 — 9 km

Powerboats

Another interesting way to see the islands is by small rental powerboat. Although this requires some basic seamanship skills, you don't have to be a salty dog to give it a whirl. Many people are pleasantly surprised at how affordable this option is. A 40-hp, outboard-driven, open, 18-ft boat can rent for less than $150 a day; a 22-footer goes for around $300 a day. Most companies (but not all) require you to top off the fuel tanks at the end of the day—remember, marine fuel is expensive here. A small deposit is usually required, as is a major credit card. Some companies restrict rentals to persons 25 and older. Hint: slow boats are cheaper, safer, and just as much fun as the fast ones. All U.S. boats come with good anchoring gear, as well as all United States Coast Guard–required safety equipment. A couple of safety rules to remember: Don't ever "beach" the boat even momentarily, since sand (like sandpaper) scratches and isn't very good for Fiberglas hulls. In shallow water, be especially careful not to nick the prop—and thus lose your deposit. Watch your engine gauges (for overheating or low oil pressure), as well as the color of the water ahead to avoid running the boat aground.

Points to Ponder on the Seas

Whatever type of boat you charter, make sure that it's allowed to go where you want it to go. The USVI and the BVI are parts of separate countries with distinctly different marine, customs, tax, and immigration regulations. Not all charter vessels in the BVI are legally allowed to visit the USVI. Some BVI bareboat companies actively discourage their customers from entering USVI waters. Check on marine and other regulations in advance. Also, read all charter contracts carefully so that you're fully aware of your liability and insurance responsibilities from the start. When you head out be sure that you understand which VHF channels are important and how to use each properly. If you plan to fish, check on permit requirements and fishing restrictions. Be sure you're aware of anchoring, diving, and other restrictions as well. Finally, drinking and driving—on the water as well as the land—is a bad idea. The legal limit for recreational boaters is .10 blood alcohol content; it's .04 for USCG-licensed captains. (Indeed, such captains cannot drink *any* alcohol within four hours of stepping aboard their vessels).

Below the Waves

Reefs, wrecks, and rife vegetation make the islands as interesting underwater as above. Convenient anchorages, conditions suitable to different levels of ability, and a plethora of dive shops add to the appeal of scuba diving and snorkeling here.

Scuba Diving

Scuba divers are required to show certification of training—a C-card—to rent air tanks, get air refills, and join others on guided dives virtually anywhere in the world. If you're an old hand, then diving on your own—off a boat or from a beach—is just a matter of renting filled air tanks. Even experienced divers, however, often hire guides, if only for their knowledge of local attractions and for the convenience of well-equipped dive boats.

Physical requirements for diving are general fitness and the ability to swim comfortably. You can accomplish the entire 32- to 40-hour open-water certification course in as few as three days of vacation, but it's hard work. Professionals suggest that you take a two-part approach: do the classroom study and pool exercises (basic swimming and equipment skills) through a dive school or a YMCA program at home. Then, with a transfer form from your home instructor, certified Virgin Islands dive instructors will lead you through four open-water dives and check your qualifications for a C-card. Most dive operations are connected to retail/rental shops and are affiliated with the National Association of Underwater Instructors (NAUI) or the Professional Association of Diving Instructors (PADI). The latter is most evident in the Virgin Islands.

All certification courses stress diver safety. But the basic rules for safe diving are simple; fools ignore them at their own peril. Serious diving accidents are becoming increasingly rare these days, thanks to the high level of diver training. However, they *do* still occur occasionally. Surfacing too rapidly without exhaling—or going too deep for too long—can result in an air embolism or a case of the bends. Fauna is another concern. Though sharks, barracuda, and moray eels are on the most-feared list, more often it's sea urchins and fire coral that cause pain when you accidentally bump them. Part of any scuba-training program is a review of sea life and the importance of respecting the new world you're exploring. Dive professionals recognize the value of protecting fragile reefs and ecosystems in tropical waters, and instructors emphasize look-don't-touch diving (the unofficial motto is: take only pictures, leave only bubbles). Government control and protection of dive sites is increasing, especially in such heavily used areas as the Virgin Islands.

Many hotels promote a package deal or have a direct line to a nearby dive shop. But, be aware that the experience could be discouraging, particularly if you find a bored instructor handing out ill-fitting equipment and sloppy advice. There are several simple questions to ask yourself and the staff to assess a dive operation. Are the facilities neat, clean, and businesslike? Are the boats custom-built for diving? Is the rental equipment in good shape? Are the instructors interested in providing you with a quality dive experience and not constantly trying to sell you another dive gadget? Do they repair their own gear in their own workshop? Do they dive frequently, and are all dives guided? Are they safety conscious and rescue trained? Do they know (without the slightest hesitation) where the nearest hyperbaric chamber is—and how to get there fast? Is the boat captain properly licensed, and does the vessel have a tank of oxygen aboard? Is the information on the dive sites precise and specific? Is the staff friendly, knowledgeable, and helpful? The answers to all these questions should be "yes."

Snorkeling

Scuba diving always requires advance planning; snorkeling, on the other hand, can be a far more casual affair. There's no heavy, expensive, complicated equipment involved. There's usually no need for a boat, since many of the finest snorkel sites are adjacent to a beach. Because most tropical marine life lives fairly near the water's surface, there's no link between the depth of a dive and your enjoyment. Many avid water-sports enthusiasts progress from swimming to snorkeling to scuba—and then gradually drift back to snorkeling. The Silent World is even quieter without the hiss of a two-stage regulator.

Few places on this planet are as convenient to snorkel as the Virgin Islands, and many dive shops rent snorkeling gear and offer some training. It can't hurt to go in knowing a few tricks, though: To see whether or not a mask fits, hold it up to your face and breath in gently through your nose. It should stick there for a moment. If not, try another. Fins should fit well: if they're too loose they'll fall off, and if too tight they'll give you blisters. Usually, any snorkel with a mouthpiece that doesn't leak is OK.

To prevent your mask from fogging, spit in it and rub the saliva on the inside of the lens. (A drop of ordinary dishwashing liquid or commercial "mask defoggers" also work.) Warning: it's difficult to walk in fins. Some people walk into the water backwards with them; a better idea is to put them on while sitting in shallow water. Practice clearing your snorkel (with a sharp blow of air) in very shallow water, bracing yourself with your hands on clear sand. This will help you develop confidence before venturing into deeper waters.

The dangers of snorkeling are few and easily avoided. As when scuba diving, don't touch red or reddish brown coral; for that matter, don't touch *any* coral. Don't put your hands into dark holes—unless you want to play "patty cake" with a defensive moray eel. Ignore sharks and barracudas unless they act particularly aggressive; if so, retreat calmly without excessive splashing. Don't wear shiny jewelry. Never snorkel alone, at dusk, or at night. Avoid areas with heavy surf or strong currents.

Snorkel as far away from boats as is practical. Avoid busy harbors, dock areas, or navigational channels. If you hear a motorized vessel approaching, resurface immediately and clasp both hands together over your head. This makes you clearly visible and means "Diver Okay." (Waving your hands rapidly back and forth over your head means "Diver in trouble. Need Help!") In addition, make sure you don't get hit by one boat while watching another. Sound direction can be confusing underwater. Finally towing a floating dive flag is your best protection against being run down.

–Gary Goodlander

Longtime Virgin Islands resident Gary Goodlander has lived aboard sailing craft for much of his life and currently resides with his wife and daughter on his 38-ft S&S sloop *Wild Card* in Cruz Bay, St. John. He's a freelance marine journalist for *Sail, Yachting World,* and other publications and is the author of both *Chasing the Horizon* and *Sea Dogs, Clowns & Gypsies.*

United States Virgin Islands Dive and Snorkel Sites

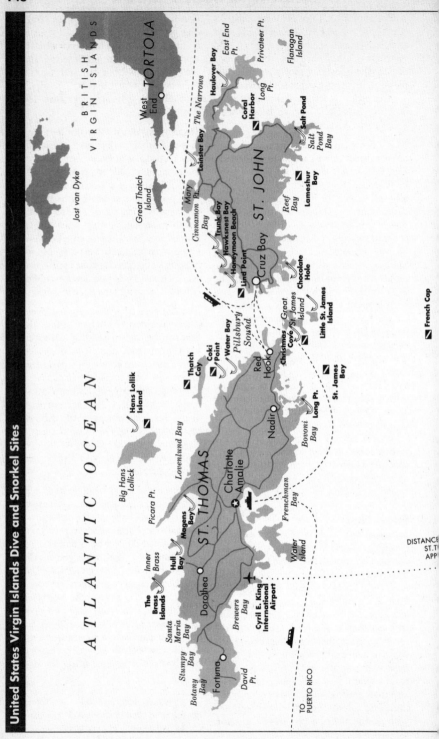

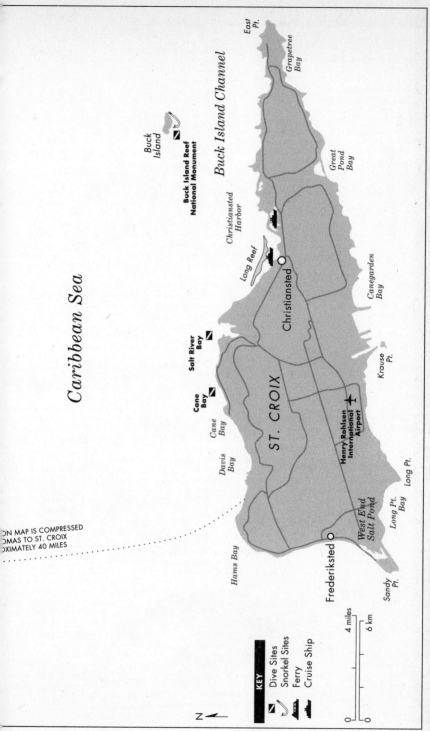

Caribbean Sea

Buck Island Channel

East Pt.

Grapetree Bay

Great Pond Bay

Buck
Island

**Buck Island Reef
National Monument**

*Christiansted
Harbor*

Long Reef

Christiansted ○

*Canegarden
Bay*

**Salt River
Bay**

**Cane
Bay**

*Cane
Bay*

ST. CROIX

*Krause
Pt.*

*Davis
Bay*

**Henry Rohlsen
International
Airport** ✈

Long Pt.

ON MAP IS COMPRESSED
OMAS TO ST. CROIX
OXIMATELY 40 MILES

Hams Bay

Frederiksted ○

*West End
Salt Pond*

*Long Pt.
Bay*

*Sandy
Pt.*

KEY
Dive Sites
Snorkel Sites
Ferry
Cruise Ship

N

0
4 miles

0
6 km

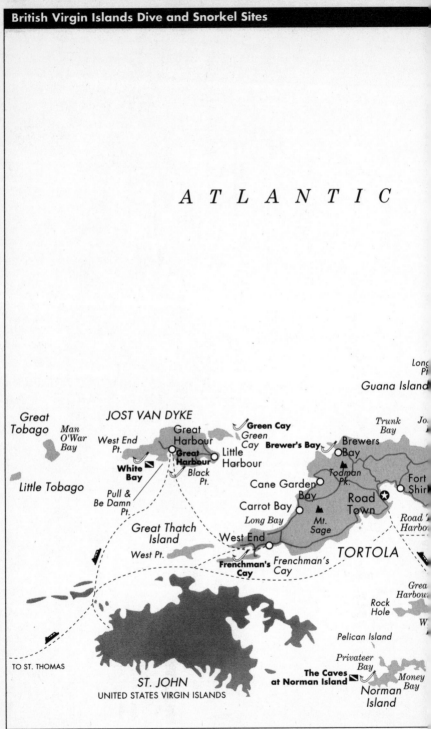

A T L A N T I C

Long
Pt.
Guana Island

**Great
Tobago**   *Man
O'War
Bay*   JOST VAN DYKE   *Trunk
Bay*   *Jo*

*West End
Pt.*   **Great
Harbour**   ✓**Green Cay**
*Green
Cay*   **Brewers
Bay**

**White
Bay**   O**Great
Harbour**   **Brewer's Bay**~   O Bay

**Little
Tobago**   *Black
Pt.*   *Little
Harbour*   *Todman
Pk.*   **Fort
Shir**

*Pull &
Be Damn
Pt.*   Cane Garden O
Bay   **Road
Town**   *Road
Harbor*

*Great Thatch
Island*   Carrot Bay O   *Mt.
Sage*

West Pt.   **West End**   *Frenchman's
Cay*   **TORTOLA**   *Grea
Harbour*

**Frenchman's
Cay**   *Long Bay*

*Rock
Hole*   *W*

Pelican Island

TO ST. THOMAS   *Privateer
Bay*

ST. JOHN
UNITED STATES VIRGIN ISLANDS   **The Caves
at Norman Island**⌐   *Money
Bay*

**Norman
Island**

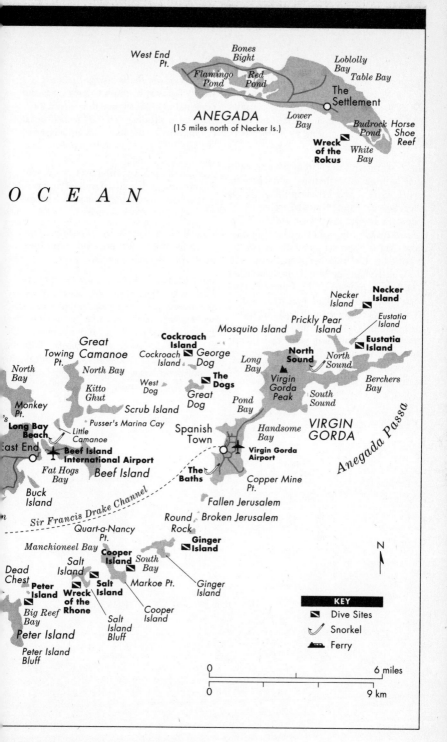

West End
Pt.

Bones
Bight

Loblolly
Bay

Table Bay

*Flamingo
Pond*

*Red
Pond*

The
Settlement

ANEGADA
(15 miles north of Necker Is.)

*Lower
Bay*

Budrock
Pond

Horse
Shoe
Reef

**Wreck
of the
Rokus**

*White
Bay*

O C E A N

Necker
Island

**Necker
Island**

*Prickly Pear
Island*

*Eustatia
Island*

Mosquito Island

**Eustatia
Island**

*Great
Camanoe*

*Towing
Pt.*

**Cockroach
Island**

*Cockroach
Island*

George
Dog

*Long
Bay*

**North
Sound**

*North
Sound*

*North
Bay*

North Bay

**The
Dogs**

*Berchers
Bay*

*North
Bay*

*Kitto
Ghut*

*West
Dog*

Great
Dog

*Pond
Bay*

Virgin
Gorda
Peak

*South
Sound*

*Monkey
Pt.*

Scrub Island

Pu   sser's Marina Cay

Spanish
Town

*Handsome
Bay*

**VIRGIN
GORDA**

**Long Bay
Beach**

*Little
Camanoe*

Anegada Passa

ast End

**Beef Island
International Airport**

✈ **Virgin Gorda
Airport**

*Fat Hogs
Bay*

Beef Island

**The
Baths**

*Copper Mine
Pt.*

*Buck
Island*

Sir Francis Drake Channel

Fallen Jerusalem

*Quart-a-Nancy
Pt.*

Round
Rock

Broken Jerusalem

Manchioneel Bay

**Cooper
Island**

*South
Bay*

**Ginger
Island**

N

*Dead
Chest*

*Salt
Island*

**Salt
Island**

Markoe Pt.

*Ginger
Island*

**Peter
Island**

**Wreck
of the
Rhone**

*Cooper
Island*

*Big Reef
Bay*

*Salt
Island
Bluff*

Peter Island

*Peter Island
Bluff*

KEY	
◣	Dive Sites
⌇	Snorkel
🚢	Ferry

0 ——————— 6 miles

0 ——————— 9 km

FURTHER READING

If you have the time before your trip, read James Michener's *Caribbean;* it will enhance your visit. *Don't Stop the Carnival* by Herman Wouk is a classic Caribbean book, though some of its 1950s perspectives seem rather dated.

Once you get to the Virgin Islands, take time to book-shop; there are some prolific USVI writers and artists publishing on every subject from pirates to architecture. Look for books, art prints, and cards by Mapes de Monde, published by Virgin Islands native son Michael Paiewonsky, who splits his time between Rome and the USVI. Mapes de Monde also publishes *The Three Quarters of the Town of Charlotte Amalie* by local historian Edith Woods. It's richly printed and illustrated with Woods's fine pen-and-ink drawings. Photography buffs will want to look for the book of internationally known St. Croix photographer Fritz Henle. For BVI history buffs, Vernon Pickering's *Concise*

History of the British Virgin Islands is a wordy but worthy guide to the events and personalities that shaped the region. Pickering also produces the *Official Tourist Handbook* for the BVI. Pick up a copy of *A Place Like This: Hugh Benjamin's Peter Island,* the charming and eloquent personal account of the Kittitian's past two decades in the British Virgin Islands. The book was written in collaboration with Richard Myers, a New York writer.

For children there's *Up Mountain One Time* by Willie Wilson, and a *St. John Historical Coloring Book.*

For linguists, *What a Pistarckle!* by Lito Valls gives the origins of the many expressions you'll be hearing, and historians will enjoy *St. John Backtime* by Ruth Hull Low and Rafael Valls, and *Eyewitness Accounts of Slavery in the Danish West Indies* by Isidor Paiewonsky. For sailors, Simon Scott has written a *Cruising Guide to the Virgin Islands.*

INDEX

Icons and Symbols

★ Our special recommendations

✕ Restaurant

🏠 Lodging establishment

✕🏠 Lodging establishment whose restaurant warrants a special trip

👶 Good for kids (rubber duck)

☞ Sends you to another section of the guide for more information

✉ Address

☎ Telephone number

🕐 Opening and closing times

💷 Admission prices

Numbers in white and black circles ③ ❸ that appear on the maps, in the margins, and within the tours correspond to one another.

A

A. H. Riise Alley, *29*
A. H. Riise Caribbean Print Gallery, *30*
A. H. Riise Gift Shops, *30–31*
A. H. Riise Liquors, *33–34*
Abe's Little Harbour ✕, *122*
Accessibility, *xx–xxi*
Admiral's Inn 🏠, *6, 19*
Agave Terrace ✕, *23, 35*
Air travel. ☞ *See* Plane travel.
Al Cohen's Discount Liquor, *34*
Alexander's Café ✕, *24*
All Saints Anglican Church, *37*
American Caribbean Museum, *37*
American Yacht Harbor (shops), *29*
Ample Hamper (shop), *108*
Amsterdam Sauer (shop), *32*
Anchorage 🏠, *20*
Anegada, *4, 123–125*
Anegada Beach Campground, *124*
Anegada Reef Hotel ✕🏠, *124*
Anegada Reef Hotel Boutique, *125*
Annaberg Plantation, *6, 77*
Apartment rentals, *xxiv*
Apothecary Hall, *62*
Apple Bay, *104*
Aquariums, *40, 59*
Arabella's (shop), *32*
Arawak (shop), *108*

Areana Villas 🏠, *100*
Art galleries, ☞ *Also* Museums.
St. John, 74
St. Thomas, 30
Tortola, 107–108
Virgin Gorda, 119
Arts Alive (festival), *83*
Asolare ✕, *71*
ATMs, *xxvi, 85*

B

BVI Boat Show, *129*
BVI Emancipation Festival Celebrations, *129*
BVI Sportfishing Tournament, *129*
BVI Spring Regatta, *129*
BVI Tourist Board, *132*
Baci Duty Free Liquor and Tobacco, *57*
Bajo el Sol (art gallery), *74*
Bamboula (shop), *75*
Basketball, *107*
Bastille Day, *83*
Bath and Turtle ✕, *6, 116, 119*
Baths (beach), *5, 117, 120*
Beaches, *4, 5*
Jost Van Dyke, 122
Peter Island, 5, 123
St. Croix, 52–53, 60
St. John, 5, 71–72
St. Thomas, 5, 25
Tortola, 5, 104–105
Virgin Gorda, 5, 117–118, 120
Bed & Breakfast Caribbean Style 🏠, *20*
Bed and breakfasts, *20, 46, 66*
Beef Island, *5, 104–105*
Beni Iguana's ✕, *22*
Bercher's Bay Beach, *118*
Bicycling, *xii*
St. Croix, 53
St. Thomas, 26
Big Bamboo ✕, *125*
Big Planet Adventure Outfitters (shop), *74*
Bing's Drop In Bar, *109*
Biras Creek ✕, *116–117*
Biras Creek Hotel 🏠, *5, 114*
Bird-watching, *86*
Bitter End Yacht Club and Marina 🏠, *114, 119*
Bitter End Yacht Club's Competition Series, *129–130*
Bitter End's Emporium (shop), *119*
Blazing Villas 🏠, *20*
Blue Carib Gems (shops)
St. John, 76
St. Thomas, 33

Blue Moon ✕, *6, 52, 58*
Bluebeard Castle 🏠, *16–17*
Boating. ☞ *See* Sailing and boating.
Bolongo Bay Beach Club & Villas 🏠, *19*
Bomba's Surfside Shack (nightspot), *6, 109*
Book shops
St. Croix, 55
St. John, 74
St. Thomas, 30
Bookie (shop), *55*
Boolchand's (shop), *30*
Bordeaux Mountain, *77*
Bougainvillea Boutique, *74–75*
Boulder formations, Virgin Gorda, *117, 120*
Brandywine Bay ✕, *6, 104*
Breakfast Club 🏠, *46*
Breezez ✕, *51*
Brewers Bay, *104*
Brewers Bay Campground, *100*
Brewer's Beach, *25*
British Virgin Islands, *3–4, 91–132*. ☞ *Also* Anegada; Jost Van Dyke; Peter Island; Tortola; Virgin Gorda.
business hours, 128
Cooper Island, 125
electricity, 129
emergencies, 129
etiquette, 129
festivals and seasonal events, 129–130
Guana Island, 125–126
guided tours, 131
language, 130
Little Thatch Island, 126
mail, 130
Marina Cay, 126–127
money matters, 130
Necker Island, 126
passports, 130
precautions, 131
price categories, 98, 101
telephones, 131–132
transportation in, 132
transportation to, 127–128
visitor information, 132
Bryan's Bar & Restaurant ✕, *24–25*
Buccaneer 🏠, *46*
Buccaneer's Bounty (shop), *108*
Buck Island, *52*
Buck Island Reef National Monument, *60*
Bus travel, *xii, 89, 132*

C

C and F Restaurant ✕, *101*
Café Roma ✕, *71*

Cafe Wahoo ✕, 23
Camera shops, 30
Cameras and photography, xii–xiii
Camille Pissarro Art Gallery, 30
Campgrounds, xxiv–xxv
Anegada, 124
Jost Van Dyke, 121
St. John, 67
Tortola, 100–101
Cane Bay, 52, 53
Cane Garden Bay, 104
Caneel Bay, St. John, beaches, 71
Caneel Bay Resort ⌂, 5, 66, 76
Caneel Beach, 71
Canvas Factory (shop), 75
Capoon's Bay, 104
Capriccio di Mare ✕, 102
Captain's Table ✕, 102
Car rentals, xiii–xiv
British Virgin Islands, 128
U.S. Virgin Islands, 80–81
Car travel, xiv–xv
British Virgin Islands, 128–129
U.S. Virgin Islands, 81–82
Caravan Gallery (shop), 76
Caravelle Arcade (shops), 55
Caravelle Hotel ⌂, 46
Cardow's (shop), 33
Caribbean Chocolate Shop, 31
Caribbean Corner Spice House (shop), 108
Caribbean Fine Arts Ltd. (art gallery), 107
Caribbean Handprints (shop), 108
Caribbean Marketplace (shop), 32
Carnival, 83
Cathedral of St. Peter and St. Paul, 37
Catherineberg Ruins, 77
Ceta's Place (nightspot), 109
Charlotte Amalie, St. Thomas, 5, 35–40
guest house, 20
hotels, 16–17
restaurants, 21–23
shopping, 29–34
transportation, 89
Chateau Bordeaux ✕, 69
Chenay Bay Beach Resort ⌂, 46–47
Chez Bamboo ✕, 116, 119–120
Children, xv–xvi
attractions for, 38, 39, 40, 41, 42, 61
China shops, 30–31
Christiansted, St. Croix
hotels, 43–46
nightlife and the arts, 58
restaurants, 50–51

shopping, 55–57
sightseeing, 58–60
Churches
St. Croix, 57, 62
St. Thomas, 37, 38, 39
Cinnamon Bay, 71
Cinnamon Bay Campground, 67
Classics in the Atrium (concert hall), 110
Classics in the Garden (festival), 83
Climate, xxxii
Clothing shops
St. Croix, 55–56
St. John, 74–75
St. Thomas, 31
Tortola, 108
Virgin Gorda, 119
Clothing Studio (shop), 75
Club Paradise ✕, 122
Club St. Croix ⌂, 49
The Clubhouse ✕, 117
Coach Boutique, 33
Coastal Islands (Virgin Gorda), 120
Coconut Coast Studios (art gallery), 74
Coconut Coast Villas ⌂, 68
Coconut Vine (shop), 55
Coki Beach, 25
Colombian Emeralds (shops)
St. Croix, 57
St. John, 76
St. Thomas, 33
Tortola, 109
Colony Cove ⌂, 49
Commissary and Ship Store, 119
Compass Point Marina, 41
Computers, xvii
Condominiums
St. Croix, 49–50
St. John, 68
St. Thomas, 20
Consumer protection, xvii
Cooper Island, 125
Cooper Island Beach Club ✕⌂, 125
Copper Mine Point, 120
Coral Bay, St. John, 71, 77
Coral Bay Thanksgiving Regatta, 84
Coral Reef Swim, 83
Coral World Marine Park, 41
Cormorant Beach Club ⌂, 48
Cosmetics shop, 109
Cosmopolitan (shop), 31
Cost-U-Less (shops), 32, 56
Cottages
St. Croix, 49–50
St. John, 68
Crafts shops
St. Croix, 56
St. Thomas, 32
Virgin Gorda, 119
Craig & Sally's ✕, 24
Cramer's Park (beach), 53

Crawl (beach), 118
Credit card abbreviations, xxvi
Cricket
Tortola, 107
Virgin Gorda, 119
Crucian Christmas Festival, 83
Crucian Gold (shop), 57
Cruises. ☞ See Ship travel.
Cruz Bay, St. John, 77–78
Cruzan Rum Distillery, 57
Crystal shops, 30–31
Customs and duties, xvii–xix
Cycling. ☞ See bicycling.

D

D. Hamilton Jackson Park, 59
Danish Consulate Building, 37
Danish Customs House, 59
Davante (shop), 34
Dead Man's Bay, 5, 123
Deadman's Bay Bar and Grill ✕, 123
Deep Bay (beach), 118
Diamonds International (shop), 33
Dining. ☞ See Restaurants.
Dinner with Andre ✕, 71
Disabilities and accessibility, xx–xxi
Discounts and deals, xxi–xxii
Dive BVI (shop), 119
Divi Carina Bay Resort ⌂, 47
Diving. ☞ See Scuba diving and snorkeling.
Dockside Bookshop, 30
Dog Islands, Virgin Gorda, 120
Donald Schnell Pottery (shop), 75
Down Island Traders (shop), 32
Drake's Anchorage Resort Inn ⌂, 114, 117
Drake's Seat (mountain lookout), 41
Duffy's Love Shack ✕, 23, 35
Dutch Reformed Church, 37

E

Eclipse ✕, 103
Ecotourism, xxii
Educators Park, 37
Edward Wilmoth Blyden Marine Terminal, 7
Elaine Ione Sprauve Library and Museum, 78
Electricity, 82
Electronics shops, 30
Elizabeth Beach, 104
Ellington's ✕, 70, 76
Elysian Beach Resort ⌂, 17
Emancipation Garden, 37
Emergencies, xiv
British Virgin Islands, 129
U.S. Virgin Islands, 82

English Shop, *31*
Enid M. Baa Public Library, *37*
Enighed Estate Great House, *78*
Epernay Bistro (bar), *34*
Estate Concordia ⊠, *67*
Estate Mount Washington Plantation, *61*
Estate St. Peter Greathouse & Botanical Gardens, *41*
Estate Whim Plantation Museum, *61*
Estate Zootenvaal ⊠, *68*
Etiquette and behavior, *xxii, 83, 129*

F

Fabric in Motion (shop), *33*
Fabric Mill (shop), *75*
Fallen Jerusalem Island, *120*
Ferry service
British Virgin Islands, 132
U.S. Virgin Islands, 79–80
Festivals and seasonal events
British Virgin Islands, 129–130
U.S. Virgin Islands, 83–84
Fish Trap ✕, *70*
Fishing
St. Croix, 53
St. John, 72
St. Thomas, 26
Tortola, 105
tournaments, 83, 129
Virgin Gorda, 118
Flamboyance (shop), *109*
Fluke's (shop), *108*
Flying Iguana ✕, *116*
Folk Art Traders (shop), *56*
Food shops
St. Croix, 56
St. John, 75
St. Thomas, 31–32
Tortola, 108
Virgin Gorda, 119
Fort Burt, *110*
Fort Christian, *38*
Fort Christiansvaern, *59*
Fort Frederik, *61*
Fort Recovery, *110*
Forts
St. Croix, 59, 61
St. Thomas, 38
Tortola, 110
Virgin Gorda, 120
Foxy's Tamarind ✕, *122*
Foxy's Wooden Boat Regatta, *129*
Frederick Lutheran Church, *38*
Frederiksted, St. Croix, *61–62*
hotels, 47–48
nightlife and the arts, 58
restaurants, 52
shopping, 55–57
sightseeing, 61–62
Frederiksted Hotel ⊠, *47–48*

Fred's (nightspot), *76*
Free Bird Creations (shop), *76*
Frenchman's Cay, *110*
Frenchman's Cay Hotel ⊠, *99, 106*
From the Gecko (shop), *55*
Fruit Bowl (shop), *32*

G

Galleon ✕, *51–52*
Gallows Bay, St. Croix, *55*
Gallows Point Suite Resort ⊠, *68*
Garden By the Sea Bed and Breakfast ⊠, *66*
Garden Restaurant ✕, *103*
Gardens
St. Croix, 60, 62
St. Thomas, 29, 37, 41, 42
Tortola, 110, 129
Gay and lesbian travel, *xxiii*
Gift shops
St. Croix, 56
St. John, 75
Tortola, 108–109
Virgin Gorda, 119
Giorgio's Table ✕, *117*
Gladys' Cafe ✕, *22*
Golf
St. Croix, 53
St. Thomas, 27
Gone Tropical (shop), *56*
Gourmet Gallery (shop), *32*
Gourmet Galley (shop), *108*
Government House (Charlotte Amalie), *38*
Government House (Christiansted), *59*
Grand Hotel Court, *38–39*
Grandpa's Korner Emporium, *34*
Great House at Villa Madeleine ✕, *51*
Greenhouse Bar and Restaurant ✕, *21, 34*
Guana Island, *125–126*
Guavaberry Spring Bay Vacation Homes ⊠, *115*

H

H. Stern (shop), *33*
Haagensen House, *39*
Handicrafts. ☞ *See* Crafts shops.
Happy Laurry ✕, *122*
Hard Rock Cafe ✕, *22*
Harmony ⊠, *66*
Harris' Place ✕, *122*
Harvey's ✕, *50*
Hassel Island, *39*
Havensight Mall, *29*
Hawksnest Beach, *71–72*
Hay Point Beach, *118*
Health concerns, *xxii–xxiii, 84*
Hervé ✕, *22*
Hibiscus Beach Hotel ⊠, *48*

Hiking
St. Croix, 53–54
St. John, 73, 77, 78
Hilty House ⊠, *46*
Historic sites, *4*
Holiday Inn St. Thomas ⊠, *17*
Holidays, *84, 130*
Home exchanges, *xxv*
Home rentals
St. Croix, 50
St. John, 68–69
St. Thomas, 21
Tortola, 100
Virgin Gorda, 115
Horse racing, *29*
Horseback riding
St. Croix, 54
St. John, 73
St. Thomas, 27
Tortola, 105
Horticultural Society Show, *129*
Hotel Caravelle ⊠, *46*
Hotel Castle Maria ⊠, *98*
Hotel 1829 ✕⊠, *6, 17, 22, 39*
Hotel on the Cay (nightspot), *58*
Hotels, *xxv, 5–6*
Anegada, 124
Cooper Island, 125
Guana Island, 125–126
Jost Van Dyke, 121
Little Thatch Island, 126
Marina Cay, 127
Necker Island, 126
Peter Island, 122–123
price categories, 16, 98
St. Croix, 6, 43–50
St. John, 5, 63–69
St. Thomas, 6, 16–21
Tortola, 5, 93–100
Virgin Gorda, 5, 114–115
Houses, historic
St. Croix, 60, 61
St. John, 77
St. Thomas, 39
Housewares, *56–57*
Hull Bay, *25*

I

Icons and symbols, *153*
Iggies (bar), *35*
Indies ✕, *50, 58*
Inn at Blackbeard's ⊠, *17*
Inn at Tamarind Court ⊠, *76*
Insurance, *xiii, xxiii–xxiv*
International Plaza (shops), *29*
International Regatta, *83*
Invitational Regatta, *130*
Isaac Bay, *53*
Island Newsstand, *30*
Island Silhouette in Flax Plaza (shop), *119*
Island View Guest House ⊠, *20*
Island Webe (shop), *56*

J

J. R. O'Neal Botanic
  Gardens, 110–111
J. R. O'Neal, Ltd. (shop), 108
Jewelry shops
St. Croix, 57
St. John, 76
St. Thomas, 32–33
Tortola, 109
Jolly Dog (shop), 75
Jolly Roger (bar), 109
Jonna White Gallery, 30
Josiah's Bay, 104
Jost Van Dyke, 4, 6, 121–122
  beaches, 122
  campground, 121
  festivals, 129
  hotels, 121
  nightlife, 5, 122
  price categories, 98, 101
  restaurants, 121–122
Judith's Fancy (house ruins),
  60
July 4th Celebration, St.
  John, 84
July Open Tournament, St.
  Thomas, 83

K

Karavan West Indies (shop),
  57
Karl and Marie Lawaetz
  Museum, 62
Kayaking, 28, 54, 73
Kendricks ✕, 50
Kicks (shop), 57
King's Alley Hotel 🏨, 43–46
Kings Alley Walk (shops), 55
Kmart, 57

L

La Tapa ✕, 70
Lambert Beach Resort 🏨, 100
Lameshur Bay, 72
Last Resort ✕, 104
Latitude 18 (shop), 108
Le Cabanon ✕, 101
Le St. Tropez ✕, 52
Leather goods shops
St. Croix, 57
St. Thomas, 33
Legislature Building (St.
  Thomas), 39
Leverick Bay, 118
Leverick Bay Hotel 🏨, 115
Libraries
St. John, 78
St. Thomas, 38
Lighthouse ✕, 116, 120
Lime Inn ✕, 70
Lime 'n' Mango ✕, 102
Linen shops, 33
Liquor shops
St. Croix, 57
St. Thomas, 33–34
Little Apple Bay, 104
Little Dix Bay 🏨, 114–115,
  120

Little Dix Bay Pavilion ✕, 117
Little Fort National Park, 120
Little Planet (shop), 74
Little Princess Estate, 60
Little Switzerland (shop), 31
Little Thatch Island, 126
Little Trunk Bay, 120
Local Color (shop), 31
Lodging. ☞ See Hotels.
Long Bay, 118
Long Bay, Beef Island, 104
Long Bay Beach Resort 🏨, 5,
  99, 107
Long Bay West, 105
Lord Rumbottoms Club, 35
Lover's Lane (shop), 31

M

Mad Dog's ✕, 116
Magazines, xxv, 30
Magens Bay, 5, 25
Maho Bay, 72
Maho Bay Camps, 67
Mail and shipping, xxv
  British Virgin Islands, 130
  U.S. Virgin Islands, 84
Mango Bay Resort 🏨, 115
Mango Tango (shop), 30
MAPes MONDe (shop), 74
Maria's Hotel by the Sea 🏨,
  98
Marina Cay, 126–127
Marina Market
St. John, 75
St. Thomas, 32
Market (Christiansted), 59
Market (Frederiksted), 62
Market Square (Charlotte
  Amalie), 39
Marriott's Frenchman's Reef
  and Morning Star Beach
  Resorts 🏨, 19–20
Meal plan abbreviations,
  xxiv
Medical services. ☞ See
  Emergencies under specific
  islands.
Memorial Moravian Church,
  39
Mrs. Scatliffe's ✕, 102–103
Mr. Tablecloth (shop), 33
Modern Music (shop), 34
Molly Malone's ✕, 23
Money matters, xxv–xxvi, 85,
  130
Mongoose Junction, St. John,
  30, 74
Mongoose Restaurant ✕, 70
Moorings-Mariner Inn 🏨, 98,
  107
Morgan's Mango ✕, 70
Morning Star Beach, 25
Mt. Eagle, 60–61
Mt. Healthy National Park,
  111
Mountain Top, St. Thomas, 42
Museums. ☞ Also Art
  galleries.
St. Croix, 61, 62

St. John, 78
St. Thomas, 37, 40
Tortola, 111
Music shops, 34
Myett's ✕, 103, 109

N

National Park Headquarters,
  42, 74
Native Arts and Crafts
  Cooperative, 32
Necker Island, 126
Neptune's Treasure ✕🏨, 124
Newspapers, xxv, 30
Next Wave (shop), 119
Nicole Miller Boutique, 31
Nightlife and the arts, 5, 6 ☞
  Also under specific islands.
99 Steps (staircase "street"),
  39
Nisky Center (shops), 29
North Shore, St. Croix, 48–
  49
North Shore Shell Museum,
  111

O

Off the Wall ✕, 52, 58
Old Mill Entertainment
  Complex, 6, 35
Olde Yard Inn ✕🏨, 115, 117
Ole Works Inn 🏨, 100

P

Packing for the trip, xxvi–
  xxvii
Palm Plaza (shops), 74
Palm Tree Gallery (shop), 119
Pan Am Pavilion (shops), 55
Paradise Beach Resort 🏨,
  115
Paradise Cafe ✕, 51
Paradise Point Tramway, 42
Paradiso ✕, 70
Parasailing, 27
Parks, national
St. Croix, 52, 60, 61
St. John, 5, 6, 73
St. Thomas, 42
Tortola, 111
Virgin Gorda, 120–121
Parrot Fish Records and
  Tapes, 34
Passports and visas, xxvii,
  85, 130
Pat's Pottery (shop), 125
Pavilion Gift Shop, 119
Peace Hill, 78
Pelican's Pouch Boutique,
  119
Perfume shops
St. Croix, 57
St. Thomas, 34
Tortola, 109
Peter Island, 4, 122–123
Peter Island Resort and Yacht
  Harbour 🏨, 122–123
Photography, xii–xiii

Pink Papaya (shop), *75*
Pissarro Building, *39*
Pizza Mare ✕, *51*
Plane travel, *x–xii*
to British Virgin Islands, 127
to U.S. Virgin Islands, 78–79
within British Virgin Islands,
   127, 132
within U.S. Virgin Islands, 78,
   89
Plaza Extra (shop), *32, 56*
Point Pleasant Resort 🏨, *18*
Point Udall, *60*
The Pointe at Villa Olga ✕,
   24
Polli's ✕, *24*
Pomato Point ✕, *125*
Port of Sale (shops), *29*
Post Office Building
   (Christiansted), *59*
Price categories
British Virgin Islands, 98, 101
U.S. Virgin Islands, 16, 21
Prospect Reef Resort 🏨, *107*
The Pub ✕, *101, 109*
Pueblo Supermarkets, *32, 56*
Purses and Things (shop), *33*
Pusser's Company Store
Tortola, 108
Virgin Gorda, 119
Pusser's Deli (bar), *109*
Pusser's Fort Burt Hotel, *98*
Pusser's Landing ✕, *102, 110*
Pusser's Marina Cay Hotel
   and Restaurant ✕🏨, *127*
Pusser's Road Town Pub ✕,
   101
Pusser's Tropical & Nautical
   Co. Store, *31*

Q
Quito's Gazebo ✕, *6, 103,*
   110

R
R&I Patton Goldsmiths, *76*
Radio stations, *xxv*
Raffles ✕, *6, 23, 35*
Red Hook, St. Thomas, *6, 42*
Reef Bay Plantation, *78*
Reef Bay Trail, *78*
Reeftique (shop), *119*
Reichhold Center for the Arts,
   35
Renaissance Grand Beach
   Resort 🏨, *18*
Rest rooms, *xxvii*
Restaurants, *xix–xx, 6*
Anegada, 124–125
Cooper Island, 125
Guana Island, 125–126
Jost Van Dyke, 121–122
Marina Cay, 127
Peter Island, 123
price categories, 21, 101
St. Croix, 6, 50–52
St. John, 6, 69–71
St. Thomas, 6, 21–25

Tortola, 6, 101–104
Virgin Gorda, 116–117
Rio Cigars (shop), *34*
Ritz-Carlton, St. Thomas 🏨,
   5, 18, 35
Road Town, Tortola
hotels, 98–99
restaurants, 101–102
sightseeing, 111
visitor information, 132
Rock Café (bar), *120*
Rolex Cup Regatta, *83*
Romanos ✕, *23*
Roosevelt Park, *40*
Royal Caribbean (shop), *30*
Royal Dane Mall, *29*
Royal Poinciana (shop), *56*

S
Safety precautions, *xxvii–*
   xxviii, 85, 131
Sage Mountain National
   Park, *111*
Sailing and boating, *xii*
boat show, 129
regattas, 83, 84, 129
St. Croix, 54
St. John, 72
St. Thomas, 25–26
Tortola, 105
Virgin Gorda, 118
St. Croix, *3, 5, 42–62*
beaches, 52–53
business hours, 80
car rentals, 80–81
cottages and condominiums,
   49–50
emergencies, 82
festivals, 83
guided tours, 85–87
hotels, 6, 43–50
nightlife and the arts, 6, 57–58
pharmacies, 82
price categories, 16, 21
private home and villa rentals,
   50
restaurants, 6, 50–52
shopping, 55–57
sightseeing, 58–62
sports, 53–55
transportation, 78, 79, 81, 87,
   89
visitor information, 89–90
St. Croix Aquarium, *59*
St. Croix Ironman Triathlon,
   83
St. Croix Landmarks Museum
   Store, *56–57*
St. Croix Landmarks Society
   House Tours, *83*
St. Croix Leap, *62*
St. George Village Botanical
   Gardens, *62*
St. John, *3, 5, 62–78*
beaches, 71–72
business hours, 80
campgrounds, 67
car rentals, 80–81

emergencies, 82
festivals, 83–84
guided tours, 85–87
hotels and inns, 5, 63–69
nightlife, 76
pharmacies, 82
price categories, 16, 21
restaurants, 69–71
shopping, 30, 74–76
sightseeing, 76–78
sports, 72–74
transportation, 79, 81, 89
villas, condominiums, and
   cottages, 68–69
visitor information, 89–90
St. John Editions (shop), *75*
St. John Inn 🏨, *67*
St. Patrick's Church, *62*
St. Paul's Anglican Church,
   62
St. Peter Greathouse. ☞ *See*
   Estate St. Peter Greathouse
   & Botanical Gardens.
St. Thomas, *3, 5, 12–42*
beaches, 5, 25
business hours, 80
car rentals, 80–81
emergencies, 82
festivals, 83
guest house, 20
guided tours, 85–87
hotels, 5, 6, 16–21
nightlife and the arts, 6,
   34–35
pharmacies, 82
price categories, 16, 21
private home rentals, 21
restaurants, 6, 21–25
shopping, 29–34
sightseeing, 35–42
sports, 25–29
transportation, 79–80, 89
villas and condominiums, 20
visitor information, 89–90
St. Thomas–St. John
   Agricultural Fair, *83*
Salt Pond Bay, *72*
Salt River Bay National
   Historic Park and
   Ecological Preserve, *61*
Samarkand (shop), *109*
Sandcastle ✕🏨, *121*
Sandcastle on the Beach 🏨,
   48
Sandy Cay, *122*
Sandy Ground Estates 🏨,
   121
Sapphire Beach, *25*
Sapphire Beach Resort &
   Marina 🏨, *18–19*
Sapphire Village 🏨, *20*
Savan (Charlotte Amalie), *40*
Savannah Bay, *118*
Scale House (Christiansted),
   59
Schooner Bay 🏨, *49*
Schooner Bay Market, *56*
Scratch/Fungi Band Fiesta,
   130

Scuba diving and snorkeling, *xxiii*
St. Croix, *54–55*
St. John, *73*
St. Thomas, *27*
Tortola, *106*
Virgin Gorda, *118*
Sea excursions, *27–28*
Sea kayaking, *28, 73*
Sea Urchin (shop), *108*
Sebastian's (nightspot), *110*
Sebastian's on the Beach ⛺, *100*
Secret Harbour, *25*
Secret Harbour Beach Resort & Villas ⛺, *19*
Senior-citizen travel, *xxviii*
Serendip ⛺, *68*
Serendipity/Domino (shop), *108*
Seven Arches Museum, *40*
Ship travel, *xvii–xviii*
to British Virgin Islands, *128*
to U.S. Virgin Islands, *79–80*
Shipwreck Landing ✕, *69*
Shipwreck Landing (shops), *74*
Shopping, *xxviii, 5*
Anegada, *125*
St. Croix, *55–57*
St. John, *28–29, 74–76*
St. Thomas, *29–34*
Tortola, *107–109*
Virgin Gorda, *119*
Sib's Mountain Bar and Restaurant ✕, *24*
Sip and Dip Grill ✕, *116, 120*
Sir Olva Georges Square (Road Town, Tortola), *111*
Skinny Legs Bar & Restaurant ✕, *6, 69, 76*
Skyworld (observation tower), *6, 111*
Skyworld ✕, *103*
Smuggler's Cove, *5, 105*
Snorkeling. ☞ See Scuba diving and snorkeling.
Softball, *107*
Sonya's (shop), *57*
Soper's Hole, Tortola, *107*
Soul of Africa (shop), *55–56*
South Shore, St. Thomas, *19–20*
South Shore Cafe ✕, *52*
Spaghetti Junction ✕, *102*
Spanish Town, Virgin Gorda, *120*
Sports. ☞ Also specific sports.
St. Croix, *53–55*
St. John, *72–74*
St. Thomas, *25–29*
Tortola, *105–107*
Virgin Gorda, *118–119*
Spring Bay beach, *5, 118*
Starfish Market, *75*
Stargazing, *28*
Steeple Building, *59*
Students, *xxviii–xxix*

Submarining, *28*
Sugar Beach ⛺, *49–50*
Sugar Mill Hotel ⛺, *99*
Sugar Mill Restaurant ✕, *6, 103*
Sun Dog Cafe ✕, *70*
Sunglasses shops, *34*
Sunny Caribbee Art Gallery, *108*
Sunny Caribbee Herb and Spice Company (shop), *108–109*
Sunterra Carambola Beach Resort ⛺, *6, 48–49*
Sydney's Peace and Love ✕, *122*
Symbols and icons, *153*
Synagogue of Beracha Veshalom Vegmiluth Hasidim, *40*

T

Tamarind Reef Beach, *53*
Tamarind Reef Hotel ⛺, *47*
Tavern on the Waterfront ✕, *22*
Taxes, *87, 131*
Taxis
British Virgin Islands, *131*
U.S. Virgin Islands, *87–88*
Telephones, *xxix*
British Virgin Islands, *131–132*
U.S. Virgin Islands, *88*
Television stations, *xxv*
Tennis
St. Croix, *55*
St. John, *73*
St. Thomas, *28*
Tortola, *106–107*
Texas Society Chili Cook-Off, *83*
Textile shops, *57, 108*
Textiles with a Story (shop), *57*
Theater, *35*
Thee Artistic Gallery, *119*
Tillett Gardens, *29, 42, 83*
Time zone, *xxix*
Timing of the trip, *xxxii*
Tipping, *89, 132*
Tivoli Gardens ✕, *51*
Tobacco shops, *33–34, 57*
Tommy Hilfiger (shop), *31*
Top Hat ✕, *6, 50–51*
Top of The Baths ✕, *116*
Tortola, *3–4, 5, 93–111*
beaches, *104–105*
campground, *100–101*
car rental, *128*
emergencies, *129*
festivals, *129*
guided tours, *131*
hotels and inns, *5, 93–100*
nightlife and the arts, *6, 109–110*
price categories, *98, 101*
private home and villa rentals, *100*

restaurants, *6, 101–104*
shopping, *107–109*
sightseeing, *110–111*
sports, *105–107*
visitor information, *132*
Tours and packages, *xxix–xxx*
British Virgin Islands, *131*
U.S. Virgin Islands, *85–87*
Toy shop, *34*
Tradewinds Restaurant ✕, *123*
Transportation, *xxx*
British Virgin Islands, *127–128, 132*
U.S. Virgin Islands, *5, 78–80, 87, 89–90*
Travel agencies, *xxx–xxxi*
Traveler's checks, *xxvi*
Tropical Memories (shop), *32*
Tropical Optical (shop), *34*
Tropicale (shop), *75*
Tropicana Perfume Shoppes, *34*
Trunk Bay (St. John), *5, 72*
Trunk Bay (Tortola), *105*
Turtle Dove Boutique, *108*
Turtle's Deli ✕, *52*
Tutto Bene ✕, *51*
Tutu Park Shopping Center, *29*
2 Plus 2 Disco, *58*

U

U.S. Post Office (Charlotte Amalie), *40*
U.S. Virgin Islands, *3, 7–90.* ☞ Also St. Croix; St. John; St. Thomas.
business hours, *80*
electricity, *82*
emergencies, *82*
festivals and seasonal events, *83–84*
guided tours, *85–87*
language, *84*
mail and shipping, *84*
money matters, *85*
passports, *85*
price categories, *16, 21*
telephones, *88*
transportation, *89*
visitor information, *89–90*
USVI Open/Atlantic Blue Marlin Tournament, *83*
Undercover Books (shop), *55*
Unique boulder formations, Virgin Gorda, *112, 115*

V

Valley Trunk Bay, *120*
Vendors Plaza (Charlotte Amalie), *29, 40*
Victor's New Hide-Out ✕, *24*
Vie's Snack Shack ✕, *69*
Villa Madeleine ⛺, *47, 51*
Villa Morales ✕, *52*
Villa Santana ⛺, *17*

Village Cay Resort and
Marina 🏨, *98*
Villas
rentals, xxiv
St. Croix, 50
St. John, 68–69
St. Thomas, 20
Tortola, 100
Virgin Gorda, 115
Villas of Fort Recovery
Estates 🏨, *6, 99*
Violet's (shop), *108*
Violette Boutique, *57*
Virgilio's ✕, *6, 22–23*
Virgin Gorda, *4, 5, 6, 111–
121*
beaches, 4, 5, 117–118
car rental, 128
emergencies, 129
festivals, 129–130
guided tours, 131
hotels and inns, 5, 111–115
nightlife, 6, 119–120
price categories, 98, 101
*private home and villa rentals,
115*
restaurants, 116–117
shopping, 119
sightseeing, 120–121
sports, 118–119

Virgin Gorda Craft Shop, *119*
Virgin Gorda Festival, *129*
**Virgin Gorda Peak National
Park,** *120–121*
Virgin Gorda Villa Rentals
🏨, *115*
Virgin Gorda Yacht Harbour,
120
Virgin Islands National Park,
73
**Virgin Islands National Park
Headquarters,** *42, 74*
Virgin Queen ✕, *101*
Visitor information, *xxxi*
British Virgin Islands, 132
U.S. Virgin Islands, 89–90
Vixen Point Beach, *118*

W

Water Island, *40*
Water sports, *5*
Waves at Cane Bay 🏨, *49*
Weather, *xxxii*
Web sites, *xxxi–xxxii*
Weibel Museum, *40*
West End Beaches, *53*
West End Salt Pond, *62*
Westin Resort, St. John 🏨, *66*
Whale-watching, *86*

Wharfside Village, St. John,
30, 74
Whim Greathouse (concert
hall), *58*
White Bay (Jost Van Dyke),
121, 122
White Bay (Peter Island), *123*
White Bay Campground, *121*
White House (shop), *56*
Wicker, Wood and Shells
(shop), *75*
Wickham's Cay, Tortola
(shops), *107*
Windsurfing
St. Croix, 55
St. John, 74
St. Thomas, 28–29
Tortola, 107
Virgin Gorda, 118
Wine Cellar and Bakery
(shop), *119*
Woody's (nightspot), *76*
**Wyndham Sugar Bay Beach
Club & Resort** 🏨, *19*

Z

Zenaida's of West End
(shop), *108*
Zora's (shop), *33*

NOTES